TRACKING BODHIDHARMA

TRACKING
Bodhidharma

a journey to the heart of chinese culture

Andy Ferguson

COUNTERPOINT · BERKELEY

Library of Congress Cataloging-in-Publication
Data is available.
HARDCOVER ISBN: 978-1-58243-825-2
PAPERBACK ISBN: 978-1-61902-159-4

Quotations from *Zen's Chinese Heritage* are
copyright 2000 by Andy Ferguson, and are used
by permission of the publisher, Wisdom Publications.
Interior and cover design by Gopa & Ted2, Inc.

COUNTERPOINT
2560 Ninth Street, Suite 318
Berkeley, CA 94710
www.counterpointpress.com
Printed in the United States of America

Contents

Introduction

THIS BOOK TRAVELS a path at the heart of Chinese culture. It follows the tracks left by Bodhidharma, a fifth-century Indian monk and important religious figure remembered as the founder of Zen Buddhism. I trace his path in China to unearth forgotten stories that shaped a civilization and reveal the roots of the religion that dominated East Asia for fifteen centuries.

This is also a personal journey, for it explores the origins and significance of Zen, a tradition I have practiced and studied for several decades.

The trail also leads into some little-known corners of Chinese history, places in the shadows of East Asia that continue to influence the region's development.

Bodhidharma, an Indian Buddhist missionary, traveled from South India to China sometime around the year 500 CE. Although his Zen religion spread relatively quickly from China to Korea and Vietnam, it was another seven hundred years before Zen finally took root in Japan, the country Westerners most frequently associate with the religion.

While Bodhidharma's teachings are known in the West as *Zen*, a Japanese word, the term is equivalent to the modern Chinese word *Chan*. This book uses the word *Zen* because it is familiar to Western audiences. Bodhidharma was the "First Ancestor" or "First Patriarch" of the Zen (Chan) sect in China.

Zen claims that successive generations of teachers have relayed its essential insight by "mind-to-mind" transmission. The religion's founding myth claims that this transmission started when the historical Buddha, Shakyamuni, sat before a crowd of his followers at Vulture Peak, a place in ancient India. There, says the legend, he held up a flower before the assembly. In response to this gesture, his senior disciple Mahakasy-apa smiled, whereupon the Buddha uttered the words that purportedly set in motion centuries of awakening:

> I have the treasury of the true Dharma Eye, the sublime mind of nirvana, whose true sign is signlessness, the sublime Dharma Gate, which without words or phrases is transmit-ted outside of the [standard Buddhist] teachings, and which I bestow upon [my disciple] Mahakasyapa.

The Zen tradition thus declared and originated its essential insight into the "signless" mind of nirvana, which can be interpreted as the nature of normal human (or any sentient being's) consciousness, which by nature is outside of time and space. In the story, the Buddha meta-phorically refers to the field of consciousness (which is usually translated as "mind") as the "Treasury of the True Dharma eye."

As Zen developed in China, it claimed that Bodhidharma taught a refined summation of this essential Zen teaching. Bodhidharma purportedly said, "Not setting up words, a separate transmission outside the [scriptural] teachings, point directly at the human mind, observe its nature and become Buddha." (不立文字，教外别传，直指人心，见性成佛。)

The Zen tradition that coalesced from this perspective held sway as China's dominant and orthodox religion for the next fifteen hundred years. The cultural impact of Zen on East Asia can hardly be under-stated. This impact is perhaps best known as underlying the aesthetics of much East Asian art and literature, where landscape paintings, poetry, and other arts often reveal Zen's spare perspective.

In China, Bodhidharma taught his Zen to a Chinese disciple named Huike (pronounced *Hway-ka*). This "Second Ancestor" is credited to have transmitted Bodhidharma's teachings to others in that country. Some records indicate that China's religious and political establishment initially rejected Bodhidharma's Zen movement, persecuting Bodhi-dharma and Huike as heretics. Accounts claim that certain religious rivals poisoned Bodhidharma and that others denounced his disciple Huike to the authorities. Those authorities reportedly executed Huike, then cast his corpse into a river.

Trouble with high authorities notwithstanding, Bodhidharma and his movement had wide impact even during his lifetime. A reliable record indicates that the sage traveled widely, and that his followers were "like a city." Having a large following and operating outside the political and religious establishment is often, of course, highly dangerous, so accounts of Bodhidharma's persecution by religious rivals and political circles seem credible.

Bodhidharma's legendary life grew in mythical detail as time passed and his religious message gained acclaim. This book examines the traditional account of his life. It also offers a different perspective, a view removed from prevailing religious and scholarly orthodoxy about Bodhidharma held in East Asia and the West. The narrative reinterprets and pieces together evidence to support a new perspective about this critical figure's life and importance. The accounts make use of the most reliable sources and shed new light on why later generations regarded Bodhidharma as such an important religious leader.

This is not simply an academic question. The ramifications of Bodhidharma's life and what he symbolized to China are only now becoming fully clear, and they extend to events that have shaped recent East Asian history. On the macro level, unraveling Bodhidharma's story reveals the roots of a narrative still being argued and even fought over in East Asia.

Besides Bodhidharma, two other figures who lived at or about his time play prominent roles in this narrative. One is China's great Tang dynasty Buddhist historian and scholar Daoxuan (pronounced *Dow Swan*) (596–667 CE). This remarkable man not only personally unified much of Chinese Buddhism but also chronicled in detail its people, thought, and movements. We can thank him for keeping Bodhidharma's life planted on the earth instead of floating in mythical clouds. Daoxuan's historical records play heavily in this story.

The other figure is an emperor. At the core of Bodhidharma's legend is his fabled encounter with Emperor Wu of the Liang dynasty, called the Bodhisattva Emperor (in East Asian Buddhism, a bodhisattva is an exalted spiritual being). Wu's reign (502–549 CE) represents the fusion of the Buddhist religion with Chinese state power and authority. Emperor Wu wedded his brilliant understanding of Buddhist tradition and theory with Confucian statecraft. The result served as the ideological basis of Wu's empire and reverberated through East Asian history. No thorough understanding of China and East Asia can overlook the critical developments that came from Emperor Wu. For this reason, this book looks at Emperor Wu's life in some detail. His intriguing story is the essential counterpoint to Bodhidharma, and the significance of each of these historic figures cannot be calculated without an understanding of the other.

As I said, I explore these questions while tracking Bodhidharma's ancient trail through China. Along the way are places that Bodhidharma lived and taught, places that reveal the cultural aftermath of his passing.

People with little prior knowledge of Zen may here have a first look at part of this deep wellspring of Chinese and East Asian culture. For readers with more prior knowledge of Zen history, the book should throw new light on the tradition's early years. But I hope that thoughtful readers with no knowledge whatsoever about Zen, about Bodhidharma, or even about Chinese history can here find an illuminating account of a critical story of East Asia history, a story that informs a better understanding of that region.

Zen, often called the "essence" of Chinese culture, had an important political component. This is not surprising. Politics has always engaged or lurked near the heart of religious movements. This is not to say that the Zen spiritual tradition is not important or that its insight is without gravitas. The tradition is engaging on both the spiritual and aesthetic plain, and its observations reach the limits of our understanding of the human condition. Arguments advanced by some modern physicists and even cosmologists fall in line with what the old Zen masters and the Buddha himself said about the world—that it is created by the mind. Scientists and philosophers still debate whether this is true only metaphorically or in some far stranger sense.

The Zen cultural tradition has bequeathed to the world a treasury of fine art, prose, and poetry. A solitary moon suspended in the void, a sweet-watered spring, a lonely mountain peak—the old Zen masters used such metaphors to suggest the nature of "signless" mind. The tradition's intimate love of nature and natural metaphor conjures a scenic trail in both fact and imagination. Bodhidharma's China road affords the traveler a chance to see how ancient landscapes of the Earth and the mind are withstanding China's exploding population and modernization. That critical question alone makes tracking Bodhidharma compelling. It is only one of the important questions an examination of his life and ancient path evokes.

Andy Ferguson
The Tao Po Hermitage
Port Townsend, WA
August 16, 2011

TRACKING BODHIDHARMA

1. An Auspicious Date

From high above,
Sublime the vision,
Islands beneath the rising sun.
—*Poem composed by Emperor Hirohito of Japan in 1939,*
submitted as his contribution to an imperial poetry contest

ON DECEMBER 7, 1941, Japanese Zeros flew out of the rising sun of a Hawaiian morning to rain destruction on the U.S. Pacific Fleet in Pearl Harbor. Personally planned and approved by Emperor Hirohito, the attack plunged the United States into the most catastrophic war in human history. But the date that flashed across the screens of Japan's war propaganda films celebrating the attack was not December 7, but December 8, the date that had already arrived in Japan when the first bombs fell in Hawaii.

The date was not serendipitous. Emperor Hirohito selected December 8 as particularly auspicious and meaningful, for according to Japan's Buddhist tradition, that date corresponds with Buddha's enlightenment day, the day when the historical Buddha Shakyamuni sat in meditation as dawn approached, then suddenly experienced enlightenment as he observed the morning star that accompanied the sunrise.

The symbolic date of the attack punctuates the role that Buddhism and its doctrines played in Japan's militarist and imperial ideology. Recently the historian Brian Victoria has detailed how Buddhism, including Zen Buddhism, played a critical role in the ideology of emperor worship in Japan before and during the war. The religion meshed deeply with native Shintoism to underpin the country's war propaganda. How, one might ask, did a pacifist religion, known as dedicated to peace and brotherhood, travel so far from its fundamental teachings to become a weapon in Japan's arsenal of imperial war?

These strange developments belie the notion that Buddhism has unerringly sided with pacifism and opposed armed conflict. As a Zen practitioner and researcher for the past three decades, I confess that Brian Victoria's narrative of the events of WWII presents me with a troubling set of questions that beg for an explanation.

Fully understanding Zen and its perplexing history has led me here to Hong Kong where I sit today on the shore in Kowloon watching the Star Ferry shuttle back and forth to Hong Kong Island under a bright autumn sun. I plan to follow the long overgrown trail of the figure credited with establishing Buddhist Zen in China, a legendary and enigmatic Indian holy man named Bodhidharma. What, after all, did he stand for?

Much about Bodhidharma's life remains obscure, and scholars debate almost everything about him. What we know comes from old Chinese records of varied reliability, complemented with legends and folklore blown up to mythic proportions.

Bodhidharma (?–528?), a Buddhist missionary from South India, arrived in China about fifteen centuries ago near where I write these words. His ship sailed into China on the Pearl River, the waterway that flows past the Chinese city of Guangzhou (previously called Canton) and empties into the South China Sea. He would ultimately be remembered as the First Ancestor of Zen, China's dominant religious tradition. Many in China say that Bodhidharma and the Zen masters that followed him, his "spiritual descendants," comprise the essence of Chinese culture.

Guangzhou, where he landed, has long been a gate of intercourse between China and the world. It is where British gunboats compelled China to import British opium, a drug that helped anaesthetize Chinese resistance to Western and Japanese imperialism, in the infamous Opium Wars of the mid-nineteenth century. Guangzhou is also where Sun Yat-sen and other luminaries of the 1911 Republican Revolution organized a failed attempt to introduce Western-style democracy to China.

Bodhidharma's influence on China was far greater than the Opium Wars or even the Republican Revolution.

Who was he? We know little of certainty about his origins beyond that he was a Buddhist monk who was born a Brahman, India's highest caste. He reached China after years at sea had thinned his cheeks, but his eyes, says his legend, matched the ocean's blue waves. They may have betrayed a Greco-Aryan bloodline. Perhaps his ancestors came from where Alexander's army rolled across India and his soldiers settled to intermarry with the local population. The earliest statues of the Buddha, which appeared where Alexander's colonies prevailed, look more like Greek gods than Hindu deities. The Chinese nicknamed Bodhidharma the "Blue-Eyed Barbarian."

Other South Asian monks besides Bodhidharma braved the tortuous currents and typhoons of the South China Sea to spread Buddha's teachings. Modern historians call those ancient sea lanes the Ocean Silk Road, the trading route that passes between South and East Asia through the Strait of Malacca.

Bodhidharma stepped ashore in a China fractured with ethnic rivalry, feudal fiefdoms, and a prolonged civil war between the country's north and south. In the centuries before his arrival, China experienced conflict, disintegration, and chaos. The people who embraced Bodhidharma's teaching had endured much and suffered more. They had already known Buddhism for several centuries before Bodhidharma arrived. Yet his Zen caught the imagination of the world-weary populace, and so rulers, aristocrats, and commoners eventually embraced religious practices connected with his name. The teachings of one lonely sramana (holy man) who walked up a gangplank in Guangzhou into a chaotic country eventually conquered it, then spread far beyond its borders. I'll start my search for Bodhidharma's traces by going to where he stepped ashore.

LOWU STATION, ON THE BORDER BETWEEN
HONG KONG AND CHINA'S GUANGDONG PROVINCE

The white incandescent bulbs of the immigration hall cast pallor on the faces of people in slow moving lines waiting to cross the border into China.

There is a short, pock-faced Chinese man with a leggy girlfriend standing ahead of me. She displays Italian fashion from hair to high heels, the shoes making her a head taller than her boyfriend. She is intently focused on everything he says. The man's pocked face and eyes convey menace, and his tailored suit sticks out among a ragged line of people wearing street market clothes. His eyes skip back and forth, parodying some shifty-eyed stereotype. I remember news stories of Hong Kong triad godfathers and gangs and so avoid staring at the odd couple. My mind drifts to thoughts about the trip that lies before me.

But my thoughts are scattered by a shrieking sound. It takes a few startled seconds to realize that I'm hearing the sound effects from the shower scene in Alfred Hitchcock's *Psycho*. It's the *ree, ree, ree* part where a shadowy figure is steadily swinging a broad-bladed knife under a gray light, plunging it into the naked body of Marion Crane (played by Janet Leigh) in the Bates Motel shower. I turn and look for the source of the sound. Then it grows louder, and I turn back to see that the pock-faced man has pulled his mobile phone from his jacket. He presses the button to talk. The shrieking sound stops. "*Wei!*" (Hello) he says. He begins talking in Cantonese. None of the other people in line pays any attention. Welcome to new China.

When I first traveled this route into China in 1978, there were no stampeding crowds. On that morning a humid fog lifted on the Hong Kong side to reveal a landscape of ragged shacks and fish ponds where limp Kuomintang flags hung defiantly within sight of the border. After a few hours' ride from Kowloon Station, our creaky train rolled across a splintered trestle to stop at the bare-brick Lowu checkpoint. Our group, a "U.S.-China People's Friendship Tour," looked excitedly at the rice paddies. Then, with entry chops pressed in passports, we rolled into the direct aftermath of the Cultural Revolution. The rice fields and shacks that met us just across the border in 1978 are now the supercity of Shenzhen, the export manufacturing zone that China's leader Deng Xiaoping dreamed of when he said "to get rich is glorious."

Many Westerners, if they've thought about Zen at all, associate it with Japan. But the tradition flourished in China for about seven hundred years before it finally took root in the Land of the Rising Sun. By then its original incandescence was dimmed by devotional religious practice and literary artifice. Politicians, poets, and dilettantes laid claim to the religion. Even in that age, the word *Zen* was thought to be cool and hip, something hard to define, imparting an attractive and enigmatic air to anyone believed to understand it.

Although after many centuries Zen suffered decline in China, it found a strange, fresh new life by leaping across the East China Sea to Japan. There its impact was widespread, stretching deeply into the country's cultural life. It spawned enduring arts well-known today, such as ornate tea ceremonies, austere rock gardens, and poignant flower arrangements.

In China, Zen interacted with China's native Confucian and Taoist culture, and this meeting had a deep and lasting influence. The religion spread not just because of its engaging insight, but also because its literature coincided with the development of woodblock printing. In its late literary heyday, Zen rode this technological wave, then caught another with the Chinese invention of movable type by an alchemist named Bi Sheng.

Zen is a Sinicized form of Indian Buddhism. The hybrid came about partly because translators introduced Buddhist ideas from India to China using Chinese words already pregnant with meaning. The meanings came mainly from China's nature-loving, magic-imbued Taoist philosophy. For example, when Buddhism arrived in China, the country already used the phrase "The Way" to describe an exalted path of philosophical or aesthetic insight and practice. "Attaining the Way" was a phrase imbued with both Taoist and Confucian ideals, China's native modes of thought. Buddhism exploited this phraseology, and "attaining the Buddha Way" nimbly introduced Buddha's enlightenment to a Chinese audience. Chinese language and thought molded and culturally reinterpreted Buddhism in China. This pattern was widespread and long-lived.

Buddhism was long established in China before "Zen" became its dominant current. The religion arrived about five hundred years before Bodhidharma sailed up the Pearl River. In fact, even Zen and Zen practice were common in China before Bodhidharma reached its shores and was crowned Zen's "First Ancestor." So a major question about Bodhidharma concerns why it was he, and not any of his many Zen predecessors, who got that sobriquet.

Some commentators suggest that Bodhidharma was called the First Ancestor of the Zen school because he was the first to emphasize directly observing the nature of the mind. But I haven't found evidence that this is so, for "observing mind" and equating the mind with Buddha's teachings was taught in China before Bodhidharma arrived there. Evidence suggests that as novel as Bodhidharma's approach to teaching

Zen may have been, it was his politics that secured his importance to the tradition.

Bodhidharma's spiritual descendents flourished in China and spread his message to Korea and Vietnam within a century or so of its arrival in China. Now there are Zen teachers and students in China, other East Asian countries, and many other places. In the West, Zen has a small but growing group of followers.

THE TRAIN TO GUANGZHOU

On the fast new train to Guangzhou, a train attendant passes out complimentary bottles of water. She hands two bottles to a middle-aged Chinese man sitting next to me and he offers me one of them. I thank him in Chinese, and he says, "You must live in China." I tell him I'm just a tourist, and he says, "No, you speak well. You must live here." I ask him where he's from. He says he's from Guangzhou and is returning from visiting his son in Hong Kong. We chat a little about what we're doing. His name is Li. He's over sixty and is a businessman with a factory in Guangzhou that makes metal products. He sells die-cast parts and castings to some big-name tool companies in North America.

He says he recently visited the United States as a tourist.

"What did you think?" I ask him.

"You have a nice environment in America, with lots of land and not many people." Then he says, "Here in China, we have too many people. That's the biggest problem. Many other problems come from that."

While we chat, a young boy a few seats away sits entranced with a video game. He erupts with an exclamation. Mr. Li looks at the boy for a long moment then turns to speak to me again.

"Ah! When I was a boy, I lived in a poor village. We had to make up our own games. We didn't have toys or even a radio. We would make straw figures or mud balls. Even if we only had mud balls, we would play all day and half the night. I remember that the best thing was when some grown-up would dress up in a costume and walk around on high stilts. We kids would run down the street after him, all excited, jumping up and down, pointing and yelling. That was our entertainment."

After we talk a while more, I ask Mr. Li a question. "Do you know who Bodhidharma is?"

"I do," he says. "When I was a child, my grandmother kept a little shrine in the house where she prayed. The statue in the shrine was of the bodhisattva Kwan Yin, but a little figure that sat next to it was Bodhidharma. She called him "Saint Bodhi." That's what I remember. The figure was carved out of wood."

2. Guangzhou

IN THE EARLY AFTERNOON, the train arrives at Guangzhou Station, and I find my way to a nearby subway station and make my way to my hotel. Unlike the barren and broken city that met me in 1978, in the truly new China of free enterprise there are many small hotel chains. My lodging tonight is typical, an inexpensive but comfortable chain named Like Home.

When first I arrived here in 1978, Guangzhou and the entire mainland lay crushed under the debris of the Great Proletarian Cultural Revolution. Then there were no evident traces of Bodhidharma in the city where he arrived in China. The night streets of Guangzhou in 1978 were quite literally dark, for even streetlights were rare. We walked long boulevards illuminated only by the headlights of an occasional public bus or belching truck. The Chinese pedestrians still sported the blue or gray Mao jackets of the day. But even then, just before economic reforms were unleashed, things were changing. One night I walked with two young women from the tour past a dark intersection. Emerging from the drab landscape, we discovered an advertisement for a local business hotel's coffee shop (Guangzhou was already the site of China's annual foreign trade fair). The ad was a near-life-size, cutout figure of a Western woman with long, wavy blond hair, the word *welcome* printed awkwardly on her torso. It was a portent of the future. "Look," said one of my feminist companions dejectedly, "she's windswept!"

We found little else of interest in Guangzhou then. The tour visited the Wampoa Military Academy where, in the early twentieth century, cadets of Sun Yat-sen's nationalist army trained to help build a new Chinese nation. We walked the barracks and looked at old photos above the spartan beds, sad shots of young men born in an unfortunate time, most fated to die in China's early but aborted attempt at modernity.

I remember a banquet we attended. It was in a well-known restaurant used by foreign traders and local officials. A high-level Communist cadre came to join us for dinner. He didn't say much but seemed to relish the good meal being paid for by our Beijing-based guides. I ventured to try out my Chinese language skills on him by asking him the following bit of nonsense.

"Wasn't the smashing of the Gang of Four important because the failures of their radical policies only dampened the peasants' enthusiasm for socialism?"

He didn't look up as he slurped his soup, a few drops glistening on his chin. "Yes, yes, of course," he mumbled. "That is fundamental . . ." He slurped another spoonful and stuffed a dumpling in his mouth, then repeated himself. "That is fundamental."

Whether in 1978 or today, knowing how to read and speak Chinese is almost necessary for traveling alone in China, since there are few English or other European language signs to help guide you through the country. Yet some language facility is no panacea. I've spent considerable time searching for places shown on maps that are maddeningly hard or impossible to locate. Locals don't always know the places I'm looking for and, anyway, seldom provide good directions to find something. Asking directions often goes like this:

Me: "Excuse me, can you tell me where Western Happiness Temple is located?"

Direction-giver: "Go straight."

Me: "Is it on the right or left?"

Direction-giver: "Just go straight."

To "go straight" means that you are going in the right direction but doesn't necessarily mean there are no further corners or intersections to be navigated correctly and provides no clue about how much longer you need to keep going. Similarly, I might be in a big department store that covers an entire block in China and ask a clerk where I can find a camera shop. He or she is likely to say, "Next door," without any indication of which direction one should go to find the store "next door."

But my schedule and route for the next couple of days will be without such problems. An old friend of mine who is now abbot of a famous Zen monastery in Northern China has made introductions on my behalf. Bright Sea, of whom I'll speak more later, called a friend of his named Yaozhi (whose name means "Brilliant Wisdom"), the abbot of Grand

Buddha Temple here in Guangzhou. He explained the reasons for my coming and asked Yaozhi to assist me. So now I call Yaozhi on my mobile phone, and he already knows who I am and why I've come. He's ready to help me search for Bodhidharma's trail and will be at my hotel tomorrow morning at nine.

There's no restaurant in the Like Home. I spend twenty minutes or so walking in the area of the hotel to find a restaurant, but there doesn't seem to be anything that offers passable vegetarian food. Finally I go back to the hotel and ask the desk clerk to direct me to a supermarket where I can buy some things to hold me over. She directs me to a big modern place about eight blocks from the hotel. I eventually find it tucked in a shopping center that offers the usual array of dress shops, sneaker stores, and ginseng sellers that abound in China. I ride an escalator to the second floor to where the market offers a wide variety of groceries, a fair portion of them imported. Well-dressed shoppers move up and down the aisles with brimming carts. Visiting stores in China's big cities today is no different from such places in any modern city in the world.

After buying a few things, I return to my hotel by way of the nearby Pearl River shoreline, along the banks where Bodhidharma came ashore in China.

The most widely believed account of Bodhidharma's life claims that he arrived in China in the year 527 in Guangzhou. He then immediately traveled to Nanjing at the invitation of Emperor Wu of the Liang dynasty. Emperor Wu believed deeply in Buddhism, elevating it to the status of a state religion. He invited Buddhist teachers from all over Asia to visit his palace and teach the religion's philosophy, and tradition says that Bodhidharma was likewise invited to perform this service. The central story that Zen has preserved about Bodhidharma is that when he met Emperor Wu in Nanjing at the latter's invitation in 527 CE, the two did not have the same views about proper Buddhist theory and practice. Emperor Wu expected Bodhidharma to praise him for the material and public support he had provided to Buddhism, but instead Bodhidharma rejected the emperor's religious activities. This was, of course, a big affront to the "Bodhisattva Emperor." Thereafter, says this traditional account, Bodhidharma crossed the Yang-tse River (folklore says he did so on a single stalk of bamboo) and proceeded north to live at Shaolin Temple in North-Central China. He allegedly lived in a cave on a mountain behind Shaolin Temple for nine years before dying in the year 536. This traditional story claims that Bodhidharma was then buried at Dinglin ("Samadhi Woods") Temple, a place west of the ancient city of Luoyang.

FIGURE 1. Bodhidharma Arrives in South China in the Year 527 CE (Traditional Story).

This widely believed traditional story, which is first seen in texts from about four hundred years after Bodhidharma lived, is almost certainly not an accurate account of Bodhidharma's life.

Serious scholars believe that a book called the *Continued Biographies of Eminent Monks* (which I'll hereafter call the *Continued Biographies*), a book written around the year 650, a time much closer to when Bodhidharma lived, provides a far more reliable account of his life. The author, the monk Daoxuan, probably knew Zen monks who were Bodhidharma's second generation of disciples. Daoxuan's book is written in a terse and hard-to-read style of classical Chinese writing, difficult even for well-educated Chinese scholars. Despite its obtuseness, prying information out of Daoxuan's old text is essential for getting the best understanding about Bodhidharma and his early disciples. Through examining this old text carefully, and reviewing commentaries about it by Chinese scholars, I have discovered some new clues about Bodhidharma. Those clues figure heavily in my plans for this trip along his path in China.

Daoxuan's *Continued Biographies* were called "continued" because the text followed a similar book that appeared a hundred years earlier. That earlier text, called *Biographies of Eminent Monks*, was written during the time Bodhidharma lived but makes no mention of him. This is an important first clue about Bodhidharma's life in China, for it indicates that official and literary circles didn't know much about him, perhaps, it seems, because he purposefully avoided them.

Daoxuan was a towering figure in both the history of Chinese Buddhism and Chinese scholarship. He established his own "South Mountain" Buddhist sect that, in its heyday, had enormous influence and prestige in China's imperial establishment. His Buddhism emphasized the "precepts," the rules of discipline by which Buddhist monks and nuns live. But as time went on, his sect shrank in size, losing ground to Zen and other Buddhist schools. During the early twentieth century, his Chinese Precepts school (also commonly referred to as the Vinaya school) nearly died out, but has recently started growing again.

To know the most reliable story we have about Bodhidharma, we must look at what Daoxuan had to say about him. Here's what he wrote in the *Continued Biographies*:

> Bodhidharma: A Brahman from South India. His spiritual wisdom was expansive. All who heard him became enlightened. He was devoted to the Mahayana practice of the profound solitary mind. He attained high comprehension of all aspects of meditation. Through compassion for this place [China] he taught the Yogacara [teachings]. He first arrived in South China during the Liu-Song dynasty [before the year 479]. At the end of his life he again traveled to live under the Wei [the dynasty that ruled North China]. Wherever he went he taught Zen. During his time he taught throughout the entire country. Upon first hearing the samadhi [meditation] teaching there were many who reviled him. [But] there were two monks named Daoyu and Huike who became his disciples. Although they were older [than typical new disciples] they were highly astute. Upon first hearing the teaching they immediately realized the Way and took their vows [became Bodhidharma's disciples]. They studied closely with him for four or five years, receiving his instruction. [Bodhidharma] understood their sincerity and conveyed to them the true Dharma, such as pacifying the mind [by the method of] meditation while facing a

wall, such as undertaking the practice known as the "Four Methods," such as liberating beings in the face of criticism, and such as not using [demons to scare people] as an expedient. [Bodhidharma said,] "There are many paths to enter the Way, but essentially there are only two, which are [entering through] principle and [entering through] practice. [The first is] accepting the enlightened doctrine that all beings possess the same true nature which is obstructed [from our view] by worldly attachments. [This doctrine] leads us to forsake the false and return to the true by sitting and facing a wall, with no self or other, [and where] sacred and mundane are the same; resolute and unmoving, not pursuing some external teaching, remaining solitary in non-action in accordance with the mysterious Way, this is called "entering the Way through principle." Entering the Way through practice entails four essential practices derived from ten thousand . . .

[The "Four Practices" are then summarized, and may be shortened as (1) accepting your karmic conditions, (2) endeavoring to practice with the conditions one encounters, (3) seeking nothing more than this, and (4) adhering to Buddhist teachings.]

". . . Bodhidharma, with these methods, converted [the people of] the Wei [the dynasty that ruled North China]. The noble who recognized the truth honored him, and turned to enlightenment. Records of his teachings circulate in the world. He personally said that he was one hundred and fifty years of age. His task was traveling and teaching. It's not known where he died.

A few things should be noted from this account. First, Bodhidharma was a real person, with a wide following, who taught in both Southern and Northern China. Second, the passage has no specific mention of Bodhidharma directly meeting any emperors or high officials, so his legendary meeting with Emperor Wu is not mentioned in this early, relatively reliable record.

Third, this account, as well as later texts, claims Bodhidharma arrived in China by sea. Although the *Continued Biographies* record doesn't

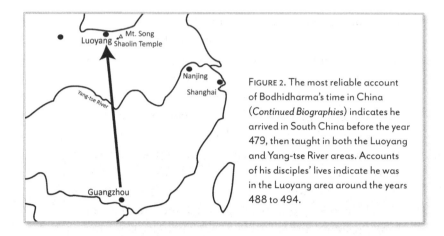

FIGURE 2. The most reliable account of Bodhidharma's time in China (*Continued Biographies*) indicates he arrived in South China before the year 479, then taught in both the Luoyang and Yang-tse River areas. Accounts of his disciples' lives indicate he was in the Luoyang area around the years 488 to 494.

give a specific location, its statement that he "arrived in South China" supports the idea that the Indian holy man did indeed step ashore here in Guangzhou, the biggest port in South China of his age.

While in college, I was intrigued by the strange account of Bodhidharma "crossing the Yang-tse River on a single blade of grass" (usually depicted in paintings as a stalk of bamboo). Fleeing from Emperor Wu's court, the old sage is shown floating over the wide Yang-tse's blue waves, his bare feet balanced on the slender stalk of the plant. There are countless depictions of this legendary event in Chinese art, and Chinese who know little else about Zen are familiar with the scene. Bodhidharma's ride over the waves, escaping from the influence of Emperor Wu, evokes a feeling of inspired defiance. Such depictions also suggest a rejection of the world's folly and of crossing over the river of existence to the "other shore," a Buddhist metaphor for liberation.

In Hong Kong during the 1970s and early '80s, I perused Chinese antique stores for paintings or other depictions of Bodhidharma's famous crossing. It was one of my two favorite Chinese artistic themes, the other being depictions of carp leaping through the Dragon Gate on the Yellow River. The latter, a very ancient story, is intimately connected to China's birth as a civilization, but it has connections to Bodhidharma as well. The carp traditionally symbolize China's first dynastic king, known as King Yu. In paintings and other arts that depict the scene, Yellow River fish turned to dragons if they successfully swim upstream and conquer the river's rapids. Likewise, King Yu became the first "Dragon

Emperor" when he conquered the Yellow River for the Chinese people by dredging and building dikes to control its notoriously silting and flooding currents.

Once during a visit to Hong Kong in 1982, I purchased works related to these legends. One was a tiny vase dated to the year 1915 that shows Bodhidharma, his jaunty face posed defiantly, riding his slip of bamboo across the Yang-tse's bouncing waves. The other work I bought that day, a traditional painting, shows three carp, one of which has successfully leapt beyond the waves of the Yellow River to attain dragon status. The painting, dated with a signature of a famous Chinese painter of the late fifteenth century named Lu Zhi, is a fake. But it's a very nice fake that is probably more than one hundred years old. Following Bodhidharma's path will take me to where both of the events depicted in those two pieces of art took place.

Since Bodhidharma arrived here in Guangzhou, the Pearl River has changed its course many times. In his time, a maze of marinas and docks crowded the riverbank, using all available real estate for loading and unloading bundled trade goods that flowed to and from ancient kingdoms that surrounded the South China Sea and beyond. Now the container freight that passes to and from the waterway does so through immense terminals and wharfs located outside Guangzhou city proper, leaving the banks here less cluttered if also less scenic.

Sitting on a stair that leads into the water and serves as a landing for small pleasure boats, I shade my eyes against the sunset to watch a tugboat pass. I wonder how many of Guangzhou's citizens, many of whom crowd the shore around me to enjoy the fall evening, are aware of who Bodhidharma was, and that he started his religious mission in China at this place.

3. Hualin Temple

AT NINE IN THE MORNING, a black SUV rolls up to the front door of the Like Home Hotel. I open the door behind the driver and hop in the backseat of the vehicle. There, next to me, sits abbot Yaozhi [pronounced *Yow Jer*] of Grand Buddha Temple. He greets me warmly. A monk sitting in front next to the driver also introduces himself; his name is Ruxin (pronounced *Roo Sin*), and he's a senior monk at the temple. Yaozhi gives the instant impression of being a very friendly and humble individual. His round face holds sympathetic eyes and a quick smile. He welcomes me to Guangzhou and asks if everything at my hotel is okay. I tell him that the Like Home Hotel is fine and really does try to make you feel at home. Except, I say, it's not really like home, because they'll do your laundry for you. Yaozhi and Ruxin laugh politely at my lame joke, and Ruxin says that I shouldn't feel bad, as in China husbands also have to do their own laundry these days.

It's only a few blocks to Hualin Temple, the place where tradition says Bodhidharma started teaching in China. We soon exit the SUV and enter a pedestrian-only walkway called Jade Street, a place where locals and tourists buy jewelry and ornaments made from China's most famous gemstone. In the midst of the tree-shaded street is a pretty fountain that sits before the front gate of the temple. Waiting at that gate is a middle-aged monk who will act as our guide.

After some introductions, I explain to the small entourage that I have visited the temple on some previous occasions but now want to dig deeper into the legend of Bodhidharma, to try to sort out facts from folklore.

There's a part of Chinese culture and demeanor that I would describe as "no need to dig too deeply." The idea is that it might be better not to investigate something too deeply just for the sake of doing so. This attitude is part of the immense patience that dwells deeply in China. It's

FIGURE 3. Guangzhou Temples: Hualin Temple, located a few hundred meters north of the Pearl River in downtown Guangzhou, is where Bodhidharma is said to have first taught in China. Legends say he also lived at Guangxiao Temple.

a practical view that exists to help maintain social harmony and face-saving. The attitude helps explain why the Chinese are in no hurry to excavate the tomb of Qin Shi Huang, the first emperor of China. They say that technology needs to improve before such a thing is attempted, and if that means waiting for a few score more years, then so be it. The idea is that "this situation will eventually change, so let's not get too worked up about it."

So, when a foreigner like me shows up and wants to poke deeper into some myths that are important to people, I may meet a bemused reaction. Who cares if the sign on the front of Hualin Temple says Bodhidharma came here in 527, even though this contradicts the most reliable historical sources about his life? Does questioning any of this change the Bodhidharma story or what he stands for? Just practice what he said and forget about the details!

Okay. Some other religions depend on the truth of their original teacher's divinity to prove their worth. To Christians, Christ must be the Son of God and to have risen from the grave after three days. But Buddhism doesn't require such validation. Zen doesn't direct its belief system to something outside (well it can, but that's not the important bit). What does it matter if some particular person was the one who said some truth? Someone said it, so who cares who it was? In light of this viewpoint, which is admittedly hard to contest, what's the difference if the old stories about Bodhidharma are a little contradictory and confused?

What makes Bodhidharma's story interesting is that it appears to express a desire for freedom in the Asian context. The fuzzy contradictions and mystical bits of Bodhidharma's life may detract from taking the story seriously. But his life and its aftermath cover too much ground and tell too much about how the world works. It touches territory spreading from the dark corners of human ignorance to the leading edge of science. It's a good narrative for looking at some old questions in a new light.

FIGURE 4. The Bodhidharma Memorial Hall at Hualin Temple.

Our guide leads us into the Five Hundred Arhats Hall, where five hundred life-size "arhats" (Chinese: *lohan*), disciples of Buddha, are displayed. There are no genuine records, of course, that list five hundred disciples of Buddha who directly studied with him, and the figures here are accretions that showed up over the centuries. All of them have associated stories that convey moral object lessons of one sort or another. The figures in the hall are full-size and displayed in various poses and expressions related to their legends. The guide explains that all the original statues were destroyed during the Cultural Revolution, but the hall and the stands remained, so after the temple was reopened, the statues were replaced.

While the Cultural Revolution was an orgy of senseless destruction, it was certainly not the only time that Buddhism has been persecuted and nearly wiped out in Chinese history. Similar, if less extreme, episodes were not uncommon even in Bodhidharma's time. Around the year 600, the situation for Buddhism appeared so precarious that many important monks like Daoxuan thought that Buddhist teachings might soon disappear. To prevent this, Buddhists started a project to carve the entire Buddhist canon, literally hundreds of books of scripture, onto stone tablets. The stone tablets were then placed in sealed caves so that after Buddhism had been outwardly destroyed, the scriptures could again be found. This immense project, involving the carving of thousands of large stone tablets, continued over an eight-hundred-year period and was perhaps the longest single project ever undertaken in human history. I often accompany groups to view the tables, at a place called Yunju Temple, about an hour outside of Beijing. So, while the destruction of the Cultural Revolution was severe, it is only a blip in the long timeline of Chinese Buddhist history. After the Cultural Revolution spent itself, the tablets of Yunju Temple were uncovered to a country again open to Buddha's teachings.

At one side of the Five Hundred Arhats Hall, there is an odd statue sitting among the many Chinese-looking figures. The guide points to it and says, "There's Marco Polo." Sure enough, sitting next to Dizang, one of the four great Chinese bodhisattvas, there is an odd-looking statue with exaggerated Western features. It's strange to see the famous Venetian adventurer sitting in a pantheon of Buddhist legends. Yet it is not too surprising. Chinese have always welcomed foreigners, so the fact that they've given Marco Polo the status of an arhat, one of Buddha's disciples, is not extraordinary. After all, he came from the "West," someplace in the sacred direction of the Western Paradise, where Buddha lived, and the source of the sacred scriptures! Anyway, this religious inclusiveness between East and West has worked both ways. During the early days when the Roman Catholic Church sent missionaries to China, the pope recognized the Buddha as a Catholic saint. It seems that the Holy See figured that it would be easier to offer salvation from the top down. If you simply change the god that people were worshiping into a Catholic saint, then their prayers will automatically become legitimate.

As we gaze at Marco Polo, a bystander overhears me talking and says something like "Oh, this foreigner can speak Chinese!" I turn to say hello and see a look of surprise on the man's odd-looking face. I say hello again, but he's now speechless and seems shocked. The abbot and other monks appear embarrassed and start moving me away from this odd denizen of the temple.

"I recognize you," I say. "Yes, you're Ji Gong! You're very famous."

"What? No, no," says the man. "That's not me!"

Everyone politely laughs at my feeble joke. Ji Gong was a legendary monk in Hangzhou that lived during the Song dynasty. He reportedly often violated the Buddhist precepts by getting drunk, eating meat, and showing up late for morning temple services. At Nanhua Temple, the Dharma seat of the famous Sixth Ancestor of Zen, there's a statue of Ji Gong by a window in the Buddha Hall where services are held every day. He's sneaking in after the door was locked for latecomers. Despite his famous shortcomings, Ji Gong supposedly performed miraculous feats and became known as a "living Buddha." He's often depicted with a face that looks like the man who now tags along with our group, a face sculpted by a hard world.

We emerge back into the temple's courtyard. There stands a "Śarīra tower," a type of pagoda structure about fifteen feet tall. In the 1960s, construction crews were moving the structure from a location in a local park when an underground vault was discovered beneath it. In the vault was a box that reportedly contained sacred relics of the Buddha, the jewels that remained after his body was cremated. The relics were retained by the local historical society, and the Śarīra tower was moved inside the Hualin Temple grounds.

We talk about the origin of the name of Hualin Temple. *Hualin* means "Flowered Woods." The place is named after the garden where Emperor Wu is believed to have met Bodhidharma. This occurred in Jiankang, capital of the Liang dynasty, the city now called Nanjing. Flowered Woods was mainly a private park at the rear of the palace grounds for the emperor and his family. It was also the venue for several of Emperor Wu's great religious events.

In passing, I mention to my hosts that I'm interested to know more about the many monks who came to China on the "Ocean Silk Road." While the Silk Road that passes through the desert is more famous, the sea route that passes through the Strait of Malacca were a well-traveled and important part of China's Western contacts in ancient times.

Yaozhi says, "There's a scholar who's just written a book about that!" In a few seconds he's pulled out his cell phone and started dialing, apparently following up on my interest.

On the other side of the courtyard is the back door of a large hall facing south toward the Pearl River, which is about a thousand meters away but obscured by city buildings. In ancient times that river is said to have flowed even closer to where we now stand, and thus this is the approximate place where Bodhidharma is said to have come ashore. What is unexplained, of course, is why Bodhidharma would build his teaching spot at virtually the very spot where he first stepped on land. I'd think the stevedores loading and emptying boats with their goods-laden shoulder poles might overrun him. Anyway, that's the story.

The big hall at the center of Hualin Temple is the Bodhidharma Hall, and it is a model of traditional Chinese Buddhist architecture, sporting ornate wooden roof beams and fishtail gables, all supported by columns wrapped with carved dragons. We walk around to the front door on the south side of the building and look in to see a twenty-foot-tall statue of Bodhidharma at its center. The guide says it was cast using three layers of bronze that were stacked one on top of the other and then sealed and polished to form the complete figure. The whole statue weighs nearly ten tons. It's an impressive work of modern statue making. Of course casting technology these days is nothing compared to what the Chinese of ancient times were capable of doing. In Beijing there is something called the Yong Le Bell, a Buddhist bell ordered cast around the year 1426 by Emperor Judi of the Ming dynasty, the same emperor who built the Forbidden City. The single casting from which the bell is made weighs an astonishing fifty-four tons (forty-eight metric tons), and on its internal and outer surfaces are two hundred and fifty thousand Chinese characters integrally cast in the bell body, all displaying text from Buddhist scriptures. Anyone who knows about bronze-casting technology and the difficulties involved in making such a one-piece masterpiece is at a loss to comprehend how this giant Buddhist bell was made in ancient times. It still hangs on public display at the Big Bell Temple museum in Beijing and is rung during the Chinese New Year celebrations.

The situation with Hualin Temple is like many other temples in China that are in an urban setting. After 1949, when religions came under pressure, much of their original land was appropriated by the government and used to create housing and other purposes, their area squeezing into smaller and smaller compounds. Finally, during the Cultural Revolution, they were closed completely, their contents generally ransacked or destroyed. After 1980 the temples began reopening, and with help from sympathetic local governments, many are getting back some of the land that was taken from them. Hualin Temple is expanding again, albeit slowly. When I ask how long this will take, my hosts laugh a little nervously. I say, "Well, Chinese are patient. Even if it takes a hundred years, that's okay." Ruxin smiles in agreement. He says that maybe it could even take several hundred years to complete. As the story of the stone tablets of Yunju Temple shows, Chinese have patience and a different sense of time. The old joke is that when two Chinese people meet, one will ask, "Where is your hometown?" The other then answers, "In Hebei Province." "When did you leave Hebei?" says the first person. "Six generations ago."

We then walk back to the temple gate and into the pedestrian street out front. Along Jade Street, shops sell every manner of jade ornaments and jewelry. We walk south along the street for a short distance and make a turn to pass under a *paifang*, one of those big ornamental Chinese gates made from stone. It commemorates and marks the spot of Bodhidharma's arrival in China. The characters written on the stone cross beam at the top of the *paifang* literally read WEST COMING FIRST PLACE. A small paved plaza sits on the other side of the gate, nestled between some buildings. At one end of the plaza is a cement railing enclosing a small area. Within the enclosed area, five round cement blocks lie on the ground. Each is a wellhead of an ancient water source. The well with its five round wellheads is called the Five Eyes Well. Four of the holes covered by the cement blocks form a square with the fifth hole placed in the center of the others. The guide explains that the hole in the center was the well discovered by Bodhidharma, while the four around the outside were enlargements dug by Bodhidharma's disciples. A legend says that after arriving in Guangzhou, Bodhidharma was walking along near the shore of the river, then struck the ground with his staff and said, "There's treasure there!" Some men standing nearby heard these exciting words from a foreign holy man and started digging on the spot. Instead of gold, sweet water came up from the ground in the middle of the brackish tidal area. The well, I'm told, continued to be used as a

FIGURE 5. "West Coming First Place" Gate. The legendary place where Bodhidharma is said to have come ashore in China by the Pearl River, Guangzhou. Now a pedestrian shopping street.

unique source of fresh water in the brackish soil around the city until 1953, when the government installed water pipes to area homes.

After a group picture, our car pulls up on the side street nearby and we climb inside, ready to proceed to visit my host abbot Yaozhi's Grand Buddha Temple.

Whether or not Hualin Temple has any real connection to Bodhidharma is tenuous. While tradition says that Bodhidharma set up a hermitage and started teaching after his arrival in Guangzhou, nearly everyone would admit that simple logic defies this story. First, there are no contemporary records that say exactly when or where Bodhidharma arrived in China. Even the most reliable record, the *Continued Biographies*, was written roughly 160-odd years after it claims Bodhidharma arrived. It says he came during the Liu-Song dynasty. That dynasty fell in the year 479, nearly fifty years before the sign on Hualin Temple says Bodhidharma first arrived at this place. One very strange thing is that the temple claims to have been established in the year 526, a year before an often-cited version of Bodhidharma's legend says he even arrived in the country. Hualin Temple definitely raises more questions than it answers about Bodhidharma and his real story.

Bodhidharma's life has been hotly debated by scholars. Most of his traditional story comes from accounts and legends created after he lived, most of it long after. This tardiness led to some Japanese and Western scholars downplaying his importance during the time he lived or even denying that he existed. In the post–World War II period, scholars in Japan and the West "deconstructed" East Asia's prevailing myths, especially the divinity of the Japanese emperor, lately the cause of so much misery and pain. Bodhidharma's was among the stories reexamined in the glare of new intellectual fashions such as "postmodernism" and "deconstructionism." In my view, the result was that Bodhidharma was cut loose from his cultural and religious moorings to become, not just in the eyes of scholars but even the Western Zen tradition, a sort of placeholder—just a symbol in history's parade. Though he was the founder of arguably the main religious current in the world's longest surviving civilization, his life has been strangely marginalized, demoted to the status of a footnote appended to an obscure place and time. Bodhidharma's "deconstruction" by scholars is reflected in pronouncements like the following by the Buddhist scholar Bernard Faure: "Bodhidharma does not . . . deserve attention as a historical person . . . [and] should be interpreted as a textual and religious paradigm and not be reconstructed as a historical figure or a psychological essence."

Influenced by such writings, even people who practice Zen and consider themselves familiar with the tradition express surprise when I tell them there should be no doubt that Bodhidharma actually existed. He wasn't a mythical figure made up later or a composite of other religious figures cobbled together by later writers. That he may represent a certain "paradigm" is true enough, but that is just a fancy way to say he lived in and was a product of an age, of causes and conditions that can be examined. He most definitely was a flesh-and-blood person who walked on China's yellow soil. To divorce his "paradigm" from his "historical person," whatever that is supposed to mean, is simply a postmodernist attempt to eviscerate him as a flesh-and-blood person whose life's story meant something and is worth considering.

Admittedly, what we can say about the facts of his life is limited, but even those limited facts, meager as they are, are not without value.

During the ride to Great Buddha Temple, Yaozhi and I get better acquainted. He is one of many young abbots now running Chinese temples. With a good education and dedication to the Dharma, he and young abbots like him are working hard to get the Chinese Buddhist tradition back on track after the problems of the twentieth century and despite continuing obstacles in the twenty-first.

Chinese Buddhism, called *Hanchuan* Buddhism or "Han transmitted" Buddhism, is generally different from Tibetan Buddhism or much of the Buddhism practiced in Japan. Having developed much earlier than in either of those places, Chinese Buddhism retains some religious practices that have disappeared or been overlooked elsewhere. The most obvious difference between Han Buddhism and the Buddhist tradition of Tibet and Japan is the former's strict observance of vegetarianism. Chinese Buddhist monks avoid eating *hwun*, meaning meat or foods derived from animals. *Hwun* also includes some vegetables like onions and garlic, believed to give rise to sexual energies and thus also proscribed. Han Chinese Buddhist monks and nuns are vegans. Emperor Wu, the same emperor who had the legendary encounter with Bodhidharma, was instrumental in the spread of vegetarianism in Chinese Buddhism. Contemporary records of his day claim that monks of the old Hinayana school of Buddhism ate meat under certain conditions. Supposedly they believed that if the meat in question did not come from an animal specifically slaughtered for the monk who was going to eat it, then it could be consumed without violating the Buddhist precept against killing, one of the "commandments" for proper behavior. But Emperor Wu and Chinese Buddhism rejected this idea and decided instead to interpret literally the precept of "don't kill or cause to kill." Thus they avoided all meat consumption. Emperor Wu was the first Chinese emperor to widely promote this view, and his influence was lasting. This was just the beginning of his long-lasting influence on Chinese Buddhism and society.

As we ride, Yaozhi talks to me about other key differences between Japanese and Chinese Buddhism. In particular, many Japanese Buddhist monks marry and have children. Japanese government reforms carried out during the late 1800s directed that Buddhist monks could marry (in part to make the country stronger in an age of imperial conquest), and ultimately this practice was widely adopted by heretofore celibate monks in that country. Japanese monks could not only marry but might even own temples as personal property. Through selling religious services on the venue of these properties, they derived personal income. So by allowing monks to marry, own property, and earn money, the line between Buddhist monks and lay people became blurred. Through this blurring of a clear distinction between the life of a Buddhist monk and a lay person, the status of the clergy was naturally degraded, its sacred legitimacy placed in doubt. Thus the word *priest* was adopted to describe them and help differentiate their spiritual status from that of the lay community.

In the course of our conversation, Yaozhi says that the differences between Japanese and Chinese Buddhism became embarrassingly apparent during the late 1980s when certain Chinese monks went to live in Japan. Yaozhi says, with a slight grin, "One person went and three came back." In other words, some Chinese monks traveled to Japan to live and practice their religion and returned to China with a wife and child.

Yaozhi tells me that the Chinese Buddhist Association then spoke to these issues by stating that "Japanese Buddhism is Japanese Buddhism, and Chinese Buddhism is Chinese Buddhism." In other words, a clear demarcation would be made between practices in Japan and China, and China would adhere to its own tradition of demanding that "home-leavers" remain celibate.

While I was studying and sitting at San Francisco Zen Center during much of the 1990s, I didn't give a lot of thought to the differences between Japanese and Chinese Zen. If anything, I simply thought that the way the practice is done in Japan and the West is more modern and nonsexist than the traditional way in China. I think my views coincided with new prevailing social mores that came from the '60s, and seemed to be a proper and "modern" perspective.

But my perspective on this question began to change when I visited Chinese Zen temples in earnest during the 1990s. On my second or third visit to a temple where a famous ancient Zen master named Zhaozhou (Japanese name Joshu, 778–897) once lived and taught, the issue came to the fore.

At the time of my visit, the abbot of the temple was a monk named Jinghui ("Pure Wisdom"), a prominent teacher now widely known in China. The temple's head monk, whose position was immediately under Jinghui in the temple's administration, was named Minghai ("Bright Sea"). Bright Sea was immensely welcoming and helpful each time I came to the monastery to visit. He is the same individual who set up my meeting with Yaozhi.

It was during one such visit to the monastery that Bright Sea invited me to give a talk to a class of Buddhist monks there. I asked him what he wanted me to talk about, and he said it would be good if I spoke about the development of Zen Buddhism in America. I reflected on this a moment, then told him I didn't really consider myself qualified to speak on this topic, since I was only somewhat familiar with only one Zen Center in the United States (San Francisco) and knew about others only through reading or occasional visits to a few places. Bright Sea assured me that what I knew would be enough for the talk.

In the end, the talk went badly. I told the sixty or seventy young monks assembled in the monastery classroom about various Zen centers in the United States, the names of their teachers, and how they mostly originated from lines of Japanese Zen teachers. I talked of what I knew about Shunryu Suzuki, the founder of San Francisco Zen Center, plus a Kamakura-based Japanese lineage derived from the Japanese teacher Yamada Roshi, and a few other Japanese teachers like Taizan Maezumi of Los Angeles. But I sensed as I gave the talk that my knowledge of the subject matter was entirely insufficient and I was definitely not connecting with the audience. The monks sat quietly with blank looks on their faces, and when I asked for questions, almost nothing was forthcoming.

When I finished speaking, Bright Sea thanked me and I returned to my guestroom in the monastery. I lay on my bed there, wondering about the deeply unsatisfactory feeling I carried away from my first attempt to communicate with a big group of Chinese monks. There was a knock on the door. I opened it to find a little monk standing there, looking at me rather timidly. He asked if he could ask a question. I said of course he could, and then he said, "Is it true that in America monks get married?" I was taken aback by the question, and it took me a few moments to realize its import, but then I managed to mumble something about how monks in America usually married persons of the opposite sex who were also monks or at least interested in Buddhism. This answer simply stumbled out of my mouth in an attempt to fill the void that the monk had exposed. When I told this story to someone later, they said the monk had simply pointed out the eight-hundred-pound gorilla in the classroom where I gave the lecture, as I had abjectly failed to notice it.

Our SUV is traveling in a nice shopping area. Yaozhi is explaining some points about how the Buddhist religion is surviving today, in the wake of the Cultural Revolution. He says that that event, although a tragedy for China on virtually every level, nonetheless provided Buddhism in China with one thing of value. For centuries, from the time of the Western Jin dynasty (265–316 CE) until the rule of Emperor Shun Zhi in the Qing dynasty (died 1661), monks in China were required to pass stringent examinations in order to enter the Buddhist orders. They needed to commit to memory long passages of Buddhist scriptures, plus they were required to understand and speak in an informed fashion on points of doctrine. Emperor Shun Zhi ended the examination system in a bid to have more people enter the Buddhist orders. The result, says Yaozhi, actually harmed Buddhism greatly. Without standards of knowledge, standards of conduct also declined, and improper behavior or practices reared their heads. After Japanese Buddhism underwent fundamental changes during the Meiji era in the late 1800s, changes that allowed monks to marry, inherit property, and so on, such phenomena started to spread and take root in China as well. I remember that some of the things Yaozhi is talking about were described in a book I read on pre-1949 Buddhist practices in China. The Cultural Revolution, says Yaozhi, caused harm to China, but it also had a certain beneficial effect. It allowed the Buddhist community there a chance to purify and reinvent itself, to reestablish stricter standards of conduct for its home-leaving monks. Yaozhi says this has been positive, as Buddhism has become ever more popular in China. Today, the need for Buddhism to provide a moral compass for society is recognized even by the nominally atheistic government. Accepting and following the traditional Buddhist precepts, the guidelines for moral behavior, is now seen as contributing to the rebirth of a "spiritual society."

Suddenly, a large *paifang* (an ornamental gate like the one where Bodhidharma came ashore) indicates we've arrived at Grand Buddha Temple, one of the five great Buddhist temples of Guangzhou. We exit the car on the traffic street and walk up a lane leading to the first hall of the temple. What greets us is typical of what one finds when entering a Zen temple in China, and is called the Heavenly Kings Hall.

4. The Layout of a Traditional Chinese Temple

ZEN MASTERS OF OLD often talked in a manner that seems, at first blush, like a riddle. Take for example this old story about a Zen master named Linxi (pronounced *Lin-see*):

A monk asked Zen Master Linxi, "What is the essence of your teaching?"

The master said, "Mountains and rivers."

The monk then asked, "Who lives among these mountains and rivers?"

The master said, "Behind the Buddha Hall. In front of the temple gates!"

This story doesn't make any sense unless you are familiar with some basic ideas of Zen Buddhism and also familiar with the typical layout of old Zen temples. The arrangement of the buildings in those temples, oddly, provides a basic lesson in Zen Buddhist psychology. The positions of the main halls and gates have special significance, and their symbolism is enhanced by the placement of the Buddhist icons and statues, or lack of such items, inside the halls.

To understand this we need to step back for a moment and look at a little of the philosophical background of Zen Buddhism. Different Indian Buddhist traditions influenced the growth of Zen in China, but the Yogacara school of Indian Buddhism was a key contributor to the Zen world view. A fundamental idea in Yogacara (I'll call adherents of Yogacara the "Yogis") philosophy was called the Three Natures (*San Xing*). These "natures" were three different ways of looking at human perception, the way the mind observes the world.

There was one other school of Buddhist philosophy that had a big influence on Buddhism during Bodhidharma's time. That school was called the Madhyamaka school, and it emphasized the idea of

FIGURE 6. Heavenly Kings Hall at Yun Men Temple, Guangzhou Province.

"emptiness." I'll call people who emphasized this idea the "Empties" from now on, because we'll see their influence come up again in Zen and Buddhist discussions. The point to remember is that there were Yogis (people emphasizing "mind" as their essential idea) and "Empties" (people emphasizing "emptiness" as the essential idea) in the Buddhist tradition of Bodhidharma's age.

Bodhidharma's famous teaching (at least it is credited to him) instructed people to observe the "nature of the human mind," and this idea dovetails nicely with the Three Natures teaching. So what are the Three Natures that correspond to Zen temple architecture? We'll take a quick walk through an old Zen temple to make this clear.

THE FRONT HALL OF HEAVENLY KINGS: THE "NATURE" OF SELF AND OTHER

The main front hall of Zen temples, called the Heavenly Kings Hall, is a representation of the "first nature" of consciousness (for anyone who cares, the Sanskrit term for this "nature" is *parikalpita*). The hall contains an arrangement of statues of certain deities toward whom Chinese

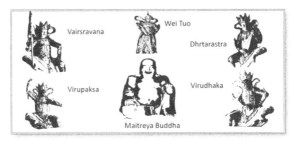

FIGURE 7. Heavenly Kings Hall Typical Layout.

people often prayed (and still do) to receive benefits and blessings. The "Heavenly Kings" referred to in the name of the hall are four mythical deities that guard the "four continents" of the world, as believed and taught in the ancient Upanishad tradition of India. Each statue of a heavenly king occupies one of the four quadrants of the hall. At the center of the hall, facing you as you come in the front door, there is typically a statue of the big fat happy Buddha widely recognized in both East and West. Even if you've never visited a Chinese temple you've seen this happy fat Buddha, named Maitreya (in Japan, this Buddha is called "Hotei"), in East Asian restaurants or your local garden supply where he's often sold as a yard ornament. For centuries, Chinese people have prayed to the deities in this hall for blessings and assistance. The "nature" of people's relationships with these deities is that of "self and other." This can be understood as "I'm here and there's a deity over there that I'm praying to, and I want some blessing to come from him." This "self" and "other" relationship characterizes normal human thinking about the world and how we see it. This sort of thinking also typifies usual religious belief and practice.

THE BUDDHA HALL: THE "NATURE" OF DEPENDENT CO-ARISING

The second main hall of a traditional Zen temple, which corresponds to the second of the Three Natures, is the "Buddha Hall." The "nature" associated with this hall can be translated as "Dependent Co-arising Nature" (Sanskrit: *paratantra*). Note that *para* means "supreme" and *tantra* originally meant "to weave," which we may understand by extension to mean "intertwining," a word with obvious links to the tantric

FIGURE 8. Buddha Hall Typical Layout.

sexual practices of some other traditions. In this hall we find "Dependent Co-arising" to be Buddhism's view of the ultimate "intertwining." Here, visitors typically find one to three statues of different types of Buddhas, plus other statues of Buddha's disciples as well as bodhisattvas. The latter, unique to East Asian Mahayana ("Great Vehicle") Buddhism, are honored as compassionate deities that appear in the world to relieve suffering. Typically, in ancient times and today, at the very center of the Buddha Hall sits a statue of the historical Buddha, also named Shakyamuni ("Wise One of the Shakya Clan"), who lived in India in 500 BCE or so. "Dependent Co-arising," the second "nature" of the Three Natures, is the idea that consciousness is a unitary experience that is divided by the brain into "self" and "other." Although there is no division of the sensations in the five senses, due to our biological evolution and adaption, the brain naturally separates the sights, smells, and other sensations of our senses, as either part of the "self" that is thought to exist in our body, or "other," things that are outside of us. Naturally, our biological evolution demanded that we recognize what needed to be preserved and protected so procreation could happen. The teaching here is that the division between the "self" and "other" is, despite our attachment to it, a fiction created by our brain. At this point I won't go into all the ramifications or a detailed explanation of this. Traditionally, Zen regards meditation as the main way for people to see and understand this "nature," the mind.

Of course, the idea that the "self" is a fiction created by our brains is not at all unique to Buddhist thinking. Innumerable religious books and figures, plus countless philosophers of East and West, have taught this idea for a very long time. For example, in a college philosophy class, I studied a book by the existentialist Jean-Paul Sartre entitled *The*

FIGURE 9. Dharma Hall Typical Layout.

Transcendence of the Ego. In the book Sartre argued that the ego was a creation of the brain's flowing consciousness. He said individuals are deluded into believing in the self by looking back on their stream of consciousness and projecting the existence of an "ego" onto the stored sensory data. Perhaps the most famous expounder of this idea in the West was the great Scottish philosopher David Hume, who brilliantly expounded this idea in his *Treatise on Human Nature* in the eighteenth century. But while many other religions and philosophical schools have talked about the illusory nature of the "self," it's probably the Buddhists who, over many centuries, have refined and defined this point of view most carefully and, in the case of Zen, most metaphorically and poetically.

THE DHARMA HALL: THE "PERFECTED NATURE" OF CONSCIOUSNESS

The third main hall of the traditional Zen temple, lying *behind the Buddha Hall,* is the Dharma Hall. The *Dharma* can be translated as the "Law," which broadly means both Buddhist teachings and the underlying moral component of life, the nature of the "wheel of birth and death." This hall symbolizes the third "nature" of conscious activity, the "Perfected True Nature" (Sanskrit: *Parinispanna*). This refers to normal consciousness that, having understood the "dependent co-arising nature" taught in the Buddha Hall, is no longer overly attached to ideas of an inherent "self" and "other."

In the Dharma Hall, there were typically no statues or symbols of devotion. In this hall of Zen's highest teaching, it's the nature of one's own mind that is honored, not outward symbols of religiosity. This absence of symbols or icons is connected to the idea of signlessness, an important idea that underlies Zen Buddhism. It equates Zen with people's "ordinary mind," the mind that doesn't seek any salvation beyond what is revealed by examining one's "self."

The founding myth of the Zen tradition is a story of the Buddha giving a teaching at a place called Vulture Peak in ancient India. What the Buddha said emphasizes the importance of the "signless" idea very clearly. According to the story, the Buddha held up a flower before his followers and said, "I have the Treasury of the True Dharma Eye, the sublime mind of nirvana, whose true sign is signlessness, the sublime Dharma Gate, which without words or phrases, is transmitted outside of the [standard] teachings, and which I bestow upon Mahakasyapa." Mahakasyapa was Buddha's disciple credited with understanding this teaching by the Buddha, where an upheld flower was the "signless" symbol of the teaching. I translate the Chinese *wu xiang* used in this and other Zen passages as "signless" instead of the more common translation "formless," partly because the Buddha held up a flower. Using a flower to represent the signless teaching is apt. A flower, though beautiful, is not something extraordinary or other worldly, and therefore it best conveys the idea of signlessness. A flower is not "formless." Translating the phrase in question as "formless" leads to an unwarranted and un-Zen-like emphasis on "emptiness" and an incorrect nihilistic interpretation of Zen teachings.

Examining the Zen *koan* I mentioned before, the apparent gibberish recited by the Zen master Linxi starts to make sense. He declared that his teaching was about "mountains and rivers," a traditional Zen symbol of "signlessness"—of something beautiful and yet ordinary. The people who live in the realm of his teaching are said to be "behind the Buddha Hall," that is, the location of the Dharma Hall where signlessness dominates, and "in front of the temple gate," meaning the ordinary everyday world of people who live outside the temple's religious activities. These are Zen's signless places, the places where people live their life without being corrupted by external religious symbols. Linxi's great teaching is not found in the Buddha or Heavenly Kings Halls, where the "signs" of religiosity abound.

One final note on this subject. There are indications in early records that certain very early Zen temples, such as the one established by Zen

Master Baizhang (about whom I'll speak more later), had only a Dharma Hall and did not have the other two halls I've discussed. Other records from the same period mention all three of the halls in the temples of famous Zen teachers. Perhaps some early Zen temples, especially private remote temples that were not generally open to the public, emphasized Sudden Enlightenment and eschewed the "stages" on the path to enlightenment that the other two halls represent.

5. Grand Buddha Temple

GRAND BUDDHA TEMPLE, like so much else in China, is currently under renovation and reconstruction. And like other temples in China, it has slightly changed the traditional layout of the three main halls I've just discussed. While the Heavenly Kings Hall and Buddha Hall have remained in the positions they formerly held, the Dharma Hall has lost its position of importance and, at the time of my visit, seems to have been eliminated altogether. This departure from the traditional layout has become increasingly common in modern times. Temples today often no longer have a formal Dharma Hall positioned where it used to be. Now the importance of written scriptures is emphasized more, and in place of a Dharma Hall there may be, for example, a Sutra Storage Hall. I think this change in the layout of many modern Zen temples directly reflects the loss of early Zen teachings, the idea that meditation reveals something outside the traditional (read "scriptural") teachings. Instead of following Bodhidharma's instruction about just observing, practitioners everywhere now focus on the words and phrases of Buddhist scriptures.

Grand Buddha Temple's existing Buddha Hall is over a thousand years old, certainly one of the oldest structures of its kind in China. It is still used daily for morning and evening services. A service is being conducted as we pass the building, with drums beating and bells ringing, the monks chanting and bowing before a grand statue of Shakyamuni Buddha.

We enter the temple's secondary buildings built around its perimeter. There, in a guest-reception room at the top of some stairs, I'm introduced to a bespectacled and earnest-looking man holding several books. I learn his name is He Fangyao (何方耀), the man who recently wrote about the famous monks who passed through Guangzhou on their way to and from India in ancient times. Upon receiving a message that a foreign guest had expressed an interest in the subject of his work, he dropped everything and ran over to Grand Buddha Temple to deliver his book to me personally. This typical kindness and solicitous response to my interest afforded me the opportunity to ask him some questions. Suffice it to say that the book Professor He (pronounced *Huh*) wrote is extremely detailed and will be a useful part of my picture of how Zen Buddhism came to China.

Professor He can't stay long because of some personal matters, so we thank him for taking time to meet us, and he goes off leaving us signed copies of his book. Then the abbot proposes that Ruxin and I have some lunch while he attends to some other pressing matters. Before we go to the temple restaurant, I follow Ruxin on a tour of the building. He leads me into an impressive library that the temple offers not only to its Buddhist members but also to the general public. Its books cover a wide range of subjects, including Western literature and philosophy, as well as topical subjects like business management and computing. Ruxin explains, "Buddhism always flourishes when China flourishes, and now China is flourishing again, and we are following suit. It's natural that we offer subjects that are timely, not only related to Buddhism, but to society at large."

In ancient times, monks of both East and West were often society's most literary group, and writing and printing was society's advanced technology of the day. The trend to stay on the cutting edge of things seems to be continuing here.

Ruxin takes me to the temple restaurant where we walk between two lines of lay workers and attendants greeting us and other patrons at the door. They all cheerfully clap their hands and welcome us with shouts of "*Huanying!*" ("Welcome!"). The inside of the place is very pleasant, with bamboo and water art and accents. We enter a small private dining room off the main hall, tastefully and subtlety decorated with natural fibers and plant motifs, conveying the vegetarian theme of the restaurant.

The food offered in the temple restaurant is top tier. I find it especially satisfying after having endured a breakfast of flavorless noodles in boiled water, the only "vegetarian" fare they could scrape together at the Fragrant Beef House across from my hotel. The temple restaurant offers platters of mushroom and vegetable dishes, plus "chicken" drumsticks that taste like the real thing, all followed by a fine nonalcoholic apple brandy.

The food here is a great leap forward from the innumerable banquets I experienced as a businessman in China, where I was forced to "bottoms up" the ghastly *bai jiu* ("clear alcohol") that is widely and mysteriously celebrated here. I simply couldn't drink the stuff. Even partaking of a small glass caused anything I ate to remain in my stomach like a rock for twelve hours.

A couple years after I started learning Chinese, President Nixon went to China. The comedian Bob Hope went along on the trip, and I remember his stand-up comedy routine that was televised from the Great Hall of the People or some such place. Imagine a big hall filled with Communist Party officials listening to Bob Hope tell jokes through an interpreter! The audience reacted with a dreadful silence to his routine, failing to comprehend his subtle, self-effacing wit so beloved by Americans. Bob Hope was dying up there, not just in front of all those Communist Party members, but also in front of an international satellite audience that had no laugh machine to leaven the deadly silence of the hall. At one point of his routine Bob poked fun at China's national alcohol, called *mao tai*, that he was forced to drink at the state banquet. He said something like "And your alcohol here! I heard it comes in two grades, regular and ethyl!" The interpreter looked puzzled, then turned to the audience and said, "He's saying something about gasoline but I don't understand what he means." The audience let out their first big laugh of the night, thinking it funny that the interpreter was confused. Bob Hope, on the other hand, took their laughter to mean he finally connected with the sea of blue Mao jackets in front of him, and he smiled broadly at the TV camera that was broadcasting the event around the globe.

As we are eating, an attendant enters and asks whether we want to hear a lecture being given in the next room by a Chinese man who is giving a talk in English. He's a teacher at the temple. I beg off so that we can finish eating. But a while later the attendant reappears and says the man has finished the lecture and asks if we would like to meet him. Behind the waiter an elderly and very distinguished looking Chinese gentleman enters the room and introduces himself as Jimmy Lin. His English is excellent, and I soon learn that Jimmy's English skills once led him to work for the United Nations. He says he's retired, but on his business card I see the impressive titles that he still retains, including "Chief Editor" of a publication called the *Golden Tripod*. He has a list of other titles including "Honorary President of the China Vegetarian Association."

"Maybe you can tell me where to find vegetarian restaurants here," I say.

"I know them all," he answers.

For the next several minutes, Mr. Lin and I get acquainted. His life is impressive. He was a lay disciple of the Buddhist teacher Xuan Hua (pronounced *Swan Hwa*), who, although virtually unknown in the United States, is famous in Chinese Buddhist circles for establishing a large Buddhist monastery near Ukiah, California, called the City of Ten Thousand Buddhas.

"In that case," I say, "Your teacher's teacher was Empty Cloud." Empty Cloud, a Chinese Buddhist monk who died in 1959 at the age of 120 years old, is the most famous Buddhist monk and practitioner in China of at least the past five hundred years.

Mr. Lin's face lit up at the mention of Empty Cloud. "I actually met Empty Cloud myself," he says. "I was 18 years old at the time and Empty Cloud was 108. He was still very healthy and robust at that age, like a healthy middle-aged man, and he was doing a lot of projects. My teacher Xuan Hua was there then too. He was then just 22 years old."

"Maybe Empty Cloud lived so long and was so healthy because he was a vegetarian," I say.

"Also the result of a lifetime of meditation practice," says Jimmy. "But during his whole life he never ate meat a single time."

Having read Empty Cloud's autobiography, I know many bizarre stories about that famous teacher's life. One story tells how once while he was giving a sermon, a cow came into the building from the street, came up to the seat where Empty Cloud sat, and got down on its knees as if paying homage to him. A butcher chasing the cow came into the hall, and upon seeing the animal prostrated in front of Empty Cloud as if seeking refuge, he renounced his profession and converted to Buddhism. Such stories about Jimmy's "spiritual grandfather" Empty Cloud are widespread in China, and there are thousands of people alive today who swear they witnessed such incredible occurrences.

"How long have you been a vegetarian?" I ask Jimmy.

"I've been a vegetarian for more than sixty years, since I was thirteen years old," says Jimmy. "At that time my whole family became Buddhists, and at the same time we all became vegetarians."

Jimmy tells me that he has another appointment. So after we agree to continue our conversation over lunch the next day, Ruxin takes me back to my hotel where I pore over some old texts about Bodhidharma during the time that many Chinese take an afternoon siesta.

Around two thirty, Yaozhi and Ruxin swing by, and we're off again to visit Guangxiao Temple, probably the oldest and most famous temple in Guangzhou. During the ride, Yaozhi asks me a pointed question.

"In America people are mostly Protestants or Catholics. Are there really any Buddhists?"

"The number of Buddhists is tiny," I tell him.

"And aren't most of those Buddhists followers of the Dalai Lama? Don't they follow Tantric Buddhism like from Tibet?"

"You're right," I agree. "There are more people interested in Tibetan Buddhism than there are Zen practitioners. But on the question of whether most people in the United States are Protestants or Catholics, maybe if you ask them, 70 to 80 percent of the U.S. population will say they are one or the other, but maybe only about 35 percent or so go to church regularly."

"What do you think?" he asks. "Is Christianity like Buddhism?"

"My view is that they aren't the same. Other religions usually seek something 'outside,' but Buddhism is about observing something 'inside.'"

Yaozhi expresses his agreement with a slight nod and smile.

During our conversation I repeat a view that I first heard spoken by Dr. Lew Lancaster, then the head of Buddhist Studies at Cal Berkeley, many years ago. He said that the three teachings of Buddhism, Taoism, and Confucianism are three legs of a tripod for Chinese society. Buddhism concerns the mind, Taoism concerns the body, and Confucianism concerns social relationships. The three philosophies cover pretty much everything. But Yaozhi looks as though he's heard this idea before. Maybe this isn't one of Dr. Lancaster's many original personal insights, as I had thought.

Our conversation is interrupted when we suddenly pull into the back gate of Guangxiao Temple.

6. Guangxiao Temple

GUANGXIAO (meaning "Bright Filial") Temple is famous in Zen history for several reasons. Perhaps most important is that this is where the Sixth Ancestor, a pivotal figure in Buddhist history and Chinese culture, took tonsure as a monk. An old bodhi tree, a type of ficus tree under which the historical Buddha realized enlightenment, marks the spot where the Sixth Ancestor's tonsure ceremony took place at the rear of the temple. The current tree is the offspring of the original that was planted in the fifth century.

One very famous legend about Guangxiao Temple is that it was here the Sixth Ancestor settled a debate about a flag waving in the wind in the courtyard. According to the story, one day while the temple abbot, Yin Zong, was giving a talk, the wind came up and was blowing a flag on the temple grounds. Somehow an argument broke out about whether it was the wind that was moving or the flag that was moving. The Sixth Ancestor, who at that point was still a lay person, famously settled the argument by saying, "It's neither the wind nor the flag that is moving. It is your mind that is moving."

A young attendant of Guangxiao Temple's abbot appears as we stand beneath the famous bodhi tree. It will be a few minutes before the abbot can meet us, he says. So we decide to take a look around. He leads us to the meditation hall at the rear of the grounds and peeks in the window to make sure we don't bother anyone before we go inside. As we pass through the canvas door at the front of the building, I first see a large statue of Shakyamuni Buddha at the center of the hall. With a bow, I follow our guide around the perimeter of the large room. It is set up in the traditional style, with an elevated bench with cushions adjacent to the wall for meditators to sit on. Here in the hot, humid south, I don't see the usual blankets available that are wrapped around the legs up north to keep the meditators warm. I also notice that above the meditation platforms are large wooden signs with beautifully written and embossed Chinese characters that hang in a row stretching around the top of the walls. Each has a phrase, such as ATTAINING THE UNSURPASSED MIND or THE DHARMA WHEEL TURNS ETERNALLY. The guide explains that the handsome calligraphy was individually brushed and presented to the temple's abbot by other abbots of other temples upon his installation in his position during the grand "Mountain Seat" ceremony that marks such occasions. One of the signs was made and presented by Yaozhi, the abbot with me now, to the abbot we are about to meet upon his "ascending the mountain seat" of this temple.

Before we leave the hall, the guide shows me a piece of split bamboo about five inches wide. It's an apparatus used by meditators in the south of China to keep cool on hot days. The bamboo is placed on the lap, hollow side down, with the hands resting on top of it. This allows the heat to dissipate much better from the body. Chinese meditation is not meant to torture its practitioners!

The differences between the Chinese and Japanese ways of meditating tell something about each culture. While the Japanese tend to be rigid and quite formal in their meditation style and ceremony, the Chinese often appear more relaxed. Between periods of sitting meditation that are signaled by hitting a board with a wooden hammer, Japanese meditators walk slowly in a single circle, sometimes at an excruciatingly slow pace that to me is tedious beyond all reason. Chinese, on the other hand, do such walking meditation in a relaxed way, each person walking at their own pace in a wide circular area, swinging their arms and making a good healthy hike out of it.

The individual teaching styles of some Chinese Zen teachers can approach the rigid Japanese way of teaching. But the fact that the Chinese can be less formalistic about such things was particularly revealed on an occasion when I sat with an American Zen group in a Zen meditation hall on top of a famous mountain in China. The abbot of the temple where we were visiting, a very friendly and engaging old fellow, helped us all get set up in our sitting meditation positions, carefully laying blankets over our laps and showing us how to tuck them in so that we would be comfortable. Our group, accustomed to meditating in the Japanese style, was lined up around the perimeter of the hall on the meditation platform. We faced the center of the place unlike in Japan where they sit facing the wall of the room. After we were all set, the little old abbot picked up a wooden mallet and unceremoniously whacked the wooden board signaling the start of the meditation session. As we all looked on, he then took out his false teeth, placed them next to a little statue of the Buddha next to his seat, hopped up on the platform, and sat down. We all had to stifle a laugh. This definitely didn't seem like the Japanese way, with its intricate bowing and ceremony!

A short stroll from the Guangxiao Temple meditation hall brings us to the Bowl Washing Well. This is the place where Bodhidharma is said to have washed his begging bowl during his stay at Guangxiao Temple. Under an otherwise unremarkable little gazebo is a screened hole where the well sits. Another place, it seems, that connects Bodhidharma to wells, sources of pure water.

Soon the abbot Sheng Ming of Guangxiao Temple makes his appearance. He greets us in a friendly fashion and ushers us into a meeting room that adjoins the area by Bodhidharma's well. We sit at the middle of a long conference table. The abbot seems welcoming enough, but I sense he has other important things to do, especially on a Sunday, when he might otherwise be resting. I really feel awkward about meeting such people. On the abbot's card there are literally nine different titles and positions listed. Among his titles are "Representative at the National People's Congress," "Vice Chairman of the National Buddhist Association," etc. All I offer is a card with the name of my little travel business, South Mountain. I can imagine him thinking "Who is this strange-looking lay foreigner, and why is he taking up my time?"

I try to explain that I organize tours of foreigners to come to China and visit famous historical temples. Perhaps, I think, that is a worthy-enough activity to merit his using part of a Sunday to meet with me. Another thing I know might engage his interest is the question of how Buddhism is evolving in the West. I sense that that question is secretly a hot topic, though no one will admit to this openly.

After an exchange of some pleasantries, the topic does indeed turn to the situation in the West. The abbot is interested to know if the Platform Sutra, a pivotal work said to have been expounded by the Sixth Ancestor Huineng, has been well-translated and widely disseminated in the

West. I tell him that my friend Red Pine (Bill Porter) and others have provided excellent translations of this "sutra," (a term normally reserved for words of the Buddha but in China also applied to this work).

The "Platform" mentioned in this scripture's name refers to an ordination platform where Huineng conveyed his Signless Precepts to monks and lay Buddhists. Because these precepts were sufficiently unique and central to Chinese Buddhist thought, this "sutra" is considered a sacred text, unique to Chinese Buddhism. More on this later.

We talk about the Signless Precepts of the sutra. I ask the abbot if he is aware that some Japanese and Western scholars have claimed that the Platform Sutra was not composed by Huineng but by someone perhaps far removed from that famous figure of Chinese religious history. The well-known Japanese Zen scholar Yanagida has claimed, for example, that the Platform Sutra was composed as a forgery many decades after Huineng died.

The abbot's face looks annoyed at my question. He says that he doesn't care what scholars have to say about the subject. The important thing, he says, is the sutra's content. Of course he's right about that, and I tell him so.

Anyway, there's one thing that scholars of Zen history do agree about, and that is that virtually all the old records of Zen are at least partly suspect. At best, scholars in the field cannot do much more than make educated guesses about much of the lives of Huineng, Bodhidharma, and other early Zen figures.

I don't want to keep the abbot from his weekend rest, so before long I beg off and say I should leave the abbot to his important duties. After a group photo in front of the Bowl Washing Well, Yaozhi happily returns me to my hotel.

The next morning before noon, I follow directions Jimmy Lin gave me in order to meet him at the Buddha World vegetarian restaurant, located about a hundred yards from the International Red Cross building in Guangzhou. I find Jimmy sitting at a large table on the fourth floor. The place is a typical Chinese-style restaurant, and everyone is talking at once. People at the tables around us are talking so loud that Jimmy and I have to lean close and nearly yell in order to hear one another. After living in Hong Kong, I'm pretty used to restaurants of this type, but this one is particularly bad, and I strain to hear details of Jimmy's life.

Elderly Chinese always have stories from the war, and Jimmy is no exception. But while many stories from the war are tinged with regret and bitterness, Jimmy seems happy that his difficulties gave him a deeper insight into how he should live his life.

He tells me that his father worked for a British firm during the 1930s and worked his way up to became a branch manager for the company in Tianjin, a big port city on the coast not far from Beijing. In 1931, renegade Japanese officers faked an attack on a Japanese mining railroad in Manchuria (The Mukden Incident) and used this as an excuse to invade Manchuria without authorization from the government in Tokyo. Six years after occupying Manchuria under these false pretenses, Japan invaded other parts of North China, including the city of Tianjin. That time left an indelible impression on Jimmy.

The Japanese army confiscated virtually all the food grown around Tianjin. Food prices skyrocketed, and starvation soon spread. Jimmy's father made a good salary for his day, but it still only paid for a minimal existence when food prices soared. Only seven years old, Jimmy saw starved bodies on the street every day. The suffering made a deep impression on him. In the midst of such hardship, Jimmy's father still concentrated on teaching Jimmy to speak English. When the war ended in 1945, it took months for Kuomintang troops to reach Tianjin. American troops, however, landed in Tianjin almost immediately and were warmly greeted as liberators. Jimmy's dad soon got a job as an interpreter for the American forces.

Twenty years later, during the Cultural Revolution, Jimmy suffered due to his father's previous relationship with foreigners. Well-educated and fluent in English, he was designated one of the "stinking ninth category" and sent down to the countryside to be "re-educated" with the peasantry. Buddhist Jimmy took this in stride.

"I liked working with the farmers. They were very nice. I liked planting vegetables and growing things. But many people from the city, especially young people, hated farming and couldn't wait to return to their homes. They especially hated southern rice farming, where they were forced to wade in deep mud and endure parasitic bites.

"All during that time, of course, I didn't dare say that I was a Buddhist believer. All religions were being persecuted, not just Buddhism. We had to be quiet until the reforms came along in 1978 under Deng Xiaoping.

"When I was eleven years old, during the Japanese occupation, my whole family took lay Buddhist vows, and we all became vegetarians. We just all went down to the local temple and took lay vows and then stopped eating meat. I think the experience of the war brought my parents to this step. At that time the Japanese had set up a phony Buddhist Association that promoted their control over Buddhist practice. But we, like everyone else, knew that the Japanese organization was phony, and we wouldn't have anything to do with them. The temple we went to was run by an old Chinese monk we'd known a long time.

"After the Cultural Revolution, I studied many Buddhist scriptures and more or less understood them. However I never really studied the Shurangama Sutra. In the 1980s I communicated with my Buddhist teacher Dharma Master Xuan Hua, who was then in the United States. He said that of all the sutras, the most important was the Shurangama Sutra. Of all the sutras, it was the one I really didn't understand, but the City of Ten Thousand Buddhas [in Ukiah, California] gave me a copy of this sutra in English, and I found that although I couldn't understand the Chinese version, the English version was very clear. I finally understood this sutra, and oh, it was like the whole universe had revealed itself to me! When I finally understood that sutra, I felt like the luckiest person on the planet!

"In the 1980s, I got a job as an interpreter with the United Nations, and this allowed me to travel to places like South Africa. Have you been there? In the city of Durban, there's a big population from India and many people are vegetarians. Out of a population of two hundred thousand people, about seventy thousand are vegetarians!"

After lunch Jimmy invites me to come to his office at nearby Hai Chuang ("Ocean Banner") Temple. The temple grounds serve as a wooded park, and Jimmy does his translation work in a small office there. He also gives lectures on Buddhism to the local community.

Inside his sparse office, he uncovers a large pile of red books and hands me one.

"Here is the Shurangama Sutra. I published these books myself."

It's nice to see someone like Jimmy living his life in relative freedom and ease after so many tribulations. The government leaves people like him alone, letting him practice a religion that doesn't hold any political threat.

After a short visit, I return to my hotel.

7. Another Visit to Hualin Temple

THE FOLLOWING MORNING I walk to Hualin Temple to do some more exploration on my own. In the early morning light, a thick cloud of smoke hangs over the temple courtyard, generated from countless bundles of flaming incense. I slip past the haze to stop in front of a little stand selling bricks within the temple grounds. The bricks will be used to build the new Buddha Hall planned for construction when surrounding apartments are torn down. For ten yuan, about a buck fifty, you can write your name in ink on one of the bricks along with a bit of text that will bring you good luck. Actually, you only get half a brick's surface to write on and must pay twenty for the whole thing. Examples of various auspicious sayings you can copy from are helpfully offered on a piece of paper. I pull out fifty yuan and write a few Chinese characters on the brick. My Chinese calligraphy is primitive, but the people selling the bricks, like Chinese people everywhere, have a bottomless reservoir of polite good will, and so they say, "Oh, how beautiful." This is, of course, utter nonsense.

I beat a retreat from the brick stand and continue my stroll around the temple. Nearby I enter a room open to the temple courtyard. Inside I find it is lined with small memorials for lay temple patrons that have died. A gentleman of about seventy years old sits doing calligraphy at a desk near the entrance. He greets me pleasantly, and I play the newcomer and ask him about Hualin Temple. As he explains the standard history of the place, I turn the conversation toward his personal involvement with Buddhism. "I'm a Buddhist believer," he says. "When Chairman Mao was alive, I studied Marxism-Leninism. All of us intellectuals did that. But that doctrine was really a 'fool-people-ism,' a 'harm-people-ism.' We all studied it. But then eight or nine years ago, I retired from teaching at the university. A friend of mine had some books on Buddhism. He gave me some of them. These were old books from feudal times. We never paid them any attention when Chairman Mao was alive. We thought those books were worthless, but such books gradually came back after Deng Xiaoping's reforms [in 1978]. These were religious books about Buddhism, Taoism, and other traditional teachings. The central authorities had suppressed the books, but they couldn't suppress people's belief in these things. They couldn't resist people's need for these teachings, people's demands for these teachings. The influence of these books on people was very great. They couldn't stop this influence.

"My grandfather was in the Kuomintang Army, so we had a lot of trouble. I tried to follow the correct political line, whatever it was. During the bad times, we first beat the landlords. Then later people would denounce each other, even their friends. Families were divided against themselves with brothers beating brothers and wives beating husbands. I beat people. I even beat my friends. We thought it was Marxism-Leninism, but really it was just 'harm-people-ism' that we were doing. Sometimes it was even 'kill-people-ism.'

"Mao was the emperor. Whatever he commanded, or what we thought he commanded, that's what we did. In ancient times the emperor was like a god to us Chinese, and Mao was no different. Whatever he said, that's what we did. We claimed it was scientific, but really it was just the same old thing. The emperor was giving commands. We were following them.

"Anyway, that's all behind us now. Now I study these Buddhist scriptures. Now, I'm retired. But I'm learning the history of this temple. We're reconstructing the history and making it available for people. People need to know their real history. Our ancestors from thousands of years ago laid down how people should behave toward one another. Buddhism explains how people should behave toward each other. We need to emphasize this now. After that time of trouble, people don't have anything left—just get more money! Get a better life! But after people get more money and get a better life, what do they do? What do they have? People need those old books to tell them how they should live their life, give it some real meaning—some real insight."

The old scholar's story is not unusual in China. Even the Chinese government and the Communist leaders have proclaimed the need to build a "spiritual civilization," to foster new moral values. But the spiritual civilization that China wants to foster today is blocked by corruption, and that in turn is protected by a closed political system. That makes many people cynical and self-centered.

Can a society that always took orders from the emperor, from the center, ever embrace real democracy? Some think that if the people of China seize democracy, much good will naturally follow suit. But I think this view is simplistic and doesn't reach the real problem blocking China's progress.

Chinese people are smart, and they do understand the idea of democracy. What they don't have any real experience with, however, is federalism. Modern democracies operate with layers of representative government, like the states in the United States, cantons in Germany, or provinces in Canada. Local governments operate with their own set of laws outside central government control. The Chinese understand the idea of democracy, but the idea of "states' rights" is a completely alien concept in a country where the emperor's rule was absolute throughout the country. My Chinese friends are quite interested when I tell them how the federal government in the United States had to arrest Al Capone on tax-evasion charges, not murder. The U.S. federal government was not set up to prosecute criminal law, and the U.S. central government's greater role in local law enforcement is a relatively new phenomenon.

China is a big and diverse country, with countless local dialects and conflicting interests. Some form of federalism seems necessary to keep the place from flying apart politically. But as long as there is still an "emperor" running the country, it will never take its place among democratic nations.

I thank the old scholar for his time and make my way back toward the temple gate. Last night I invited my new friends, including Jimmy, Yaozhi, and Ruxing, to lunch at Grand Buddha Temple restaurant, and I have a few errands to do before we meet.

Around eleven o'clock, a taxi drops me at the temple restaurant. When I called Yaozhi and Ruxin and invited them last night, they weren't sure they could make it. So now I'm facing the Chinese "host's dilemma"— how much food should I order? In China, it's taken for granted that if the guest eats up all the food offered by a host, the host really loses face. It means the host didn't care enough about the guest to make sure there was enough food (or even worse—he or she's a cheapskate). If, on the other hand, there's food left over after the meal, it means the food offered wasn't good enough to eat. Either way, the host is disgraced. Being a host in China is a no-win situation.

I'm only certain of me and two other people attending, but I order six dishes plus appetizers and noodles. You lose the least amount of face if there's so much food they couldn't possibly eat it all, and this is how the situation is usually handled. That's why so much food gets wasted in China, and attempts to change the country's wasteful culinary habits have not been very successful.

Just when I've got the food ordered and everything set, Mr. He the scholar arrives, and Jimmy Lin shows up right after him. Jimmy has brought another guest, a Mr. Chen, who works in the travel business and wants to meet me. I'm happy I ordered the extra food. A few minutes later Ruxin turns up. I start to get a little nervous.

As lunch starts, Jimmy Lin is already in fine form, regaling the table with stories about the Japanese occupation many years ago at Tianjin, about how he became a vegetarian during the occupation, and how Einstein was definitely a pacifist and a Buddhist his whole life. I'm not sure about the last bit, but I'm happy that Jimmy's enjoying himself and everyone is pulled into the conversation.

I compliment Mr. He on the impressive scholarship that went into his book. He and Ruxin talk about the fact that the Japanese academic community had to take up the slack in Buddhist studies for a long time (i.e., during the Cultural Revolution) when the mainland Chinese Buddhist academic world stopped working. Before World War II, China had many world-renowned scholars, most educated in famous Western universities like Harvard. Their names were household words in China. These illuminati included scholars like Hu Shi, Lin Yutang, and Tang Yongtong. Then things went south, and China's academic community was destroyed by politics. But since the 1980s, the pendulum of Chinese history scholarship has been quickly swinging back from Japan and the West toward China.

Then a new guest appears. A young woman enters the room and says "I'm sorry I'm so late." She introduces herself as a friend of Jimmy's named Everny (she says it's a French name). I take a quick panicked look across the table and see that there's still quite a lot of food left, but things may get tight. Everny turns out to be a devout Buddhist and says she makes a living teaching students to play the Chinese lute. While we talk, Everny sits quietly, eating an astonishing amount of food for such a small person. It's touch-and-go, but just when I'm ready to order more dishes, she suddenly lets up and joins the conversation. She talks about a recent trip she made to Tibet where she circumambulated a sacred mountain with Tibetan Buddhists while carrying a photo of her late father. The Tibetans spoke no Chinese, and she spoke no Tibetan. Despite everything, she says (and here I think she was referring to the political situation) the Tibetans totally accepted her into their group of religious pilgrims and helped keep her going over precarious mountain terrain. I often hear Chinese say how much they respect Tibetan people and their religion.

I mention that I intend to visit Yunmen Temple in north Guangdong Province in a few days, and Everny exclaims that it is the temple where her Buddhist teacher lives, and how when she goes there it is like going home.

Before I know it, two hours have passed, and I can tell Ruxin needs to do other things. I thank him for coming and see him to the door of the little dining room. Then I try out a Chinese phrase that I've never used before. I say, "*Xie xie nide shang lian.*" It is a polite expression that means "Thanks for giving me face by coming." I look carefully to see if this expression causes any reaction with Ruxin or the other guests. They don't seem surprised, but I'm suspicious.

When I speak Chinese or (especially) Japanese, I must sound like something out of a Monte Python bit. Decades ago on the night I first arrived in Japan, fresh out of my college Japanese classes, I asked a young man at the Haneda Airport train station about how to find my hotel in Tokyo. I used a verb form that is extremely formal and polite to address him. He looked taken aback and said, "Oh, you speak Japanese very well." What I said probably sounded like "Good morrow, cousin!" My Japanese is very weak, but I'm pretty sure that during all the rest of the time I spent in Japan then and in subsequent years, I never heard anyone use the polite verb form I used that night.

Soon everyone has excused themselves and made their way into the sunny afternoon. I'm left alone and am extremely pleased to find the right amount of food left on the table. The right amount is slightly more than if everyone left something out of politeness.

8. Traveling North

TODAY I LEAVE GUANGZHOU behind and travel north by coach to the city of Shaoguan, about four hours away. My exact destination is a famous spot called Nanhua Temple, the teaching seat of Zen's Sixth Ancestor named Huineng.

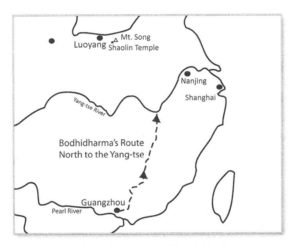

FIGURE 10. Bodhidharma Travels North.

While the taxi lurches through a crush of cars and pedestrians, I again contrast the scene in the Guangzhou streets now with my first visit in 1978. The Chinese word for *contrast* is *fancha*. It's a word applicable to the contrast between China's urban and rural lifestyles, the new rich and the old poor, and the country's pristine and polluted environments. China's many *fancha* constitute a sort of social bipolarity. Naturally the biggest *fancha* is the contrast between the new and the old. Among the massive amounts of new in the city of Guangzhou, there is still an island of old that hasn't surrendered to the modern, a place I used to find it impossible to avoid.

The word *Stalinesque* may sound trite, but it aptly describes China's postrevolutionary train stations. Monuments to socialist triumphalism, they evoke no other suitable adjective. During the last ten years, many cities have renovated these old mausoleums, but some others, Guangzhou included, have kept them in service, at least as I write these words.

The old train stations are showcases for the problem that Mr. Li spoke about on the train from Hong Kong, China's massive population. His assertion that many other problems come from China's overpopulation crisis are there revealed as understatement. The huge population places all of China's modernization under a cloud, but the problem is most apparent in public transport.

Even today, the wide concrete plazas in front of the old train stations serve as campgrounds for legions of peasants migrating to China's cities to escape poverty in the countryside. They also convey masses of travelers making their way back to their family's village during the country's holidays. The Statue of Liberty has witnessed only a minute fraction of the number of huddled masses that cross China's railroad landscapes on a single day.

My experience on Chinese trains in the early '80s made a lasting impression on me about China's population. In those days, air flights between Chinese cities were few and infrequent, and the current highway system was still unimagined. Travel meant using the train.

I was once in Guangzhou on business, and I needed to leave the next day for the city of Changsha, a few hundred miles to the northwest. From my hotel I made my way by taxi to the Guangzhou Train Station early on a gloomy winter evening to buy a ticket for a train the next night. I struck up a conversation with the taxi driver who was happy to talk to a "foreign friend."

We arrived at the square in front of the station to see a huge crowd that covered all available real estate and spilled into the streets in each direction. Lines to buy tickets were hundreds of feet long. I was worried and unsure what to do. But then the driver kindly offered to buy the ticket for me and return it to the hotel. I said I'd pay him for the service, and we came to some agreement. But when he came to the hotel hours later, I discovered he had not obtained the *ruan wo* (soft sleeper) ticket I asked for but instead had obtained a *ying zuo* (hard seat) ticket. He said the soft berths and seats were sold out. Also, the train was listed on the ticket as a "local," not the express I'd requested.

So the next night I joined the Chinese masses for my journey north. Ugly in the daylight, at night Guangzhou Station was hell's maw. Milling crowds moved through the musty caverns of the place under dim lights interspersed with dark voids. About 11:00 PM we surged as one from the huge waiting room onto the train for the overnight trip. From the beginning, and for the entire journey, the train was crowded beyond belief. In the "hard seat" car, I was wedged with five other people on benches meant for four, three of us facing three others across a tiny table. The aisle was jammed tight with passengers. The train blew its whistle, the train shuddered, and we crawled north through a black night unrelieved by rural lighting.

Every ten or fifteen minutes, the train stopped at another station where a large portion of the local masses pushed mightily against the doors in a futile attempt to get onboard. Too compressed by other passengers to keep my arms by my side, my elbows were pressed together over my stomach. As the night grew long in lurching weariness, I let my forehead drop over my hands to rest and bounce on the tiny table. When the situation is hopeless and the body exhausted, it mercifully retreats to sleep. The next thing I knew I had slept five or six bouncing hours in this position—vertical, arms tucked elbow to elbow, my forehead on the table. Dawn broke.

As the sky slowly brightened, the train still stopped frequently and the crowds trying to get on the train got even larger. The hardiest souls occasionally managed to get aboard by squeezing people into almost comical distortions. No one seemed to want to get off.

Despite our pitiful circumstances, the others around the little table were friendly and curious about the foreigner that rode with them. They spoke with a heavy dialect accent, but I could understand enough to carry on a conversation. We made cramped small talk. One young man, slightly heavyset and rough-hewn, asked me where I was from.

"America," I said.

Without hesitation he said, "Is it true that in America people are free?"

"It's like everywhere," I said diplomatically. "If you have money you have freedom."

He looked thoughtful for a few moments and then said loudly, "That's right. It's the same here! If you have money, you have freedom!" He emphasized this by nodding at the others and saying, "Right?"

They responded with a noncommittal facial expression, common to countries with many secret police, that lies between a smile and a grimace.

We rumbled and rocked our way north. At the next station, the crowd was somehow larger than ever. Some young men in the human tide trying to board the train started yelling "*Shang che!*" ("I'm getting on!"), pushing as hard as they could toward the immovable doors. It was just then that I said something in Chinese to the effect of "My God, this train is crowded" to the young man who earlier asked the question about freedom.

"Yes, it's crowded," he said. "And not just this train. The whole country is crowded. There are too many people." His raised his voice as he looked around. "Everything is crowded! There are too many Chinese! We need a big war to reduce the population! Really! I'm not kidding. We need a really big war!" He looked around again. The same noncommittal expression covered people's faces.

Finally, the train came to a small country station where the crowds were mercifully smaller. Here, several wheeled carts approached the train to offer little white boxed breakfasts of *shui jiao*, boiled dumplings that are usually stuffed with minced pork and vegetables. People opened the train windows and a brisk business ensued. Passengers near the windows bought the boxes for themselves and others and passed them into the train car.

With some effort I managed to squeeze my arms under the table to retrieve a small bag I'd brought with me that contained an apple, some nuts, and a few candy bars. I pulled out the apple and joggled it into a position where I could get a few bites. Some moments later, a woman sitting across from me suddenly said, "This is terrible! How can they sell us this stuff?" A chorus of agreement issued from the other passengers who had sampled the dumplings. The next moment someone said, "Give it back to them!" and several people started throwing the boxes with uneaten dumplings out the window onto the train platform where they rolled every direction and scattered their contents. The passengers had had it. They were tired and miserable, packed like sardines in the train, the weather cold and gloomy, and now the dumplings were inedible. The cart vendors hid behind big cement pillars on the train platform as people hurled the *shui jiao* and curses at them, tumbling dumplings and detritus across the cement. "Give 'em back to them!" people yelled.

My arms, resting uncomfortably in front of me due to the crowding, held my apple core. I considered simply swallowing the thing, then remembered something about arsenic in apple seeds. Suddenly the young man who decried China's population spoke directly at me. "Throw it out!" Some others chimed in, "Throw it out! Throw it out!" I looked out across the field of rubbish on the platform. "Throw it out!" Hesitantly, I tossed the apple core out the window into the scattered boxes of dumplings. Several people clapped their hands, happy that I had joined the masses' spontaneous rebellion. Chairman Mao said, "Where there is oppression, there is also resistance." The train jolted, and in a few seconds we began to roll north into the fog.

Back in the present, my taxi has moved past the Guangzhou Station of my memories to reach the Guangzhou bus terminal. My timing is lucky, and I'm soon on the right bus heading north on China's modern highway system. What used to be a six- or seven-hour trip to the city of Shaoguan is now covered in less than half that time on a modern highway.

As we leave the city, I remember the abbot Yaozhi's quote that "Japanese Buddhism is Japanese Buddhism and Chinese Buddhism is Chinese Buddhism." But didn't the Zen of both countries come from Bodhidharma?

9. Zen at War

THE AUSTRALIAN SCHOLAR and Soto Zen priest Brian Victoria published his book entitled *Zen at War* in 1997. That book and subsequent writings by the same author and others provide a shocking exposé of the support provided to Japan's WWII war effort by the Buddhist community, including the Zen community, in that country. Victoria provides evidence that Japan's Buddhist sects were not simply passive participants in the rise of Japan's militarism but provided foundational ideas and influence that helped the spread of fascist ideology.

Victoria's writings show that Japanese Buddhism embraced emperor worship, nationalism, and militarism. During the 1930s and '40s, simply put, Zen ideas were used as a tool for promoting political extremism and imperial war. Victoria's book reveals that the Japanese emperor assumed the status of the historical Buddha, and his likeness took a place of honor and worship on Buddhist temple altars. This relationship between Buddhism and the emperor contributed to unthinking obedience and fanaticism, much like the fanaticism the old scholar at Hualin Temple described when he talked about Mao's status in the Cultural Revolution.

Sugimoto Goro, a Japanese army officer who is credited with helping establish the state of Manchukuo (occupied Manchuria) was only one of many Japanese warriors who rallied the nation with Buddhist rhetoric. In a book called *Great Duty*, Sugimoto said, "The wars of the empire are sacred wars. They are holy wars. They are the Buddhist practice of Great Compassion." Brian Victoria cites the following related passage from the book:

> The reason that Zen is necessary for soldiers is that all Japanese, especially soldiers, must live in the spirit of the unity of the sovereign and subjects, eliminating their ego and getting

rid of their self. It is exactly the awakening to the nothingness (*mu*) of Zen that is the fundamental spirit of the unity
of sovereign and subjects. Through my practice of Zen I am
able to get rid of my self. In facilitating the accomplishment
of this, Zen becomes, as it is, the true spirit of the imperial
military . . .

Sugimoto's reference to *mu* comes from an old story associated with
Zen Master Zhaozhou, the ancient teacher at the Cypress Grove Monastery. That's the same place where I gave the lecture about American
Zen I mentioned earlier. Penetrating the *mu* gate is a form of Zen study
originally from China but now employed mainly in Japan and elsewhere
as part of Zen spiritual training. Sugimoto, in a strange and twisted
way, used this central Zen *koan* (story) as a rationale for emperor
worship.

Other things Victoria reveals in *Zen at War* are also shocking. During
the 1930s, an Imperial-Way faction of radical young Japanese army officers assassinated high-ranking officials who tried to control them. One
of these young radicals, Aizawa Saburo, regarded his Zen training, the
study of the Buddha Dharma itself, as a means of training for giving up
his ego and "sacrificing himself for his country." According to Victoria's
account in his book *Zen War Stories*, on August 12, 1935, Aizawa assassinated the politically moderate Major General Nagata Tetsuzan in the
latter's Tokyo office using a sword and afterward expressed shame that
he didn't dispatch his victim with a single stroke, like in some romantic
Zen samurai legend.

Victoria's research demonstrates that Zen and Buddhist support for
the war effort generally was not piecemeal, half-hearted, or exceptional
but with a few minor exceptions nearly universal and marked by great
enthusiasm. The war was not simply a national project to be supported
by patriotic Buddhists but was a projection of Japan's self-proclaimed
unique and authentic "True Buddhism" onto the world stage. War apol-
ogists in that country argued that the world must be led, by means of
war, to appreciate Japan's uniquely authentic Buddhism, which they
claimed was the only true Buddhism in the world.

Through these and other examples, Victoria's book *Zen at War* (and
subsequent writings by Victoria and others) show convincingly that

Japanese Zen institutions, teachers, philosophers, and self-proclaimed Buddhist individual soldiers and monks played key roles in promoting and supporting Japan's war of aggression against China and other countries.

Buddhists widely quoted two Buddhist scriptures to help provide a doctrinal basis for Buddhist militarism. Prominent members of Japan's Nichiren Buddhist sect, a major Japanese Buddhist organization that bases its teachings on a scripture called the Lotus Sutra, embraced Imperial-Way Buddhism by name. They formed the Association for the Practice of Imperial-Way Buddhism. The association claimed the following:

> Imperial-Way Buddhism utilizes the exquisite truth of the Lotus Sutra to reveal the majestic essence of the national polity [national identity]. Exalting the true spirit of Mahayana Buddhism is a teaching which reverently supports the emperor's work . . . that is to say, Imperial-Way Buddhism is the condensed expression of the divine unity of Sovereign and Buddha.

Victoria writes that Sugimoto cited from a text called the Nirvana Sutra, a well-known Buddhist scripture. He quotes Sugimoto as writing of the need for "protecting the true Dharma by grasping swords and other weapons." Sugimoto then claimed that "the highest and only true Dharma in the world exists within the emperor."

Even before Victoria's first book unleashed a wave of controversy and self-examination in both Western and Japanese Zen circles, I had long wondered about the appearance of martial training and even combat as part of the Zen tradition. This association is clearly seen at Shaolin Temple, the purported home of Chinese Zen, which is also the home of the Chinese martial arts. Shaolin Temple and its promoters also claim that Chinese kong fu (martial arts) came from Bodhidharma himself, who taught such martial skills to monks between periods of meditation.

In a similar fashion, Japanese Zen is widely associated with the famous feudal samurai, swordsmen who often steeled themselves for battle with Zen meditation. The samurai's counterparts in the Japanese imperial army employed rhetorical Zen-like ideas like the "emptiness of self and other" to rationalize killing. The idea of "Bushido," which means "Way of the Warrior," was infused with "Zen."

The biggest incongruence of Zen's being caught up with militarism is apparent when one considers the religion's much-vaunted Bodhisattva Path. That path is constantly emphasized by teachers at Zen temples and Zen centers, as well as by teachers in the Tibetan and other Mahayana Buddhist traditions. The ideal can be likened to a personal orientation to do good. People who vow to follow the Bodhisattva Path orient their lives and goals to fulfill the Bodhisattva ideal of helping all beings, an ideal expressed in a special vow taken by all aspiring bodhisattvas. The Bodhisattva Vow, recited at all Zen temples and centers in the world, goes like this in its basic translation into English:

Though the many beings are numberless, I vow to save them,
Though delusions are inexhaustible, I vow to end them,
Though the Dharma Gates are numberless, I vow to enter them,
Though Buddha's Way is unattainable, I vow to embody it fully.

Without seriously questioning it, for decades I considered the Bodhisattva Vow to be a highly commendable, if not ultimate, orientation for good. It certainly conveys a grand and laudable commitment. I deeply appreciated that Shunryu Suzuki, the founder of San Francisco Zen Center, brought this vision to America's shores from Japan and set up a community motivated by such a noble sentiment. A passage in one of Shunryu Suzuki's lectures encapsulates the absolute devotion and confidence that Mahayana Buddhists invest in the Bodhisattva Path: "Even if the sun were to rise in the West, the bodhisattva has only one way."

It was only after reading Brian Victoria's book that my views on the Bodhisattva Path developed some foundational cracks. Victoria's research convincingly demonstrates that Japanese Zen, during the war period, saw no contradiction between its Bodhisattva Path and the path of war. My previous assumption, which was that "honest Buddhists" in Japan must have opposed the war effort there, was based on entirely erroneous assumptions. By and large, Japanese Buddhists, including Zen Buddhists, saw the war effort as an attempt to spread "true Buddhism" to the rest of East Asia and the world. The idea that that Japanese Buddhists were forced to decide between maintaining Buddhist beliefs or supporting the war effort is a false dichotomy. The war effort in Japan was, to most Buddhists there, an attempt to give "true" Buddhism to people in other benighted countries that didn't grasp Japan's true Buddhist doctrines. Victoria's research shows that the Japanese Buddhist teachers who transmitted Zen to U.S. audiences, despite claims to the contrary, did indeed support Japan's war effort. Many of those Zen teachers were enthusiastic supporters of Japanese nationalist sentiment and militarism.

For these and other reasons, I had to face the fact that I didn't really understand the whole Zen picture, at least as I had learned it from teachers in the United States. I had already begun studying early Zen texts from China and was becoming aware that the Zen story was far more complicated and nuanced than I had theretofore understood.

How is it that in modern times a religion that proclaims such noble bodhisattva-style rhetoric, and is often described not just as one sect of Buddhism but as the "crown jewel" of the religion itself, could have developed such strong ties to militarism and violence? Most important, could anything that had embraced the evident fascism described in Victoria's books be considered part of genuine Buddhism or even understood as rational?

My doubts peaked when I participated in a three-week intensive meditation session at San Francisco Zen Center in 2001. At that time I had already read Victoria's book. I rationalized that even if the Japanese tradition had for a certain period strayed from Buddhist ideals, the U.S. branch of the tradition had the good sense to remain true to ideals of nonviolence and antimilitarism. The United States, after all, has no emperor to be exalted, so how can Chinese or Japanese emperor worship enter the picture there?

Yet there was a tension around the whole issue, and this tension bubbled up on the last day of the meditation period when I had visions of Japanese Buddhist monks being transformed into soldiers and doing banzai charges against the American and Chinese armies. I decided to start doing a lot more personal research into Zen, its origins, and its real meaning.

FROM GUANGZHOU TO SHAOGUAN

The bus is full of people. Most of the passengers are young, perhaps workers from the many factories in Southern China that have closed due to the recent economic recession. Perhaps they are returning to visit their relatives or are simply traveling to someplace new to try to make a new start during tough economic times.

For the first hour or so north of Guangzhou, we pass through flatlands of semitropical rice paddy culture, farmlands interspersed with hills and vegetable gardens surrounded by banana palms. Then we enter the hilly terrain typical of much of South China, with steep bluffs of greenery surrounded by low-lying terraced fields. In ancient times this area was called Ling Nan, meaning "south of the mountain range," and the residents in this region, populations not far removed from Vietnam and other Southeast Asian areas, are a little shorter and darker than northerners. Northerners once dismissively called them "barbarians" and exiled disgraced court officials to this area as punishment.

It was one such "barbarian," a spiritual successor of Bodhidharma six generations removed from him, who should be examined to understand what Bodhidharma's Zen came to mean in China. I first mentioned him during my visit to Guangxiao Temple, and now we'll stop at his teaching seat to look at his life in a little more detail.

10. The Platform Sutra of the Sixth Ancestor

THE PLATFORM SUTRA of the Sixth Ancestor is the text that records a famous sermon and ordination ceremony performed by Huineng, Zen's famous "Sixth Ancestor." It tells a story about how this sixth teacher in Bodhidharma's teaching lineage, as an illiterate and impoverished young man on the outskirts of society, understood and then came to represent Zen's most essential insights. His famous story served to solidly shoehorn Zen into the Chinese mindset. As an illiterate, Huineng had no way to read Buddhist scriptures, and thus his knowledge is connected to the idea of a Zen "outside the scriptural teaching." Buddhism came to China from India along with a mountain of scriptural works. One way to view the Zen sect is that it was a practical Chinese reaction to the mountain of literature that Buddhism developed over preceding centuries. Zen was China's reaction to Buddhism's universe of literature and metaphysics, a reaction that said, "Great, now could you boil the whole thing down to something manageable, preferably a phrase or two?"

The fact that Huineng began his spiritual quest as an impoverished boy with no social status also conveys the Mahayana (which, again, means "Great Vehicle") idea of extending the Buddha's teaching to everyone, not just the privileged, the rich, and the literate.

The Platform Sutra also narrates a ceremony where Huineng provided Chinese Zen a key innovation called the Signless Precepts. In this ceremony, home-leaving monks and lay people take the same religious vows. The ceremony departs from tradition by asking the vow takers to seek Buddha in their own minds. They are asked to remain true not to some external system of rules or metaphysics but instead to the awakening that comes from observing the nature of consciousness itself. Because there are no symbols or metaphysical ideas that can mediate this inward turning of attention, Huineng's precepts are called "signless."

In the ceremony, Huineng states, "Wisdom is only found by observing mind, why waste effort seeking metaphysical ideas?" (菩提只向心见, 何劳向什求玄?)

The Signless Precepts followed logically from Bodhidharma's emphasis on meditation and "observing" and not following the teachings of the religious establishment and metaphysical doctrines taught by organized Buddhism.

The Signless Precepts ordination ceremony Huineng conducted was likely performed outside during daytime, because the number of people taking part seems to have been very large indeed. Chinese historians have pointed out that such large public ordination ceremonies were fairly common in ancient times, with participants numbering in the thousands. The Platform Sutra's ceremony was apparently just such a grand convocation.

As important as the Platform Sutra is to Chinese Zen, I've found that properly translating that work into English is problematic. Translations of this "sutra" have long suffered from this problem. The tricky part is translating words like *signless*, a key word that echoes the origins of Zen in Buddha's legendary teaching at Vulture Peak, in a way that makes sense to Westerners while remaining true to the original meaning. Many translators use the term *formless* instead of *signless*. But I think the word *formless* falls short, since it implies that there is something that has no form. Signlessness, on the other hand, is what is found in things just as they are.

11. Nanhua Temple: The Sixth Ancestor Huineng's Dharma Seat

THE SHAOGUAN BUS STATION lies on the east side of the Zhe River in downtown Shaoguan City. I emerge into the clear fall day and walk down the steps to the boulevard next to the river. There I hail a taxi to travel the six miles or so to Nanhua Temple, outside the city's southeast corner. The first indication of the temple is a broad cement plaza that sits in front of its entrance gate. I direct my taxi past the front of the plaza and then to turn left on a small road that passes some shops selling giant sticks of incense and souvenirs for the many pilgrims who come here. The taxi lets me out by an electronic gate where the attendant on the other side, seeing me with luggage, pushes the button to open the apparatus. He then invites me to come into the guardhouse for a cup of tea. While he calls the monk in charge, named Guo Zhi (pronounced *Guo-jer*), I drink Iron Kwan Yin tea and watch flashy scenes of Chinese opera on the guardhouse TV set. Presently a monk appears and motions me to follow him. A short distance away through a grove of trees and across a large pond rests the newly completed Nanhua Temple Guesthouse. It is a big building indeed and built in traditional Chinese architectural style, with a paved courtyard surrounded on three sides by imposing wings of the building.

Nanhua Temple was established in the year 502. It existed before Huineng came here and gained fame as a Zen master. The place still has a special position of importance in Bodhidharma's tradition. Moreover, the place promises to reveal, in the next few days, an important aspect of Emperor Wu's influence on Chinese culture. I've arrived in time for the annual Water and Land Festival, a traditional event directly traced to Emperor Wu and with important implications for understanding the object of my trip.

I'm led to my accommodations. Set amid the quiet trees of a hill near

Nanhua Temple, the guesthouse is a comfortable if somewhat overbearing building. But the environment around the place is serene, broken only by occasional construction noises nearby where a new guest meditation hall is in the making. A long covered walkway stretches up the hill through the trees leading to the temple proper.

My guide Guo Zhi doesn't seem too overjoyed to see me. I don't know if this is just his personality or whether he's simply bored with dealing with visitors. At China's most famous temples, there's an endless stream of tourists showing up to disrupt the spiritual practice of the occupants. Now, while preparations for the Water and Land Festival are in full swing, it's especially understandable that he may be impatient. Everyone is probably overworked and stressed out, even here at a Zen temple.

Emperor Wu, the same emperor famous for meeting Bodhidharma, created the Water and Land Ceremony that is at the heart of the festival. Most Zen students know that Wu built many Buddhist temples and promoted Buddhist scriptural study, but the full impact Emperor Wu had on Chinese history is still not well-known. This important part of Bodhidharma's story offers colorful sights and sounds that stretch from Emperor Wu's time until today.

Chinese Buddhist tradition says that Emperor Wu started the Water and Land Ceremony after having a dream in which a monk advised him to call on spirits in the higher realms to assist those who suffer in the lower realms of existence. At the emperor's request, the ceremony was designed by a monk named Baozhi, one of the most famous of Emperor Wu's Buddhist teachers. It was first held at Jinshan Temple, a very old temple near Zhenzhou City in Jiangsu Province, east of Nanjing. Jinshan Temple still exists and is very active today.

The ceremony is a highly elaborate and expensive undertaking in which Buddhist monks do prayers and rituals that beseech gods and bodhisattvas in the higher realms to journey into the lower realms to give succor to the inhabitants there. The Buddhist "Six Paths" of existence figure into the ceremony. Those paths, comprised of different realms of beings, include the (1) heavenly or godly realm, (2) the realm of asuras (highly evolved beings), (3) the human realm, (4) the animal realm, (5) the "hungry ghost" realm, and (6) the hell realm. Days of purifications, special offerings, and rituals lead up to the biggest ceremonies on the final day of the festival. That day, things get especially interesting.

Lots of people come to the temple to take part in the grand event or just to see the spectacle. Previously when I've witnessed this ceremony in China, I've noticed people from the lay Buddhist community taking an active support role for the proceedings, performing all types of services like preparing vegetarian banquets, making decorations and floats for a parade, playing music, and so on. Guo Zhi tells me that the main ceremonies will occur tomorrow. Yet many activities are already under way.

Guo Zhi leaves me to my own devices with instructions about where and how to join other lay people for meals at the temple dining hall. He promises to give me a tour later, but right now he's preoccupied with other jobs.

Flagship temples like Nanhua in relatively rich Southern China don't lack financial support. Rich patrons who have made fortunes in export trading have lavished funds on some of them, and Nanhua, due to the fame of the Sixth Ancestor, may be the richest temple in all of China. The new guesthouse suggests this. With more than two hundred rooms, it is the size of a big hotel. Yet even during the current big celebration there are not more than a handful of people staying here. Most of the crowds of people at the temple are local day-trippers.

I settle into my new digs and pull out a bag of ground coffee beans. I'm surprised to find that my guesthouse room is new and equipped with a Western bath and new furniture. It's hardly different from a hotel room, with two comfortable beds instead of the usual four or more typical of Chinese monastery guestrooms. Most amazing, the room has an Internet connection. I spend a half hour or so trying to get connected, eventually appealing to the building attendant to help me. She claims it's all working fine, but finally she realizes that she's turned off the server in a different part of the building.

An hour or so later, Guo Zhi returns and offers to give me a tour of the temple. I'm interested to see what's new, so we set off.

Nanhua Temple holds perhaps the most sacred relic of Chinese Zen, the "True Body" of the Sixth Ancestor himself. It's traditional for devout Buddhists upon arriving at the temple to first go to the hall of the Sixth Ancestor at the rear of the temple and bow to him before going back to the central Buddha Hall and bowing to the Buddha or any other statues. Even on a normal day, the temple is crowded with visitors from near and far, but special occasions like this make the crowds exceptional. Not that many foreigners come to Nanhua, so I get the requisite number of stares from people who hardly ever see a *lao wai*, literally "old outsider." (Don't get the wrong idea from these words. The word *old* in China is always meant as a compliment, a sort of honorific that is analogous to the word *honored*.)

I'm happy to note that the statue of Ji Gong (I mentioned this figure during my visit to Hualin Temple) remains in front of one of the windows inside the Buddha Hall. He's still showing up late for morning services! I manage a surreptitious photo in violation of the sign against photo taking.

Guo Zhi tells me that the temple abbot won't be able to meet me, as he is caught up in activities related to the ceremonies at hand. But I'm happy that I'm offered a chance to meet the temple superintendant, a young monk named Fa Qi (pronounced *Fa-chee*) at a reception room in the new Zen Academy located on the temple grounds. Such academies are all over China, both connected and unconnected to major temples. It's not clear exactly what the curriculum is in these places. Some, like the one at Cypress Grove Temple in North China, publish books of old Zen records, or at least they used to before the Internet became the preferred medium for disseminating Buddhism in the country.

The meeting will be first thing the next morning, so I spend some time writing and researching from the Chinese Internet.

The Chinese Buddhist Internet is a lively place with thousands of related Web sites and galaxies of information about events, Buddhist history, scholarly papers, sutras, and an array of related information. If someone invents high-quality automatic translation software for Chinese to English, then Western practitioners are in for a shock about how big the Buddhist electronic community in China really is and what a vast information ocean it offers.

The next morning Fa Qi welcomes me very warmly, and I can see he's a different sort than Guo Zhi. On the table in the reception room, there is a traditional Chinese tea set up, a slotted bamboo tea basin, on which sits a Yixing (pronounced *Yee-sing*) tea pot and two cups. Yixing tea pots are made with special clay from the city of Yixing in Jiangsu Province. Though plain and unglazed, when properly fired this clay is ideal for making tea pots because it retains heat very well. The material is also slightly porous, and if a pot is used for a long time to brew one type of tea, the residue in the clay can be used to brew tea even if you have run out of tea leaves.

Fa Qi draws hot water from an electric water bottle and performs his tea *kong fu*, the traditional way of pouring tea for a guest. He is about thirty-something years old, well-spoken, and obviously well-educated. I give him a short introduction about my purposes on this trip. He then goes into a fairly long recitation about the role of Nanhua Temple in Chinese Buddhism, the importance of the Sixth Ancestor, and how this place is "representative" of the essence of Chinese Buddhism. At one point he says that in the Chinese Buddhist world there are still very many people who are hazy on this issue. I reveal some surprise at this idea and relate how in the first college class I ever had on the subject of Chinese Buddhism, the main thing taught was the importance of the Sixth Ancestor Huineng. I also say that it's my impression that North American practitioners of Zen would be unanimous in recognizing the importance of Huineng in the tradition. At some point he realizes that I didn't just fall off the rice wagon, and he pauses for a thoughtful moment. Then he says, "During the Cultural Revolution, this tradition was completely wiped out. Now it's fallen to us, the younger generation, to find whatever pieces are left and put the tradition back together. You can say we're still "*mo shitou guo he*," (literally, "probing the rocks to cross the river").

I sympathize with his problem. I once met a famous Buddhist master named Tiguang ("Body of Light") who lived at the ancient Dharma seat of Zen Master Qingyuan (Japanese: Seigen; died in 740), one of the main students of Huineng. I asked him, "Wasn't the persecution of Buddhism during the Cultural Revolution like that that occurred in the Northern Zhou dynasty, or during the suppression that occurred in the late Tang dynasty?"

"Not the same!" he glowered. "Back then there was not the complete destruction of the religion. During the Cultural Revolution, everything was destroyed, and all monks and nuns were laicized. They didn't just come once to the temple and close it down. They repeatedly came and destroyed everything they could lay their hands on. Nothing like that had ever happened before."

At Nanhua Temple, the destruction was like what Master Tiguang described to me. However, through courage and luck, certain temple treasures were saved. The "True Body" of the Sixth Ancestor, according to a story I've heard a few times, was dragged through the streets of nearby Shaoguan City by the Red Guards, who decried it as a fake. Someone threw rocks that hit the lacquered body, breaking off a piece of its shoulder and damaging its stomach. A piece of bone was exposed. This scared even the Red Guards, who realized that this was an actual body that had apparently remained intact for fifteen centuries. Even they were superstitious about what might happen for damaging a real corpse, so they dragged it back to the temple and left it there. Secretly, a senior monk named Foyuan retrieved the body and hid it in a cave on the mountain behind Nanhua Temple. After the Cultural Revolution had passed, the body, along with the hidden lacquered bodies of two other historic abbots of the temple, were again brought out and put back on public display.

Perhaps the fact that Chairman Mao had once praised the Sixth Ancestor Huineng influenced the Red Guards' decision to not destroy the body. According to old records, Huineng lived among and highly praised the common people. Chairman Mao once quoted Huineng as having taught a leftish-sounding teaching: "Among the lowest people is the highest wisdom." (下下人有上上智) Foyuan and other monks saved other famous Nanhua Temple relics as well. Among them was a large sign over the monk's dining hall that was famously painted by "China's Shakespeare," a Song dynasty poet-statesman named Su Dongpo, about eight hundred years ago. A monk quick-wittedly retrieved the sign when the Red Guards came, saving it by using it as a bed board under his thin mattress during those times of chaos.

Fa Qi is indeed like other young Buddhist monks I've met in China. He tells me he was a businessman, but in his late twenties decided to become a monk. Now, despite his age, he has a position of considerable responsibility in one of China's most important temples. He seems enthusiastic about the task the lies before him.

After two cups of tea, I excuse myself. I know Fa Qi has a lot to do. In the afternoon the main ceremonies of the Water and Land Festival will be under way. He thanks me for coming and tells me he will be happy to welcome any groups that I bring to the new guesthouse.

Back in that guesthouse, I get my camera and make ready to observe the main ceremony that will start soon. I make my way to the big Buddha Hall once again and find that things already seem to be in full swing. The Buddha Hall is full, and the onlooking crowd is surrounding the place. Once the monks and lay practitioners are inside, no one is allowed to enter or leave until the ceremony is finished. But the front doors of the big hall remain open, and so I join the spectators who are all standing there taking photographs, pointedly ignoring signs that say no pictures are allowed.

The chanting and bowing in the main Buddha Hall proceeds for a long while. The sounds of sutra chanting and prayers are broadcast through speakers with terrible acoustics, and even though I speak Chinese, I can't understand what's being said. This goes on for nearly an hour, and I'm getting tired of standing on the pavement listening to what I don't understand. Then I hear a traditional Chinese band start to play near the Heavenly Kings Hall a distance away. I go over to investigate and find a line of people and objects preparing for the final procession that will be the culmination of the ceremonies. Hundreds of lay Buddhists are gathered around a traditional instrument band that is making a ruckus. The music and chanting all crescendo for another twenty minutes, until it finally and suddenly stops. Then the monks who were leading the ceremonies in the Buddha Hall emerge in a procession that moves toward the front of the temple. At the front of the procession, paper-mache figures of the Heavenly Kings on horseback and a big paper boat with a statue of Kwan Yin at its helm are held aloft by lay people. The senior monks, dressed in bright yellow robes and special hats, trail behind the statues that are lifted aloft. As the colorful figures and monks proceed, the other monks of the temple and crowds of lay people fall behind them in a parade, myself among them.

The procession of three hundred or so monks from inside the Buddha Hall, along with the crowd of lay people, move south toward the temple gate. Generally, monks in China do not wear hats. But for this ceremony, the leading monks wear the same crown as that worn by Dizang, the bodhisattva that has specially vowed to liberate beings from hell. They also walk under large yellow umbrellas festooned with auspicious Chinese characters held by their assistants. The Chinese band has fallen in and now serenades the scene with the din of Chinese funeral music.

Cymbal and drum players punctuate the squeal of the brass *suona*, a trumpetlike instrument, as the spectacle marches along. We all pass to the far side of the wide plaza that stretches a couple of hundred feet in front of the temple gate, arriving at the highway that runs past the front of the area.

At the front of the parade is the paper-mache boat, about twenty feet long, that carries Kwan Yin. The idea is that she will captain the craft on its mission into the lower realms and ferry the benighted beings there across the bitter sea to the shore of happiness. The Heavenly King figures precede the boat to protect it. There is also a statue of Guan Gong, China's most famous historical army general from the Three Kingdoms era. I know that the Taoists long ago deified Guan Gong, but I don't remember seeing him around many Buddhist temples. He probably shows up for special occasions. Today, all the gods are pitching in for a good cause.

The high squeal of the *suonas* sends a message to denizens of the hell realms that we're coming to set them free. At the highway the long line turns right and makes a short trip alongside the road. It then crosses the road at a place where all traffic has already been stopped by a police barricade and enters a large field that contains a long, wide cement slab. Hundreds of people in the long line file into the area, and the paper boat and figures of the gods are placed on the cement area and made ready for their send-off to the lower realms. People scramble back and forth taking pictures of the spectacle. A lot of people in the crowd come up and heap "hell money" on and around Kwan Yin's ferry boat. That special printed money is meant to be conveyed on the craft to hungry ghosts and others on the other side who can use it for whatever essential goods and services are for sale in hell.

As the statues are made ready, the leading monks beneath the big yellow umbrellas bless messages that are also placed on the boat. When the boat is full to the point of capsizing, additional boxes of more hell money get placed next to it, along with personal messages of good will to deceased relatives. Finally everyone steps back and a flame is produced. Within seconds, the boat, figures, money, and messages are emitting flames that shoot skyward, conveying the compassion of this world to the other five realms. The bodhisattva Kwan Yin, for a few moments, stands tall amidst the fire and smoke that consumes the boat, then is consumed in the conflagration to rise in the big column of smoke into the sky.

I'm standing fairly close to the flaming boat trying to get some good photos. Suddenly a blast of heat strikes me like a wave, and I'm forced to jump back so as to avoid being an inadvertent offering. To add drama, someone has placed a long string of very loud firecrackers in the ship. Reaching a more distant vantage point, I turn to watch a massive cloud of smoke rise over the picturesque farmlands in front of Nanhua Temple. A timeless ceremony in a timeless valley.

Ceremonies like this have probably gone on here since before recorded history. People of the assembled crowd, having seen it all before, begin to retreat before the last of the firecrackers have popped under the afternoon autumn sky.

SHAOGUAN CITY

The taxi driver in Shaoguan City is perplexed. I've told him the hotel I'm looking for is called the Handy Economic Hotel and its address is at the corner of Feng Cai ("Graceful Bearing") Street and Xin Zhonghua ("New China") Street. He knows Feng Cai Street well enough, since part of that road is the main pedestrian shopping street in Shaoguan City. But New China Street seems to be a mystery. We ask another cab driver who points us down a side street called Feng Du ("Wind Passing," but not in its pejorative sense) Street. There we find a tiny *paifang* over an alley that says NEW CHINA STREET on top. However, there's no hotel called "Handy Economic" to be seen. Maybe my source for this information was an Internet dead end, a Web site abandoned years ago. I decide to hop out of the taxi and look around and then notice a big greeting sign over the door at a different building that says NANA EUROPEAN-STYLE HOTEL and decide to check it out. It turns out to be a smallish but clean and respectable-looking place, with scores of European art prints framed on the walls and a campy Romanesque nude female statue prominently displayed on the second-floor landing. There's no lift, but the price is right. A decent double room, Internet-ready computer included, is about $23 a night.

An hour or so later, I get the call I'm expecting from Everny, the music teacher who crashed the lunch at Great Buddha Temple. She had sent me a message through Jimmy Lin that she was going to visit her Buddhist teacher at Yunmen Temple and asked if I wanted to go there with her. Yunmen Temple is about an hour from Shaoguan. I'd like to visit there again, so I agreed to meet her at the bus station where we can take the local fourteen-seat minibus directly to Ruyuan City, a short taxi ride from the temple.

12. Yunmen Temple

ZEN MASTER YUNMEN was among the most uncompromising of all the old Zen masters. He adamantly rejected metaphysical and mystical thinking among his students. He even scolded people for hanging around temples, criticizing them for searching out any religious claptrap that some teachers have "chewed on and spit out" and then "putting it in their own mouth." Here's an example of how Yunmen talked:

Yunmen said to the monks, "Why are you wandering around here looking for something? I just know how to eat and shit. What else is there that needs to be explained?

"You here have taken pilgrimages everywhere, studying Zen and asking about Tao. But now I ask you all, what exactly have you learned in all these places you've visited? Bring it out for us to see, and we'll check it out! And after all this, what is it that the master of your own house has attained? You've all chased after some old teachers, picking up something they have already chewed on and spit on the ground, then putting it in your own mouth and calling it your own. Then you say, 'I understand Zen!' or 'I understand Tao!' I want to ask you—even if you can recite the whole Buddhist canon, what can you do with it?

"The ancients didn't know when to quit. They looked at you running around, and [to try to help you] they said 'bodhi' and 'nirvana,' but this just covered you up and staked you down. Then when they saw you didn't get it, they said 'no bodhi' or 'no nirvana.' They should have made it clear from the beginning that this can only go around and around! Now all you do is look for commentaries and explanations!

"When you act like this, you destroy our school. You've

been carrying on like this without stopping, and I want to know, where has it gotten you?

"Back when I was going around on pilgrimages, there were teachers who gave me explanations. They meant well. But then one day I completely saw through what they were doing. They're just laughingstocks. If I manage to live a while longer, I'll break the legs of those teachers who destroy our sect! These days there're plenty of affairs to get involved with. Why don't you go and do them? Why are you looking for a piece of dried shit around here?"

Yunmen then got down from the Dharma seat and chased the monks from the hall with his staff.

Of course some people might think that chasing the monks out of the hall with his monk's staff is a bit over the top. Much is made about such seemingly erratic behavior by old Zen masters like Yunmen. Scholars use a fancy word to describe such strange behavior, calling it *antinomian*. The word describes the behavior of religious people who think their understanding of the truth entitles them to act with disregard toward religious convention or conventional morality.

But I think the word *antinomian* doesn't really apply to the behavior of the old Zen masters like Yunmen. While they sometimes flaunted convention, their behavior seldom rose to the level of violating Buddhist vows. In thousands of pages of the old Chinese Zen records, I've never seen passages where the old Zen masters counseled their students to violate their vows of chastity or vows against harming life, telling lies, or encouraging other transgressions that run counter to the basic precepts of the religion. What I *have* encountered, quite regularly, is a studied indifference to religious symbolism, a near total disregard of holy representations. The old Zen masters were true iconoclasts—breakers of icons; their Dharma Halls were devoid not just of religious statues but also of any manner of special signs or metaphysical speech. The old Zen masters even ridiculed such talk. Zen Master Huanglong pointedly rejected such fancy talk. One day he did so like this:

Zen Master Huanglong [1002–1069] entered the hall and addressed the monks, saying, "The dharmakaya is formless but is revealed in things. Prajna wisdom is without knowledge, but it shines in conditional existence."

Huanglong then lifted his whisk and said, "When I lift up the whisk, it is called the dharmakaya. But here it is not revealed in a thing. When I bring the whisk down, it is called prajna wisdom. But here it does not shine in conditional existence."

Huanglong then laughed out loud and said, "If somebody came up here and grabbed me, spit on me, gave me a slap, knocked over the meditation bench, and dragged me down to the floor, then I really couldn't blame them!

"Talking like this is like gnawing on the feet of pigs and dogs. What a state I've fallen to!"

Everny yells to me from across the plaza in front of the Shaoguan station, and a few minutes later we've boarded the bus that leaves every half hour for Ruyuan City. *Ruyuan* literally means the "milk's source," and I've always thought the name must have been derived from the great Zen masters that lived in the place.

As we sit on the bus waiting to leave, I chat with Everny about a famous nature park not far from Shaoguan. It's called Danxia (pronounced *Don-sya*) Mountain. The name *Danxia* can be translated as "red-hued." Mountains that are red-hued, whether due to iron in their soil or for some other reason, are not so rare, and there are several places in China that are named Danxia. My interest has been to visit the home temple of an ancient monk named Danxia Tianran (738–824). His name means the "Natural from Danxia." I've long wondered if the scenic mountain recreation area not far from Shaoguan City was connected to that monk, and whether he lived there or not. Danxia was one of the most famous iconoclasts of Zen. His legend says that when he first entered the famous Zen Master Mazu's temple, he went into the Buddha Hall and climbed up to sit atop the statue of the Buddha, his legs straddling its neck. This caused a stir, and so the old master Mazu entered the Buddha Hall to see what the commotion was about. When he looked up and saw Danxia perched on the Buddha's shoulders he exclaimed, "Oh! My natural disciple!" Thereafter Danxia's Dharma name was Tianran ("Natural"). Another story about Danxia Tianran tells how he once stayed at a temple in the cold north of the country on a winter's night, and began to burn the temple's Buddha statues to stay warm, much to the chagrin of that temple's abbot. "Why are you burning the holy icons!" said the abbot. "Oh," said Tianran, "I didn't know there were any real Buddhas inside them!"

Everny assures me that the park in question was the home of Danxia Tianran. I seem to recall that his place of practice was not here, but rather in the north of the country, somewhere near Nanyang City in Henan Province, but she claims he lived at a temple in the nearby national park that is called Bie Chuan ("Separate Transmission") Temple.

I find the name of the temple appealing. "Separate Transmission" is an obvious reference to the "special transmission outside the teachings" and indicates the temple has some affinity with Bodhidharma's Zen. When Everny tells me the exact location of Danxia Mountain, I realize it is near the likely route that Bodhidharma traveled when he came through this area. From Shaoguan, Bodhidharma probably set out toward the northeast, traveling along the Zhe River toward its headwaters near Danxia Mountain and then across more mountains into what is now Jiangxi Province. Ultimately, his northern journey would take him to the south bank of the Yang-tse River. He may have purposefully been making his way to East Woods Temple, a famous center of Buddhist worship and translation near the confluence of the Yang-tse and some other river systems. That temple was already widely famous well before Bodhidharma came to China. A famous scholar and translator monk named Huiyuan (334–416) established East Woods Temple and translated Buddhist scriptures there. When Bodhidharma traveled from here toward the north of China, he almost certainly would have stopped and stayed at the famous landmark that lies at the crossroads of many travel routes.

In that light, Bodhidharma's going past Danxia Mountain would be axiomatic. Anyway, Everny claims that mountain was home to one of his most famous spiritual descendants, so it seems a worthy stop along his ancient path.

The late afternoon bus ride to Yunmen Temple near Ruyuan stops frequently at designated places to take on passengers. It also stops at nondesignated places, including the shoulder of the road, picking up whoever successfully waves it down and can then be crammed onboard. Now that China buses are no longer publically owned and must make a profit, every fare is a good fare, and every empty space on the bus represents lost revenue. The trip is especially slow until we finally reach the edge of Shaoguan and get into more open country.

By the time we get to Ruyuan, it's late afternoon, and immediately Everny starts looking for a bus that will take us to Yunmen Temple. However, I'm aware that if we don't get to the temple soon, we'll miss dinner, and there's no village near that temple where a restaurant can be found. I hail a taxi and call on Everny to jump in. The temple is, after all, only a $2 ride away. Soon we're passing through the picturesque mountains on the north edge of Ruyuan. Then we reach an intersection where a wide road branches left toward a high mountain that backdrops the temple itself. As we approach the temple main gate, I notice a cluster of new buildings that sit on the hill behind a high wall on our left. It is a Zen nunnery, recently rebuilt and with a gleaming new pagoda nestled on the mountain behind it. We proceed past the nunnery to the main gate of Yunmen Temple, a new big *paifang*. The high mountain, after which the temple is named (Cloud Gate), has eclipsed the late afternoon sun.

We send off the taxi and approach the entrance office of the temple. Normally, visitors must pay an admission fee, but Everny's lay ordination certificate at this temple, called a *guiyi zheng*, is a passport for us to enjoy the temple's hospitality. We walk past the temple's scenic front square and a large pond (the "Liberate Life Pond" found in many temples where monks release fish and turtles saved from the market) to enter the Heavenly Kings Hall. With an immediate right turn we reach the dining room, arriving just as dinner is being served.

As I mentioned above, Chinese monastics are full-fledged vegans. Despite this they usually seem in ruddy health. Chinese temple food is usually good and satisfying. Vegetables dominate, but protein in the form of tofu, legumes, and gluten dishes are plentiful. They also offer a *zhuchi*, the foundational starchy dish that accompanies every Chinese meal. In the north of China, noodles and bread made from wheat or millet serve this purpose, while in the south of China, rice plays this starchy role. Still, Chinese monastic diets are not always low fat, since a lot of oil is typically used for cooking.

After dinner, we arrange for our guestrooms in the men's and women's guest quarters. Then Everny wants to pay her respects at the burial monument of Foyuan, the late abbot of the temple who was a disciple of Empty Cloud. He's the same person who bravely saved the remains of Zen's Sixth Ancestor Huineng from destruction during the Cultural Revolution. We climb the hill behind the guesthouse to light incense and bow before Foyuan's photo that sits before his stupa (monument). As the unusual heat of the autumn day starts to subside, Everny shows me some of the other old stupas that mark the lives of famous abbots and monks. We then walk down the hill from these burial sites and go up a separate wide path toward an area nestled at the base of Cloud Gate Mountain, a place lushly surrounded with timber bamboo. On the hill high to our left is a meditation hall. To our right the bamboo droops over ornamental ponds populated with fish and turtles. In the midst of the forest we arrive at a memorial hall dedicated to Empty Cloud. No sooner do we arrive than an old monk from the temple appears whom Everny recognizes and greets. He's carrying a big bag of peanuts and immediately starts scooping them into our hands under a beaming, nearly toothless grin. After filling our hands with peanuts he reaches into his bag to scoop out more and try to pile them on us. We jump back to keep him from stacking more peanuts on our already-full hands, and with a toothless cackle he swirls around and dances down the path we've just come up. We stuff our pockets full of peanuts, then Everny circumambulates Empty Cloud's stupa before we climb the steps to its entrance. About twenty-five feet square, it's a traditional style Chinese hall decorated in a subdued fashion, suitable for the crypt of China's most famous modern-era Buddhist teacher. In front of the hall we encounter two monks sitting in arm chairs to the left of the main door of the shrine. They seem to be shooting the breeze, talking a little animatedly about some other monk and some incident in the temple. After we have paid our respects and emerge from the small hall, Everny pauses, staring at the monks. As I walk away, I hear her criticizing them for what is to her unseemly behavior. They've been talking loudly about mundane worldly matters around Empty Cloud's shrine, a place, she says, that should remain quiet and peaceful out of respect. I'm a little shocked by this. Here's a lay woman criticizing some home-leavers. I look around and notice that they look as shocked as I am, and they immediately fall into a sullen silence. Everny is obviously very devout and takes her religion seriously. The tone of her voice toward the monks is highly critical, leaving no room for any face-saving excuses for their behavior.

I'm pretty surprised at Everny's boldness in criticizing the monks. I'm acutely aware that I would not have the courage to speak up about the monks' behavior as she did, especially as a foreigner. Anyway, at least they were sitting outside and not inside Empty Cloud's shrine as they chatted away. I remember an experience I had long ago when I was in Japan. On one occasion I visited the shrine of a very famous monk named Dogen at Eiheiji Temple near Japan's North Sea. Dogen is credited to be the founder of a line of Zen that flourished in Japan and then spread to America and other countries. His memorial shrine sits on a mountain outcropping at the back of Eiheiji Temple. I well knew, when I visited the place, about the honor his memory commands in Japanese and American Zen circles. So I was quite shocked when I first looked past a wooden guardrail at the front of his burial shrine, a place where signs said KEEP OUT to commoners like me, to see a group of resident Japanese monks horsing around inside. One was balancing a long pole on his finger and running back and forth in front of the altar, trying keep it upright in the air. Others were laughing and talking. Some Japanese lay Buddhists, standing outside the guardrail along with me, stood with shock on their faces at the monks' behavior. Was what they were doing some strange object lesson, something like the "natural" monk's behavior with the Buddha statues at Mazu's temple? That would be a generous interpretation.

Everny and I stroll down the mountain on a different path than the one we came up on. As we pass the other side of the ornamental ponds, I spy the old monk we encountered before, a broad smile on his face, standing beneath the tall bamboo, happily tossing peanuts to the fish and turtles of the murky ponds. Night begins to fall. I tell Everny that I'll be returning to Shaoguan early the next day, so we say our good-byes.

The next morning, I get up with the sun, brush my teeth, and make my way to the temple gate. The guard tells me that a bus passes every fifteen minutes or so at the main road, so I walk down the road past the nunnery and position myself at the intersection where the temple's approach road branches from the main highway.

After five minutes or so, no bus has come. A motorcyclist going my way appears and glances at me as he goes by. Suddenly he slows down and pulls over. I have only a small backpack with me, so riding on the rear of a motorbike would be no problem. Within a few moments we agree on a price for a ride to Ruyuan City, about fifty cents, and a moment later I'm holding onto my hat as we speed through the countryside.

An hour or so later I've managed to return to Shaoguan by bus, and I go directly to buy a ticket for the night train heading north. In the ticket hall there is a huge bulletin board with all the trains listed by departure time and the stops they visit. After some searching, I find there's only one train that travels to my destination, Nanchang City, five hundred miles away, and it doesn't go there directly, instead passing through intermediate and out-of-the-way places. The train departs at nine in the evening and arrives at Nanchang early the next morning. Without a better option, I get in line and buy a ticket, then go out and hop on the back of a motorcycle taxi to return to my hotel. After a breakfast of instant oatmeal mixed with nuts and dried fruit and a brewed coffee, I check out and leave my bag with the desk. Grabbing another motorbike taxi to the country bus terminal, within a half hour I board a bus traveling to Ren Hua County, the location of Danxia Mountain and Separate Transmission Temple.

13. Danxia Mountain

CHINA'S GEOGRAPHY IS quite different from the geography of North America. In the United States, traveling from west to east, the mountains, valleys, deserts, and plains are pretty well-defined. For example, traveling from San Francisco to New York, there'd be a valley (Sacramento), mountains (the Sierras), desert (Nevada/Utah), mountains again (the Rockies), the Midwest plain, mountains again (the Appalachians), and after some hills and rolling country you'd reach New York. In China, the mountains and hills are far less orderly. Aside from certain places like the "northern plain," an area stretching south from Beijing, mountains and valleys occur much more at random, especially in the south of the country. The same goes for unusual geographical features. Danxia Mountain is just such an unusually featured place. Located near agricultural areas in the south, Danxia Mountain is composed of a group of fantastic wind- and water-carved peaks and bluffs. A wide area there is now set aside as a recreational nature preserve, inaccessible to automobiles. At its center is a series of hiking trails that visit various strange rock formations and historic places. One such place is the temple I'll visit today.

"When you go there, you'll understand better about Danxia Tianran's personality," Everny had told me.

Traveling northeast out of Shaoguan, we follow the river and soon break into open agricultural land. Here again are small farms common to Southern China composed of rice paddies, vegetable gardens, banana palms, and lychee. The bus stops periodically to let passengers get off and on along the way. Interspersed with the small farms, there is the usual collection of motorcycle and tire repair shops, brick and gravel piles, small cement factories, and murky ponds. Anywhere a body of water may be large enough to support aquatic life, there's usually a casual angler trying his luck.

Before long there are some startling-looking mountains in the distance. They rise abruptly from the earth and are oddly flat on top, a little like the mountain mesas of the American Southwest.

Within an hour, the bus travels the thirty miles that separate Shaoguan from Renhua. We've barely entered the town when a wide avenue opens to our left that leads to a huge, blockade-like gate, the entrance to the Danxia recreational area. The bus lets us off, and I walk toward the huge edifice. I buy an admission ticket at the nearly deserted ticket building at the side of the street. Passing through one of many rows of deserted turnstiles, I come to a waiting area empty except for a few seated old women. They're delighted to see a foreigner come along and smile big toothless grins at me as I sit to wait for one of the small buses that ferry people into the park.

Presently, a man appears who tells us all to come with him. He's a driver, and soon we are bumping our way along the road into the mountains in an electric touring car, a sort of long golf cart with five rows of seats. The car stops at an intersection that appears to branch to a village. The old ladies jump out and give me a friendly smile and a wave as I continue alone into the park.

I examine my ticket. It is a high-quality, plastic affair adorned with the photo of an odd, very phallic pinnacle rock formation. I'm not sure what to make of the picture. A descriptive brochure I got with the ticket explains how Danxia Mountain was considered a candidate to be a World Heritage site by UNESCO, though apparently this did not ever come to pass. (Note that in China the word *mountain* can be ambiguously either singular or plural, and Danxia Mountain, like many other such places, is actually composed of many separate mountains.)

Presently the driver tells me we've reached the end of his route, a place by a large bridge that passes across the finger of a clear blue lake. On both sides of the bridge are resort facilities, including restaurants, many moored foot-paddle boats, and a bunch of tour boats and their operators. After asking around about the location of Separate Transmission Temple, I get directions to go to a cable car a few thousand yards away. A ticket taker for the paddle boats tells me to wait for the shuttle bus on a nearby bench. A bus comes along, and I climb aboard. We weave into the mountains and pass through a checkpoint where someone examines our tickets, then soon are let off at the boarding area of a big cable car that stretches up the abrupt face of a mountain.

I buy a cable car ticket, and in a few moments the attendant hustles me alone into a moving cable car for the ride to visit Separate Transmission Temple.

The massive, forested mountain form and the scene jolt a memory of another Chinese Zen master, Danxia Zichun (1064–1117), whose name is associated with Danxia Mountain. He talked about a mountain and employed the metaphor of a jewel to convey his teaching on the nature of the mind:

> [Danxia Zichun] entered the hall and addressed the monks, saying, "Within the cosmos, inside the universe, at the very center, there is a jewel concealed in Form Mountain.
>
> "Dharma Master Zhao [Zhaozhou] says that you can only point at tracks and speak of traces of this jewel, and that you cannot hold it up for others to see. But today I split open the universe, break apart Form Mountain, and hold the jewel forth for all of you to observe! Those with the eye of wisdom will see it!"
>
> Danxia hit the floor with his staff and said, "Do you see? It's [like] a white egret in the snow, but that's not its color. Nor does it resemble the clear moon, nor the reeds in the water!"

I turn around and look at the view in the other direction. Far beneath the clear sky, the fingers of Danxia Lake stretch in and out of the encircling peaks, a few large tour boats shuttling tourists along its shimmering surface.

14. Separate Transmission Temple

AT THE TOP OF THE MOUNTAIN, a summit trail winds through *ubame* oak, Chinese horsetail pine, and ficus trees that shade a series of mountaintop lookouts. Each vantage point is positioned to expose a view of the area's unique terrain, its smokestack-like mountains rising vertically from broad forested valleys. Along the path, hikers sit on log benches and enjoy lunches of fried bread and bottled water. The lone foreigner causes some interest among people enjoying their fall holiday, and I pause several times during my hike to have my picture taken, backdropped by spiraling rock columns, with honeymooning couples, giggling schoolmates, and sundry retirees enjoying this quiet corner of China.

The trails are well-marked, and I walk for a half hour or so and then ascend some nearly vertical stone stairs to reach a high lookout at the end of the mountain's ridge. There, a wide panorama of Danxia's peaks and valleys stretches in three directions. Directly below me on the mountain, perched with a western exposure, Separate Transmission Temple nestles into a hollow on the mountainside. From my overlook I can see down past the temple to where Danxia Lake winds through shadowed valleys. The whole effect is a picture of a Zen monk's retreat from the dusty world, where a "separate transmission" can be truly separate from everything else.

Retreating from the high lookout, I start down the steep mountain path leading to the temple. Soon it reaches a nearly sheer face that drops to the area off to the temple's side. Clutching a safety chain bolted into the mountainside, I descend about fifty meters down a set of steps carved into the escarpment. Near the bottom, a gazebo perched on an outcropping serves as a mid-descent resting place. After a few minutes there, I continue descending the last elevation to the level of the temple, reaching a place a hundred meters or so from its front gate but at the same level.

I circle to my left toward the front of the complex. In Chinese *feng shui*, it's considered very lucky to situate a building with "mountain behind, water in front," and Separate Transmission Temple is a classic example of this arrangement. From the small Heavenly Kings Hall that sits at the front of the temple compound, its buildings rise up the steep slope to some sheer vertical bluffs. In the other direction, the afternoon sun reflects on pretty Danxia Lake a mile or so down below.

A monk happens by, and I ask him if the abbot is in today. He nods and smiles, greeting me with his hands clasped, and then points toward some buildings that stretch east from the central temple area. It's clear that the rather squeezed area on the central axis of the temple is too small to accommodate the monks that now reside here, and the temple has expanded horizontally in the flat area along the side of the mountain to make room for its new population. The monk tells me to follow him, and we make our way through a construction area toward a newly built hall. Inside there's a statue of Dizang Bodhisattva that overlooks floor cushions where temple services are held. Passing to the hall's right, the monk leads me to a building with living quarters. He ducks into an open doorway, and a few moments later he reemerges with Separate Transmission's abbot beside him.

Happily, the abbot is just having tea with two other monks at a table just inside the door, and he invites me to enter. He introduces himself as Benchang, a name that means "Fundamental Shining." He's around forty years old and has an earnest, intelligent, and welcoming demeanor. A large wooden carving of Kwan Yin sits on a bookcase behind him, and the room is otherwise adorned with photos of Buddhist clergy and carved Buddhist figures. He adds hot water to a Yixing teapot as I explain my reason for visiting Danxia Mountain. By the time I've stopped my short introduction, he pours a cup of Iron Kwan Yin tea, hands it to me, and smiles.

"Danxia Tianran didn't live on this mountain. He lived during the Tang dynasty. This temple was set up much later, during the Kang Xi period of the Qing dynasty."

I notice the tea tastes slightly bitter.

"There's confusion around this subject because the monk that set up this temple was named Dangui ["Peace Returns"]. He had a teacher whose name was also Tianran, and people get that name confused with the monk who lived eight hundred years earlier in the Tang dynasty."

My quest to find Danxia's Dharma seat will have to continue elsewhere.

"What was Dangui's story?" I ask.

"Dangui was an official who worked during the Ming dynasty (1368–1644). When the Ming dynasty collapsed, he grew weary of the world and decided to leave it behind. He became a monk at Hai Chuang ["Ocean Banner"—the same place where Jimmy Lin has his office] Monastery in Guangzhou and later came up on this mountain and established Special Transmission Temple."

Benchang then tells me his own story. When he graduated from college in the late '80s, he first worked as a businessman but then decided to become a monk and took ordination in 1992. He studied under the famous monk Yicheng at True Thusness Temple on Yunju ("Cloud Abode") Mountain. In 1997 he was sent here to Separate Transmission Temple, where he became abbot.

I've visited Cloud Abode Temple, where Benchang was ordained, on different occasions, and I've also met his teacher Yicheng at that location. It's famous as the place where Empty Cloud lived just prior to his death there in 1959. Cloud Abode Temple is aptly named. On my first visit, the entire mountain was socked in with clouds and fog, a steady rain causing a constant downpour from the monastery's roofs. Old abbot Yicheng, once a student of Empty Cloud, was very welcoming. When I said I felt honored to be at the place where Empty Cloud lived and died, Yicheng said, "Would you like to see his sacred relics?" I was completely taken aback by his offer. A moment later he disappeared behind the altar at the center of the abbots' reception room and reappeared with a pagoda-shaped vial containing the pearl-like, round relics, some of the remains of Empty Cloud after his cremation. That he showed these sacred items to a total stranger who happened in out of the rain really surprised me. Later, when I told this story to my friend Bill Porter (a.k.a. the author Red Pine), he told me that Yicheng was famous for doing crazy things.

Benchang and I drink a pot of tea and talk about Cloud Abode Temple, Yicheng, and other topics of common interest. Obviously, Separate Transmission Temple doesn't have a known relationship with either Danxia Tianran or Bodhidharma. There are only some records indicating that monks of the Tang dynasty already lived in huts on the mountain. Apparently it's long been regarded as an ideal escape from the dusty world.

After one more pot of tea, I say I must be going, and Benchang accompanies me outside. He instructs me about taking the path down the mountain, and after we say good-bye I walk out the temple gate and turn, one last time, to look at the temple's special position on the planet. Above it on the bluffs there are big Chinese characters that have been carved into the face of the mountain over long centuries. The temple's name is carved among them, its characters accented with vermillion paint. Four other characters proclaim THE RED DUST DOESN'T REACH HERE.

A short way down the mountain the trail branches, and I'm met by a signpost, complete with photos of the sights to be seen in each direction. One trail leads to a most unusual-looking cave that is graphically depicted on the signpost. The cave has a stunning resemblance a certain private part of the female anatomy. Then I remember the unmistakably phallic photo on the park entrance ticket and realize one reason why Danxia Mountain commands special interest, especially in China's famously yin and yang culture. The place has remarkable geographic features, but the strangest ones are still a little too risqué to gain acceptance as a UNESCO World Heritage Site!

15. Nanchang City

LATE IN THE EVENING I board the night train for Nanchang. Instead of traveling northeast directly to that city, it first goes northwest to Hengyang City in Hunan Province. After picking up some passengers there around midnight, the train turns east to enter Jiangxi Province from the west, passing through ancient Zen country, a place where local dialects still use the word *Zen* instead of *Chan*, revealing the origin of the pronunciation still used in Japan and the West. The train route from Hengyang to Nanchang City passes like a belt under the belly of much ancient Zen real estate. Not far north of the rail line are many ancient temples where the most famous masters of old lived and taught. That area is my next destination along Bodhidharma's ancient path.

At 7:00 AM I drag my bags onto the platform to follow the crowd through the exit tunnel. An army of taxis waits to disperse the train's passengers through the city.

Nanchang is typical of cities in China today. As the country undergoes the hard transition from agricultural to urban society, its "midsize" cities like Nanchang have exploded. In such cities, millions of new urban workers arrive from countless villages, struggling to get a foothold in China's middle class. They are left to their own wit and devices to do this. In this nominally socialist country, there is even less of a safety net than exists in the capitalist United States.

I check into a hotel that I located on the Internet before I left Shaoguan. It will serve as my base while I explore the geographic bowels of ancient Zen during the next couple of days.

After a night on the train, I won't travel farther today but will get ready to leave for the countryside in the morning. Today I will stick around here and drop by Youmin Temple, one of the Dharma seats where Zen Master Mazu (whose name means "Horse Master") lived and taught more than thirteen centuries ago.

Mazu, who as I mentioned earlier was the teacher of Danxia, is among the most famous Zen masters of ancient times. The picture of him painted in old texts is of a big, dynamic, self-assured Zen master, reportedly with a tongue so large he could cover his nose with it. Emphasizing the teachings of the Shurangama Sutra, he forcefully expounded the teaching "Mind is Buddha," and his next two generations of disciples, numbering well over one hundred persons, spread this teaching not only throughout China but to Korea and Vietnam as well. In terms of the "three halls" analogy, Mazu's message that "Mind is Buddha" corresponds with the insight gained from the Buddha Hall.

But in Mazu, a paradox at the heart of Zen reveals itself. After preaching "Mind is Buddha" for many years, he switched his vantage point and started teaching the idea of "No Mind, no Buddha." Or another way to say this is that he moved from the Buddha Hall on to the Dharma Hall, the signless place.

Scholars apply the word *antinomian*, which I talked about previously, to Mazu. Old stories tell how he would shout at or even hit his disciples. Some claim he started this sort of strange behavior, which then spread to some of the teachers who followed him.

It's not the purpose of this book to explain these odd—and to modern sensibilities, even offensive—ways of acting. But I will offer one more observation on the antinomian criticism. Remember that Zen requires its students to look inward, not outward. They must realize *their own* nature, not carry around some idea that others have given them. In this light, a lot of the behaviors of the old Zen masters may be easier to accept. Zen teachers were sometimes abrupt and even forceful about cutting off their students' wandering minds. Seeing the nature of one's own mind sometimes occurs suddenly and may be precipitated by abrupt actions. The Zen tradition of Mazu and other spiritual descendants of the Sixth Ancestor Huineng is referred to as the Sudden school, meaning that enlightenment occurs suddenly. The way some of the old Zen teachers taught can be viewed in that context.

I once accompanied a group of Vietnamese Zen Buddhists to visit Zen monasteries in China. The group was composed of many abbots, abbesses, and lay people, mostly of Vietnamese descent, who had come from around the world to take part in the tour. One evening we met with the abbot of a famous Chinese Zen monastery for a short visit.

Having just returned from a trip out of town, the abbot had taken an hour out of his very busy and exhausting schedule to meet us. He could have made small talk and sent us on our way, but instead he sought to connect to this important group of Zen worthies by speaking directly to the heart of the matter, by talking about an important Zen insight to these long-time practitioners. I think he surprised the group, or at least he surprised me, by stating openly that Zen did not subscribe to Marxist "dialectical materialist" philosophy. He also said that contrary to widespread belief, Zen also did not subscribe to the opposite philosophical idea, the philosophy of the mind called "idealism" in traditional Western philosophy. Instead, he said, Zen is based on the perception that the nature of the mind cannot be known in any philosophical way. The way that Zen views things is "not material, not mind, things not separate, things not united. Not one, not two." Awakening, the abbot said, was of a place beyond all such categories, in fact liberated from such categories, and it might come about suddenly. The abbot went on to explain that the methods Mazu and others sometimes employed, like blows and shouts, must be understood in context. "Such methods can't just be taken up randomly," the abbot said. "You can't just take some ignorant person and hit them or shout at them and expect anything to come of it. People subject to this sort of behavior must be ready for it, perhaps through long meditation and study. They must be prepared for this experience for it to have any meaning."

Another aspect of the antinomian idea relates to how Zen masters treated sentient life. I know of two old stories where Zen teachers are said to have intentionally killed other beings. In one story a Zen master kills a snake in the garden. But the most famous such story is about Mazu's disciple Nanquan, and in my view the incident involved was not "antinomian" at all, but a purposeful teaching about a vitally important Zen principle, taught with an extreme example of violating the precept against taking life. That story is entitled "Nanquan Kills the Cat," and is recorded in Zen records as follows:

> The monks of the temple were arguing about a cat. Nanquan picked it up and, brandishing a knife, said to the monks, "Say the appropriate word, and you'll save the cat. If you don't say it, the cat gets cut in two!"

The monks were silent. Nanquan cut the cat in two.

Later, Zhaozhou returned from outside the temple, and Nanquan told him what had happened. Zhaozhou then removed his sandals, placed them on his head, and left.

Nanquan called after him, "If you had been there, the cat would have been saved!"

First of all, this classic Zen story could be considered exhibit A for demonstrating how Zen's down-to-earth and personal stories often appear, on their face, utterly stupid and illogical. Taken alone and out of context, such stories seem totally bizarre. But in the proper context, when they are personalized for the reader or listener, their meaning becomes clear, and their wisdom is conveyed.

We don't know for certain whether this incident actually occurred or was created later to make a point. Certainly if it describes a real event, it is an especially astonishing story. Nanquan, a great Zen master, appears to willfully kill an innocent sentient being because his students couldn't say an "appropriate word." What the hell could this mean?

Simply put, matters of life and death depend on our ability and willingness to acknowledge and speak the truth. Whether we're talking about ninth-century China or our twenty-first-century world, life-and-death matters require that we see the truth for what it is and then speak immediately and truthfully about what we see. This might be called the social aspect of Bodhidharma's "observing."

When Nanquan's student Zhaozhou, the same Zhaozhou famous for the *mu koan* previously mentioned, placed his sandals on his head and walked out of the room, he really demonstrated transcendent understanding. But how?

Zhaozhou's action had two essential aspects. On the one hand, he "went out," demonstrating that it is the one who stands outside the wheel of birth and death, the one who in both a symbolic and literal sense goes out—that is, "leaves home"—who can best speak the "appropriate word." When the Great Lie is promulgated, it's the one who has not accepted its definitions, the one who isn't invested in the lie, who can speak clearly and with authority to expose it. Zhaozhou also put his sandals on his head. This just reinforces the previous point, for it is the one who is not in a defined position, someone whose shoes are not positioned where the world has defined them as appropriate, who can and must speak the word required to save life.

All Zen *koans* teach about something very close to us. They are personal. This story, like all Zen stories, is about something so close we tend to overlook it. Buddhist monks are home-leavers and, at least in the ancient world if not the modern world, their views commanded some respect simply because people knew they didn't speak from a position of personal self-interest.

Nanquan's age, like all ages, was in a critical political way not so different from ours. Who is it, then and now, who will speak the appropriate word and save the cat?

16. Youmin Temple

YOUMIN TEMPLE, jammed between buildings in the central part of Nanchang City, is all but deserted. In years past several monks lived and practiced here, but it seems that as country monasteries have opened, many monks have left the noisy environment of the city to practice in the quiet of the mountains. But I enjoy visiting here because it retains all the traditional three halls I've previously described. At the back end of the temple complex, a large Dharma Hall remains standing. Unlike other halls, inside there are no big statues of Buddha or other figures, just some works of calligraphy and art on display and a place where people can sit and hear lectures from a teacher.

I've mentioned that such halls were "signless," without statues of Buddhas and the like. But there was, strictly speaking, one sign of the Dharma that could be seen there. The old Zen master who spoke to the monks would wear his formal robe. The robe, a patchwork of squares traditionally said to represent fields of rice or grain, was an important symbol that monks wore to signify the Dharma. However, it should be noticed that even in this example the robe represented the signlessness of the teaching. It did not reveal some arcane symbolism but was simply a representation of ordinary life, made up of a patchwork that represented the checkered fields where farmers work their crops. In Zen Buddhism, just that ordinary signless place, shown in the assembled patchwork of the Buddha's robe, is taken as the ultimate "signless" symbol, worn by someone who has left the rest of us behind.

17. The Trip to Baizhang Temple

AROUND ELEVEN O'CLOCK in the morning, the Nanchang central bus station is concealed behind a mass of people. The taxi driver motions me toward where there must be a ticket office, but I can't see it in the churning crowd. Weaving and dodging, I squeeze my gear between buses, bicycles, and every other manner of motorized and nonmotorized vehicles that are all pinched into the street. I look for the entrance to the bus station, but, failing to see it, I simply push in the direction of some buses I see parked behind an iron fence. I pass through a gate into the bus yard and realize I've just gone through an exit gate and so now must walk through the parked buses to get to the doors of the main terminal building. Reaching there, I see that I've entered the main station without buying a ticket or passing through security. I pause to buy a bottle of water from a vendor and ask her where the ticket office is. She motions toward the area outside of the security X-ray machine, so I pass the security checkpoint going the wrong direction into the ticket-selling area. There I find five ticket-selling windows, but four are empty, and the one window manned with a ticket seller has a very long line. The line ends at a small stack of luggage and bags, which seems to indicate that someone is holding their place in line with these objects. I stand behind them, and within moments some people walk in front of me and take a position in line in front of the bags. I mutter something in Chinese about "not understanding proper etiquette" and move close behind the newcomers so that no more people can crowd in front of me. After some time, I reach the front of the line and ask for a ticket to the country town of Fengxin (pronounced *Fung-sin*). I buy my ticket, and the woman behind the window says I should "go outside and down the street" to catch the bus. Her talk is garbled by the bad microphone-speaker setup, but I dutifully go outside into the street again and ask some attendants at a taxi stand where the bus will arrive. They motion toward a nearby bus stop. Then I see a bus whose front sign says it is going to Fengxin, but it's apparently already departed, and my ticket says my bus doesn't leave for another half hour. The bus in the street doesn't look too promising anyway. It's stuffed with people and covered with a thick layer of dust and grime. I watch the bus attempt to run the blockade of vehicles in front of the station. It's having a hard time. After about ten minutes it finally clears the area. In the meantime I'm subjected to a passenger bus that's just arrived from the countryside that has a man unloading live pigs from inside bags in the luggage compartment under the passengers. Some of the pigs, sensing they've arrived at their doom, are squealing inside the bags. A few have escaped from their bags but are groggy and confused, apparently from the heat of their ride next to the bus engine. I recite a mantra for their benefit and retreat in the crowd to a place next to a noodle restaurant and snack stand. After I've stood there a few minutes, one of the locals ventures a "hello" in English, and I say hello back. Before long, I'm surrounded by a crowd of people all delighted to chat with a foreigner that speaks Chinese. Laughing and joking with them takes my mind off the pigs. When one of them asks where I'm going, I say Fengxin, and he motions to a bus stop farther down the street. Soon I manage to break away from the crowd by threatening to take everyone's picture. They scatter, and I walk to the other bus stop. But there I don't see anything to indicate that my bus will arrive. As the departure time on my ticket draws close, I figure something is wrong. No intercity buses have stopped at this bus stop. With only a couple of minutes to go, I return to the "exit" where I went in before and go toward the buses. There's an attendant there and I show him my ticket and ask where my bus will load. He points me to a place on the far side of the bus parking lot, and I realize for the first time that there's a second bus terminal there, down the street and close to where I was standing outside at the bus stop. I suddenly realize that the bus stop I'm supposed to go to is in that second terminal, not on the street, and so I hurry across the wide parking lot toward that terminal. My bus will leave any second. Frantically I read the destination on every bus parked along the boarding area. There it is! A bus to Fengxin! I dash over to the bus and the bus conductor, seeing me coming, yells to me to get aboard and grabs my ticket out of my hand, saying, "I'll get it punched for you." Naturally I haven't gone into the second station properly either, haven't gone through security, and haven't gone through the line where you get your ticket punched before you board the bus. I fall panting into an empty seat at the rear of the bus. Seconds later the ticket conductor rushes down the aisle toward me, my punched ticket in her outstretched hand. The door closes. The bus lurches, then crosses the wide parking lot toward the exit. The road leaving the bus station passes a flower store over which a sign inexplicably reads DESPOT FLOWERS in both English and Chinese (a gift for your favorite despot?). We bounce into the confusing and tightly jammed chaos of the main street. Another trip into the Chinese countryside successfully begins.

Three times previously I've tried to go to Baizhang Temple, and each time I was forced to turn back due to road construction. It's been two years since my last attempt, and I'm hopeful the roads are fully passable now. Twenty minutes out of Nanchang City, the bus crosses the Gan River and heads west on a four-lane highway. Some previous trips in this area have caused me to dread this stretch of road. Two lanes run each direction, east and west, and although there is a divider between lanes going in opposite directions, it is only intermittent, apparently so cars can turn across the other lanes to exit the highway. The trouble is that it is common for drivers impatient with the progress in their own lanes to pass completely into the two lanes going in the opposite direction and go headlong toward oncoming traffic whenever they think they can get away with it. Then the divider appears again, and they are stranded going the wrong direction, and everyone is forced to squeeze together to avoid head-on collisions at high speed. I'm pretty used to China's wild highways. Now I hardly notice things that once seemed shocking and still scare the daylights out of other foreigners. But I've never gotten used to this particular stretch of road, the Zen Country Highway of Death.

The highway is also a nightmare because pedestrians, animals, and nonmotorized vehicles clutter its edges and are all but impossible to see in the darkness of the night or late evening. Once, as I traveled here at night in a small van with a group from the United States, we were shocked to see a small child, maybe four or five years old, walking next to the divider in the center of the lanes while cars raced by in each direction. We were in the left lane, closest to the child, and we yelled at our driver to stop. He refused. There was absolutely no way to stop without causing a pileup. One of the members of our group claimed she saw someone who was probably accompanying the child, but I didn't see that.

But today the sun is out, the weather is clear, and the road seems to be quite civilized. Happily, I don't need to travel it at night, and my route today leaves this road and turns onto a safer two-lane highway for the leg of the journey that goes to Fengxin after only a half hour or so.

The scenery is interesting if you're not paralyzed in fear by dangerous traffic. I particularly like the water buffaloes that are common here. Their calm, enduring demeanor, whether while tethered to the plow or grazing in the shade of a bamboo grove, captures some ancient grace about China's countryside. Watching them lumber along the road, dutifully following the tethered lead of a nine-year-old child who weighs less than a tenth what the animal weighs, still amazes me.

Other country scenes of rural China sweep past—a closed and crumbling bamboo-products factory; people playing cards in front of a whitewashed cement house; a young couple on parked motorbikes under the shade of a tree, a worried look on her face as if she's breaking the news of pregnancy; a truck loaded with cages of live chickens broken down in the road; and other scenes of joy, pain, and pathos reveal themselves every few seconds. A sign next to a service station says IF YOU'RE SICK, DON'T GET IN THE CAR. IF THE CAR'S SICK, DON'T GET ON THE ROAD! Frequently, on the roadside, farmers dry unhusked rice on bamboo mats under the autumn sun. Soon they will purposefully put the rice on the road itself where passing vehicles will roll over it and husk the grain.

Before long we reach Fengxin. I remember the first time I passed through this small city about eleven years ago, when it was a small, rundown country town. Now there are rows and rows of new and attractive apartment buildings surrounding a town that has exploded in size. We arrive at the bus station and I go inside. A ticket taker tells me that a connecting bus that goes all the way to Baizhang Temple has already left, and another won't be leaving until after two hours from now. It's already one thirty, and such a wait would get me to Baizhang late in the day. I opt to take a bus for Shangfu Village, an intermediate stop, which leaves in a few minutes. I should be able to get a bus or other transport from there to the temple. I buy a ticket and am directed to the Shangfu bus.

Soon I'm traveling down the highway again, at the back of a crowded coach, next to a gentleman who's taking his grandchildren home from school. It turns out he's an off-duty bus driver who actually drives the route we're taking. We chat about how the roads have improved and make other light conversation until the bus arrives in Shangfu an hour later. At one point he tells me that it will be cold up on the mountain by Baizhang Temple. This is something I hadn't considered, and I realize I'm not carrying any heavy clothing.

Finally we roll into Shangfu, a small town that is the closest I ever got to Baizhang's place on my previous attempts to visit there. When I get off the bus, the off-duty bus driver also tells me that it's too late in the day to catch another bus west, so I should take a taxi. He guides me down the street to an intersection next to a river where a group of taxis and their drivers sit languidly waiting for fares. I negotiate the hour-or-so ride to Baizhang Temple for a hundred yuan, about $12. It's a twenty-five-mile ride to the top of Great Hero Mountain, where the temple is located. I turn to the off-duty bus driver and thank him for his help, asking "What's your name?"

"It's Xie" (pronounced *See-eh*), he says.

This is both a surname and the Chinese word for *thanks*, so I say, "Many thanks! Many thanks!" Back when people in China wanted big families, this play on words would have had more meaning.

It's obvious now that I will need to spend the night at or near Baizhang Temple. What I hadn't considered was that the night would be quite cold there, nestled as it is on the top of a mountain. I hadn't brought a jacket so, before leaving Shangfu with the taxi driver, I check out the nearby stores to see if any sold something that would protect me from the cold. I dash back and forth along the street for several minutes, but amazingly there's not a single adult's coat or sweater for sale in any of the stores I can see. I decide to chance it.

I jump in the taxi and again strike out to the west. The taxi driver turns out to be very personable, and soon we're chatting and laughing as we wind along the new road next to a stream that goes into the mountains. We talk about how much pressure young people have to endure these days in China. Everything is super competitive, and times are hard for everyone. Young men trying to support families are under particular stress. China is still a little traditional in this way. While there is a surprising amount of equality between the sexes here compared to, say, Japan, the traditional role of men as breadwinners and women as child bearers still dominates the roles of young Chinese couples. Still a little more conservative than in the United States, I guess. We both agree that the drive to amass wealth is a common factor everywhere. He says, "No matter how much people make, they always want to make more." He also poses a slightly strange question, asking me, "What about public security in the United States?"

I don't know exactly what he's driving at. Is he implying that there are problems with the public security apparatus in China and wondering if the United States is different or better? Or is he just asking about whether we feel secure going about our daily lives? I sort of let the question pass without addressing it head on.

Before long we've entered a forested area where the road climbs into the mountains alongside a stream. It's getting colder, and as we climb, the landscape undergoes a clear change from semitropical rice paddy to the beginnings of a coniferous forest. In less than an hour, we have traversed the mountain switchbacks and emerge into a valley on Great Hero Mountain. The main road turns from pavement to gravel, but there is a side road that is paved, leading right into the valley. We follow it, and after a couple of fast corners we find ourselves next to a very large parking lot that is under construction. One of the workers at work placing and mortaring large cobblestones is a woman, and it appears her young son is playing near her while she works. When I get out of the taxi the boy has an astonished look on his face, so I say in Chinese, "*Wa!* A big-nosed foreigner scaring people!" The taxi driver laughs loudly as the boy appears ready to cry from the fright of seeing me. I shake the driver's hand and turn to look at Baizhang Temple.

18. Baizhang Temple

Looking up the valley past a big *paifang*, I realize that the parking lot is not the only new thing happening here. In the distance, past the front gate and across a very large plaza, I see that a very grand, very new Baizhang Temple is being constructed. In front of it are bridges and water features being built even as I watch. Beautiful new sweeping roofs also adorn what look like dormitories and other buildings.

ANCIENT TEMPLE GATES

In ancient times, there would have been three gates to pass before I could enter Baizhang Temple. These gates were called the Gate of Emptiness (空门), the Gate of Signlessness (无相门), and the Gate of Nonaction (无作门). The Chinese word for *three* (*san*) sounds very much like the word for *mountain* (*shan*). In many Chinese dialects, the words sound the same. For this reason, the two words intermingled, and "three gates" became synonymous with the phrase "mountain gate" (there is no difference between the singular and plural form in such Chinese words). The term *Mountain Gate* then became synonymous with *Zen monastery*.

The first Zen gate, called "Emptiness," is named after one of the most misunderstood and confusing terms used in the Buddhist religion. I've already explained my view that emptiness is not as important as "signlessness" and won't go into it much further. Our grammar school teachers taught us that things are made from basic building blocks called atoms (which are in turn made of quarks). Atoms form elements and molecules. Thus we learned very early that everything in the world is made of these building blocks, and things do not have some "essential" nature. This is as good an explanation of the idea of things being "empty" as anyone needs. Anyway, if you look at the human body under a microscope at ever smaller scales, you'll never find any essential "mind." There is no "mind" in the human body. The brain is just the antenna for the field of mind (there's probably not a "field" either, but that's the topic of some other book to be written by modern physicists or neurobiologists).

I've already explained the meaning of *signless*, so I'll only mention that the last gate, called "Nonaction," in part symbolized the ultimate ideal of leaving the world, not doing any more action that causes harm. A real Zen adept must pass through all three gates both physically and mentally to attain the Zen way.

I make my way through assorted work crews laying mortar and cobblestones and find my way to the front of the temple complex. I slip through a walkway leading past the Heavenly Kings Hall to find the inner temple area alive with even more activity. Construction crews are hard at work everywhere. A big mechanized scoop is moving dirt near a newly constructed Buddha Hall. I cross an area of construction and ask a man standing to one side if there is a guesthouse at the temple. He says yes and points me to the back and right of the line of new buildings. I pick my way along on construction planks, hopping over open ditches.

Soon I reach the general area where the man was pointing and run into another man who approaches me and asks if I've come to stay the night. I answer in the affirmative, and he leads me out the side of the new construction toward a group of buildings that constitute the old temple. Here we pass another Heavenly Kings Hall and enter the rectangular area of Baizhang's original temple. The temple buildings ascend a slope leading up the side of the valley, with various terraces created for the buildings. The man leads me to the guest reception hall of the old temple. Aside the wide-open door is a big poster with four pictures of Mickey Mouse, all waving "Welcome!"

Late afternoon services are under way in the old temple's Buddha Hall and there's no one in the guest reception room. The man who brought me there suggests I wait until after services have finished and someone can come to register my presence. I agree to wait. When he leaves, I walk up the hill a few yards to view the layout of the place. At the rear of the rectangular enclosure of the temple grounds there is no Dharma Hall behind the Buddha Hall. But from the look of things, it appears there was space for one there in ancient times.

ZEN MASTER BAIZHANG'S TEACHINGS

Baizhang's contribution to Bodhidharma's Zen gave the tradition staying power in China. He adhered to important principals that defined Bodhidharma's practice and then made key contributions to Zen that helped set it apart from other Buddhist sects. He wrote the Pure Rules for monastic life that formalized the independent farming and laboring existence that Zen monks followed. This gave Zen a certain independence from the emperor and ruling circles. Baizhang also defined the manual labor involved with this agricultural life as part of a Zen monk's spiritual practice. This emphasis on work and ordinary life as one's practice went hand in hand with Baizhang's conscious avoidance of philosophical speculation. He forcefully argued against allowing metaphysical interpretations of Zen and would not engage in theological debate.

There is a passage in *The Record of Baizhang* that lays out his views on such matters quite clearly. Baizhang instructed his monks as follows:

> If you cling to some fundamental [read: "metaphysical"] "purity" or "liberation," or that you yourself are Buddha, or that you are someone who understands the Zen Way, then this falls under the false idea of naturalism [i.e., something not subject to cause and effect]. If you cling to [the idea of self or things'] "existence," then this falls under the false idea of eternalism. If you cling to [the self or things'] "nonexistence," this falls under the false idea of nihilism. If you cling to the twin concepts of existence and nonexistence, this falls under the false idea of partiality. If you cling to a concept that things do not exist and also do not not exist, then this is the false idea of emptiness, and [all these ideas] are also called the heresy of ignorance. One should practice only in the present without views of Buddha, nirvana, and so on, nor with any ideas about existence or nonexistence, and so on; and without views about views, which is called the correct view; or what you have not heard or not not heard, for this is true hearing. This is all called overcoming false doctrines.

Baizhang formalized an agricultural "farmer Zen" tradition already started by Zen's Fourth Ancestor Daoxin (more on this later) so that Zen could remain outside the imperial orbit. This represented a clear break from the Buddhist precepts established in India and carried on in other Chinese Buddhist schools. In India, Buddhist home-leaving monks were required to exist on donations only and were forbidden to engage in labor. In contrast, the monks of Baizhang's monastery were required to engage in labor daily to maintain their own livelihood. This was a unique innovation in Zen Buddhism.

A key part of making labor part of a monk's life was Baizhang's creation of the Pure Rules (in Chinese, Qing Gui) that prescribed activities in the monastery. These rules were thereafter followed in other Zen monasteries. After a few hundred years, Zen economic independence became less of a factor in the tradition, and these rules died out, the original rules themselves falling into oblivion.

As I mentioned, Buddhist monks in ancient India depended on the donations, called *dana*, provided by lay people. Work of any type was strictly forbidden for Buddha's home-leaving disciples. This was not because they were seeking a life of ease. The home-leaving ideal demanded that karma-generating activities must cease, and among such activities was gainful employment. From the Protestant work-ethic point of view, this may seem rather naïve, if not selfish. But the idea was that by giving up any ideas of gain, monks would gain freedom from all vexing desires (sex, of course, was strictly forbidden as well). In India, where the climate permitted monks to live in the forest using little more than their robes for shelter, an itinerant lifestyle of little activity presented no great difficulty. Each morning, traditional Indian monks could walk into town with their individual begging bowls and receive donations from the faithful. For much of Buddhism's early history, a number of Indian monks lived and practiced in small groups in the forest, gathering in larger groups once a month under the full moon to jointly honor the Buddha. Even today, the full-moon ceremony is performed in Buddhist monasteries, a continuation of this tradition. However, in northern regions, monasteries appeared, a necessary development due to cold winters that made living outdoors impossible. This development was even more necessary in China, where winters can be extremely severe.

In China, a long-established Taoist hermit tradition showed how an individual might live apart from society. However, Taoist hermits living alone high in the mountains grew and collected much of their own food. Early on, China's Buddhists didn't regard the Taoist path to be true to their religious practice. Yet there was no *dana* tradition in China. A monk who tried to support himself by begging might starve to death in the cold.

To survive, Chinese Buddhist monks needed to build monasteries and take their meals in dining rooms made for that purpose. The Chinese, in a nod to earlier tradition, used the name conglin ("forests") to denote their monasteries. But the need for proper shelter from the harsh weather naturally won out over embracing the home-leaving, woods-living ideal.

Solving this problem had far-reaching consequences. Immediately, there was the problem of how monasteries would be financed, both for their construction and for the support of the monks who would live inside them.

An emperor, especially a newly converted one, could be approached to provide the Buddhist church with support, or even lavish wealth. With imperial help, gold leaf might shine from the Buddha statues and temple roof tiles. But isn't such a course of action contrary to a religion that idealizes leaving the material world behind?

Ironically, a tradition dedicated to "leaving home" and forsaking the karmic world thus always faced a fundamental problem of a political nature. What it boiled down to was government control. For when monks lived in a monastery, the decisions of who would lead it, how the abbot and director of the place would be chosen, and what would be taught there always came to the fore. Would the new abbot be someone who supported the home-leaving ideal, someone who allowed monks to forsake the world and practice apart from its polluted influence? Or would the abbot be chosen according to the emperor's (who was paying for it all) personal understanding and interest in Buddhist doctrines?

Understanding the dynamic between Zen and central imperial power is a vital aspect of understanding Zen's development in China. Bodhidharma seems to have been at pains to maintain independence from the court. Baizhang played a key role in this continued effort when he formalized the economic independence of Zen monks.

Baizhang's well-known dictum that prescribed the work ethic for home-leavers is revealed in this famous story from old Zen records:

> In the everyday work of the monastery, Baizhang always was foremost among the assembly at undertaking the tasks of the day. The monks in charge of the work were concerned about the master. They hid his tools and asked him to rest.
>
> Baizhang said, "I'm unworthy. How can I allow others to work in my behalf?"
>
> He looked everywhere for his tools but was unable to find them. He even forgot to eat [while looking for his tools], and thus the phrase "a day without working is a day without eating" has become known everywhere.

Although not the first Chinese Zen monastery to adopt farming to feed itself, Baizhang's monastery symbolized this way of life. One of Baizhang most famous disciples, named Guishan Lingyou, carried on this nontraditional Buddhist lifestyle at Gui Mountain, establishing what became known as the Guiyang Zen school. Guishan not only undertook gardening and tea production for his monks to live, but also was famous for retaining draft animals like water buffalo. Here again, Zen moved further away from the Indian precepts, among which were rules that forbade keeping or restraining any animals.

So in China (and perhaps in India long before), building monasteries had political overtones. How independent from the emperor could a monastic order remain? To fully appreciate Bodhidharma's life and legend in China, one needs to examine him with this in mind.

In the Zen tradition, the purity of the home-leaving ideal was diluted so that monks could practice the religion without political compromise. The need to just "observe mind" led Bodhidharma's Zen to avoid the court, but also, perhaps, to backslide on issues like growing their own food and keeping their own animals.

BAIZHANG AND THE BODHISATTVA WAY

That early Zen rejected indulging in metaphysics or making grand statements about reality is clearly shown in some of Baizhang's teachings. He warned against falling into any partial views whatsoever. He wanted to keep practice grounded in what's right in front of us. In this light, his "views" on the idea of reincarnation are especially interesting. What does he have to say about the idea of rebirth on the wheel of birth and death? For an insight into his views on this controversial doctrine, there is a famous story in old Zen records called Baizhang's Wild Fox:

Every day when Zen Master Baizhang spoke in the hall, there was an old man who would attend along with the assembly. One day when the congregation had departed, the old man remained.

Baizhang asked him, "Who are you?"

The old man said, "I'm not a person. Formerly, during the age of Kasyapa Buddha, I was the abbot of a monastery on this mountain. At that time, a student asked me, 'Does a great adept fall into cause and effect or not?' I answered, saying, 'A great adept does not fall into cause and effect.' Thereafter, for five hundred lifetimes, I've been reborn in the body of a fox. Now I ask that the master say a turning phrase on my behalf, so that I can shed the fox's body."

Baizhang said, "Ask the question."

The old man said, "Does a great adept fall into cause and effect or not?"

Baizhang said, "A great adept is not blind to cause and effect."

Upon hearing these words, the old man experienced unsurpassed enlightenment. He then said, "Now I have shed the body of a fox. I lived behind the mountain. Please provide funeral services for a monk who has died."

Baizhang then instructed the temple director to tell the monks to assemble after the next meal for funeral services. The monks were all mystified by this, because there was no one who was ill in the temple infirmary, so how could this be? After the meal, Baizhang instructed the monks to assemble by a cave behind the mountain. He then brought out the body of a dead fox on his staff and proceeded to cremate it according to established ritual.

It appears, given the magical events it relates, that this story was made up by someone to make a point. Yet the story is instructive.

Baizhang's "not blind to cause and effect" appears important because it skillfully addresses the problem of "cause and effect," which is here also the "wheel of birth and death" without sinking into a set view, a "metaphysical" understanding. Zen practitioners, like others in the Buddhist and Vedic traditions, thought this "wheel" idea to be the essential existential problem people face. Baizhang's answer about the correct way to view this idea was that, in effect, the wheel of birth and death shouldn't be thought to "exist" or "not exist." He simply says he can see it. Whether it is real or unreal, an illusion or genuine, it is nonetheless the unavoidable problem that appears to Baizhang when he looks closely. This is what is seen in the "observing the nature of mind" practice that is at the heart of Zen.

There is one other passage in *The Record of Baizhang* that is quite startling. Baizhang, one of the towering figures of Zen history and the Bodhidharma Zen lineage, specifically counseled against embracing the bodhisattva ideal. In the record of his historical teachings, the same work where he counseled against holding doctrinal views, he said, "Don't fall into the bodhisattva vehicle." He followed this instruction by saying one should "Break [the shackles of] the three phrases." The "three phrases" to which Baizhang refers in this passage were ancient explanations of what is fundamental to following the Bodhisattva Path, namely (1) bodhi-mind, (2) great compassion, and (3) every manner of expedient means (for helping beings).

Nowhere in my study of Western Zen literature do I remember anyone quoting this passage (although of course maybe someone has done this, and I'm not aware of it). In any case, it seems quite astonishing that Baizhang would make such a statement. How do we square this idea, uttered by one of the most highly honored of the old Chinese Zen masters, with the modern Western Zen tradition that fervently embraces the Bodhisattva Path and ideal? Did Zen, early on, associate the Bodhisattva Path with problems?

A TOUR OF BAIZHANG TEMPLE

After a while, services end, and a young monk appears to greet me. He says his name is Juexing ("Enlightened Nature"). He's very accommodating, and before long I've registered and have been given a futon bed in the old guesthouse. The new guesthouse, he explains, still has no electricity, so it will be best if I stay in the old one for the time being. I agree; minutes later, after I put down my things, Enlightened Nature reappears with three garments he suggests I use if I get cold. One is a massive overcoat, one is a padded vest, and the final one is a light jacket typically worn by lay workers at the temple. I thank him and slip into the jacket. The chill of the evening had been worrying me. Now, because of Enlightened Nature's thoughtfulness, everything will be fine. A bell rings, and he invites me to dinner.

The dining hall turns out to be self-service-style at dinner time. Huge pots of rice and noodles provide the base for other dishes of pickled and/or spicy vegetables from the temple garden. It's a feast.

After dinner Enlightened Nature offers to show me the important landmarks on the hill behind the monastery. I readily agree, and we wind our way up a well-constructed pathway through a forest of very tall timber bamboo. Climbing a hundred feet or so of steps, we arrive at two large boulders. Each has characters inscribed into the rock. The characters on the upper boulder proclaim THE PURE RULES BENEATH HEAVEN. The Pure Rules were of course the rules by which Zen monks would live in their monasteries as set up by Baizhang. The term *Beneath Heaven* can be translated as "known everywhere," and it is a term widely used to denote something of great fame. Enlightened Nature says the characters were inscribed in the stone during the Tang dynasty, about twelve hundred years ago, to commemorate the promulgation of the Pure Rules. Nearby there's another large, flat boulder with the words COILED DRAGON STONE inscribed on its side. According to tradition, says my guide, the Tang Emperor Xuan Zong (pronounced *Swan Zoong*) once sat in meditation on top of this flat stone. Xuan Zong was, as a young man, a student of one of Mazu's famous students, Huangbo. Huangbo once slapped him to wake him up. Thereafter, Huangbo gained fame as a Zen teacher cheeky enough to slap an emperor.

I say to Enlightened Nature that I know there is another famous story about this mountainside. "What about the Wild Fox *koan*?" I ask.

"Come this way," he says. He leads me to small crevice in the ground where some boulders sit oddly stacked and juxtaposed, forming a small cave. Here is the spot where Baizhang purportedly retrieved the fox's body from the hillside. The characters WILD FOX ROCK are etched on an overhanging boulder.

Enlightened Nature accompanies me back to the old monastery as darkness falls. He says, "The wake-up bell will sound at 4:30 AM, and morning service will be at 5:00 AM. Do you know the chants we do?" I say I don't know them but I'll try to attend the service anyway.

I return to my room and consider going to sleep. I'm already quite tired, but my watch says it's only six thirty in the evening, too early for bed. I sit and write in my journal for a while, then I hear some monks talking. I notice they are sitting on the veranda of what looks like living quarters across the garden from my guestroom window. I slip out into the darkness and go around the building to join the monks.

They welcome me and immediately pull out a stool for me join them. I notice that one of the three figures is not a monk, but the lay gentleman who met me when I first arrived and guided me to the guesthouse. Of the two monks on the porch, one is pretty young, about twenty to twenty-five years old. The other is around thirty.

From our vantage point, the outlines of the great new halls in the valley are backdropped by the mountains, a last light of the sun, and a half-moon that appears high overhead above the new temple's rooftops. A complete stillness has settled over the scene now that the workers have gone and the stars are appearing. I'm surprised at how clear the sky is. China's well-publicized air pollution doesn't seem to reach here, even though we're far from the ocean. I already like the secluded mountain setting of Baizhang Temple more than any of the other scores of temples I've visited in China. I remark to the monks about how peaceful it is. The younger monk says that here on Great Hero Mountain it's much cooler in the summer than at many other monasteries. It's the ideal mountain retreat.

The monks are interested to learn where I'm from and what leads me here. I explain that I organize tour groups of people interested in Zen to come to China and visit famous places of the tradition. They wonder if I'm connected to the City of Ten Thousand Buddhas, near Ukiah, California. As I mentioned before, that place seems far more famous in China than it is in the United States.

In the course of our discussion, the younger monk asks me if I own a gun. He is quite surprised to learn that I don't have one. He believes nearly everyone in the United States owns firearms. I ask him, "Why should I buy a gun?" He says that newspapers say Americans buy guns to protect themselves from the rampant crime that pervades our cities. The fact that Americans without criminal records can buy guns freely seems astounding to him. I tell him that it's likely that a minority of Americans own firearms, and most of them use them for hunting wild game. Certainly there are many people that have guns for protection, but my guess is that maybe only about 30 percent or so of the whole population do this. Most Americans feel quite safe where they live, I say. Though obviously some places have quite a bit of crime, the general situation for most people is not that way. I tell him that the media always likes to exaggerate everything to make a good story. He is quite surprised that we all don't live in barricaded houses, locked and loaded, ready to protect ourselves from the drug-crazed criminals that would prey on us the instant we let our guard down. Finally the older monk says, "Actually, people everywhere are about the same. It's not so different in different countries."

The topic turns to the situation for monks in China. The young monk says the situation for young home-leavers is quite good right now because they can travel from monastery to monastery and study under whatever teacher they like. "We're free to come and go as we please," he says. He pulls out a book by a well-known Chinese teacher of Pure Land Buddhism and asks me if I've read it. I say I haven't, and he hands it to me to take a look. The fact is, I've never been interested in Pure Land Buddhism. It smacks too much of the heaven and hell scenario I heard in Baptist Sunday School as a boy. Religions that counsel people to find paradise and avoid hell are too common, and while they offer countless people hope of something in the hereafter, that is more than counterbalanced by the millions of adults and children who remain more or less permanently terrorized and traumatized by the threat of eternal damnation. Talk about terrorism! Threatening someone with eternal damnation seems to me to be rather more terroristic than getting blown up by a bomb. I peruse a few pages of the book and hand it back to the young monk.

"I hear that Pure Land Buddhism is very strong in Japan," he says.

The monks are interested to learn that I know about Zen Master Baizhang, the ancient famous teacher of this place, and his importance to Chinese Zen. I tell them that even though much Zen Buddhism in the United States is derived from the Japanese Zen tradition, the traditional stories from China are widely known and studied by American Zen students. Zen practitioners in the United States know the stories of Bodhidharma, Huineng, Mazu, Baizhang, and many others through reading the *Blue Cliff Record* and a number of other books.

The older monk, whose words and speech seem thoughtful and perceptive, asks me what practice I do. I tell him I'm devoted to the practice that Bodhidharma espoused, that of just observing the nature of the mind and following whatever insights that practice offers.

For an hour or so I share the veranda of the monks' quarters and shoot the breeze with them. The unruffled quiet of the ancient evening finds them at peace, apparently happy with their lives. I want to ask them what made them give up the world, give up on the idea of getting a job, having a family, and acquiring things. How did they come to accept the wisdom of forsaking the goofy stuff the world thinks is important for the simple practices and brotherhood of religious life? I've wondered whether, in a society where homosexuality is almost a forbidden subject, many gay men embrace home-leaving so they won't be trapped in unhappy heterosexual relationships. Yet I've never seen any evidence that homosexual relationships commonly occur in Chinese temples. It would be naïve to say they do not, for I can't pretend to know everything that goes on in these places. Yet the monks I've talked to don't, as a rule, strike me as being gay. I often meet men in Chinese lay society who have effeminate mannerisms, characteristics that make little secret of their orientation. It's widely known that gay Chinese men often marry women because of the society's norms, and unhappy marriages result. Maybe most of the Buddhist monks in China have really left the samsaric world (*samsara* means, roughly, the ordinary world of pleasure and suffering we normally occupy).

In China, it's considered rude to ask a monk or nun why they left home. I don't know why this is so. Perhaps it's because their paths have resulted from some failure or loss of face they suffered in the world that is best left unmentioned. But whatever the reason, they have not abandoned the world completely. Within the parameters of their lives, they still work together to make themselves a good place to live on a beautiful mountain. They chant their chants and practice calligraphy, poetry, and even art. Monks travel and enjoy reading. They help out in times of natural disasters, going to the aid of unfortunate victims. They express a determination to pursue the Dharma for their own and others' benefit.

My day of traveling starts to overtake me, and I tell the monks I think I'll head for bed. Just then an old monk emerges from the open doorway of the building. Apparently he's been listening to our conversation. He sits on a stool next to me and we exchange greetings. His name is Shenghui ("Sacred Wisdom"). He presents me with a piece of calligraphy paper on which there are Chinese characters. He brushed them while listening to us talk and wants to give them to me as a gift. The calligraphy is truly exquisite. It is a verse. It is a poem that says that when clouds appear in the sky, they are really just some of the infinite Buddha worlds that stretch through the universe. This is a vision from a famous Buddhist scripture called the Avatamsaka Sutra that tells of countless worlds in the cosmos, each of which has a Buddha preaching the truth. In fact, the sutra says that all these worlds are composed of atoms, and on each of them is a Buddha expounding the Dharma.

Later I'm back in my room on a high kang, or platform, where I make use one of four available sleeping mats and thick blankets. The futons (flat cushions) supplied by my hosts are quite comfortable, and I'm ready to drop off to sleep when the temple drum begins to sound. Playing the evening drum in Chinese Zen monasteries is often an amazing percussion performance. The drummer climbs the drum tower to perform on the side of a very tall circular drum that sits inside the enclosure. His performance includes various rolling, rapid cadences that crescendo and recede repeatedly for about twenty minutes. I lie in complete darkness and listen to the sound roll across the mountain. Tonight, after ten minutes or so, there is a variation. The drum fades away, and the temple bell, from its opposite tower, replies in the darkness. Then a human voice joins the performance. There is a musical dialogue, a calling and answering between the bell and a monk who chants plaintively for the happiness and welfare of all beings. This duet continues for some time, the sound of the bell and voice calling to each other across the dark mountain.

I lie in bed thinking about Baizhang and what this place means to Zen. There is the old argument about the Northern and Southern schools of Zen, the north represented by Shenxiu, who reportedly promoted Gradual Enlightenment, and the Sudden Enlightenment Southern school symbolized by Huineng, the monk who became the famous Sixth Ancestor. The traditional view is that the Northern school emphasized a "gradual" path to enlightenment, whereas the Southern school believed that awakening occurs in a single moment, like "remembering something you once knew but had forgotten." Leaving that old explanation aside, it's clear the two schools were certainly different in their relationship to the Chinese court. Bodhidharma avoided contact with Chinese emperors. His Southern school kept its distance from the country's capital city, its teachers instead living here and on other mountains like this one, far removed from China's aristocratic society, making a living on their own. Baizhang didn't concern himself with what wasn't in front of him: "Just leave home and . . ."

The four thirty wake-up bell reverberates across the valley, and I feel the cold air on my scalp. I compare it to the warmness under the blankets and listen to the argument that breaks out between the two places about which way I should move.

One side finally wins out, and by 5:00 AM I am the lone lay person in the Buddha Hall. Here I participate in morning services with the temple's monks. There are about twenty of them on the other side of the aisle, in the half where home-leavers perform their timeless morning rituals. I'm comfortable with this situation, as I've attended many such services before and I know I should simply bow and stand up whenever anyone else does. Also, I know how to fall last in line when, during one part of the service, the monks circle the central altar several times. Two monks come and join me on my side, apparently concerned that I be able to see what they're doing and follow suit, and maybe so I won't feel so lonely. I can't recite any but a few of the words to the sutras that are chanted, but I know the drill. First they spend a long time chanting the names of scores of ancestors stretching from the seven Buddhas that existed before Shakyamuni, then his name, then all the ancestors, generation after generation, that followed, down to the present time. After that they recite one or two sutras, then they recite Namu Kwan Yin Pusa ("Homage to Kwan Yin Bodhisattva"), while we all walk in a circle around the central altar. A few more sutras and some more bows, and it's over. When we emerge into the courtyard, dawn has broken. Breakfast will be ready in fifteen minutes.

After breakfast I take the opportunity to take a few more photos. Then I see a monk departing with his bag. He tells me he's on the way down the mountain and that the bus to Nanchang will leave in half an hour. I return to see Enlightened Nature and tell him I should catch the 7:00 AM bus. He checks me out of my room and, before I have a chance to refuse, tells me to keep the lay jacket he'd given me the night before to stay warm. "I have many of those," he says. He also pulls out a very old copy of the Platform Sutra, an edition first published in 1952 that includes the original translation from early in the twentieth century by Wong Moulan. I can't refuse it, and anyway there's some information in that edition that I need for my own research. I thank Enlightened Nature profusely, and soon I'm weaving my way through the new temple buildings that are under construction, already alive with workers, making my way toward the village on the far side of the mountain valley.

I soon find the bus stop in the small village by the road. Cows and chickens stand around with the village early risers, people and animals all in their morning routine. Four monks are waiting for the bus to take them down the mountain. Villagers walking along the road are surprised to see a foreigner taking pictures with them. More people line up for the bus. People smile and wave. A few moments later the bus arrives. After I board I find everyone seems to be fighting to give me their seat on the bus. They won't let me refuse them, and I'm guided to a vacated seat. I put my backpack on my lap to make as much room as possible for other people to sit and take a last look at the landscape of Great Hero Mountain as the bus starts down toward the flatlands. We roll through the switchbacks that flank the mountain and follow the winding river. I dial in "Traveling Riverside Blues" on my MP3 player and ride toward the morning sun.

MOUNT LU AND EAST WOODS TEMPLE

Before my bed a moon so bright,
I thought the ground with frost was sown,
I gazed up to that lustrous light,
Then dropped my head and thought of home.
— *"Night Thoughts" by Li Bai*

夜思　　李白著

床前明月光
疑是地上霜
举头望明月
低头思故乡。

Li Bai is probably China's most famous ancient poet, and the poem I've translated here is his most famous verse. In China it's so widely known and loved that (if you read Chinese) you will notice it everywhere enameled on vases and embroidered onto pillow cases. Li Bai's persona was of a wandering poet, drunkard, and nostalgic merry-maker. So the poem quoted above should not conjure an image of someone actually in a bed, but rather of Li Bai waking in a drunken hangover at midnight upon the grass of a high mountain meadow. He probably wandered away from his drinking mates to pee, tripped over a log, and passed out. When he came to, he wrote this verse. That's my narrative, anyway.

Hiding in high mountains away from the polluted world is an idea that united Zen Buddhism with Taoism, China's native religion. To refer to Taoism as a "religion" is not quite right, as it is hard to separate Taoism from Chinese culture in general, so widespread is its multimillennial influence on the country. Taoist culture has even spread in little ways to the West. My dentist, with no other connection to China's culture, likes to talk to me about his Tai Chi exercise class, something intimately Taoist in its origins.

Taoism is the formal name of a religion with deep roots in China. On a rather high philosophical level, the religion has a certain similarity to Buddhism. Taoist philosophy idealizes the radical "nonaction" of leaving the polluted world behind to live a simple and natural life. This idea, on its face, is somewhat like the Buddhist ideal of home-leaving. But through the centuries, Taoism adopted various metaphysical ideas and philosophies that are at odds with Buddhism's outlook. Some of these ideas came from a Taoist belief that one can prolong one's life by living in harmony with the natural environment. This idea spawned all types of theories about "energies," usually translated as Qi (normally written in English as *Chi*), that underlie theories of natural health. Qi influenced exercises like Tai Chi and Qi Gong (which in the West were once called "Chinese shadow boxing") and Chinese medicine. Without debating the merit or truth of theories of Qi, which is a different question, it must be admitted that Taoist metaphysics also spawned a lot of quackery. Early Taoist alchemists, trying to make life longer through chemistry, mistakenly identified lead and mercury as important elements in any good long-life potion. Needless to say, the actual effect of their exotic products had exactly the opposite of their intended effect. After providing such untested elixirs to some gullible emperors, the Taoist alchemists abandoned chemistry in favor of a new theory called "internal alchemy." That philosophy simply counseled that one should practice to align one's "internal" Qi energies with the cosmic Qi meridians that pervade the universe, a more mysterious but also safer form of Taoist practice.

Taoist metaphysics left a lot to be desired, but China's mythical folklore is full of stories of people who allegedly discovered long-life elixirs or other edible means of gaining immortality. Typically, these figures left the world—due to some danger or tragic event—to take refuge in high-mountain vistas like those depicted in traditional Chinese landscape paintings. In these high mountains, they encountered old Taoist hermits or similar demigods who ultimately revealed their secrets, and so more and more lucky world-leavers joined the realm of the immortals. Partly for this reason, Taoism has an immense pantheon of gods and immortals, most of them legendarily connected to events of every tragic age of China's long history. For example, one of the great female immortals, named Magu, is said to have been a concubine of the first emperor and unifier of China, Qin Shi Huang. When he died, custom demanded that his concubines should be buried alive along with him. Magu decided against this fate and escaped to the mountains, there learning the secrets of the Tao. Other immortals of Taoist folklore escaped similar misfortunes in the red dust of the world. Gift stores in Chinatown offer visitors a museum of figurines depicting these ancient immortals. Many of them clutch peaches or mushrooms, two foods they often prescribed to nurture an endless lifespan.

Mount Lu, a peak in Southern China that sits not far south of the Yang-tse, is the ideal mountain setting for Li Bai's verse. Folklore from the dawn of Chinese history tells of Taoist adepts who lived (live?) happily among its caves and peaks, concealed in the mists, and dine on its magic mushrooms. Perhaps they still come out in the early dawn to look down and laugh derisively at the benighted mortal fools who cling to the world.

The Buddhist home-leaving ideal was more easily accepted in a China that already had the idea of these Taoist hermits. Leaving home and "attaining the Way" was not a difficult concept for the Chinese to grasp. Zen, in some respects, was the fusion of Buddhist home-leaving with the Taoist mountain living ideal. In Chinese landscape paintings this ideal is everywhere seen where hermits or scholars are depicted taking refuge among high cliffs. Poetry also fused Zen with Taoism. Take for example this untitled verse by Zen Master Yanshou (904–975):

> Amid high bluffs a lonely ape cries down at the moon,
> The recluse chants, a half night candle's lit,
> Who comprehends this place, this time?
> Within white clouds, a Zen monk sits.

> 孤猿叫落中岩月，
> 野客吟残半夜灯，
> 此境此时谁得意？
> 白云深处坐禅僧。

From my rock perch atop Mount Lu, East Woods Temple appears as a smallish dot on the plains below. It's the place I mentioned before, the Buddhist temple and hub where the famous translator Huiyuan lived and taught sixteen centuries ago. I arrived atop Mount Lu last night from Nanchang by bus and stayed in the high village that caters to the throng of tourists now overrunning the mountain. They've all come to see the places where Li Bai and other famous poets wrote verses amid these peaks far above the dusty world. The view from Mount Lu is beautiful indeed, but nowadays, if you want to find a place with the solitary remoteness of the poetry, you'd better find a different mountain. Here on Mount Lu the tourists stream through the trails like ants, everyone seeking the immortal solitude that Li Bai and Yanshou idealized.

I shift my position on the rock on which I'm sitting and strain to see if anything's moving at East Woods temple.

As I've said, Bodhidharma likely traveled north from South China through the mountains to Jiangxi Province, the area around modern Nanchang City. From there he would have continued north through lake country toward the Yang-tse, going directly past here, and likely stopping at East Woods Temple. That place was already famous when he passed this way and would have been his obvious stopping place. He certainly looked up at the place where I'm sitting now. Maybe he climbed up here.

An old record that claims that Bodhidharma came to East Woods Temple is in a book called *Record of the Dharma Treasury [through the] Generations*, written about the year 760 CE, more than two hundred years after Bodhidharma died. It relates a strange story that says that two of the old master's disciples traveled to China before Bodhidharma himself arrived in the country. According to the story, these two monks brought the teaching of Sudden Enlightenment to a skeptical Chinese society. For their efforts they were thrown out of all the temples in which they tried to stay and finally ended up at East Woods Temple by Mount Lu where they encountered the abbot, the famous Buddhist translator named Huiyuan. When Huiyuan asked them why they had been driven out of other temples, they explained their revolutionary doctrine to him along with the insight that "nirvana is the same as samsara." It was truly a radical idea that nirvana and samsara were the same thing, with the critical difference only existing in the mind of a deluded observer. They reportedly used an odd example to describe this idea, saying that "a hand is also a fist; a fist is also a hand." This supposedly profound insight was said to have awakened Huiyuan to the truth of the "Sudden" doctrine of enlightenment. The story goes on to say that Huiyuan helped the two monks translate a Buddhist scripture called the Zen Gate Sutra, a text that emphasizes a teaching on the Sudden way. Then the story says the two monks passed away. Word of their death eventually reached their teacher Bodhidharma, who was still in India. In order to complete their mission, Bodhidharma himself then came to China and traveled to East Woods Temple to live.

This story is fanciful, at best. Nevertheless, like many old tales, it may be based on a grain of truth. As I've explained, Bodhidharma probably did come here.

Huiyuan, the temple abbot who met the two monks in the story, is famous as one of the most important scholars of Chinese history. His translation of scriptures laid the basis for the Buddhist Pure Land sect. East Woods Temple is thus the mother temple of that widely followed branch of the Buddhist religion.

Among his many important contributions to Chinese Buddhism is Huiyuan's treatise entitled "A Monk Does Not Bow to a King." This essay strongly proclaimed that a Buddhist monk is not subject to the normal relations of loyalty and fealty required of other subjects toward their monarch. As an early statement on the need to separate church and state, Huiyuan's essay is notable and fascinating. Even more surprising is that it was widely acclaimed and accepted in many Buddhist and even official circles in the south of China during his age. The writing weighs in on the meaning of Bodhidharma legend that says he met with Emperor Wu. I'll refer to "A Monk Does Not Bow to a King" again later.

From my perch high on the mountain, I can barely make out the front gate in front of East Woods Temple on the plain far below. There's an interesting legend about that spot that concerns Huiyuan. It seems he befriended the great poets and philosophers of his time, the early fifth century. A legend tells how he had two special friends, a famous Confucian poet named Tao Yuanming and the Taoist Master Lu Xiujing, who once came to visit him at East Woods Temple. The three spent a long afternoon engaged in lively conversation. Their famous friendship symbolizes how the three Chinese teachings of Confucianism, Taoism, and Buddhism should live in harmony. As a monk that had "left the world," Huiyuan had vowed to not leave the monastery, never crossing the bridge that spanned a creek in front of the temple. As his friends were leaving, Huiyuan accompanied them to the front gate, seeing them off in the Chinese fashion. The legend relates that the trio began to cross the bridge that passes over the creek when suddenly a tiger roared from the nearby woods, as if warning Huiyuan not to venture any further and thus violate his world-leaving vow. The three friends all laughed in surprised delight, and the saying "Tiger Creek three laughs" was thereafter remembered and depicted in Chinese folklore and art.

The teachings of East Wood Temple's Pure Land sect, the same teachings cited by the young monk I talked to at Baizhang Temple, remain popular in China and elsewhere and provide a way for people in distress to find solace in religious practice. Many years ago I visited a Chinese nunnery whose inhabitants followed Pure Land teachings. The abbess, a young Chinese woman of about thirty years old, greeted me and my friend and travel business associate Eric Lu warmly, inviting us to have tea. "So, the women here practice Pure Land Buddhism?" I said to her to start the conversation. Her reply surprised me. "Yes," she said, "but of course there is really no such thing as a 'Pure Land.' We're all going to the same place. That place is enlightenment. There are just different ways to get there. It's like taking a trip to Shanghai. Some people will take a train, and other people can take an airplane." Most of the women who lived in the temple, she explained, came from situations of abuse or abandonment and had established a new and happier life in the monastic setting. I was struck by the dignity and poise of the young woman's manner, apparently the result of dedicated practice and dedication to her charges. Later, when I viewed a group photo that we had taken, I was shocked to realize she was extremely short, maybe four foot nine. Her upright poise had left me with the impression she was quite tall.

After being ravaged by the Cultural Revolution, East Woods Temple sat dormant and empty for many years, waiting for political conditions to allow it to be reopened and refurbished. Like other temples, its statues and other valuables were smashed by the Red Guards, the fanatics that attacked China's cultural treasures in a spasm of violence and bloodshed during the late 1960s. Westerners don't widely understand the reasons for the Cultural Revolution, often thinking that it was an ideological struggle where Marxism was carried to extremes in its repudiation of religion and traditional culture. The truth is a little more subtle and interesting. The Cultural Revolution was much about Mao Zedong's attempt to continue holding power when others in the Communist Party felt he should step aside. The Red Guards were not members of the Communist Party. They were youths who, at Mao's urging, decided that the Communist Party was too conservative. Mao famously called on the youth of China to "bombard the headquarters," meaning the Communist Party itself, and overthrow the officials that threatened Mao's position. In the resulting insanity, which was intense for three years and disrupted the society for another decade, life was turned on its head as countless factions were created, aligned, and dissolved, all laying claim to revolutionary purity, the disparate groups fighting with each other throughout the country.

When I first visited mainland China in 1978, ten years after the worst days of the Cultural Revolution, no revival of religious culture was yet evident. It was not until a visit to the country in 1982 that I saw religion making a hesitant reappearance. That year I visited the recently reopened and well-known Yong He Temple in the northeast part of Beijing. In the back hall, where a colossal standing statue of the Buddhist bodhisattva Avalokiteśvara is situated, a very elderly woman was prostrating herself repeatedly on some dusty old cushions before the statue. As surprising as this brave display of religious devotion was, the reaction of bystanders was more interesting. In stunned silence a large crowd gathered around the woman, watching her intently as she kowtowed in front of the statue. The surprise on people's faces betrayed the fear haunting religious expression at that time. Happily, before long, such outward displays of faith became very common, and soon a large number of important religious sites were being rebuilt and reopened.

During my earlier China trip in 1978, the country's reforms under Deng Xiaoping had not yet begun, and normalization of relations with the United States was just in the offing. I saw the country just after the steely grip of the Cultural Revolution around the country's neck began to falter, letting in a little gasp of air. The miserable conditions under which most people were existing at that time were obfuscated by political rhetoric about the then current "great leader" Chairman Hua Guofeng and the "joy of the people due to the smashing of the 'Gang of Four.'"

Then, like now, there was an uneasy relationship between the central government and local officials. At that time, local officials seemed nervous about anyone who came to visit from Beijing. As a member of a "U.S.-China People's Friendship Association" tour, we were accompanied throughout the country by Beijing guides. These guides appeared well-educated, spoke good English, and often offered bemused "read between the lines" interpretations of many things we saw in the country.

It took little effort to see evidence of the hardships that people endured. One guide suffered from chronic headaches that resulted from her persecution during political struggles. The other guide, an admitted Communist Party member, actually seemed very sophisticated. You might even describe him as "suave," with a nice-fitting Mao jacket and sunglasses. He clearly had personal ideas about how China had gone haywire.

I remember how local officials, most of them unable to speak English, were uneasy when they came into contact with these central government guides. To a person, they never deviated from parroting the official line on the current political situation, saying things like "since the smashing of the Gang of Four, production has increased by threefold blah blah blah . . ." We all understood that the "smashing of the Gang of Four" meant "since the end of the Cultural Revolution." At that time the "Gang of Four," a group close to Mao that was denounced after his death, was an acceptable target for criticism. But the Cultural Revolution was not directly denounced openly by name (a phenomenon that still lingers in China). People then were still trying to pretend that the impressive-sounding "Great Proletarian Cultural Revolution" was something other than a disaster. China groped for a face-saving way to deal with its aftermath. In this atmosphere, our questions concerning the real situation in China were deflected as skillfully as a *kong fu* fighter slips a blow. Local guides avoided meaningful conversation. I remember a guide in Guilin, the famous scenic city on the Li River, talking about the banal expressions Chinese use in everyday speech. "When Chinese people arrive somewhere, we say, '*Daole*' ['We've arrived']." Then he would laugh at his own weak joke. This was about the deepest thing I remember him saying to us.

A gruesome parroting of the then prevailing political line extended to a kindergarten we visited. I recall a group of five- or six-year-olds greeting us warmly with expressions of "*Shushu, Aiyi, huanying!*" ("Welcome, Uncles and Aunts!") and then performing skits where the boys happily brandished toy weapons to shoot the heads off of Gang of Four puppets that had been bound and subdued by the girls. To Western liberal sensitivities, recently affected by the violence of the Vietnam War and the nonviolent philosophy of Martin Luther King Jr., viewing kindergarteners act out a pageant of political violence was rather startling, to say the least. When they finished their bloody little skit, they warmly sent us off with chants of *"Shushu, Aiyi, zaijian!"* ("Uncles and Aunts, good-bye!").

Another astonishing example of the fear that our central government guides instilled in the locals occurred at a hospital we visited in Shanghai. Some of the propaganda coming from China in those times centered on the use of acupuncture and its applications in therapy. To witness this medical marvel, our tour group was led into an operating theatre in a hospital to witness the use of acupuncture as an anesthesia for serious surgery.

Apparently the hospital was originally built by Westerners and was used for education, because the operating room was a theatre where students could sit and observe surgeries. We all donned operating masks and entered the darkened theatre under poor lighting. Little did we know how accurately the term *operating theatre* matched reality.

The operating table looked like a long-overused model from the 1930s, left from when Western medicine was predominant in the hospital. Besides that and one other small table that held some instruments and acupuncture needles, there was no other furniture, not even a drug cabinet. Two buckets sat on the floor as receptacles for refuse, and there was little else. When we entered, the patient was already on the operating table, fully conscious. The guides explained that she was about to have a thyroid operation. Whether her thyroid would be removed, or perhaps have some growth excised, was not explained.

Two female nurses had erected a small stand and tiny curtain over the woman's chin. This kept her from seeing the operation that was about to be performed at the base of her neck. Then a surgeon entered with a man who seemed to be a male nurse or assistant. He picked up some acupuncture needles from the table and began applying them to some that already protruded from the woman's neck, arm, and legs. After a short time, with the woman fully conscious and her eyes wide open, the physician made an incision at the base of her neck. As he did this, a nurse placed pieces of a mandarin orange in the woman's mouth, demonstrating that she not only was not feeling any pain from the incision, but also that she was capable of enjoying a fruit snack while they operated on her. The medical miracle of acupuncture notwithstanding, the patient looked distinctly nervous.

After making the initial incision, the doctor paused and spoke some words with the other man, as though giving him instructions. The man removed some bloody gauze from the area of the incision, putting it in one of the buckets. Both men then stood quietly, occasionally muttering a few words we could not hear. After a few minutes, the doctor left the room, and the orderly appeared to be looking at something in the bucket. The woman receiving the operation remained dutifully conscious, eating an occasional piece of fruit placed in her mouth by an attending nurse.

Oddly, nothing happened for several minutes. The orderly would shuffle back and forth along the operating table, first looking at the incision on the woman, then talking to the nurse about something or other, then putting a bloody piece of gauze in the bucket. This went on for what seemed a very long time. Occasionally, the man would look up into the theatre where we were sitting and then look down again. For some reason, after making the initial incision, which was not very large, the procedure stopped and nothing more happened for perhaps a total of ten minutes or so. We didn't know what the hell was going on.

All at once one of the guides jumped up from her seat and said, "It's time to go. We are late for our next place!" She jumped out of her seat so fast that it startled me, and in a few moments we were all up and filing out of the operating theatre into the hall of the hospital.

Oddly, after beating such a hasty retreat from the operating room, we walked only a short distance before the guide told us to wait. She disappeared for several minutes, apparently arranging for us to enter the children's ward, where we were directed next. Nothing seemed to urgently require our attendance. When we finally entered the children's wing, it didn't appear that anyone was particularly expecting us. Everything seemed quite normal and relaxed.

It took me a year or so for me to finally realize what had happened in the operating theatre. It appears that perhaps the visiting Beijing guides suggested to the hospital that the foreigners see acupuncture being used as an anesthetic, and the doctors simply faked an operation for us. After making a superficial incision, the doctor was clearly biding his time for ten or fifteen minutes while waiting for us so to leave so he could sew up the unfortunate "patient." Somehow, the message that the group should leave immediately after the first incision did not get communicated clearly to the guides, and as a result we watched the doctor depart after the first cut and then the orderly do his best to stall, stall, stall, not inflicting any more cuts on the "patient" before we got out of there. When it finally dawned on our guide what was happening, she shooed us out so fast you'd have thought the building was on fire, but then we just dawdled for the next half hour or so, visiting a nursery that didn't know we were coming. China in 1978 was straddling two eras. It was about to embark on an era of important reform. But some attitudes of the earlier era, like fear of high officials, was very pervasive at that time, and I'm sorry to say it is still lurking around today.

When I visited East Woods Temple on a recent trip to China, I tried to inquire about any connection between the place and Bodhidharma. One person in the temple bookstore seemed unclear about who Bodhidharma was, and the only available monk seemed disinterested in the whole topic. As important as East Woods Temple was in Chinese history, it appears that any connection between that place and Bodhidharma today remains only in a few books. Still, I think he was there.

19. Jiujiang City

Old Shakyamuni had four great vows. He said,
"Though the many beings are uncountable, I vow to save them;
Though delusions rise without end, I vow to end them;
Though Dharma Gates are limitless, I vow to study them;
Though Buddha's way is inconceivable, I vow to embody it."
But as for me, I have my own four great vows. They are
"When I get hungry, I have something to eat; When the weather
is cold, I put on more clothes; When I get tired, I lie down and
take a nap; When it's warm, I look for a cool breeze."
—*Zen Master Baiyun ("White Cloud," active 1025–1072 CE) of Nengren
Temple in Jiujiang City, addressing the monks in the Dharma Hall*

THE YOUNG MAN who has just boarded the bus to Jiujiang and sat down
next to me looks at me expectantly and says, "You're the first foreigner
I've ever spoken to." When he saw me sitting here, he knew it was his
lucky day. Millions of Chinese are busily learning English without any
native English speakers to talk to.

For the next hour or so during our trip to Jiujiang, I give English
instruction to a twenty-year-old Chinese man trying to make his way
in the crowded world.

"Yes, I am studying at Jiujiang Technical Institute. There I study international business, management, and marketing. I like American NBA
basketball. Do you know my favorite team?"

"Is it the Houston Rockets?" I venture.

"Yes!" For someone who has never spoken to a foreigner, his English
is surprisingly good. And of course, like many young Chinese, he loves
NBA basketball and is devoted to the Houston Rockets, meaning he's
a fan of the famous Chinese NBA basketball player Yao Ming. "I want
to have a job in international business," he says.

As our bus winds down the mountain, I try to mix English-language lessons with a few practical life lessons for an aspiring international business major. "It's good," I say, "to learn not only a foreign language but some other skills as well. For example, you could learn to manage databases. That is an excellent business skill you can use with your English-language skills."

The young man pulls out a dictionary and looks up *database*. "Yes," he says. "I think this is a good idea."

We talk business and basketball for an hour or so, until the bus arrives in Jiujiang and lets us off near the Jiujiang train station. My English student offers to help me find my way to an ongoing bus to Huangmei. I decide to accept his help. Experience has shown it's always good to use local help when you can get it.

In fact, it was at this very place on a sunny morning not long ago that my ability to read Chinese landed me in a confusing situation with the local bus system. On that particular morning I emerged from the Jiujiang train station after an overnight train ride from Guangzhou. It was about 9:00 AM and the sun shone brightly on the wide plaza in front of the station. A few taxis were lined up to pick up the train's passengers. I bought some water at a kiosk, and before getting in the taxi queue I noticed a rather makeshift sign that said NANJING BUS, TEN O'CLOCK. I wanted to catch a bus to the Third Zen Ancestor's temple near Tianzhu Mountain, which was in the direction of Nanjing, so I asked the person next to the sign whether the bus stopped near that location. He said no. I then talked to a person at a ticket counter and learned that I'd need to go to the downtown Jiujiang bus terminal to find such a bus. So I returned to the taxi line and took a five-minute ride to the center of town where the main bus terminal is located. There I got in yet another line and eventually worked my up to the ticket seller behind the window. I asked her, "Is there a bus that stops near Tianzhu Mountain, or the nearby town of Qianshan?" No, she said, and there's no such bus to there from here. After checking the maps and asking more questions, I finally decided that I wouldn't go directly to the Third Ancestor's Temple. Instead I'd try to go there later in my trip after visiting Nanjing. I inquired about getting a bus ticket to Nanjing but was told it wouldn't leave until eleven o'clock. I checked my watch and saw it was about 9:35. I remembered the bus at the train station that said it was leaving at 10:00. *I can save an hour getting to Nanjing*, I thought to myself. I ran outside and hailed another taxi. Minutes later I arrived at the train station where the bus to Nanjing was advertised. I approached the person next to the sign and asked to buy a ticket. After I paid my fare, I was told I still had thirty minutes until departure because the bus was late. So I went and bought some snacks and used a restroom, and when I got back, a man with a small motorcycle was standing beside the "Nanjing Bus" sign. He motioned me to get on the back of the cycle. I was carrying a backpack and an average-size suitcase. "Where's the bus?" I asked. He explained that he'd take me to the bus. So I jumped on the back of the motorbike holding my suitcase in one hand, and off we went into the Jiujiang traffic, weaving between cars, me shifting my suitcase carefully to make sure it didn't hit someone's rearview mirror. After a while we reached a place by the Nanjing River Bridge where we stopped and I got off the motor-bike. There was a kiosk and some people standing around. After quite a wait, a bus appeared with NANJING written above the front window. The motorcyclist, who was still standing there next to me, waved to the bus. The driver waved back and pointed toward the Nanjing River Bridge, but he didn't stop. The motorcyclist told me to climb aboard the motorcycle again, and then we circled around a couple of roads to emerge onto the bridge itself. After we traveled a couple hundred yards or so onto the long bridge, the cyclist stopped and told me again to wait. About five minutes later, the bus reappeared coming across the bridge toward us. The bus driver stopped and opened the rear door of the bus. I got on, and the driver waved to the motorcyclist. Then it dawned on me that this was the regularly scheduled eleven o'clock bus I would have caught from the main station had I remained there. The driver and the motorcyclist had a little side business going, snagging passengers from the train station and pocketing their fares. This is not unusual in China, especially around certain country bus and train stations. People will "guide" you to the correct bus whether you've asked them to do so or not. They may tell you they are the ticket seller, ask for the fare, then actually buy your ticket at its correct lower price, give it to you, and pocket the difference. People in China aren't any more dishonest than anyone else, but the struggle to survive in an ocean of competitors compels them into little scams like this Nanjing bus-ticket caper.

Back in the present, the young man whom I've helped with his English gets directions and helps me find the right bus and bus stop in Jiujiang to continue my journey. I board a bus that takes me into an area in the old part of town, where the driver tells me to get off by a dusty alley surrounded by poor commercial buildings near the Yang-tse River. There, a minibus with a sign in the window that says HUANGMEI ("Yellow Plum") is nearly full of passengers. That's my bus, and it has one seat left open. After throwing my bags in the back, I wedge into the van next to a young couple with a two-year-old that exhibits an immediate curiosity for the strange-looking man with a pointed nose. A minute later, my nose firmly in the grasp of my young inquisitor, the minibus lurches, clutch squealing, out of the lane and onto the dusty avenue jammed with afternoon traffic.

Huangmei, about twenty-five miles north of Jiujiang and the Yang-tse River, has the same name today that it did when Zen's Fourth and Fifth Ancestors established their temples in that area fourteen centuries ago.

The Fourth Zen Ancestor, named Daoxin (pronounced *Dow-sin*) is another key figure in the development of Chinese Zen. His monastery, ten miles or so from Huangmei, sits beneath Potou ("Broken Top") Mountain. Before Baizhang established the "Pure Rules" for Zen monastic life, Daoxin had already set up a Zen monastery independent from China's ruling circles. Two hundred years before Baizhang formally fused Zen to manual labor, the farming way of life may have already entered the Zen religious scene at Daoxin's place.

After an hour of cramped traveling, I arrive on the south side of Huangmei. Emerging from the bus station, I cross the busy street to a small shop selling snacks and drinks. When I greet the shopkeeper in Chinese, she strikes up a conversation, curious to know why I've come to town. I explain that I'm heading for the Fourth Ancestor's temple for the night and tomorrow will participate in the opening ceremony for a new temple called Laozu Temple at Twin Peaks Mountain.

"Do you need a taxi?" she asks. Before I can answer her, she disappears out the front door and waves toward a new Toyota pickup parked nearby. A man emerges, and I soon discover that he is both a taxi driver and a member of the local Buddhist community that practices at the Fourth Ancestor's temple. After I buy a few snacks, we're on our way west of the city toward my evening's accommodations at the monastery.

20. Up or Down the Yang-tse River?

WHEN BODHIDHARMA traveled north and reached the Yang-tse River, he must have made a decision. He could either travel upstream on the Yang-tse, following its Han River tributary to the area of Luoyang and Mount Song, or he could go downstream to reach the lower reaches of the Yang-tse and the capital city at what is now the city of Nanjing.

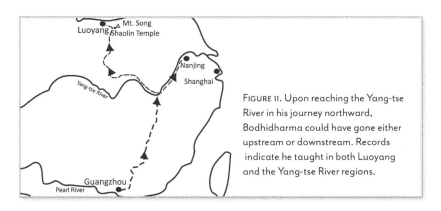

FIGURE 11. Upon reaching the Yang-tse River in his journey northward, Bodhidharma could have gone either upstream or downstream. Records indicate he taught in both Luoyang and the Yang-tse River regions.

Bodhidharma's record in the *Continued Biographies* offers no clear evidence about this. It says he arrived in the country during the Liu-Song dynasty, a time span that stretched from 420 to 479 CE. If he had a normal lifespan, he arrived toward the end of this dynasty. Various accounts of Bodhidharma's death place it sometime between the years 528 and 537. If this timeframe is correct, and he lived to the plausible age of ninety-five, then he could have arrived in China in the year 463 at around thirty years of age.

A young Buddhist missionary would need time to learn Chinese before he could begin teaching in that language. Therefore it seems unlikely that Bodhidharma would have immediately started taking disciples or publically teaching. It seems plausible, if he arrived in the country between the years 455 and 465, that he would first seek assistance and advice from a fellow countryman who had arrived in China before him, someone already famous and respected as a foreign Buddhist teacher. Gunabhadra, a famous Indian who that lived around Nanjing at that time, was just such a person.

21. Meeting Gunabhadra?

GUNABHADRA (394–468), like Bodhidharma, was an Indian monk from the Brahman class. A record of Gunabhadra's life appears in the *Biographies of Eminent Monks*, the book after which Daoxuan modeled his *Continued Biographies*. According to this record, Gunabhadra enjoyed immense fame as a Buddhist teacher and translator of scriptures. He lived, for the most part, in the city of Nanjing, where he managed the work of translating a large number of Indian Buddhist scriptures into Chinese. As he was the most famous Indian Buddhist in South China, it seems likely that Bodhidharma would have met Gunabhadra if he had the chance.

One of the many texts that Gunabhadra translated into Chinese was called the Lankavatara Sutra. This text was an early text of the Yogacara (the Yogis) school of Buddhism. It is also a text, Daoxuan states, that Bodhidharma and his successors used to spread their Zen teachings in China.

For these and other reasons, it seems reasonable that Bodhidharma, if he arrived at the south shore of the Yang-tse River prior to Gunabhadra's death in the year 468, would have traveled downstream to the capital city of Nanjing, a place where Gunabhadra and other foreign monks were received and honored. There he could find support, learn Chinese, and best begin his own missionary career in China.

BODHIDHARMA IN LUOYANG 488–494?

The *Continued Biographies* claims Bodhidharma arrived in China before 479. Another critical clue about his whereabouts in the years that followed appears in that text in the biography of Sengfu, his senior disciple. Daoxuan's description of Sengfu's life contains various clues about Bodhidharma, and I'll examine it in more detail later. For now, the critical point is that it places Bodhidharma in the Luoyang/Mount

Song area during the period 488 to 494 CE. That's the time the record says Bodhidharma accepted Sengfu as a student somewhere in that region.

I surmise that if Bodhidharma arrived in China in 460 he would have had ample time to travel and even teach in both Southern and Northern China before arriving in the Luoyang region in the north by 488.

In another section of Daoxuan's *Continued Biographies* (which, again, was composed around the year 650, more than a hundred years after Bodhidharma lived), there is a passage where the author offers his opinions about the Zen school of Buddhism. His comments in this part of the text are almost unmentioned in China and are virtually unknown in the West. Yet they provide, in my opinion, critical clues about Bodhidharma's reputation and importance during his lifetime. The text that reveals this information is difficult to decipher. The passages that are the most important are nearly impenetrable. But with the help of some Chinese scholars, I've reviewed them carefully and below offer an interpretation of their meaning.

The passage in question, which is a general description of Chinese Zen teachers of the early to mid sixth century, clearly ranks Bodhidharma as among the most important of the teachers of his age. Daoxuan also speaks about Bodhidharma and his Zen teachings with admiration, offering comments that go beyond what he wrote in Bodhidharma's biography. Daoxuan first discusses the great influence that Zen monks had during the time Bodhidharma lived. Finally he says the following:

> Bodhidharma was of this sort [of popular Zen teacher]. He converted [people to] and established the Zen doctrines in the Yang-tse and Luoyang regions. The "wall-gazing" practice of the Mahayana is the highest [teaching]. Those who came to study with and honor Bodhidharma were like a city . . . Bodhidharma would not remain in places of imperial sway. Those [in high places] who desired to see him could not draw him near them.

Notice that Daoxuan says that Bodhidharma "established the Zen doctrines in the Yang-tse and Luoyang regions," indicating that

Bodhidharma's teaching activities occurred in both North and South China. He also "would not remain in places of imperial sway" and "those who desired to see him could not draw him near them." Since Bodhidharma's followers were "like a city," it follows from the above passages that the ones who "could not draw him near them" were persons of the highest standing, namely emperors, kings, and their courts, all the people of places within "imperial sway." Other evidence in the text seems to bear this conclusion out. Clearly, Bodhidharma proselytized in the Yang-tse region, an idea absent from the widely known accounts of his life that dominated the Zen tradition later.

The Yang-tse flows from west to east through Southern China. It originates in the Tibetan Plateau, flows through the provinces of Yunnan and Sichuan, passes the central city of Wuhan, and soon turns northeast to loop over the top of Nanjing before entering the sea. For reasons that will become clear when we look at the record of Bodhidharma's senior disciple Sengfu, Bodhidharma almost certainly did not carry out his activities in the upper reaches of the Yang-tse. Instead it was the lower reaches of the river where he likely journeyed and stayed. Nanjing, as the main population center and seat of imperial power in South China during Bodhidharma's time, must be considered as the area where Bodhidharma lived and taught in the Yang-tse region. It is clear from Gunabhadra's biography and countless other sources that the imperial capital of Nanjing was then already a ferment of Buddhist activity.

All considered, from the *Continued Biographies* account we can surmise that in the course of many decades in China Bodhidharma would have had plenty of time to travel in the lower Yang-tse River area, perhaps not just a single time. Daoxuan's account indicates he probably traveled widely over an extended period of time, perhaps going back and forth several times along the Yang-tse population centers or at least remaining for an extended time in part of that area.

If Bodhidharma chose to visit Nanjing early in his time in China, it would mean he arrived there more than thirty years before Emperor Wu took power and set up his dynasty and fully fifty years before the year 527, when the most widely believed story about him claims that he arrived in China and met the emperor.

Considering Daoxuan's limited account in more detail, there is a possible clue that suggests that Bodhidharma did indeed go to Nanjing and meet Gunabhadra. That clue can be surmised from Bodhidharma's reported "not remaining in places of imperial sway."

China's imperial system of rule was set up so that the reigning emperor ruled from the main capital city, while "kings" of lower status than the emperor ruled over local provinces or prefectures. These local kings were typically one of the emperor's close relatives such as a brother, uncle, nephew, and so on, with none far removed from his nuclear family.

Around the years 450–454, Gunabhadra, at the invitation of the local king of a place called Jing Province, took up residence in what is now the city of Xuzhou (the name of this city sounds similar to Suzhou, the famous garden city near Shanghai). Xuzhou is located on the Huai River and is about two hundred miles northwest of Nanjing, the location of the emperor's throne during the Liu-Song dynasty that then ruled South China. In 454, the local king who was Gunabhadra's student rebelled and tried to seize the emperor's throne. Due to Gunabhadra's fame as a Buddhist teacher, the rebel king compelled him to join his cause, forcing him to accompany his army as it marched toward Nanjing to overthrow the emperor. The rebel exploited Gunabhadra's holy status to rally people to his rebellion. Like a cross before armies of the Christian Crusades, Gunabhadra was put in the vanguard of the advancing troops, his role like that of a mystical shield meant to legitimize the rebel as a "Buddhist" king who would establish righteous religious rule over the country.

As it turned out, the emperor crushed the rebel forces, and the rebel king was beheaded. The emperor then considered executing Gunabhadra as well for his role in the rebellion. But because of Gunabhadra's fame and position, the emperor allowed the old teacher to present evidence of being forced unwillingly to accompany the revolt. The emperor examined letters between Gunabhadra and the rebel king, finding that Gunabhadra had actually opposed the rebellion, and thus permitted Gunabhadra's head to remain attached to his body. But undoubtedly the old teacher gained a clear understanding about the pitfalls of getting mixed up in China's high ruling circles.

Bodhidharma, if he met Gunabhadra, likely learned from him about the dangers of dealing with people in high places. Even if they didn't meet, the story likely reached Bodhidharma's ears. This object lesson may have contributed to Bodhidharma's shyness about meeting royalty. Was this episode the source of Bodhidharma's disposition to "not remain in places of imperial sway"?

FOURTH ANCESTOR'S TRUE ENLIGHTENMENT TEMPLE

Traditional accounts claim the unbroken line of Zen teachers and students in China starts with Bodhidharma. Following him was his most famous disciple, Huike (pronounced *Hway-kuh*), followed in turn by his most famous disciple, Sengcan (pronounced *Sung-san*), and then his student, the Fourth Ancestor, Daoxin.

The Fourth Ancestor's teaching seat, named True Enlightenment Temple, sits in a mountain valley that is one scenic waterfall above rich Yang-tse Valley farmland. It offered the Zen master and his students an ideal balance between secluded mountain practice and land to grow food for self-support. The Fourth Ancestor's teachings and temple represent a critical step toward putting Bodhidharma's Zen on a solid and independent footing, setting the stage for it to become the dominant religious stream in East Asia.

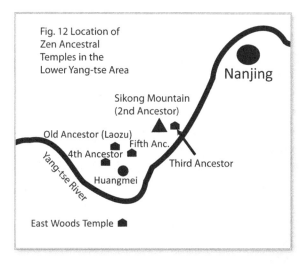

FIGURE 12. Location of Temples in the Lower Yang-tse Area.

There are two related phrases often mentioned about the temple's primary role in Zen. One phrase is *Zen, farming*, equally emphasized, and the other is *Zen and work*.

What is especially worth noting was the Fourth Ancestor's attitude toward people in high places. Echoing Bodhidharma's apparent dislike for the imperial spotlight, the Fourth Ancestor Daoxin famously refused four commands from the emperor to come to the capital and submit to court supervision. At the fourth request, the emperor's envoy threatened to cut off Daoxin's head if he didn't comply with the emperor's summons. Daoxin responded by bowing and exposing his bare neck. When his envoy reported this to the emperor, the latter finally withdrew his demand for Daoxin to submit to central government supervision.

Besides literally "putting down roots" for Zen in China by taking up farming to support his monks, Daoxin's historical importance lies in his synthesis of Zen practice with other prevailing Buddhist currents of his age, making it more understandable and accessible to the Chinese public.

Daoxin appears to have followed the instruction that observing the nature of the mind was the essential aspect of Zen practice. However, the age when Daoxin lived was rife with controversy about various Buddhist theories that seemed at odds with Zen's practice of "observing." These controversies arose because popular Buddhist scriptures introduced ideas like "Buddha nature" and an "atman" (soul) into Buddhist beliefs. The Nirvana Sutra, the scripture cited by the Japanese militarist Sugimoto, was a source of some of the most contentious of these controversies. During the fifth and following centuries, the sutra's ideas about the existence of an atman caused problems because Buddhism traditionally rejected this idea. The existence of an atman was considered impossible if everything comes about and passes away strictly due to causes and conditions. A permanent "soul" could not be possible. This argument inflamed theological discussions of the day. Another doctrine that caused wide controversy at that time was the idea of Buddha nature. Many Chinese Buddhists thought the idea that all beings possess "inherent Buddhahood" sounded suspiciously like yet another concept that fell outside of the "cause and effect" doctrine. Finally, another idea set forth in the Nirvana Sutra got people excited in a way that can be little imagined today. That was the presumed heresy of the sutra's teaching that everyone, even incorrigibly evil beings, not only had "Buddha nature" but also could ultimately become Buddhas.

The Fourth ancestor Daoxin skillfully cut short such discussions by offering a peculiarly Zen interpretation of them. He presented a Zen view on such matters by saying that all such popular notions about the nature of reality and the various Buddhist concepts then in circulation were really, after all the shouting, just descriptions of perceiving the nature of the mind. A record from the seventh century quotes Daoxin to have said the following:

> If only one sees this mind, it is the same as the true Dharma nature of the Tathagata, and it is called the true Dharma, or it is called Buddha nature, or the true nature of all Dharmas, or reality, or the Pure Land, or bodhi, or diamond samadhi, or fundamental enlightenment, or the nirvana realm, or prajna, and so on. Although there are unlimited names for it, they are all a single body that can't be observed [with characteristics], and [these terms] are [just varied] descriptions of the [practice of] observing [mind].

Daoxin emphasized the nature of this perception in the following statements:

> This [perceiving] mind continues until it suddenly becomes clear and solitary, and finally without karmic thoughts. The Prajnaparamita Sutra says, "That which is without any thought is called 'thinking of Buddha.'" (心心相续忽然澄寂。更无所缘念。大品经云。无所念者。是名念佛。)
>
> And what is it we call "without any thoughts?" It is thinking of Buddha that we term "without any thoughts." Apart from mind there is no Buddha. (何等名无所念。即念佛心名无所念。离心无别有。佛。)
>
> Apart from Buddha there is no other mind. To think of Buddha is to think of mind. Seeking mind is seeking Buddha. And what does this mean? (离佛无别有心。念佛即是念心。求心即是求佛。所以者何。)
>
> Perception is without form. Buddha is without form. Buddha has no sign or appearance. If you understand this principle, this is serene mind. (何。识无刑。佛无刑。佛无相貌。若也知此道理。即是安心。)

By continuously thinking of Buddha, karma does not arise, for it dissolves in signlessness, an undifferentiated equality. When one does not have this orientation, then the mind that perceives Buddha is lost, with not a bit left. It is just perceiving mind in this fashion that is the true Dharma nature body of the Tathagata. (常忆念佛。攀缘不起。则泯然无相。平等不二。不入此位中。忆佛心谢。更不须徵。即看此等心。即是如来真实法性。)

Daoxin termed the Zen practice of this type of meditation to be the "single practice samadhi," and called it the "single universal expedient for attaining the Buddha Way."

Daoxin's description of this mind can be confusing. Note that while he speaks of "thinking of Buddha," he doesn't mean thinking about a historical figure or personage. He means observing the undifferentiated experience of consciousness without bifurcating or otherwise dividing it up with thought or intention. Daoxin describes this mind as *ming jing*, a term that translates as "bright and pure." This is observing without an observer, perception unsullied by thought or intention, not even by the idea of "mind." Daoxin says that it "is not thinking about Buddha, nor is it grasping mind, nor is it observing mind, nor is it considering mind, nor is it engaged in thought, nor is it observing practice, nor is it [in any way] unsettled—just in this direct way [it transpires]."

In Chinese, one term that Daoxin used to explain this expedient practice, the term *nian fo*, has shades of meaning that nuance Daoxin's teaching and in a sense subvert it. On the one hand, the term means to "think of (or concentrate on) Buddha." Yet another meaning is to "chant Buddha('s name)." So in practice, although Daoxin was emphasizing that this practice was, to use Bodhidharma's phrase, just directly pointing at mind, less sophisticated practitioners interpreted the phrase *nian fo* to also mean "chanting Buddha('s name)." Thus the true meaning of Daoxin's teachings was in a sense degraded by the practice of a different Buddhist sect called Pure Land Buddhism. That sect saw the literal act of chanting Buddha's name as the path to salvation. As time went on, the prevalence of actually chanting Buddha's name itself became ever more widespread even in the Zen community, in apparent contradiction to the intent of Daoxin's teachings.

THE FOURTH ANCESTOR'S TEMPLE

When I first visited the place fifteen years ago, the road to the Fourth Ancestor's temple was truly wretched, a washboard of massive ruts that jarred passing vehicles and their occupants into a numb dizziness. I was surprised that the first taxi driver to ferry me over this road persevered and didn't turn back to save the vehicle of his livelihood. On that occasion, aside from the problem of the washboard road, we arrived in the middle of the rice harvest, and grain carts assembled to use a weigh station aside the road blocked our passage. Happily, since that time, and under the guidance of the monastery abbot, the famous and respected Chinese Dharma teacher Jinghui (the same Jinghui who was previously abbot at Cypress Grove when I gave the lecture there), the monastery and its access road have been rebuilt and transformed into a comfortable and welcoming place.

An ancient covered bridge sits aside the paved approach to the Fourth Ancestor's temple. It rests serenely above a waterfall and once served any visitors approaching the place, spanning the creek that drained the monastery's mountain valley. Now a new road bypasses the bridge, but its classic and graceful architecture hints at the gravity and importance of this ancient temple.

The Fourth Ancestor's temple faces toward the southwest, and the late afternoon sun reflects warmly off its dark yellow walls. As we approach I look high on the hill to the left, to the landmark that marks the spot where the Fourth Ancestor was buried fourteen centuries ago. His old stupa is still there, a big structure about thirty feet high that commands a view of the temple valley and surrounding peaks. According to Zen records, after the Fourth Ancestor died, his body was first placed in the stupa. A few weeks later, a storm came up and the old door to the stupa blew open, revealing that his body had not decayed. Shocked at this, his disciples moved it to a "True Body Hall," where it remained for many centuries. Eventually the body was interred in the temple, but the destruction caused by subsequent wars caused it to be lost.

While the temple is formally named True Enlightenment Temple, Chinese people usually call it by the short name "Sizu," which simply means "Fourth Ancestor." On previous visits to Sizu, I've found the place to be a very quiet, peaceful refuge from China's dusty cities. But today as I arrive the temple is alive with activity. Buses fill a new parking lot outside the temple gate, and groups of people are milling around. Everyone is here to prepare for a grand ceremony that will take place tomorrow at a place not far away. That grand ceremony is the formal opening of another rebuilt temple, the teaching seat of a teacher known as Laozu ("Old Ancestor"). Sizu, with its large guest hall and dining room, is a staging area for people who have come to join the celebrations that will occur at Laozu Temple tomorrow morning.

I pass the Heavenly Kings Hall and make my way into the monastery's interior. The monastery halls rest on the steep slope of the valley, and I have to carry my luggage up the stairs that link its big halls on the temple's central axis. From a wide plaza built in front of the Buddha Hall, I see organized groups that have come to take part in the festivities. A crowd is packed inside the hall itself, and the bells and chants of afternoon service float across the landscape and the mountain valley's greenery.

Tired from traveling, I retreat to the temple office where I encounter an old friend, a monk named Mingyi. He looks a little harried. As the temple *weina*, or director, he has a lot on his mind today. Mingyi formerly lived at Cypress Grove Monastery in North China, the place where I've spent so much time. Friendly and accommodating, Mingyi taught our visiting groups there about traditional Chinese Zen practice and meditation. A few years ago he was transferred here to the Fourth Ancestor's temple to help Jinghui, the "Old Master," carry out new construction.

"Are you alone?" Mingyi asks me.

"Yes, I'm alone," I reply.

Some relief sweeps across his face. It's clear that housing for all the visitors is a big problem that's preoccupying him. "We have a room for you," Mingyi says.

This makes me feel only slight less awkward. I know he would say this whether they have one or not. But it turns out to be true, and a little later, after dropping my bags in a special room complete with a private bath, I go out to see what's going on. The pilgrims that have arrived to take part in tomorrow's ceremonies are in high spirits. They cluster around the Buddha Hall, chanting and bowing with the proceedings. A big crowd of people is in the temple gift store and bookshop buying up everything in sight. People in China love to buy souvenirs, and whatever such goods are labeled with the name "Fourth Ancestor's Temple" appear to be in high demand.

Seeing the Buddhist religion so enthusiastically embraced in China is still a little bit of a shock. I remember, in my college days, a professor of Chinese studies saying that there would never be business or religion in China again. From the looks of the milling, excited crowd, it seems as if the Chinese were simply lying in wait for the latest political tide to subside so they could get back to doing business and being Buddhists again.

An hour later the big monastery dining room is packed with pilgrims. There are too many people for everyone to eat at once, and as some people finish eating at the long wooden tables, others pour in to take their place. The mood is festive, a contrast to the somber air of a monastery. The fare is rice and vegetables with some tofu and chili peppers on the side. China's celibate monastics avoid onions and garlic, vegetables that they claim cause sexual arousal, but they don't have any qualms about offering super hot chilies, which apparently don't have the same effect. Visitors and monks from Hunan, Jiangxi, and Sichuan, provinces where people are devoted to devouring the hottest chilies imaginable, eagerly scoop up these side dishes.

As I walk down the long sidewalk that leads from the dining room to my guestroom, I listen to groups singing in the different courtyards of the temple. It's obvious that these people haven't come around here to devote themselves to "observing the nature of the mind." They are part of China's big "intertwined" community that is again gaining steam.

22. Laozu Si, the Old Ancestor's Temple

A KNOCK ON MY DOOR at four fifteen alerts me that the morning looms.

The story of Laozu, which means "old ancestor" and refers to another Indian monk who came to China, is an incredible tale that leaves most Westerners and many Chinese shaking their heads. Although he was called "Old Ancestor," his actual religious name was Bao Zhang ("Treasured Palms"). Treasured Palms (as in the palms of your hands) was an Indian monk said to have arrived in China by way of what is now Myanmar and Sichuan Province at the end of the Han dynasty, around the year 212 CE. Astonishingly, he was said to have already attained the formidable age of 628 years at the time he arrived in the Middle Kingdom. Even more astonishing, he eventually died in China in the year 657 at the age of 1,072. Various Zen texts dating from the ninth to fourteenth centuries tell his story and refer to him as "Thousand Year Treasured Palms." There are assorted historical records that describe this monk, so, regardless of whether he really lived to be over a thousand years old, his life seems to be widely known and documented in China's Zen records.

It's said that Bao Zhang, though a Buddhist monk, did not finally realize full enlightenment until he had resided in China for 300 years. Thus, he finally achieved enlightenment when he was over 900 years of age. The reason why this bears on Bodhidharma's story is because Bao Zhang is recorded to have achieved this goal by traveling from his residence at Laozu Temple down the Yang-tse River to someplace near Nanjing. There he reportedly met Bodhidharma and asked for his teaching. Bodhidharma, who apparently was living in or near Nanjing, offered a teaching that allowed Treasured Palms to reach full enlightenment. His story goes on to say that Emperor Wu thereupon invited Treasured Palms to visit his court, honoring him because of his great age.

Being old commands respect in traditional China, so you can imagine how much respect would flow to someone who had celebrated more than 900 birthdays. Treasured Palms, even if he was, say, 150, would still have garnered huge interest. As I mentioned above, China's Taoist alchemists had long tried to make potions by which China's emperors could gain immortality, but, at least since the time of the legendary Yellow Emperor, they seem to have failed at this task. Yet here was a foreign Buddhist monk who had lived far beyond the lifespan of any ruler of China. Emperor Wu, it is recorded, received Treasured Palms with great ceremony. But then Bao Zhang's Zen philosophy, which he allegedly received from Bodhidharma, caused the two men to "not connect, as though they spoke different languages." This is an interesting story, particularly since Treasured Palms was described as a student of Bodhidharma, and the latter reportedly had a similar experience with Emperor Wu. Treasured Palms went on to eventually travel and teach farther south in Zhejiang Province, where he is said to have died in the year 657 at a mountain called Huiji near Shaoxing City. Thereafter, during the Tang dynasty, a ditty circulated throughout Eastern China that described Treasured Palm's meeting with Bodhidharma and his final fate:

> In Liang City he met his sage,
> With Zen attained the ground of mind,
> Then journeyed to the land of Zhe,
> By lovely streams he left the world behind.

I'm entirely uncertain what's in store at the "Blessing" ceremony that I'm to attend at Treasured Palms's old temple. The woman in charge of the temple guestrooms told me that breakfast would be served at 5:00 AM and the buses would leave at 5:30.

"Where exactly is this place we're going to?" I asked.

She said, "Old Ancestor's Temple!"

"And what are we doing there?" I ventured.

"An official blessing! You know what a blessing is, don't you?"

"Yes, of course I know," I said. Well, actually I have only a vague idea what a blessing is. I know that high-ranking monks open new temples, new meditation halls, and so on by performing "blessings," but I don't

know exactly what is involved. "Blessing" is not a very good translation of what's going on. But I can't think of a better way to say it right
now. A "blessing" is sort of another way of saying "christening," but
that term obviously isn't a good way to translate the official reopening
of a Buddhist temple. It's the opening ceremony or inauguration of the
place, but neither of those terms seems to convey the right meaning
either. Maybe the literal translation of the Chinese characters is best.
They mean "Open [the] Light."

So when the attendant knocks on my door at 4:20, I roll out of bed
and brew myself a cup of coffee to stiffen me against the morning chill.
Then I dress, splash some water on my face, and walk to the dining hall,
which I find is a busy scene indeed, with hundreds of people serving
themselves bowls of rice gruel from large wooden pots, topping off the
gruel with spicy pickled vegetables ready-cooked from plastic packages.
I manage to gulp down a bowl, which surprisingly tastes not half bad,
perhaps because my body is still too asleep to know the difference. Soon
the coffee has taken full effect, and I'm ready to go.

But there's one more problem. Bright Sea, the abbot of Bai Lin Monastery, called me last night at about ten thirty, waking me from a deep
sleep. He asked where I was, and when I told him I was at the Fourth
Ancestor's Temple, he said, "Fine! Tomorrow we'll go up to Old Ancestor's Temple together." He didn't say where he was, and I assumed he
was at the same temple where I'm staying. Now, with an array of buses
sitting in front of the temple loading pilgrims and Bright Sea nowhere to
be seen, I need to decide whether to board the buses with them or wait
for my promised ride. I try calling Bright Sea on my cell phone, but there
is no answer. So I approach one of the monks directing traffic near the
buses and ask him, "Do you know if Abbot Bright Sea is here?"

He says, "Bright Sea is already up on the mountain."

Okay, I think, *in that case I'd better get on one of the buses.* I pull out
my cell phone and text a message to Bright Sea that I'm going with the
buses to Treasured Palms Temple. Then I make my way to the parking
lot where a bevy of buses is already loading pilgrims to ferry them to
the day's events.

As the sun starts to come up, my bus of pilgrims grinds its way up
the winding mountain road to the ancient residence of the Old Ancestor.
Although the place is located only a few miles away over the mountains

from where we're staying, the circuitous road to the place requires more than an hour to drive. Not far up the final mountain ascent, someone starts handing plastic bags from the bus's overhead rack to passengers at the back of the bus. I notice that some people are retching from motion sickness. I'm doing fine, but soon, from right behind me, I hear a number of disturbing sounds being emitted.

The bus weaves and climbs through the scrub pine forest, occasionally offering a lookout over mountain valleys where a water reservoir sits far below. After an extended ascent, we pass a sign that says SCENIC AREA, accompanied by some worn-looking guesthouses. The plant life on the mountain changes as we ascend, from semitropical undergrowth to coniferous forest, and the temperature drops noticeably. Most of the buses in the caravan stretch out along the highway, but we remain close to the bus winding up the hill in front of us. Finally, we come to a group of buildings and an intersection where cars are parked along the road. We slow to a crawl, an apparent indication we've drawn near to our destination. However, the bus in front of us continues straight through the intersection and up the mountain, and our bus follows. After another mile or so, it becomes clear that neither the bus in front of us nor ours is on the right road. No other buses can be seen, and the road seems to be diminishing among a few ragged buildings. We finally turn around and go back down the mountain toward the intersection, arriving there to see many other vehicles and a fair number of people all clustered on the road. The bus stops, and we are instructed to get off and walk on the road that branches from the intersection. Apparently we'll walk the last couple hundred feet or so to the Old Ancestor's Temple. Maybe 120 people, from the two buses, walk together from the intersection toward the temple.

The mountaintop's dawn sky changes to a thick gray fog. The road weaves around outcroppings covered with ficus and pine trees. After twenty minutes we find ourselves strung out along the mountain road with no temple in sight. Some people are older and having trouble walking the long distance. Suddenly a large drop hits the pavement in front of me, and I realize that what looked like fog has evolved into threatening rain clouds. The rain begins to fall steadily. We all have no idea how much farther it is to the temple, but we know that it's a twenty-minute walk back to the intersection. Some people start running. I pull my broad-rimmed travel hat from my backpack. One man pulls a large broad leaf from the undergrowth and holds it over his head. The rain falls harder. Everyone's moving fast, and some people notice that that road is now descending through switchbacks and it may be possible to take shortcuts down the mountain between the corners. Many people try this, slipping and sliding down the mountain on the wet leaves and rocks. Some fall down in the effort and land on the muddy paths, soiling their clothes. I decide to remain on the road, but without the temple or any other shelter in sight, things start looking a little worrisome. Then, thankfully, the rain starts to let up and within another minute or two has almost ceased. People calm down.

Several vehicles now start to pass us on the road, and I realize that dropping us off at the intersection seems to have been a spur-of-the-moment decision by someone who didn't know how much farther we needed to go. The other buses apparently had kept going on the road and delivered the passengers directly to the temple. After another ten minutes or so, we reach a pretty mountain valley. At last, I spy some large red balloons with Chinese characters rising from what appears to be a group of buildings in the distance. Then the sound of drums and symbols rings across the mountain, and I realize that the vanguard of our strung-out group is being welcomed into the temple grounds. Our destination finally comes into view, nestled against a mountain, and on its left there is a blue lake contained by peaks on its far side. Two nearby peaks rise to the same altitude, quite close to one another. We've reached Twin Peaks and Treasured Palms's old temple residence, now newly rebuilt and ready for its blessing. We walk into its big parking lot to the cadence of two long lines of welcoming drummers, all lay women. They are dressed in festive red sweaters and black slacks, each keeping time on a small drum draped over her shoulders.

To the left of the women, opposite the front of the temple, is Produce Wood Lake. A legend says that when the old ancestor Treasured Palms's temple was first being built, logs needed for construction miraculously appeared in the lake's waters. Similar legends abound in China, often connected with the building of important temples. On the far side of the parking lot, I see other pilgrims disembarking from buses, and a long line of people is filing toward me as I stand aside the temple gate.

A total of seven peaks surrounds the mountain valley where Old

Ancestor's Temple sits lofty and remote. The seven peaks are together called Lotus Peak since they appear arranged to match the petals of that sacred Buddhist flower. Thus hidden, Old Ancestor's is the type of place a Zen temple should be, far from trouble. It's clear why the Old Ancestor and other monks of the Zen tradition made their way to this remote mountaintop to live and teach. Besides being a place of great natural beauty, it conveys the feeling described in the old Chinese saying that says "heaven is high, and the emperor is far away."

Ceremonies have begun by the time I reach the temple. Monks, lay practitioners, and officials fill the Buddha Hall and the surrounding area, all under the watchful eye of a large number of police and public security officials. Decorative banners hang throughout the place, and big balloons shaped like traditional Chinese lanterns are tethered to the earth with wide banners that display more slogans.

Part of the art of surviving in China's political ferment has been about knowing exactly what to say and knowing what political line is currently fashionable. One bright banner hanging from a balloon juxtaposes religion and politics, saying TAKE THE BUDDHA DHARMA AND MIX IT INTO SOCIETY: TAKE THE INDIVIDUAL AND MIX HIM INTO THE MASSES! Another says FACE THE WORLD WITH A GRATEFUL HEART; HARMONIZE WITH OTHERS WITH AN INCLUSIVE MIND.

It's impossible for me to understand the speech issuing from the loud-speakers, especially under the din of the large crowd that is part watching the proceedings and part just chatting and enjoying the day with their friends and relatives. I circle the perimeter of the crowd to see if Bright Sea is anywhere to be seen. I can't find him, though he may be inside the hall where ceremonies are being conducted by a big contingent of monks. As I stand looking at the crowd, I notice that there are defined contingents of people, different groups, each with its own flag, from a variety of famous temples in Southern China.

I consider going back out the front of the temple for a few photos of the outside and so move toward the front gate. As I make my way through the crowd, I suddenly see Bright Sea, along with a small contingent of people from Cypress Grove Monastery, enter the temple. One of his aides points me out and he turns to greet me.

His first question is "Have you seen my *shifu* [teacher] here?" He's referring to his teacher Jinghui, the former abbot of Bai Lin Monastery who now leads the Fourth Ancestor's Monastery. I tell Bright Sea I haven't seen him although he may be inside the Buddha Hall where I haven't been able to enter.

In their terrific enthusiasm for participating in today's religious event, some lay people go a little overboard in their desire to show respect for the high-ranking monks that are about. As I talk to Bright Sea, several people who recognize him literally start prostrating themselves to show their respect on the wide sidewalk where he is standing. I've seen this happen before when high-status Chinese monks appear in public, and I feel a little uncomfortable talking with Bright Sea in a normal conversation while several people are prostrating themselves toward us. It's like Bright Sea was the actual Buddha or something. To their credit, monks don't encourage or seem to like this sort of thing. They usually say "Don't bow. Don't bow!" to people who nonetheless refuse to quit doing so. Sometimes the monks give up trying to stop this behavior, not because they like it, but because it's futile to do so, so it's better to just act normal. Bright Sea simply ignores the scene around him. He seems very much at ease and happy. He takes my hand and says to his entourage, "Come on! Let's take a look around."

We make our way through the crowd and circle to the rear of the Buddha Hall. Bright Sea explains the story of the Old Ancestor, the millenarian, to me. He was yet another foreigner that the Chinese greatly honor. I can't help but reflect again about how China has accepted and honored a wide array of foreigners into their society down through the centuries. The idea that China has always been a closed society, contemptuous of things from outside, is simply wrong. That perception of China comes in part from modern events, from the strong reaction China developed against the encroachments by the imperial powers in the nineteenth and twentieth centuries. That relatively short historical era and the xenophobic ideas projected by Westerners toward China gave birth to the ridiculous ideas that the Chinese are insular and inscrutable. In fact, Chinese are open and welcoming, appreciative of foreign ideas and customs. In ancient Chang An, the capital of China's great Tang dynasty, there were so many foreigners arriving over the Silk Road that the emperor gave them a special market where they could conduct their business. This "foreign" market was on the west side of the market area, and the traditional Chinese market was on the east side of the same. If you were going shopping, you would say you were going to buy, literally, "east-west" (*dong-xi*) by visiting those east and west markets. Since that time, thirteen hundred years ago, the word *east-west* has taken on the meaning of a "thing," a meaning derived from buying things in those ancient foreign and domestic shopping centers. The fact that the word *east-west* means "thing" in Chinese has long baffled new students of that language, but it is actually an early indication of the Chinese welcoming foreigners into their society.

Foreign people and things have deeply influenced China, Bodhidharma being a case in point. Moreover, the idea of respecting and following the customs of others when visiting them is widely accepted in China. Confucius counseled this path by saying, "When in another country, follow its customs," a well-known saying almost matching the phrase "When in Rome . . ." from Western cultures. Certainly, everywhere I travel in China today, I'm welcomed with the utmost enthusiasm and warmth. Of course this is not unique to China, as people in many countries do the same thing. The Chinese are generally no different.

As we tour the temple, a familiar face appears. It is a monk named Mingji, a former resident of Cypress Grove Monastery and fellow student with Bright Sea under Jinghui. He says some words to Bright Sea, who suddenly grabs my hand and leads me back toward the Buddha Hall. A minute later Bright Sea is pulling me behind him as he enters a side door of the hall. I try to hold back, but he is insistent. As we enter, instead of turning toward the center of the hall itself, Bright Sea leads me out the front door to a wide rostrum where rows of chairs filled with high monks and officials are sitting. Now I really try to stop and go the opposite direction, but several people, including Mingji, push me toward an empty chair only a couple of rows back from front center stage. I notice that there are television crews and camera people shooting the scene. I nearly panic, but now I dare not embarrass everyone by taking flight. I stand for a few moments with everyone else, trying to maintain a facial expression solemn enough to make up for my unshowered, unshaven face and unkempt hair. I think it then becomes apparent even to Mingji, who is standing close to me, that I don't want to be here. Perhaps having a token and bedraggled foreigner on the platform isn't that important, so he doesn't say anything as I turn and walk to the back of the rostrum. Someone then grabs my arm and leads me along the back row to another open seat at the far side. At least here I'm out of the range of the TV cameras, but I still try to avoid sitting down with the high-ranking monks assembled beside me. Yet my hosts are insistent, so I finally sit down in a proffered chair and try to be unobtrusive. Several different officials and high monks now get up, one after another, to address the crowd through a microphone at the front of the wide rostrum. I notice that front and center is Jinghui, the Old Master and abbot of Sizu.

I first met Jinghui in the '90s when I sought out and found Cypress Grove Monastery. I'd gone looking for the place where the famous Zen master Zhaozhou once lived. A guide book I had said that nothing remained of the old temple site except a broken-down pagoda that marked Zhaozhou's grave along with some old cypress trees. As I roamed the streets of Zhaoxian, a provincial town where the temple was located, I noticed a big new temple. I went there and inquired about where I could find Zhaozhou's old temple site and learned that this was the very place, as a new temple had recently been built on the old site. This was where I later gave the fateful lecture on American Zen. Bright Sea was then only in his late twenties or so and actually looked hardly older than a college student. In contrast to his now photogenic presence, he then seemed rather diminutive. In that first visit to Cypress Grove, Bright Sea arranged for me to meet Jinghui. I learned that some very high officials had been in the temple during the past couple of days, including the fourth-ranking official of the central government. Then I met Jinghui face-to-face. The abbot of one of China's most important temples, who had just finished talking with high government officials, warmly welcomed a foreign stranger who had wandered in the front gate of the monastery with the status of a tourist.

The families of several high-ranking Communist officials visit and even study with high-ranking Zen monks. And while it is not widely publicized, high-ranking Communist officials sometimes formally study Zen teachings. Zen is regarded even by the party as an important part of China's cultural and spiritual landscape. It's regarded as the "orthodox" Buddhist religion of China. The government calls on some Zen monks to refute the heresies of various groups that might threaten political security. Cults that are influenced by Taoist ideas are especially anathema to the government and are targeted for elimination. The reasons for this go deep into history. Taoists have long tended to believe in occult powers, especially embracing things like magic amulets or spiritual mantras that they believe confer protection from harm on their practitioners. I already mentioned the Taoist love of long-life elixirs. Taoist-influenced cults often were involved in political rebellions, thinking they had special powers to protect them from the arrows or bullets of government troops. Such groups appear more dangerous to the government than Buddhists, who are usually content to practice their religion quietly and who tend to emphasize meditation over confrontation. Taoists are bigger political threats than Buddhists.

This is not to say that Buddhists haven't led any rebellions. At various times Buddhist monks have been rabble-rousers. This was particularly true around the time that Bodhidharma visited China, the period covering about 470 to 530 CE. Then, under the Wei dynasty that ruled Northern China, several revolts broke out where Buddhist monks rallied peasants against the government. More on this later.

Jinghui, the Old Master, is the most honored guest and main speaker at the event. Finally, he rises to speak to the crowd. I seize the opportunity to grab my camera from my backpack and retreat completely from the rostrum under the pretext of taking his photograph. Freed at last from the spotlight, I relax again. Jinghui delivers his remarks and his congratulations for the reopening of the temple, and thereupon a cascade of fireworks is set off above the temple's front gate, signaling an end to the day's formal activities. As the crowd disperses, a monk motions me to a door leading upstairs to a dining room. Ascending the stairs, I see Bright Sea and members of the Cypress Grove Monastery delegation and join them to enjoy a buffet lunch.

After we're done eating, Bright Sea pulls me toward the exterior walkway that runs along the side of the building. "Let's go see him," he says. I realize that there's a crowd clustered there, all waiting for the chance to see the Old Master, Jinghui. I feel like an imposter as the crowd opens to let Bright Sea and me pass. But anyway I go along, and soon we find ourselves in a guest reception room where Jinghui sits in front of an enthusiastic crowd of admirers. I go forward to pay my respects. He's seated and looks up at me as I approach him.

"Do you remember me?" I ask.

"Feng Keqiang?" he asks, saying my Chinese name.

I'd like to ask Jinghui a few questions, but the crowd is pressing into the meeting room. Jinghui's celebrity now draws throngs of well-wishers. After a few moments Bright Sea and I retreat to a nearby reception room for some photo taking. Soon it's time to leave, and I fall in with Bright Sea's entourage to push through the crowd to the front of the temple. We board a waiting bus that fills up quickly behind us. Minutes later we are winding down the mountain en route to the city of Huangmei. After we arrive at Bright Sea's hotel, he kindly arranges for his private car to return me to the Fourth Ancestor's Temple.

While I was dealing with festivities at Laozu Temple, my longtime friend Eric Lu has arrived back at the Fourth Ancestor's Temple and is waiting for me there upon my return. Eric and I have traveled widely in China together for more than a decade. A college graduate who majored in English, Eric speaks that language with complete fluency. He's joined me to visit the next few stops on Bodhidharma's trail.

Among the early Zen places in this region, there is the temple that claims to be the residence and teaching seat of the Third Ancestor of the tradition, and there is also a mountain where Zen's Second Ancestor, Huike, Bodhidharma's main Dharma heir, is said to have lived.

Scholars mostly ignore these places because there are no early texts like the *Continued Biographies* that confirm that the Second and Third Zen ancestors lived here. The references to these places are all found in later texts that many Western and Japanese scholars dismiss as fictions. Many scholars regard the idea that the Second and Third Ancestors lived in these places as highly dubious, probably just later attempts to create a Zen mythology. I think the facts we know support the idea that the old ancestors really lived in these places, but that is an argument for a different book.

BODHIDHARMA LEAVES THE LUOYANG
MOUNT SONG REGION IN 494?

As I mentioned previously, while much of Buddhism, including certain currents of Zen, submitted to and was tainted by the wealth and power of the court, Bodhidharma's band of followers appears to have stayed away from the intoxicants of fame and royal praise. This is indicated in the *Continued Biographies* where it says he would not remain in "places of imperial sway" and "those who loved to see he could not draw him near them." That this was part of Bodhidharma's Zen tradition is also indicated by the refusal of the Fourth Ancestor to answer multiple summons from the emperor.

The Chinese scholar Yang Xiaotian has written a paper about Bodhidharma's life that emphasizes this point. He points out that the fact that Bodhidharma's disciple Sengfu left the Luoyang area in the year 494 is significant. Yang shows that this time coincides with the decision by Emperor Xiao Wen, of the Northern Wei dynasty, to move his court from the northern city of Pingcheng to Luoyang, the place where we know Bodhidharma and his disciple were living at that time. Sengfu's biography says he left the area at that time and went to Nanjing. Evidence indicates Bodhidharma also would have had good reason to leave.

Emperor Xiao Wen, who was of the Tuoba ethnic group, was everywhere adopting and incorporating Chinese culture into his "barbarian" northern empire. Moving from the northern city of Pingcheng, near the Tuoba people's traditional northern home, to Luoyang, a place with a long history as China's capital, was a political move designed to cement the Wei's legitimacy with the Han Chinese population.

Emperor Xiao Wen, like other Chinese emperors, was a believer and promoter of Buddhism. He spent lavishly to build monasteries and support the religion in various ways. A famous landmark of his support for Buddhism is the Yungang Grottos, the site of stunningly beautiful and artistic Buddhas carved into the stone cliffs and caves near modern Datong City in North China. That site, better preserved but less famous than the Longmen Grottos near Luoyang, remains as evidence of the astonishing artistic skills of carvers who believed that carving beautiful Buddhas secured you a better future life. Emperor Xiao Wen, who fashioned himself to be an incarnation of the Tathagata (the Buddha), commissioned the Buddhist statues that were carved into the cliffs in both Yungang and Longmen.

When Emperor Xiao Wen moved his capital from Pingcheng to Luoyang around the year 492, work on the Yungang Grottos near Datong was stopped. The work then started again at Longmen ("Dragon Gate") along the Yi River near Luoyang. For the next two and a half centuries, the Longmen site saw the creation of literally thousands of Buddhist carvings in caves that overlook the river. That place is now a famous

UNESCO World Heritage site visited by thousands of tourists every day.

The *Continued Biographies* reveals that Sengfu left Luoyang just when Emperor Xiao Wen moved his court there. A coincidence? Bodhidharma's biography in the *Continued Biographies* indicates he was roundly criticized for the type of practice he advocated. He did not fit in the Buddhist establishment of Emperor Xiao Wen's court. In fact, Emperor Xiao Wen issued a directive demanding that Buddhist scriptures be publically taught by Buddhist monks. Bodhidharma, an independent teacher outside the religious establishment, could well have suffered criticism if not persecution for not joining the emperor's efforts to spread scriptural study.

During the time of Emperor Xiao Wen's rule (471–499), monks were definitely not supposed to operate outside the religious establishment and direction of the court. The reason for this is clear from historical records. During the first two decades of Emperor Xiao Wen's rule, at least three uprisings against him and his court were led by Buddhist monks. The last such rebellion in the year 490, shortly before the Wei capital moved to Luoyang, occurred when a monk declared himself the new messiah and marshaled the Han Chinese peasants against the Tuoba "foreign" oppressor. Emperor Xiao Wen brutally crushed this rebellion and executed the "messiah" and his commanders.

For these reasons it seems logical that Professor Yang's ideas are right, and that Bodhidharma and his band of independent misfits decided they should get out of Luoyang, while a new gang, the emperor and his establishment monks, was taking over their turf in the Luoyang area. They likely left the Luoyang area around 494, as Sengfu's biography indicates. They departed the area where the Northern Wei dynasty was setting up a new capital and headed south, down the Han and Yang-tse Rivers into the area where Xiao Yan (Emperor Wu) would soon overthrow the boy emperor Baojuan and set up the Liang dynasty.

If Professor Yang's idea is indeed correct, and Bodhidharma and his disciples left the Luoyang area at that time and traveled south, then many pieces of the Bodhidharma puzzle fall into place. This possibility provides a possible explanation for tantalizing references to Bodhidharma and his disciples living in the southern part of the country, especially around Nanjing. It also explains where Bodhidharma and

Huike lived and taught during the long thirty-plus-year gap in their history that the *Continued Biographies* leaves open, a gap that stretches from the year 494, when they were in Luoyang, until the approximate date of Bodhidharma's death sometime around the year 530. In this long period of time, there would have been ample opportunity and means for Bodhidharma's group to migrate to the southern Yang-tse River region and take up residence there.

As I mentioned earlier, the people who established the Wei dynasty that ruled Northern China at that time were originally of the Tuoba ethnic group. They were foreigners, not Han Chinese. Since the third century, their invasion of Northern China drove many ethnic Han Chinese to migrate from the north to the south of the country. One of the main routes for these migrations started from the area where Bodhidharma and his disciples lived around Luoyang and proceeded south through the Fu Niu Mountains. After a relatively short distance, this migration route reached the Han River, which flowed downstream to meet the Yang-tse. Commerce and travel was well-established on these rivers, and so the great majority of the distance between Luoyang and Nanjing could be traveled by boat. The idea that Bodhidharma and his disciples could have followed this well-established migration route to the south is entirely plausible. Their route, going downstream on the Han River, would have carried them through the vital trading and political city of Xiangyang (pronounced *Hsiong-yong*), the same city where Military Governor Xiao Yan (the future Emperor Wu, who we'll examine in detail soon) lived around that same time biding his time, planning his rebellion against the last Qi dynasty emperor in south China.

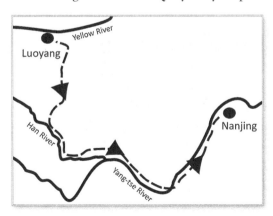

FIGURE 13. Bodhidharma and his disciples leave Luoyang and travel down the Han and Yang-tse Rivers to the Nanjing region in the year 494.

The precise reasons why Bodhidharma avoided imperial contacts can only be surmised. Naturally, as a Buddhist home-leaver, he might be expected to leave society behind and avoid its temptations. Yet the fact is that Bodhidharma traveled at great personal danger for an enormous distance to proselytize in China. Clearly he was not simply of a home-leaving mindset that ignored the world. He wanted to convert people to his vision of Zen and willingly traveled in the world to do that.

In light of the idea that Bodhidharma seems to have avoided the Wei emperor Xiao Wen (and later, as I will show, Emperor Wu), the likelihood that Bodhidharma met Gunabhadra and learned from the latter's harrowing experience with royalty seems even more plausible. Buddhism teaches that life can be both mesmerizing and transient, and where more so than among the competing ruling elites and their bitter struggles for power? At the top of the list of those to be avoided would be an emperor and his immediate kin. Gunabhadra's bitter experience as a political hostage showed that no matter how such people profess affection for the Dharma, they are still tactically minded, always jock-eying for advantage in the fearful maelstrom of politics. Emperors and kings maintain their positions through lethal force.

Daoxuan clearly says that Bodhidharma taught in the "south and north" of China, citing the areas of Luoyang and the Yang-tse. Teaching along the Yang-tse, in my view, must mean that he taught in the most important region of the Yang-tse, the area around Nanjing. Therefore, any analysis of Bodhidharma's life must show whether and how he could have resided in that area.

Eric and I will go to Nanjing and see what clues it holds about Bodhi-dharma's life.

The different dates pertaining to Bodhidharma's possible presence in the Nanjing area are a fascinating part of his puzzle. The two Nanjing-area places most plausibly connected to Bodhidharma, places that have the best claim of a direct historical connection to him, are Dingshan Temple, where he supposedly stayed for up to three years, and True Victory Temple in the nearby city of Tianchang. There, local records claim he established a teaching seat in the year 520. These are places I need to explore in Nanjing.

23. Nanjing City

FROM A WIDE, twenty-first-story hotel-room window, I look across a broad swath of downtown Nanjing City. My view roughly encompasses the area where the Tai Cheng Palace, Emperor Wu's ancient home, lies buried a few meters beneath the cityscape and its autumn morning traffic jam. This is the locale at the heart of Bodhidharma's story.

Nanjing, whose name means "Southern Capital," has had other names during its long history. One of Nanjing's early names was Jinling, meaning "Gold Hills" or "Gold Mounds." The name comes from a legend that says an ancient king who ruled this region from a different place buried gold in the Mufu Mountains that lie to the north of the

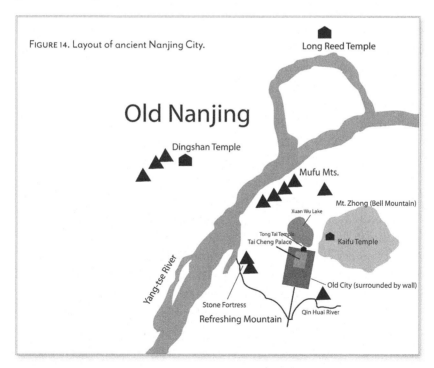

FIGURE 14. Layout of ancient Nanjing City.

Long Reed Temple

Old Nanjing

Dingshan Temple

Mufu Mts.

Xuan Wu Lake

Mt. Zhong (Bell Mountain)

Tong Tai Temple
Tai Cheng Palace

Kaifu Temple

Yang-tse River

Old City (surrounded by wall)

Stone Fortress

Refreshing Mountain

Qin Huai River

city to disrupt the favorable *feng shui* the city enjoys. Such a place, he feared, could easily give rise to talented men who would challenge and overthrow him. The city's *feng shui* is indeed very good. Around the old city proper, the Yang-tse, approaching the city from the southwest, passes up and over the city, providing arched protection from invaders approaching from the west or north. On the east side of the city sits Bell Mountain, which, along with some lesser peaks, offers an excellent high-ground defense against invading armies from the east. Finally, the Qin Huai River, flowing from east to west beneath the city and emptying into the Yang-tse, defended the city's southern approach.

The Mufu Mountains, a line of rocky bluffs riddled with white dolomite limestone, rest along the bank of the Yang-tse, providing high, defensible ground and even more protection from any invader attempting to cross the river. If all this weren't enough, within the upper semicircle formed by the Mufu Mountains and Bell Mountain rests Dark Warrior Lake. This beautiful natural lake provided a huge reservoir of fresh water within the city's defensive perimeter, allowing it to withstand a long siege.

Along a portion of the Qin Huai River that loops around the bottom of the city, another group of hills called the Stone Fortress gave the city more high ground to repel invaders that might attack the city from upstream positions.

Along with these ideal natural defenses, a high man-made wall surrounded the old city proper. And finally, within the northern area of the old city, another rectangular high wall protected the Tai Cheng Palace.

The layout of the Tai Cheng Palace, where Emperor Wu presided over his dominions, was much like the Forbidden City we can see today in Beijing. Oriented toward the south, grand halls met a visitor coming in through the main gate, eventually leading to the emperor's living area at the north of the complex. From the well-defended throne of the Taiji Dian ("Great Ultimate Hall") inside this imperial seat, emperors ruled a number of Southern Chinese dynasties beginning with the Eastern Jin dynasty (317–419) and ending with the Chen dynasty (557–583). Emperor Wu, the key player in Bodhidharma's legend, established the Liang dynasty and ruled from this place beginning in the year 502 and continuing for the next forty-seven years.

In modern times Nanjing played a key role in the formation of modern China. The city was the seat of Sun Yat-sen's Nationalist Government established in 1911. Today, a grand memorial site to the "Father of the Nationalist Revolution" lies on the wooded slopes of Bell Mountain.

Nanjing's formidable natural defenses notwithstanding, it lies atop the detritus of measureless triumphs and tragedies. One infamous tragedy happened only recently. The "Rape of Nanjing" by Japanese imperial forces is still remembered by older citizens of the city who lived during the late '30s, the period preceding the United States's entry into World War II. The Nanjing Peace Museum commemorates that gruesome stain on human history by receiving and educating thousands of visitors each day. The museum, about three blocks long, is filled with disturbing photographs and documents about Japan's brutal occupation of the city. China will not let the Rape of Nanjing slide into history's dustbin and be forgotten.

24. Emperor Wu and Imperial-Way Buddhism

The Jade spring is nearly exhausted,
The palace splendor diminished,
Surrounded by heavenly music,
Everywhere the chants flow forth,
The body cleansed in tepid baths,
Penitence purifies the mind,
The rushes again luxuriant,
Falling flower petals splendidly blanket the ground.
—*"Taking the Buddhist Refuges with the Crown Prince,"*
by Xiao Yan (Emperor Wu)

和太子忏悔　　　萧衍著

玉泉漏向尽
金门光未成
缭绕闻天乐
周流扬梵声
兰汤浴身垢
忏悔净心灵
萎草获再鲜
落花蒙重荣。

EMPEROR WU (ruled 402–449), whose personal name was Xiao Yan (pronounced *Hsiow Yan*), was a devout Buddhist who ruled China's Liang dynasty after seizing power in a rebellion against the Qi (pronounced *Chee*) dynasty. He initiated and led a bloody war against the Qi emperor Baojuan, a young man only seventeen years old.

The boy emperor Baojuan assumed the throne upon the death of his father, the Qi emperor Ming Di. The boy was then still in his early teens and considered too young to wield power, and a group of officials was established to rule the country in the boy's name. But soon the boy, spoiled and temperamental, demanded to exercise the full prerogatives of his position. When he was denied such power, he reacted by forming a secret alliance with court eunuchs, ambitious military men, and corrupt courtiers to strike against the officials who held the reins of the state.

In a ruthless bid for power with his unsavory allies, the boy executed the country's two highest officials and slaughtered their families at the imperial Tai Cheng Palace in a single morning of bloodshed. Following that event, the youth systematically tortured and murdered any court officials he and his court toadies thought might oppose him. This threatened the lives and families of scores of officials and aristocrats of high standing.

As the bloodbath spread with ever greater ferocity, some retired generals and others launched rebellions to dethrone the deranged boy. Two major attempts to topple him ended in disappointing failure at the foot of the Tai Cheng Palace wall. Strange misadventures caused the rebellions to fail, leading that superstitious age to believe that heaven had intervened to protect the occupant of the throne. Even Baojuan believed himself to have supernatural protection. Imagining himself invulnerable, he and his corrupt clique carried out ever-greater outrages of murder, debauchery, and mayhem against the cowering aristocracy, and the circle of his victims widened to include commoners unlucky enough to come to his attention.

This turbulent era spread its effects into far reaches of Chinese culture. Baojuan owned a favorite concubine, a beauty named Jade Slave. Her tiny, delicate feet aroused the boy's extreme passion. Baojuan was so enraptured by Jade Slave and her miniature feet that he routinely traveled to her father's house to pay the man special honors, even acting as the man's servant. These bizarre expeditions spread terror, for any commoners unlucky enough to remain in the street when the imperial caravan passed on the way to Jade Slave's house were summarily murdered. The boy's episodic madness terrorized everyone. Aristocrats, trying to survive the boy's rule, made a show of embracing his perverted tastes. Some historical accounts say the foot binding of ancient China was started due to Emperor Baojuan's infatuation with Jade Slave's tiny feet.

One night while Baojuan, Jade Slave, and their friends were enjoying themselves at the house of Jade Slave's father, fire broke out in the Tai Cheng Palace, destroying scores of halls along with the apartments of the imperial concubines. The unlucky women were unable to escape the conflagration because gates that enclosed their living quarters could not be opened without the emperor's direct command. Thus well over a thousand women, girls, and their servants perished. When Emperor Baojuan returned and viewed the carnage, the bodies "stacked like cordwood," he reportedly said, "Now I can build the palace I have wanted!" He then ordered ornate new halls to replace what was lost, undermining the country's already crippled finances. As a special gesture to his beloved Jade Slave, inside one of the new halls he built a special pathway where lotus flowers, sculpted in relief using ivory and jade, marked where her tiny feet passed each day.

Meanwhile, a man named Xiao Yan, the aristocratic military governor in the distant city of Xiangyang, watched developments warily. As an official appointed as a result of his connections and distant blood relationship with the crown, he had long loyally served former Qi emperors. But he knew the situation the country now faced was indeed dangerous. The civil chaos and rebellion that wracked the country since Baojuan began his campaign of terror was threatening on many levels. Besides blanketing the country in a treacherous state of fear, it could open the door to invasion by the rival Wei dynasty of Emperor Xiao Wen that ruled North China. The Wei dynasty, ruled not by Chinese but "foreign" peoples called the Tuoba, was considered a barbarian state and must not be allowed to conquer all of China.

In years prior, as a young official climbing the imperial ranks, Xiao Yan was a close friend of a royal Qi dynasty prince who ruled as king of a prefecture called Jingling. Xiao Yan and seven other literary-minded aristocrats met with the king to share literature and talk philosophy, practicing the then fashionable pastime of *qing tan* (pronounced *ching tan*), meaning "pure conversation." The king often invited eminent Buddhist monks to lecture to the group, and Xiao Yan became deeply familiar with Buddhist thought.

When the Emperor Baojuan seized power and started his crimes, Xiao Yan was already famous as a military commander for his actions against the Wei dynasty. A brilliant battlefield tactician, he had routed an enemy force with a surprise night attack by creating the illusion of having a large military force.

Xiao Yan's older brother, Xiao Yi, was a high-ranking military general who commanded forces loyal to the Qi throne. As the situation with the murderous boy emperor went from bad to worse, Xiao Yan tried to get his brother to join him against the youth on the throne, but his brother would have none of it, clinging instead to the ideal of Confucian loyalty to one's sovereign. Xiao Yi refused to turn against the dynasty he had long served, so Xiao Yan, failing to persuade his older brother, quietly found other allies and secretly laid aside stores of war materials.

Finally, events took a momentous turn. Xiao Yan's brother Xiao Yi led a royalist counterattack that crushed the second rebellion against the throne. When the Tai Cheng Palace in Nanjing was surrounded by rebels, Xiao Yi crossed the Qin Huai River from the south in a lightning strike, routing the rebels' perimeter defense, then killing or scattering insurgent fighters who had besieged the palace. This brilliant military victory should have earned Xiao Yi a lifetime of honors, but this was not to be. Within a month the emperor's corrupt courtiers and eunuch allies, who dreaded Xiao Yi's sudden status and power, trumped up empty charges of disloyalty against him. They convinced Baojuan that Xiao Yi coveted the throne, leading the boy to treacherously execute his military commander for treason.

Upon hearing of the execution of his brother, Xiao Yan marshaled his secret allies and declared a new rebellion. Using stores of timber, he fortified warships he had secretly built in estuaries of the Han River near Xiangyang, then launched his forces downstream on that waterway, a tributary of the Yang-tse that would carry his forces to Nanjing.

After more than a year of battles and a brilliant campaign, Xiao Yan's forces arrived at the banks of the Huai Qin River, southeast of the city. That place, named New Woods, was where the bulk of the force defending the capital lay awaiting his arrival. In a brilliant flanking movement, Xiao Yan routed the city's defenders at this spot, then marched on the capital itself to lay siege to the imperial palace and its young emperor, who even now continued to believe that his protector deity would rescue him.

Xiao Yan established his command post at the spot called Stone Fortress, on a string of hills west of the city, then laid siege to the enemy force that still defended the Tai Cheng Palace. All the while the young emperor inside continued to make merry, believing himself divinely protected. Xiao Yan's headquarters at Stone Fortress gave the benighted people of the city hope, providing the siege an air of inevitable success as time went on. The population waited anxiously for Xiao Yan's final victory.

At last the siege and war had its intended effect, for two generals who were defending the palace and its mad prince turned against the boy and capitulated. Baojuan was still partying when a soldier ran into his palace to chase him down. The boy ran out a back door of his musk hall (a room saturated with male deer musk, said to enhance virility) trying to escape. He tripped and fell and was overtaken by the soldier. One story describes him as arrogant and defiant to the end, saying to his assailant, "What is this then? A rebellion?" The soldier and others who ran to the scene then stabbed the defiant emperor to death.

Upon the death of Baojuan, it fell to Xiao Yan to dispose of his property, including his substantial number of concubines. Records indicate that he selected certain of the women to be his own consorts, but Jade Slave did not appear among the survivors. One account says that Xiao Yan wished to keep this country-toppling beauty for his own, but his subcommanders demanded the death of a woman associated with so much murder and misery. Reluctantly, Xiao Yan sentenced her to die by the executioner's sword.

Xiao Yan, who would soon become Emperor Wu, demonstrated the strange convergence of Buddhist sensibilities and marshal prowess that ran through Chinese ruling circles. Devotion to Buddhism and the tools of war and intrigue required to seize and maintain the throne might seem contradictory, to say the least. But in this Xiao Yan was typical, not exceptional. Like other emperors before and after him, he paid homage to Buddhist ideals while manipulating every means necessary to seize and retain power. But he would carry this fusion of Buddhism and state power to a level previously unseen in Chinese history. This transformation would proceed further than those gone before due mainly to Xiao Yan's skillful fusion of Buddhist and Confucian ideals, especially the literature and rituals of these two seemingly contradictory philosophies.

After Baojuan's death, Xiao Yan secured the imperial throne by methodically eliminating, mainly through execution, all the brothers and other male family members of the deposed boy monarch who might try to reestablish the vanquished dynasty. Thereafter, Xiao Yan, who would be known as Emperor Wu, ruled continuously for forty-seven years, an unusually long imperial reign in China's long history.

25. Tianchang City and Bodhidharma's True Victory Temple

ERIC AND I LEAVE OUR Nanjing hotel on Huangpu Road and take a taxi to a small bus station that offers routes to nearby cities. The air is bad. Low fog fuses with the stagnant haze to reduce visibility to a few hundred feet and is a tangible presence on the nostrils and tongue. After a taxi ride through the morning gloom, we arrive at a bus station and soon await a bus to Tianchang (the name means "Long Sky"). Other waiting passengers sit with us on bright red plastic seats beneath prominent signs put up by the bus company to guide employee and public behavior. One surprisingly detailed sign says FIX THE ROAD, FIX MORAL VIRTUE, BUILD A BRIDGE, BUILD WEALTH, DO THINGS PEACEFULLY, CREATE NEW ENTERPRISES. Other such signs exhort people to all other manners of country-building activities. I wonder how much longer the Chinese people, who are intelligent, creative, and perceptive, will put up with patronizing slogans. Just then a bus driver yells into the building so sharply that Eric and I both nearly jump out of our seats. Then we realize he's just making the last call for a bus that's departing. The driver must have inspired the "do things peacefully" part of the wall propaganda.

China has long recorded its history in official records. Each emperor had archival and court historians. But a separate type of historical record was kept in local provinces and prefectures concerned solely with local affairs. These local records are called *difang zhi* (pronounced *dee-fong jer*), meaning "area record" or "gazette." What remains of these old records, and they are numerous, offer a wealth of detail about events and life in old China.

A paper by a Chinese scholar uncovered just such an old record that says that a temple once existed in a place called Tianchang County, a temple established by Bodhidharma. According to the record, a temple named True Victory Temple was built in the second year of the Putong era (the year 522), a time when Emperor Wu's Imperial-Way Buddhism was in full flower. However, the scholarly paper says the record comes from the Qing dynasty (1644–1911). This is a late record in the scheme of things. However, it is interesting because it doesn't follow the "official story" of Bodhidharma that was developed earlier. Instead of saying he arrived in China in 527, it indicates he was already in China before that time, and so it agrees time-wise with the more reliable record of his life found in the *Continued Biographies*. This is worth investigating. Another compelling facet to this story is that the place in question, Tianchang, is about sixty miles north of Nanjing. This places Bodhidharma in the general area of Nanjing during the time when Emperor Wu was in power.

After first reading about this old record, I spent three years searching for clues about whether anything might be left of the old temple to which it refers. No "True Victory Temple" is listed among the famous temples of the era in question. Nor is there any record of the temple in general Zen literature. Finally I stumbled across a document online that is published by the Tianchang City government. It says that an old well still remains from the old temple and the well is located on Liuli Street in Tianchang. This is the place Eric and I have set out to find today.

The buses at this terminal in Nanjing are not full-size long-haul coaches, but smaller vehicles for short service routes. I notice one that is decorated with the words VENICE TOUR BUS on its side.

Soon, a door opens under a sign that says TIANCHANG, and we board and take our assigned seats. Presently the driver edges us into the Nanjing traffic jam, and we press our way toward the Yang-tse River Bridge that will lead us to the north side of the river and on to our destination.

The Yang-tse River Bridge was constructed in 1968, during the heyday of revolutionary fervor in China. At that time China had quit its revolutionary alliance with the Soviet Union and the latter had withdrawn all its technical advisors. The construction of the Yang-tse River Bridge by Chinese engineers was a great symbolic victory meant to show that China could, through "self-reliance," achieve greatness in feats of engineering without outside assistance. The "self-reliance" idea evolved into a political slogan that spread into every part of Chinese society, often with absurd consequences. Even in times of natural disasters, the "self-reliance" motto reigned, resulting in serious hardships for people needing assistance. This movement helped isolate China's people from each other and the world. When the reforms of 1978 started the process of "opening," years of "self-reliance" had spawned political provincialism and competition between localities, a situation whose effects continue in China today.

But in 1968 the great Nanjing River Bridge symbolized a triumph of modernism, with two lanes running in each direction, a bus stop in the middle, and formulaic statues of revolutionary heroes portrayed as building the New China. Unfortunately the bridge builders did not foresee a China where private autos and trucks would jam the highways, making the four-lane bridge far too narrow to handle a modern city's traffic flow.

The final block before the bridge takes about ten minutes to navigate, with every vehicle jostling for each inch of competitive position. At last our bus makes it onto the span, and we move fairly steadily toward the Yang-tse's distant shore. After another fifteen minutes, we are moving steadily along a multilane highway through a large residential and industrial district called Liu He, or "Six Harmonies." The name comes from an old mountain there and is based on some Taoist philosophy. I know this is where Bodhidharma is said to have come ashore after he crossed the Yang-tse on a "single blade of grass." It will be part of later explorations.

As our bus exits a cloverleaf interchange to get on a major thruway, traffic comes to a dead stop. The long line of trucks filling both lanes in front of us doesn't look good. Our driver lights a cigarette and hops out to check out the situation. I see him make his way forward through the traffic and he disappears for several minutes. After a time he returns, starts the engine, and somehow manages to turn our bus around and head back the opposite direction in the oncoming lanes of the turnpike we just entered. I clutch the edges of my seat hoping that some large trucks don't appear around the corner as we proceed the wrong way on the highway. Luckily, no vehicles that can't get out of our way appear, and the driver soon crosses the divider to ultimately end up on an exit ramp that leads to some side roads. For the next half hour or so we get an unscheduled tour of the back roads of Six Harmonies, bouncing through potholed pavement next to assorted construction sites and industrial facilities. At last we emerge back onto the turnpike we exited farther south. Traffic going our way now seems normal, and I wonder if the detour was worth it.

Tianchang is another one of the typical Chinese cities with a population of six or seven hundred thousand people that the outside world has never heard of. We get off the bus at the downtown station and start looking for a place to eat lunch before we proceed with our expedition. After a fruitless search up and down a couple of streets, we stumble into a new, fast-food-sort of franchise place with a Korean name. Oddly, a Korean fast-food restaurant has apparently beaten out McDonald's to set up shop in this big city. We order some items, and while we're eating the young man who owns the restaurant engages us in conversation, curious about the rare foreigner. We explain we're looking for the site of an old temple said to have once existed in the city, and we think now there is only a well remaining where it once stood. We want to find out more information about it. The young man, whose name is Huang, says he knows the spot, and furthermore he tells us his old classmate is the editor of the local *difang zhi*. If we want to find out anything from the old records, he can make an introduction for us. *Guangxi* (relationships) like Mr. Huang's are the lifeblood of Chinese society.

So after lunch Mr. Huang accompanies us in a taxi to the seat of local government where we intend to find the *difang zhi* bureau. We arrive to find a very colossal set of government office buildings, their polished granite reflecting the morning sun. The big buildings also reflect a strange thing that lingers all over China. The imperial mindset of government officials leads them to spend a big chunk of the people's money on grandiose government office buildings, the better to show off government authority. Tianchang is almost unknown in the wider scheme of the world, but the building directory indicates it has a foreign-trade bureau, an external cultural-affairs office, and other huge bureaucratic wings of a city administration that doesn't like to skimp on itself. The wide cement plaza in front of the main high-rise of this bureaucratic Disneyland is a few hundred meters across, decorated with an immense metal globe of the world at its center. On many occasions I've heard Chinese people swear under their breath at the vast sums spent to enhance the government's stature. Tianchang offers an egregious example of this phenomenon.

But when we peruse the big building directory that indicates the presence of almost every manner of government bureau, the *difang zhi*, where local historical records would be kept, is nowhere to be found. After numerous inquiries with different desks, Mr. Huang informs us that the *difang zhi* was never transferred here when the new buildings were built and remains at its old location a few blocks from his restaurant where we ate lunch.

Not long after, we exit our taxi in front of an alley in the center of the city. Mr. Huang leads us past some buildings into a parking lot where some workers are enjoying their afternoon break, dancing to some pop rhythms played on a CD player. A little farther on we reach the old *difang zhi* office. Mr. Huang had gotten the telephone number of the place, and so his former classmate, a woman named Chu, meets us at the door and invites us in.

Once in her office, I explain to Ms. Chu what we're doing. I tell her that there is a gap in the record of Bodhidharma's life in China. After the year 494 there is no clear record of where he lived or taught until he died, presumably around the year 530. I'm looking for hard evidence that Bodhidharma spent at least part of this time in the Nanjing area. While several places in the area claim a connection with the old sage, they offer no unimpeachable evidence. The myths and supernatural events that accompany some accounts make them implausible. Certain other stories are clearly false since they associate Bodhidharma with temples that didn't come into being until later times. However, the story of True Victory Temple is different. The local *difang zhi* (historical records) provide the date of the temple's construction and connect it directly with Bodhidharma. *Difang zhi* are widely considered reliable because they are not "histories" but simply local records of events, untainted by politics and myth. So this place, almost unknown in China and the West, may truly be where Bodhidharma established a Dharma seat and expounded his Zen teachings in China.

Ms. Chu listens to the story for some time before commenting. When she does, she seems very accepting that the version of events I've put forth may have merit. She explains that in ancient times Tianchang was a well-populated, relatively rich agricultural area that was a crossroads between North and South China. Its *feng shui*, with "mountains behind and rivers in front" conformed to ancient ideas of an ideal habitat.

Then, while we wait, Ms. Chu retrieves the story of the temple in question from the local electronic records. Soon she comes up with the description: "Our records of this temple come from the Jia Qing era of the Ming dynasty [circa 1480]," she says. That record refers to even earlier records from the Ming dynasty (circa 1380) that say that True Victory Temple was constructed in the second year of the Putong era (522) by Bodhidharma, and its name was later changed to Liuli Temple. (*Liuli* means "glazed tile" and is also an old word for colored glass). Ms. Chu is particularly adamant that because the records are *difang zhi*, they would not have been fabricated without any basis. Indeed, even skeptical Western scholars regard China's *difang zhi* as dependable. They were simply records, not propaganda created to extol historic events, legendary or otherwise.

Ms. Chu then goes on to offer more reasons why Tianchang would have been a good location to set up such a temple in ancient times. Old records indicate that several other temples existed in the area, a sign that there was enough local wealth to support such activities. She says she's heard stories that the temple we're talking about once had large murals depicting Bodhidharma and many statues of him as well. However, no one has ever paid much attention to the old record because the date of the temple construction doesn't fit with the prevailing story that Bodhidharma arrived in China in the year 527. Since the local record doesn't fit with other widespread accounts of Bodhidharma's life, no one has been certain how to interpret it. In particular, the dominant account of Bodhidharma, which does not say he lived in the area of Nanjing for an extended period, is completely contrary to what this old local record indicates.

I then ask Ms. Chu about the old well that is said to still exist where the temple once stood.

"That well is right in front of that building over there." She points out a large building that sits between the office bureau where we're sitting and the main street (Liuli Street, the same name that the old temple had) we came from earlier. "There's a movie theatre and an appliance store in that building. In front of them is the well. Before, the wellhead had a protective cover that was about a meter high. After some new construction was built, what remains is only a few inches off the ground now, but it's still there."

It occurs to me, as I look out the window at the building in question and consider our south-facing direction, that where we're sitting was likely inside the original perimeters of Bodhidharma's temple. In fact, given the layout of China's old temples, we might be sitting where the abbot's quarters once stood, the place where Bodhidharma would have lived.

After we exchange cards and promise to exchange information in the future, Ms. Chu accompanies us to the front door. "That's the building right there," she says pointing to the south. "You'll find the well in front of it."

A couple of minutes later, we reach the street and almost immediately see a rimmed hole in a small red-brick plaza in front of the appliance store that Ms. Chu told us about. The hole is less than a meter across and has a grating just below the ground's surface to allow water to drain into it. The rim around it is only a few inches high and, given its location on a busy sidewalk on a major street, it's amazing that it has been preserved, as someone could easily trip over the edge and fall into or across the thing in the dark. The same architectural artifact in the United States would have surely led to a lawsuit. Somehow, when this major modern street and modern shops were built, someone decided the old well was worth hanging onto, even though there is no indication that this well holds cultural significance.

Eric and I both start taking pictures of the well, and this draws a lot of curious observers wondering what the heck the foreigner and his friend sees in the otherwise unremarkable hole in the pavement. Then we take pictures of each other standing next to it and of the surrounding buildings, eliciting more stares and surprised looks.

The colossus of today's China sits upon an incalculably large pile of history. Certainly some of the old culture remains intact or well-reconstructed, but it is such a tiny fragment of what the country has known that it can't even suggest the infinite dramas and pathos of the civilization. Occasionally a fragment of the old grandeur simply juts out of the ground. I remember looking for the remains of the temple where a famous ancient Zen master named Deshan (Japanese: Toku-san, 782–865) lived and taught. The day I arrived looking for the place was the same day that a large backhoe was knocking down the temple cemetery where Deshan and other old high-ranking monks were buried.

FIGURE 15. Bodhidharma's wellhead positioned in front of an appliance store in Tianchang City. Photo taken in October 2009.

An old woman guided me to the spot where his burial stupa had been removed moments before. "Deshan was there," she said. The old woman then took me to where an apartment complex had been built on the site of his old temple. Some stone lions, once the guardians of the temple's Buddha Hall, now jutted out of the ground between two buildings. No one had bothered to retrieve them from the new soil of progress.

Likewise, here on the pavement in front of an appliance store on a busy street, is the last tangible remnant of a temple reportedly occupied by Bodhidharma. Somewhere, someone who understood its significance had made sure it was not totally abandoned to modernity. Unseen forces work to preserve.

A light rain begins to fall harder, so Eric and I finish our photos and hail a taxi, making our way back to the bus station. This is but the first of Bodhidharma's traces I plan to ferret out in the Nanjing area.

26. Linggu Temple on Bell Mountain

TWO DAYS LATER on a comfortable and sunny fall afternoon, Eric and I are stooped over examining the soft ground, brushing soil and leaves off old stones to read faded inscriptions. We are standing in the soft dirt of Bell Mountain's forest among old monuments that protrude from the fallen leaves and autumn undergrowth. On close examination we realize that the old monuments are stone carvings eulogizing old Zen masters of the Caodong (Soto) Zen school whose remains were placed here a couple hundred years ago.

Virtually everything older, including any tangible remains from Emperor Wu's time, fifteen centuries ago, is now removed, decayed, or lost beneath Bell Mountain's forests. The mountain has seen so many battles, fires, and other misadventures over long centuries that only the mind's eye can imagine the grandeur that once presided amid its trees and meadows.

The place we're exploring is called Ling Gu ("Departed Spirit Valley") Park. It now serves mainly as a war memorial, as there were pitched battles around this location during World War II. The original temple that stood here, called Departed Spirit Temple, was built in the year 514 by Emperor Wu to honor Baozhi, the famous monk who helped Emperor Wu establish the Water and Land Ceremony and who also was an early Zen foil to Emperor Wu's religious questions.

Even though he lived before Bodhidharma's Zen tradition took root in the country, the monk Baozhi is remembered as the quintessential Zen personality. His biography is filled with fanciful stories. The emperor often questioned Baozhi about the meaning of Zen, and his odd answers displayed a teaching style made famous by China's later generations of seemingly enigmatic Zen masters.

Once Emperor Wu asked Baozhi, "My mind is still plagued with troubles and doubt. Why can't I rid myself of them through practice?"

To this Baozhi is said to have answered, "Twelve."

This was a typical Zen-like response. Baozhi's record says he was referring to the twelve hours of the Chinese day. Ancient Chinese divided a day into twelve time periods of two hours each. Baozhi meant that as long as Emperor Wu's "practice" was concerned with actions in the twelve hours of the day, the karmic realm of time, of cause and effect, he could not solve his troubles. In Zen, even time and space are regarded as empty karmic abstractions.

According to one legend, Baozhi also performed some magic for Emperor Wu so that he could see former emperors suffering in hell for their misdeeds. Other bizarre stories are sprinkled in the record of Baozhi's life.

A stupa dedicated to Baozhi rests near where Eric and I are looking around. It is not the original stupa that Emperor Wu made for him. That one succumbed to long-forgotten disasters that have plagued this place. Actually, this one isn't even near where the original one sat. That place, a few kilometers from here around the slope of Bell Mountain, became a burial ground for the first Ming dynasty emperor. I guess he was jealous of the good *feng shui* of that spot and took it over, as emperors were allowed to do. So now this new stupa honors Baozhi. The old rocks and monuments that Eric and I spy beneath the bushes and undergrowth are just an echo of an echo, tiny tailings of the splendor of ancient Bell Mountain.

27. Emperor Wu, the *Chakravartin* King and Bodhisattva Emperor

ON THE EIGHTH DAY of the fourth lunar month of the year 502, Xiao Yan ascended an outdoor platform at the summit of a mountain south of Nanjing and proclaimed his acceptance of heaven's mandate to rule the land. He would be known to history as Emperor Liang Wudi, a name that translates as "Martial Emperor of the Liang Dynasty." The date Wu accepted heaven's mandate to rule was not picked at random. It coincided with the Buddha's birthday, long celebrated by Buddhists with a ceremony that includes bathing a statue of the baby Shakyamuni Buddha, and it signified a new political and religious beginning.

From the start of his rule, Emperor Wu used Buddhism as his reigning ideology, exploiting its dates and symbols in this manner. Deeply sincere in his personal belief and devotion to Buddhism, he unerringly played the role of the august and wise Buddhist sovereign fighting the forces of Mara (delusion and evil) in a Buddhist universe. He immediately began to build Buddhist temples and increase the number of monks and nuns in the country. He invited translators and eminent monks from around China and abroad to live and teach in new or newly refurbished temples as well as in his own palace, where they translated or retranslated uncounted Buddhist scriptures that flowed into the country from the home of Buddhism in the Asian subcontinent.

Emperor Wu was less interested in the affairs of state than to devoting himself to the study of Buddhist scriptures. He personally selected the texts that his retinue of "house monks," as he called his favorite clerics, must study and translate. This core group of monks, numbering about twenty, directed extensive translation work on a wide range of scriptures. Among the group were several monks who gained great distinction for their work and contributions.

The Sanskrit word *chakravartin* literally means "[one] whose wheels are turning," and in India it was anciently applied to a king whose chariot wheels went everywhere spreading the Buddha's teachings. A chakra, or spoked wheel, symbolized a king's righteous Buddhist rule and his actions to spread the religion. The famous early example of such a Buddhist king was the Indian monarch Ashoka (304–232 BCE), who first used Buddhism as the reigning ideology of a wide empire. The chakra not only symbolized Ashoka's rule, but also remains the symbol of political rule today in modern India. The idea of "turning the wheel of the teaching," often cited in Buddhism, is connected with the idea of the turning wheels of the *chakravartin* king's chariot, and thus the propagation of the Buddha Dharma or law.

According to Emperor Wu's imperial propaganda, a *chakravartin* in the mold of India's Ashoka the Great had now ascended the throne in China, and this was an event of millennial importance.

Among the first scriptures that Emperor Wu had translated and propagated was the King Ashoka Sutra. That scripture purported to be the prophetic words of the Buddha praising Ashoka, who of course was born long after the Buddha's death. Wu made a point of holding up King Ashoka as his righteous predecessor. On the twenty-sixth day of the eleventh month (lunar calendar) in the year 513, the translation of the King Ashoka Sutra was begun under the direction of an Indian missionary house monk in Emperor Wu's court named Sanghabhadra. Emperor Wu attended this event and personally made notes on what was said. The full translation of the sutra translated by Emperor Wu's monks is preserved in the Taisho canon, the one-hundred-volume collection of Buddhist writings compiled in the 1920s to honor the reign of Emperor Hirohito. It remains as the definitive collection of Mahayana Buddhist scriptures used by scholars throughout the world today.

Ashoka is remembered and honored even today in India and in Buddhist history as a great humanitarian ruler who spread Buddhism's influence far and wide. Stone monuments created during his reign tell some of his story and indicate that his Buddhist teachings even reached the shores of ancient Greece. He famously established burial stupas that housed the cremated remains (known as "sacred relics") of the Buddha's body. According to legend he divided up and left tiny remnants of these relics at eighty-four thousand places throughout the known world. Various places in China, drawing from the legend of King Ashoka, claim to have been among the places where King Ashoka consigned sacred relics for later generations to venerate (though there are no early records in China that confirm this). Recently Nanjing archeologists unearthed a jade stupa repository, several feet tall, purportedly holding relics of the Buddha, that was interred during the reign of Emperor Wu. It's likely that Emperor Wu obtained and venerated these relics to strengthen his association with his revered predecessor, Ashoka the Great.

While the *chakravartin* ideal that Ashoka represented was used by Chinese emperors before him, Emperor Wu went to the greatest lengths to reinforce his connection to that Indian monarch and enhance his own reputation as a *chakravartin* emperor. He may have found this necessary because Huiyuan's famous treatise entitled "A Monk Does Not Bow to a King" caused Buddhists in Southern China to be less deferential to kings than Emperor Wu demanded. Emperor Wu strengthened his religious role by compiling and even retranslating scriptures that enhanced his religious position. He also directed the country's citizens, including the aristocracy, to embrace Mahayana Buddhism and even personally expounded Buddhist scriptures and philosophy in grand public assemblies.

Emperor Wu utilized other symbols to build his Imperial-Way Buddhism. Tellingly, after gaining power he constructed his first of many Buddhist temples at New Woods, the site where he defeated the main body of Baojuan's forces southwest of the capital. He named it Dharma King Temple, evoking a story of the Dharma King (Buddha), who was likened in scripture to an enlightened sovereign. The exact scriptural passages used to justify this fusion of politics and religion came from the famous Lotus Sutra, which proclaimed, in the most widely used translation of that day, the following:

> And so the Tathagata [Buddha] appears, utilizing the strength of samadhic power [literally "Zen," or meditative concentration], to obtain the land of the Dharma realm, becoming the king of the three worlds [past, present, and future]. And when the demon kings refuse to submit to him, the Holy One and his generals give battle with them . . . And so the Tathagata appears in the midst of the three worlds as the *Great Dharma King*, using the Dharma to save all beings [emphasis mine].

Moreover, the term *Dharma King* was the name of an important Buddhist scripture, the Dharma King Sutra, which espoused the Bodhisattva Precepts with a Confucian twist. I'll talk more about that interesting sutra later.

Equating himself and his specific battle to seize power with the actions of the Dharma King in this fashion was typical of Wu's fusion of political with religious symbols to enhance his own status.

The Buddhist scriptures that Emperor Wu promoted and spread often contained thinly veiled political meaning that was interpreted to nurture Imperial-Way Buddhism. A cornerstone of Emperor Wu's Buddhist order was the Lotus Sutra, cited above, a text that effusively praises the role of bodhisattvas in the world and links those exalted beings to wise kings. This was the same text that the Nichiren sect in Japan used to justify their praise of the Japanese emperor during World War II.

Among the house monks who helped lead the translation, building, and other religious projects undertaken by Emperor Wu was the monk Zhizang (pronounced *Jer-zong*). He resided at Kaishan Temple, where the most honored of the house monks lived. Zhizang was among the two or three highest-ranking monks who taught the Buddha Dharma to the emperor and his family. He was the preceptor for the emperor's oldest son, Crown Prince Zhao Ming (pronounced *Jow Ming*, meaning "Shining Bright"), when the youth himself ceremonially accepted the Bodhisattva Precepts. Zhizang is often included in the lists of monks from Kaishan and other temples who lent their efforts to Emperor Wu's translation and other Buddhist projects.

The teachings set forth in these and other scriptures were not accepted by the entire Buddhist community uncritically. Some Buddhists of the day criticized doctrines advanced by Mahayana Buddhism (bodhisattva-style Buddhism) as being fundamentally non-Buddhist in nature. Such critics were often in the Precepts school, and they were dismissively referred to by Mahayanists as "Hinayanists" (small-vehicle Buddhists that are concerned only about their own salvation, not with saving all beings). Concepts of "Buddha nature" and "emptiness" advanced in the Mahayana texts that Emperor Wu emphasized, like the Nirvana Sutra and Prajnaparamita Sutra, were highly contentious, for they suggested metaphysical ideas that seemed to transcend the basic Buddhist teaching of cause and effect. But Emperor Wu was undeterred by the doctrinal contradictions some Buddhists found in the scriptures he promoted. He glossed over the delicate theological questions Mahayana Buddhism's metaphysics created and embraced its messianic vision. Metaphysics had always been part of the mysticism used to extend Chinese imperial rule. Astrology, *feng shui*, and medicine were all products of China's long-developed metaphysical proclivities. In such a society, it wasn't too hard for these new Mahayana Buddhist metaphysical ideas to gain acceptance.

Emperor Wu ranked the sutras in importance, composed his own commentaries on them, which he espoused publically, and placed them solidly in the ideological foundation of his rule. He saw this as the proper exalted role, after all, of a *chakravartin* and bodhisattva monarch in China's burgeoning Buddhist society.

The Bodhisattva Path that was so exalted in Emperor Wu's era represents a critical divergence between Mahayana Buddhism of East Asia and Theravada Buddhism, the branch of the religion that remains dominant today in certain South and Southeast Asian countries. The split between these two groups might be traced to different views among the earliest factions of Buddhist sects and how they viewed the historical Buddha. Some scholars suggest that Mahayana Buddhism may have developed with an emphasis on supernatural occurrences credited to or associated with the Buddha, either miracles reportedly performed by him or strange phenomena associated with events in his life. For example, flowers were said to rain from the sky when he spoke, and an earthquake was said to have occurred at the time of his death. On the other hand, Theravada Buddhism tended to emphasize Buddha's more mundane side, especially the practical guidance and logic found in his teachings.

As time went on, the role of a bodhisattva, who in early times was seen as a person who was nearing the apex of Buddhahood in his cycle of lives, took on more supernatural aspects. Eventually certain branches of Indian Buddhism believed bodhisattvas were able to undergo magical transformation and to take on any of a number of different bodies to accomplish their great mission of helping beings. Thus they might appear as a lay person or cleric, male or female, a child, or even an animal. The bodhisattva Kwan Yin, who is worshiped extensively in East Asia, for example, is traditionally said to appear in the world in thirty-two different incarnations, including all of the above.

In the year 504, three years after assuming power, Emperor Wu became disenchanted with Taoism. He had long engaged that native Chinese philosophy, along with its idealistic vision of naturalness and immortality. Taoist ideas, after all, lay at the heart of Chinese medicine and much else in the culture, and the religion was naturally part of most people's concern with their own health and well-being. But Emperor Wu decided to make a formal break with Taoism's philosophy and much of its alchemical hodgepodge. As time went on and his faith in Buddhism grew more fervent, he issued an edict ordering people to turn away from Taoism and support the Buddha Way instead. He also composed a vow entitled "Forsaking the [Taoist] Way, Turning to Buddha," and led twenty thousand clergy, aristocrats, and commoners in a public ceremony where the vow was recited.

By the year 513 or so, the emperor had become a strict vegetarian. Around that time he also ceased engaging in sex. The *Book of Liang*, the dynasty's official history, says he "did not visit the women's quarters." Obviously this left the hundreds of concubines that spent their lives hoping for a liaison with the emperor in a hopeless situation. But records say Emperor Wu released most of his harem from captivity, allowing them to return to their old families. He apparently maintained his commitment to celibacy and vegetarianism until his death in the year 549.

Emperor Wu himself took the Bodhisattva Vow on at least four occasions in grand ceremonies. Perhaps the grandest and most significant of these ceremonies occurred in the year 519, when he underwent this ceremony at a place called No Impediment Hall in the Flowered Woods Garden at the rear of his palace.

But the Bodhisattva Vow he recited and the ceremony that the emperor underwent publically in the year 519 were different from what had taken place before. In the years leading up to that grand ceremony, the emperor's house monks had created a new version of these precepts distilled from many previous different versions, and the ceremony was altered. While in former times the vows were designed for and taken by home-leaving monks, Emperor Wu emphasized the still-controversial idea that people who had not left home could also take these precepts. He gave them a new official name, the "Home-Abiding, Home-Leaving Bodhisattva Precepts."

In 521, Emperor Wu built Tongtai Temple, a place that would thereafter be an important stage for his religious activities. The temple's location, directly across the street from a rear gate of the palace wall, was convenient, allowing the emperor to pass his double life as emperor and monk out of the public eye. In the years 527, 529, and 546, he repeated his acceptance of the Bodhisattva Vow at this location. After each such event he took up residence in Tongtai Temple as a monk, studying and doing chores with the other clerics who lived there.

Each time Emperor Wu relinquished his position as emperor, he created a crisis for his family and the rest of the aristocracy who enjoyed their high positions through his patronage. The ruling factions that depended on him were then compelled to cough up a big sum of money, essentially a ransom, given to the Buddhist Church, to return the emperor to formal power. After the ransom was paid, the emperor would go back across the street to the palace and resume his imperial duties. But even in the palace, he'd retain his monkish lifestyle, sleeping on a floor mat in an unadorned room of the inner chambers.

Emperor Wu's personal lifestyle and commitment to Buddhist principles faithfully followed the Confucian ideal that a king must be a model for his subjects. Though he spent lavishly on building monuments to his religion, his personal lifestyle appears to have remained simple.

As I mentioned during my visit to Nanhua Temple, until Emperor Wu's time monks of the Buddhist tradition were able to eat meat under certain circumstances, such as if the animal was not killed specifically for the monk to eat. The idea behind this was that the evil karma arising from violating the first precept, the avoidance of killing of sentient life, would not apply to the monk himself. However, Emperor Wu rejected this idea and enforced a ban on all meat-eating among monks. That ban has continued more or less uninterrupted until today in China's Buddhist monasteries.

28. Emperor Wu and His Family

WHY WOULD A SUCCESSFUL military general and man of letters, a person who had reached the pinnacle of power, embrace a pacifistic religion like Buddhism?

It's doubtlessly true that Emperor Wu saw, in Buddhism's doctrines, a place to find personal refuge from his bloody age. But he also used Buddhism as a way to consolidate his rule using a religious ideology, a divine and popular metaphysic of liberation that provided cover for more mundane political interests. Buddhist doctrines offered a coherent view of life, and combining Buddhism with Confucianism, a philosophy that reinforced social relations and familial solidarity, was especially useful and important. The combination of these two faiths fused ideas of social harmony (Buddhism) and loyalty (Confucianism). These were ideal models for promoting stability in a feudal society.

Less cynically, Buddhism offered a relatively progressive, one could even say "rational," set of beliefs in a superstitious age. In the years after Emperor Wu seized power, he largely rejected Taoist ideas in favor of Buddhist doctrines. His personal conversion was deeply sincere, not the thin religious profession that can be expected of a politician, then and now. Emperor Wu's conversion to Buddhism bordered on revolutionary. It involved unprecedented scale and cost. Why such devotion?

Doubtless, Emperor Wu's experience with the Jinling Eight, his official and royal friends who met for "pure conversation" about Buddhism many years prior, led him toward his faith. He also developed a deep belief in an afterlife. Where this belief came from is especially telling.

A legend that helps explain Emperor Wu's deep conversion concerns his wife Lady Shao (464–499). The only woman that the emperor ever married, Lady Shao bore him three daughters but no sons. She died prematurely at the age of thirty-six from an unknown illness just prior to Xiao Yan's two-year campaign to dethrone the mad boy emperor Baojuan.

Prior to Lady Shao's death, Xiao Yan brought a single concubine into his household, a young woman named Ding. Lady Shao despised and resented her husband's new mistress. According to the story, her venomous loathing for the woman led to an event that had deep impact on Emperor Wu's religious beliefs and long effect on Chinese culture. The story says that soon after Emperor Wu occupied the throne, his late wife appeared to him in a dream, begging for his help. She explained to him from the dream that before she died she had secretly persecuted his new young concubine. As a result she suffered rebirth in the body of a snake, a huge boa constrictor like that "found in the South Seas." Lady Shao begged Emperor Wu to do something to save her from her unhappy rebirth as a reptile.

Shocked by this experience, Emperor Wu more deeply accepted Buddhist teachings about the "wheel of birth and death," and directed his Buddhist teacher Baozhi and others to create a special Buddhist ceremony on behalf of his late wife. In the ceremony for Emperor Wu's wife, much of it composed by Wu himself, the emperor and his Buddhist monks prayed to liberate Lady Shao from her snake's body to a higher realm of rebirth. And Emperor Wu's intercession with the Buddha to help his wife gain a more auspicious birth was reportedly successful. Even today, the Water and Land Ceremony references Lady Shao's experience as part of its inspiration, but the impact of this story spread even more widely.

The ceremony Emperor Wu established to save his wife led to the wide celebration of the Hungry Ghost Festival throughout China. This holiday was thereafter celebrated as a sort of Chinese Halloween. Even today many Chinese, on that holiday, make offerings to deceased ancestors who have purportedly been temporarily let out of hell to wander the world. These unhappy spirits try to satisfy their insatiable appetites as they roam city streets. With big stomachs and tiny necks, they are unable to satisfy their hunger, the karmic consequence of excessive greed during their earthly lives. Thus a folk holiday was born from Emperor Wu's dream and its religious significance, a celebration recently resurrected in today's China.

CROWN PRINCE ZHAO MING (ALSO NAMED XIAO TONG)

At the time he seized control of the country, Emperor Wu had a seven-month-old son by his concubine Ding. The boy's name was Xiao Tong (501–531), and he is famously known in Chinese history by his posthumous title, Zhao Ming. As a youngster Zhao Ming devoted himself to studying the Chinese classics and Buddhist scriptures. Brilliant and precocious, he gained wide fame while still young as the compiler of China's first literary anthology, a translator of Buddhist scriptures, and a composer of poetry. Tragically, he suffered a premature death at the age of thirty. The young prince's verses are still read and studied in China, and localities associated with his life remember him with monuments and libraries.

Emperor Wu and his family affected China in other ways, far surpassing in importance foot binding, hungry ghosts, and literary anthologies. Emperor Wu and Zhao Ming elicited an unprecedented embrace of Buddhism throughout the country. Other emperors had exalted the religion and worked to spread its teachings. But Emperor Wu went so far as to demote China's other great spiritual tradition, Taoism, and made profound changes to Buddhism to integrate it deeply into the fabric of China's culture and politics.

29. Emperor Wu and the Temples of Bell Mountain

Buddhist monks 'midst mountain peaks,
For others' sakes their chants are loud,
But distant city folks there see,
Just peaceful white and drifting clouds.
—*"Visiting the Brothers and Sisters in the Mountains"*
by Wang Wei (701–761)

山中寄诸弟妹　王维著

山中多法侣
禅诵自为群
城郭遥相望
义公习禅寂。

FROM MY OPEN cable car gondola, I look over a wide swath of Bell Mountain's thick forest. The mountain's ancient name must have come from all the Buddhist bells that once rang across these pretty valleys, pealing out each morning from scores of Buddhist temples that nestled in its shady hollows and slopes. In Emperor Wu's age, the mountain offered one of the grandest spectacles of ancient history, a fairy tale–like vista of sedate temples floating high in the clouds. My long cable car ride goes all the way to Bell Mountain's summit, where Love and Honor Temple once stood. Grandest of all the mountain's temples, it was one of Emperor Wu first great projects, constructed in the early years of his reign—an architectural wonder undertaken with utmost reverence as an act of filial piety toward his late father.

A boy, fifteen or so, shares my three-seat gondola with me. He periodically waves and shouts to his three friends in the car ahead of us, no doubt wishing he could have shared the long ride to the top of the mountain with them instead of with a boring foreigner.

"Have you come up here before?" I ask him.

He looks surprised, then nods. "A few times," he says.

In recent years China's press and Internet have witnessed a lot of discussion about the "post-1980" generation, Chinese young people born after 1980 who have a different view of the world than their parents. Those doted-upon children, raised without siblings under China's single-child policy, enjoyed an unprecedented level of attention and were called "little emperors." More recently the "born after 1990" generation has been recognized and has moved into the limelight. That newer generation, with significant disposable income, is driving new fashions and commercial campaigns by Chinese manufacturers and retailers, much like what has happened in Japan and Western countries in the decades since World War II. The post-1990 group is truly a harbinger for change. Eric's son, Kevin, like the boy in my cable car, is in that age group. When Eric speaks of Kevin and that generation, he simply shakes his head and says, "They know everything!" And Eric's description is not meant as the usual cynical remark that the old heap upon the young. In critical ways, the new generation really does "know everything." The brightest among them understand how their elders messed up the world and why their parents are clueless about where the world's going and what wonders it may hold in store in the new digital and biomedical age. They are technically savvy. I wonder if the boy next to me is in the "know everything" camp, or whether he might instead be one of the many denizens of China's new "opium dens," the Internet bars. In those smoky places, many of China's young men drape themselves languidly across chairs, chain-smoke cigarettes, and blast virtual Nazis with virtual machine guns and rocket launchers.

"Why are you visiting here?" the boy asks me.

"I think this place is important for Chinese history," I reply. "Have you ever heard of Emperor Wu?"

"Of course," the boy says. "He was the most famous emperor who lived here. He built many temples on this mountain and made Nanjing a famous city in ancient times."

"Oh, you know a lot," I say. "Do you study Emperor Wu in school?"

"In school we study Nanjing history, and also my parents told me stories and gave me some books."

I gather that the young man in the cable car is in the "know everything" group.

Emperor Wu's temple-building campaign on this mountain and other locations was a fundamental part of his effort to spread Buddhism. Aristocrats and commoners both contributed to the building effort and worshipped in the new temples. Famous Buddhist monks, "Dharma masters," lived and taught in these places, some receiving public acclaim close to rock-star status. A poem written two hundred years after Wu's time by a famous Tang dynasty poet named Du Mu paid tribute to that brilliant era and its Buddhist landscapes, saying, "Four hundred eighty temples of the Southern dynasty, so many pavilions and terraces amid the fog and rain." The actual number of temples even surpassed what Du Mu described. A memorial to the throne written in the year 522 indicated that more than five hundred Buddhist temples then existed around Nanjing alone. Other ancient records indicate that within the entire territory of the country (including only Southern China because the Wei dynasty controlled the north) a total of 2,846 temples were officially recognized. The list included only temples large enough to be officially noted. Smallish temples and shrines, too numerous to account for, were not included.

In that age around eighty large temples sat amid Bell Mountain's forests and meadows. Unfortunately, all of them are now gone, victims of penurious centuries and in a few cases of modernity and political passions. Only a few of the ancient sites where they stood have been excavated by Chinese archeologists, though more digging is planned. The tumbled underbrush and soft soil below the cable car may reveal more clues about Bodhidharma etched on cold and forgotten monuments, toppled and buried in forgotten upheavals.

We know something about these old religious habitats. The *Continued Biographies* offers some information about these old temples and their illustrious inhabitants. It was in these temples that Emperor Wu assembled and supported his well-educated and highly talented coterie of monks from home and abroad, tasking them to undertake Buddhist translation and other projects on an immense scale.

One of the early famous temples on this mountain, built before

Emperor Wu came to power, was called Dinglin Temple (*Dinglin* means "Samadhi Forest"). That temple, which served as home to several famous Buddhist teachers, housed a large library of Buddhist texts that its inhabitants had collected, composed, or translated. Another temple was later built down the slope from Dinglin and was thus called Lower Dinglin Temple. The two Dinglin Temples were widely famous. Both figure heavily in Emperor Wu and Bodhidharma's histories.

When Emperor Wu came to power, he wanted to make use of Upper Dinglin Temple's important library and moved much of it to a new hall that he built within the Tai Cheng Palace, a big and specially built library in his imperial garden, the place called Flowered Woods. The library, called Flowered Woods Hall, was the focus of important religious and secular literary activity. It provided materials used by the Crown Prince Zhao Ming to develop China's first literary anthology and was the repository for newly created Buddhist bibliographies and reference books created at Emperor Wu's orders. Naturally, the Flowered Woods Hall also was the repository for hundreds of new Buddhist translations, the many thousands of pages of new Buddhist scripture that continued to arrive from the Indian subcontinent along with foreign teachers to expound them.

It was in this ferment of activity created by Emperor Wu that a story solidly connecting Bodhidharma's tradition to Nanjing took shape. This story, found in the *Continued Biographies*, is about the monk named Sengfu, a monk almost forgotten today who was, says the record, Bodhidharma's oldest disciple.

According to Sengfu's story in the *Continued Biographies*, he lived in two of Bell Mountain's long-lost temples, both located on the mountain's northwest side. He resided in those places during the period 494 to 524, a time that covers more than two decades early in Emperor Wu's rule and when the emperor's religious activities reached high dudgeon. Sengfu's story offers clues not only about the life of this obscure disciple of Bodhidharma but about his teacher as well. Scholars concur that Sengfu is the same monk referred in later records as Daoyu, who is described in the Zen literature to have "attained the bones" of Bodhidharma's teaching. Critical information that appears in Sengfu's biography helps piece together the hazy events that occurred before Bodhidharma's Zen became China's mainstream religion. Most important, his biography

suggests reasons why Bodhidharma became highly honored in subsequent ages. Here is the *Continued Biographies* record of Sengfu, Bodhidharma's oldest disciple, and an inhabitant of Bell Mountain during its
Buddhist golden age:

> Sengfu: His family name [before becoming a monk] was
> Wang. His home was in Qi County in Taiyuan Prefecture.
> [As a young child] he was weak and unable to do things.
> He [was also] introverted and avoided groups. As the years
> passed he studied and attained insight. Some in his village
> considered him strange. He was different from those who
> lacked humanity. Also he naturally loved quiet contemplation.
> He roamed far and wide. He packed his bag and went every-
> where, unsuccessfully looking for a teacher. Then he heard
> about Zen master Bodhidharma, whose illustrious teachings
> [were about] the practice of perception. So [Sengfu] went up
> to the cliffs and caves to ask [Bodhidharma] about deep wis-
> dom. He followed Bodhidharma and became a home-leaver
> [took his vows] with him. He embraced [Bodhidharma's
> teachings] thoroughly and never again asked about questions
> of [scriptural] doctrine. He practiced the samadhi [Zen] teach-
> ings faithfully, [as he had already] received and exhausted the
> meaning of scriptures. Moreover he understood that the truly
> enlightened do not speak [of enlightenment]. In the Jian Wu
> era of the Qi dynasty [494] he moved to Yang Nian [Nanjing].
> He resided at Lower Samadhi Forest Temple on Bell Moun-
> tain. He delighted in its forests and meadows, finding it an
> ideal place for the mind to dwell. He would stroll through the
> frost and ice [of winter]. He gained spiritual authority, and his
> only possessions were nothing more than the three garments
> and six objects [traditional articles possessed by a monk]. He
> entered [the Way] according to principle appropriate to the
> time and was taken as a model by the clerical and lay com-
> munities. [Sengfu's] fame became such that the emperor and
> his court called on him to come and speak [to them], and
> they were disappointed that he would not do so. [Although]
> only a short distance from the emperor, [Sengfu] would not

meet him. His actions were widely recognized and extolled. Emperor Wu honored his pure virtue [even without meeting him], praising him highly. [Emperor Wu] commanded craftsmen to examine Sengfu's room [at Lower Dinglin Temple] and build [a replica] at Kaishan Temple [nearby on Bell Mountain] to receive him. [The Emperor] feared Sengfu was too fond of staying in the wilderness. But each time Sengfu would arrive at the gate [of Kaishan Temple], he would lean on his staff and sigh, saying, "[It's like] obstructing one's view with a tiny window." [So the emperor] made the quarters much larger. [But Sengfu said] "Should I prefer a big, grand place over a simple thatched hut? A quiet place is all that's needed. If the ancients thought such a place adequate, why should I want more than that? That is what delights the ears and eyes!"

Sengfu wished to travel to Min [Sichuan] to visit Mount Emei [a famous scenic mountain that is the legendary home of the Bodhisattva Samantabhadra]. He met with Xiao Yuanzhao [elder brother of Emperor Wu and the governor of Sichuan] and traveled to Sichuan. There he traveled widely to wherever he pleased, but though the road was difficult, he never forgot the "Three practices" [of Zen Buddhism, namely perception, meditation, practice], [and he] did not promote scriptural teachings. Only holding this [Zen teaching] did he pass his days and nights there. [In this way] Zen teachings flourished in Sichuan. After a long time [Sengfu] returned to Jinling [Nanjing], where he again lived at Kaishan Temple . . . Soon afterward [Sengfu] died at Kaishan Temple. He was sixty-one years old. The date was the fifth year of the Putong era [524]. He was buried in front of the main gate of Lower Dinglin Temple. The Emperor [Wu] mourned him and submitted gifts [to the temple to honor him]. At the time [Sengfu] became ill, there were some who urged him to take expensive treatments. [But] Sengfu propped himself up [on his deathbed] and firmly said, "Prolonging one's life through expensive means is far from the Way! Anything left in my room should be distributed to the monks. After I die my body should be discarded in a mountain valley. Isn't it best that it provide

food to birds and beasts? Don't make a fancy coffin for carrying my body." But his disciples wept and could not bear to
follow [his instructions]. A memorial was carved [in stone] to
commemorate his virtue. Princess Yong Xing [Emperor Wu's
oldest daughter] proclaimed acceptance of Buddhist vows in
a public ceremony honoring Sengfu. She asked the Crown
Prince [Zhao Ming] to compose [the words of the memorial].
He ordered King Xiangdong [a relative to Emperor Wu] to
make the monument. It was erected at the temple.

It's fascinating that while so much attention is traditionally paid to the
meeting of Emperor Wu and Bodhidharma, the relationship between the
emperor and Bodhidharma's oldest disciple, reliably recorded above, is
hardly known in Zen circles. Why is this so? No doubt it's because this
old record directly contradicts the official Bodhidharma story derived
from later literature and passed down through generations until today.
The biography quoted above is an early (circa 650 CE) and relatively
impartial account of Sengfu's life that connects him with Bodhidharma
in the "cliffs and caves" of the Luoyang area about forty years (about
487–489) before the official Bodhidharma story says the latter arrived
in China (in 527). But the Sengfu biography agrees time-wise with
Bodhidharma's story in the same book, enhancing the reliability of each
account. Sengfu's story also suggests that Bodhidharma had a wide
reputation as a teacher, as Sengfu must have received such honor from
Emperor Wu at least partly through his association with his teacher. By
locating Bodhidharma in the mountains near Luoyang at the time in
question, it suggests the possibility that Bodhidharma occupied his cave
on Mount Song even before Shaolin Temple was formally established
there by the Northern Wei dynasty emperor around the year 496. Perhaps it was Sengfu, not Bodhidharma's more famous disciple Huike, that
originally sought out Bodhidharma in his cave (more on this later). Its
location on Mount Song, long China's sacred central mountain, would
have been a natural place for a missionary monk to live and practice,
with Buddhist and Taoist temples already occupying its many slopes
and valleys.

As I ride the cable car, I can see the general area where Lower Dinglin
Temple, Sengfu's first residence, sat on Bell Mountain's slopes. The exact

site of that temple remains unexplored, and prospects for digging there remain uncertain because it currently sits on a closed military reserve. Another temple site within my field of vision, close to Lower Samadhi Temple, was Kaishan Temple, the place referred to in Sengfu's biography as where Emperor Wu cajoled Sengfu to come and live. Kaishan was an especially important temple in Emperor Wu's world. There the emperor invited his most eminent house monks to reside. Thus it is very noteworthy that Emperor Wu prepared a place at that temple for Bodhidharma's oldest disciple, and that Sengfu did in fact spend many years of his life there. Given this scenario, it seems unlikely that Emperor Wu did not know of Sengfu's teacher, Bodhidharma, and would not have invited him to present himself at the court if this were possible.

As I look down from the cable car, the big question posed by Sengfu's biography is obvious. If Sengfu died in 524 and spent a good portion of the previous thirty years living on the slopes of Bell Mountain, why did he never, even once, respond to invitations to visit Emperor Wu's court? I can see both temple locations and the place where the palace once stood quite easily from my perch in the cable car. Why did Sengfu's devotion to the "way of the ancients" keep him from even once visiting the most famous center of Buddhist activity of his age, along with its "Bodhisattva Emperor," brilliant Buddhist crown prince, and its rich collection of Buddhist scriptures and other texts? All these things were only a short walk from his longtime home!

Our gondola finally reaches the top of the mountain and my co-rider happily joins his waiting friends. I look around the mountaintop and quickly realize that nothing appears to remain of Emperor Wu's grand Love and Honor Temple project except massive boulders, jumbled rocks, and scrubby trees. One could never guess what stood here once. But while the mountaintop itself has little to offer related to its ancient fame, the view in every direction is beautifully expansive. It's clear today, and the vista covers hundreds of square miles, encompassing most of Nanjing and every other direction.

The peak has a lot of uneven ground. It's hard to imagine that about fifteen hundred years ago a huge monastery occupied this place where there is now so little flat area. The mountain seems to have only a small crown and the slopes around it are steep. But records indicate the monastery here in the year 510 CE housed more than one thousand monks and covered two hundred acres. Descriptions tell of scores of large and small halls and pavilions, with many monuments and stupas tucked in the mountain's crevices. The place reportedly had grand dining and ceremonial halls. A passage describes the temple perched on the high mountain to appear "like heaven itself." The temple's basic completion required nine years, plus several more years to finish auxiliary structures like a famous seven-story pagoda. The number of people needed just to carry the building materials up the high mountain must have been enormous. And that was just the beginning. Maintaining a thousand monks high in the clouds was no small logistical feat. Somehow the temple's Buddha statues, recorded to be fifty feet tall, had to be brought up here and either propped up or assembled. Now what remains of the entire colossal undertaking is nothing but rocky landscape. All things, say Buddhism, arise and pass away due to causes and conditions. Apparently there's been a lot of erosive conditions on this mountain during the past fifteen hundred years.

While this was Emperor Wu's most ambitious temple project, it was far from being the only big one. During his forty-seven-year reign he built roughly ten new Buddhist temples every year. Hundreds of temples already existed in his empire from previous centuries, but the scope and speed of construction and renovation under Emperor Wu was unprecedented. The sums spent on buildings and grand Buddha icons evoked intense criticism from later Chinese historians.

30. Mufu Mountains and Bodhidharma's Nanjing Cave

IT'S ANOTHER COLD November morning in Nanjing. A recent cold snap dropped temperatures all over North China by twenty-five degrees almost overnight. The inch or so of the snow that fell last night heralds colder days ahead. I wait until things warm a bit then leave my hotel on Huangpu Road, east of where Emperor Wu's palace once stood, and walk north, then turn to walk west along Zhujiang ("Pearl River") Road. After a short distance I cross the bridge over Clear Creek, a waterway that once ran around the northeast perimeter of Emperor Wu's palace, and continue west on a small street comprised mainly of small eateries. Here is where the north protective ramparts of the palace once stood. A row of pastry shops, laundries, real estate offices, and sundry kiosks line the small road where battlements presided over siege armies.

I turn right and cross another bridge above Clear Creek then continue west along its opposite shore beneath some tall buildings. Around here is where construction crews reportedly uncovered some Liang dynasty ruins while they were doing work in 2006. Workmen uncovered the remains of old posts and other detritus about two meters deep. Experts claimed they were remains from Tongtai Temple. This was the temple where Emperor Wu lived each time he renounced the throne. Legends are not unanimous about whether Emperor Wu met Bodhidharma here at the temple location or at the Flowered Woods Garden within the rear of the palace walls, likely just to the south of where I am.

Emerging from the walkway along the creek onto Peace Avenue, I hail a cab. I tell the driver I want to go to the Mufu Mountains, the low mountains that follow the Yang-tse River around the north side of Nanjing. He asks for a more specific location, but I'm at a loss to know exactly what to tell him. My map shows a spot called Labor Mountain in the midst of the Mufu Mountains, so I point at that. He nods, and after a ten-minute ride I emerge from the cab on a broad street, separated from the Mufu Mountains by new apartment construction. "I can't get any closer," the driver says. I pay him and walk up a lane through the developments, trying to find my way to a foot trail that the map indicates leads through the scrub forest on the hills' slopes. As I walk back and forth at the end of the street, someone helpfully points me toward a trailhead, and I make my way up the steep grade. Along the hill are trails and small roads that appear ideal for hikers. At the top of the first hill I encounter a broad, impressive vista of the Yang-tse River flowing along the far side of the high ground; a score or more of barges and ships are navigating the river in each direction. Upriver I can see the Nanjing Bridge about four miles away. Acacia and low-lying pines line more trails that lead through low peaks to my right. In Chinese these hills are called mountains, and I suppose that in English a better word to describe them would be *bluffs* or *palisades*. On the river side of the hills their bare white rocks plunge steeply to the Yang-tse's shore. The jagged, white dolomite exposed in the cliff faces and outcroppings is the source of one ancient name for Nanjing, Baixia, a name that means "Beneath the White."

These bluffs and shores have witnessed some momentous events. When Zheng He, China's famous world navigator who, it has been suggested, circumnavigated the world before Magellan did, tested his ships for ocean voyages, he did so on the Yang-tse backwater sloughs that lie opposite these hills. From my vantage point I can see where he prepared and tested his famous five-hundred-foot-long ships.

In Bodhidharma's story, here is where he reportedly crossed the Yang-tse River standing on a "single blade of grass."

There are few other people on the hills today. I make my way along the trails to some high points overlooking the river and so get an ever-broader view of the place. For at least twenty-five centuries each of these small peaks has served as a military outpost, guarding Nanjing from military attacks. Everywhere beneath the low brush are broken rocks and shards, stuff from which ancient signal towers were constructed. Below, along the slopes facing the river, a few ghostly World War II–era pillboxes remind strollers of more recent tragic events.

The Yang-tse is a true colossus among the world's rivers. It drains a watershed immense enough to have a large number of its own species, like the Yang-tse dolphin. It is the world's third-longest river after the Nile and Amazon and is probably the world's greatest commercial waterway, for the number of ships and barges that can be seen at any point on the river is often startling. It's a beautiful river to watch.

From a high peak I look across the Yang-tse to the Liu He ("Six Harmonies") district where Zen says Bodhidharma reached the far shore after crossing the river. Now, Six Harmonies has become a wide industrial zone dotted with chemical plants. Once the subject of poetry, the place now is marked by smokestacks and natural gas flares from refineries. But time is long. I wonder if a hundred years from now a wiser planet will restore the place to honor Bodhidharma instead of building new PVC plants to make feedstock for toy factories and plumbing pipes.

I round a bend on the trail and come upon what at first seems to be some sort of homeless encampment. Then I notice that the tables and makeshift structures on the forested hillside are set under a very unusual rock formation that overhangs the place. The stone of the rock is gnarled, almost decorative, quite unlike the layered limestone in other parts of the Mufu hills. The position of this place, nestled away from the river's exposure and under tall trees, gives it a measure of protection from the rain and wind. Under the rocky overhang I spy an elderly Chinese man dressed in the blue work tunic of a monk. He turns and smiles at me with a largely toothless grin and motions me to sit on one of many chairs set up near some tables in front of what appear to be two entrances into the rock overhang. The monk apparently lives here. The entrance's makeshift doors of plastic and large wood branches lead into caves. Then I see the characters carved on the bluff between the two openings that say BODHIDHARMA'S CAVE. I sit down where the monk has indicated. He sits down across from me, smiling with a round, friendly face. I ask him about his story.

Huiyuan (the name means "Wisdom Source" and sounds the same as the famous translator at East Woods Temple) took up residence here at Bodhidharma's cave in 2002. He originally studied under a Buddhist master named Zhurong at Longchang Temple, not far from Nanjing. Longchang Temple is famous as a Precepts school temple, the same type of Buddhism practiced by Daoxuan, author of the *Continued*

Biographies. There's a resurgence of popularity for this Buddhist school in China. Longchang Temple is now the main temple of this Buddhist sect, and every year hundreds of people formally take the precepts there in grand ceremonies.

Huiyuan and I exchange information. He's happy to learn I'm from the United States, and before long I explain that I'm traveling through China looking for traces of Bodhidharma. Using an almost unintelligible local dialect, Huiyuan then starts relating Bodhidharma's story, but the version he is telling me is an odd one. There's an old text called the *Bodhidharma Biography* (达磨传) that dates from the late Tang or early Song period (around the years 900 to 1100). It's widely known to be apocryphal (a fake record). Following that story, Huiyuan says that Bodhidharma "flew from India to China in two hours," where he then met Emperor Wu. Emperor Wu didn't understand Bodhidharma's words, so Bodhidharma left. He also says that Bodhidharma then met the Second Ancestor Huike, who according to this account was teaching the Dharma somewhere in North China. Bodhidharma asked Huike where the Dharma was to be found in what he taught. This seemingly insulting question upset Huike, who responded by striking Bodhidharma in the face with his iron prayer beads, knocking out Bodhidharma's two front teeth. Bodhidharma, magically knowing that if he spit out the teeth, China would experience a three-year drought, swallowed them instead. Bodhidharma then left Huike and traveled back to Nanjing, where he discovered this ideal cave, and he remained here sitting in meditation for a period of time. Emperor Wu, knowing that Bodhidharma was located near Nanjing, sent two people to get Bodhidharma and bring him back to his palace. However, when the two people got close to Bodhidharma as he sat on this mountain, two nearby mountains suddenly slammed together, closing off their path. Indeed, near the cave where Huiyuan tells me this fantastical story sit two mountains that appear scissored together. Huiyuan points them out to me.

Although this version of events surrounding Bodhidharma is fanciful, it goes back quite far in history. From the mid-eighth century on, there are different accounts that contain parts of the above story. What is clear is that, starting from about the mid-700s, Bodhidharma became a larger-than-life figure to the Chinese Zen world, and certain myths about him became widespread. The dividing line between simple historical uncertainty and obvious myths about his life occurred around that time.

While Huiyuan is telling me the story of Bodhidharma, a man approaches us and sits on one of the other chairs around the table. When Huiyuan is finished they exchange some words, and it is obvious they are well-acquainted. I greet him and learn that his name is. Xu (pronounced *Sue*) and he comes up the mountain every day or so to deliver bottled water to Huiyuan. "The water situation here is not good," he says.

Mr. Xu, whose accent is far easier to understand than Huiyuan's is, tells me that many people come up the mountain on weekends to hear Huiyuan lecture about Buddhism. He says the table would be filled with people who normally come to hear him but for the fact that it is chilly today. Then I ask if it's okay to look in the caves, and Huiyuan says to go ahead and take a look. I stick my head in the door of the cave that appears to contain some statues inside and discover that its interior is about fifteen feet square. In the center are some carved Buddhas, while on the dirt and stone floor there are a handful of bowing and meditation cushions. At the back of the cave there is a small shrine set up to honor Bodhidharma that contains a stone engraved with his presumed likeness.

I ask Mr. Xu if people in Nanjing are aware of the special history connected with the place and want to preserve it. He answers that this is certainly true. He says Nanjing is not a big capital city like Beijing and Xian, where international sights like the Great Wall and Terra Cotta Warriors draw crowds from everywhere. Instead, Nanjing has a special historical flavor connected to certain important periods in Chinese history. One of those periods, the South-North dynasties period, the time that surrounded Emperor Wu's rule, has special importance. Nanjing people are aware of and very proud of that fact, even if people elsewhere don't appreciate it.

Could Bodhidharma really have stayed at this place? While the story is obviously silly, it might have evolved from some real geographic connection to the old sage. Because the cave is such an unusual geographical feature on the dolomite slopes of the mountains, it seems likely that later storytellers would have connected him to the place for this reason. However, if Bodhidharma actually stayed in the Nanjing area for a long period of time, as I believe he did, then this place might be one of many where he spent some time. The location, which during Emperor Wu's time was concealed in the river hills about five miles from the city, was a suitable place for him to avoid the world. Perhaps in Bodhidharma's day believers made their way into the hills to hear him speak. He did, after all, have "followers like a city," and many of them could have conveniently lived in Nanjing and visited Bodhidharma in nearby areas, much as Huiyuan's students do now. Maybe they peered quietly into the cave to see him gazing in meditation at its stone wall.

While other emperors might have made a fuss about someone refusing to come see them, Emperor Wu apparently did not take offense at this. There are many other stories related to his rule that indicate he was a man of reasoned disposition who avoided punishing people whose actions might have led other emperors to order severe punishments. Emperor Wu's oldest daughter neglected her studies and fancied a handsome aristocrat, also a close relative, who secretly wanted to gain the throne. The two visited Emperor Wu at the palace, intent on killing him, but Wu, knowing the plot, prevented it from happening while maintaining a friendly and patient manner with them. He did not punish them afterward. Such stories about Emperor Wu show he could have tolerated Bodhidharma's presence without forcing him to come to the court or punishing his failure to do so.

As the day recedes I bid farewell to Huiyuan and Mr. Xu and make my way down the mountain toward the Yang-tse. Along the riverbank, the city of Nanjing has created a park on new landfill that stretches two or three miles in each direction. When I visited the spot a year ago, the place was bare ground intersected by the foundation of a new road. Now the park and road are finished, and the ponds and traditional bridges in the park have attracted a few men who quietly try their luck fishing in the new artificial pools. I walk a few hundred yards to a new dock where some boats are moored and some large bronze statues of four horses plus a dragon appear to be coming out of the river. A story about the place says that some ancient kings of China came here on horseback. Suddenly one of the horses turned into a dragon, an omen that its rider would soon become emperor. Naturally, he did so. The spot, called Five Horses Crossing the Yang-tse, is considered one of the "forty-eight famous scenes" of ancient Nanjing. Some other statues would be appropriate here, including one of Bodhidharma standing on his stalk of bamboo and heading out over the placid waves with his imperial pursuers watching him from the shore.

Unfortunately, the new bus terminal at the site is still under construction, and without bus service or any visible taxis on the new road, I end up walking two or three miles back to the north end of Nanjing's Central Road, which stops near the river. I pause near the end of my walk to visit the slim white granite memorial stele commemorating the thousands of Chinese who were executed here at the riverbank by invading Japanese troops during World War II. Night is falling when I finally manage to wave down a taxi.

31. The Fusing of Confucianism and Buddhism under Emperor Wu

EMBRACING BUDDHISM but largely rejecting Taoism, Emperor Wu nonetheless continued to honor China's third religion, the one concerned with statecraft, known as Confucianism. Confucian philosophy emphasized loyalty and filial piety, and among the first temples the emperor built were two that honored his late mother and father.

For the first few hundred years after Buddhism arrived in China, the delineation between Buddhism and Confucianism gradually blurred. Emperors who promulgated and spread Confucian rhetoric to legitimize their rule absorbed Buddhist beliefs into their propaganda. But many Buddhists were at pains to maintain the distinction between these two movements. Previously I mentioned that Huiyuan, the famous monk and translator who lived at East Woods Temple, wrote a treatise entitled "A Monk Does Not Bow to a King," meant in part to confirm the clear boundary between the two religions. He argued that there is a difference between the home-leaver's life and the world of Confucian loyalties. Monks should not bow before kings, he said, because the realm of the home-leaver was outside normal human relationships. But such relationships were the defining feature of Chinese Confucian society. So how, it must be asked, could these two contradictory philosophies ever find harmony with one another in China? This leads to another facet of how Buddhism transformed itself when it arrived in the Middle Kingdom.

Some of the answer to this dilemma can be explained by a Confucian idea called the "Way of Kings." This Confucian concept, articulated by the Confucian philosopher Mencius (372–289 BCE), prescribed the moral behavior by which a king must guide his country.

Mencius pointed out that a king must first and foremost rule by example. His position in relation to his vassals was likened to the North

Star that sits unmoving in the sky, reposed in "nonaction" while all the other stars move around it. Thus the proper functioning of the empire, according to this astrological metaphor, must take as its model the king's personal virtue. Most Chinese emperors at least tried to project such a virtuous Confucian face to the public (while privately enjoying the benefits of absolute despotism). But Emperor Wu appears to have taken this Confucian model quite seriously. To Emperor Wu, virtuous conduct meant following Buddhism. His sincere performance as a model sovereign fused Mencius's Way of Kings with the Way of Buddha.

King Ashoka, the Buddhist king of India, also emphasized Confucian-like filial loyalty, as evidenced in his writings on old stone monuments that remain from the time of his rule. Undoubtedly, King Ashoka faced the same challenge that Emperor Wu and other Buddhist monarchs faced, which was to make sure that the idea of home-leaving was not confused with the idea of rebelling against one's parents or king. Rebellious princes who might usurp the throne were especially not to be tolerated.

Emperor Wu regarded Confucianism as the "outer" teaching, while Buddhism was the "inner" teaching. Records tell how Emperor Wu emphasized Confucian values to his son, Prince Zhao Ming. At the age of eight, the boy recited the *Filial Classic*, a Confucian text extolling filial piety, to the assembled royal court.

A key to understanding how the two conflicting philosophies of Confucianism and Buddhism merged in China can be further seen in the Buddhist scripture I mentioned earlier called the Dharma King Sutra. This text, which expounds the Bodhisattva Precepts, offered these vows with a Confucian twist, thus smoothing out any kinks in the strange weave of Confucian filial loyalty and Buddhist home-leaving. The text instructs its readers that filial piety, a very Confucian idea, is actually a Buddhist moral demand of central importance:

> At the time when Shakyamuni Buddha first attained Supreme Enlightenment beneath the bodhi tree, he explained the Bodhisattva Precepts. The Buddha expounded filial piety toward one's parents, Senior Masters, and the Three Treasures. Filial piety and obedience, he said, are the True Path [of Buddhahood].

Through this and other texts that were recorded centuries after the Buddha lived, the home-leaving ideal seems to have surrendered to the idea of obedience to one's parents as the true Buddha Way. Using the Dharma King Sutra and other texts, Emperor Wu transformed the Buddhist precepts and created his interestingly named Home-Abiding Home-Leaving Bodhisattva Precepts. This new account of the correct rules for conducting the Bodhisattva Vow ceremony killed two important political birds with one stone. First, it united the idea of loyalty to one's parents with the Buddhist precepts, in modern parlance making them "Buddhist precepts with Chinese characteristics." Second, it went far to dissolve the difference between home-leavers and householders, granting exalted spiritual status to those who did not leave home. The Bodhisattva Vow was tailor-made for the spread of Imperial-Way Buddhism. Now, the original home-leaving teachings of early Buddhism might no longer be seen as the highest ideal of religious life. A *chakravartin* king might be seen as having an even higher religious status. This precepts revolution resonated through history. Emperor Wu's allowing both home-abiders and home-leavers to gain a sort of equal status is significant. Its effects are clearly seen today in Japan and Western countries today where the Bodhisattva Precepts may be taken by both clerical and lay believers.

This point is so important that it is worth emphasizing. With this action, through imperial fiat, Emperor Wu, more than any who had come before him, blurred the distinction between home-leaving and home-abiding Buddhist believers. In a religion that traditionally honored those who "leave the world" as having taken the highest spiritual path, now everyone, whether they were home-leavers or not, could attain a sort of exalted status. Prior to this innovation, the ceremony for receiving the Bodhisattva Precepts was intended for people who would later become or who were already monks. Prior to Emperor Wu, non-home-leavers only received a shortened version of the precepts more suitable for the lay lifestyle. Thus Emperor Wu made it possible for lay people, including emperors, to gain the exalted spiritual status of full-fledged bodhisattvas even though they hadn't left home. Naturally, the most exalted of these non-home-leaving exalted beings was the emperor himself. With a status even higher than the traditional home-leaver, the emperor effectively had his spiritual cake and ate it, too. He could now demand a monk to bow before a king.

32. The Tai Cheng Palace and Hualin Garden

NO TRACES REMAIN, at least above the ground, of the Tai Cheng Palace. The Hualin Hall library where Crown Prince Zhao Ming worked with its thousands of volumes, the first such library in China, is long vanished. The Eastern Palace where learned men from throughout Asia taught Buddhist doctrines to an eager court, as well as the Great Ultimate Hall from which Emperor Wu ruled over his realm, remain, if anything at all, obscure rubble a few meters beneath Taiping Road in modern Nanjing. The same goes for the Tongtai Temple, the place behind the palace, where Emperor Wu lived as a monk after each occasion of his trying to leave the world.

I walk north along Taiping Road toward Dark Warrior Lake. According to my estimate, the street lies nearly on the central axis of where Emperor Wu's palace stood. Now, on each side of the street, modern buildings sit above multiple layers of rubble from lost dynasties. The South-North dynasties period, the time when the Liang dynasty held sway, sits somewhere in the lower levels of the debris. As I proceed north from Taiping Road's intersection with Pearl River Street, I pass over what was likely the inner palace area, the place where the Qi emperor Baojuan had his musk hall, where deer musk was applied to the walls to enhance the sexual atmosphere of the place, the site of orgiastic parties. It's where Jade Slave sexually mesmerized the teenage boy and where plots to kill high officials were spawned and approved. Nanjing's modern nightclub district stretches to the east. An area of amusement today, it is also where the emperors of old took their pleasures with their nightly selections from the imperial harem.

Two particular symbols of modernity, a Starbucks and a Costa Coffee shop, compete side by side on a corner of Taiping Street. I enter the Costa Coffee shop to order an espresso. Three young girls are working the counter, and since there are no other customers waiting, I take the opportunity to ask them a question.

"Do you ever consider that this was the place where the emperor lived during the South-North dynasties?"

The girls look at me a little shocked, partly because I asked the question in Chinese and partly because of its strange content.

One girl seems to have little idea at all about the history of the place. "When was that?" she asks.

"It was about fifteen hundred years ago," I say. "Emperor Wu lived here. From my calculations I think this spot was where his private living area was located. Over there"—I point to the south—"was his Great Ultimate Hall where he sat on his throne. That was his court. That way was his Flowered Woods Garden, where he liked to relax."

Two of the girls quickly catch on to what I'm saying and agree with me. "It's true," says one. "This is probably where the emperor lived. I can't say I've ever thought about it, but there are many people who study this and know a lot."

I get my espresso, and one of the girls gives me some advertising literature about the British chain that owns the coffee shop. On the back of the brochure it proclaims the company's slogan: "With every drop a bit of history!"

After I drink the coffee, I wave good-bye to the girls behind the counter and continue my walk north along Taiping Road. The great palace is buried ignominiously beneath pizza parlors and convenience stores. At the intersection of a little street called Yang-tse River Back Street, I see an odd clustering of pillars grouped together on the corner. It seems like either an artistic work or a memorial or both. The sixteen round pillars are grouped in receding rows and heights. Each is topped with some retro sort of traditional décor. I remember an old news story from Nanjing that described a location where some archeologists claimed to have discovered parts of the old palace, perhaps even part of Flowered Woods Garden. I ask a newspaper seller what the pillars are for. He shrugs and says he doesn't know. Maybe they don't mean anything.

Emperor Wu took the Bodhisattva Precepts in Flowered Woods Garden, perhaps just at this spot, in the year 519. Maybe the pillars mark where he lectured to the public about points of doctrine, about original enlightenment or Buddha nature. Perhaps this is where the grand ceremony was held to honor Bodhidharma's senior disciple Sengfu when he died. And maybe someone in a local university or historical bureau is figuring all this out and will make it public someday.

Some accounts say the Tongtai Temple was located about where the Beijing Road Peace Park now sits in the north part of modern Nanjing, a couple of blocks north of where I am now and just south of Dark Warrior Lake. Other scholars dispute whether Flowered Woods Garden was even inside the palace wall, although to me that view seems indefensible. My own view is that the garden had to be inside the palace, as this was the design of an earlier Han dynasty palace in Luoyang after which Emperor Wu's palace was reportedly modeled. The same general design can be seen in the Forbidden City in Beijing today, where the Ming and Qing emperors' leisure garden remains just inside the palace's rear gate.

As to the place where Emperor Wu allegedly met Bodhidharma himself, there is no solid evidence to say exactly where the event happened, if it occurred at all. So if we can't know exactly what lies buried beneath the monument at the corner of Taiping Road and Yang-tse River Back Street, it seems like the appropriate place to commemorate Bodhidharma and Emperor Wu's meeting. As far as I'm concerned, this spot and its odd artistic columns work fine as a remembrance of where their great misunderstanding might have occurred.

EMPEROR WU'S RELATIONSHIP WITH HOME-LEAVING BUDDHISM

Emperor Wu knew that to solidify his rule and enhance his Bodhisattva Emperor status he needed to bend Huiyuan's idea that "a monk does not bow to a king" to the proper imperial perspective, namely that a monk should indeed bow to a king. As I've explained, this is where the status of being a bodhisattva had particular value, for that exalted religious role did not, by definition, require that the emperor need to become a home-leaving monk in order to have high spiritual status.

But some clerics in Emperor Wu's inner circle of house monks were apparently not happy with the special spiritual position the emperor had conferred on himself. While they were no doubt pleased that their religion now dominated spiritual life in the country, there's evidence that the monks resented the emperor's high-handed religious authority, a power that eclipsed their own status as home-leavers.

In Daoxuan's *Continued Biographies* there is a biography about the monk Zhizang, a foremost Buddhist teacher and preceptor to the Crown Prince that I mentioned previously. Though he was among the most honored and famous of the emperor's favorite monks, his biography reveals serious friction between him and Emperor Wu over the latter's spiritual self-aggrandizement. Zhizang, due to the high status and honor Emperor Wu afforded him, was allowed to come and go in the palace as he pleased. In the course of elevating his own spiritual status, Emperor Wu issued an order saying that only the emperor himself would be allowed to lecture from the throne chair that served as a teaching seat in the palace. The implication of the emperor's exclusive claim to this teaching chair was clear. The emperor wished to compel the religious community to recognize that he had ultimate spiritual status, and that the idea that kings were not of the Dharma realm, as reflected in Huiyuan's dictum about not bowing to them, was not valid. The story relates that the monk Zhizang, whose former lay family had imperial connections, strode into the palace in a pique and went directly to the throne chair in question, ascended, and sat down on it. He then somewhat sarcastically declared, "I am [also] of the royal house and am not ashamed to sit in the royal seat. If the emperor wants to brandish his royal sword, he is, after all, a *chakravartin* monarch, and if he wants to kill me, he can kill me! I can go to a different realm, and even if it is hell itself, there's nothing there that can stop me from carrying on with my practice!" The story relates that Emperor Wu, thus confronted, rescinded his order about being the sole user of this Dharma-expounding throne.

This was not the only indication of Zhizang's rebellion against imperial prerogative. Another story from the biography reveals more of Zhizang's resentment toward the emperor and also throws light on the problems that arise when Buddhism is the state ideology. According to this story, a problem arose in the country because many people availed themselves of the special rights enjoyed by clergy by simply taking the Bodhisattva Vows and claiming to be monks. The rights thus obtained were indeed attractive and included, besides permanent room and board, freedom from manual labor, the avoidance of military service, and no need to pay taxes. Not surprisingly, many young men without an inheritance opted for this path. With little genuine religious conviction, these "monks" further blurred the home-leaving and home-abiding boundary by sneaking out to carouse (visiting prostitutes, drinking wine, and partaking in other forbidden behaviors) with some of their "religious brethren." Naturally, this behavior scandalized the religious community and called for some sort of action. Emperor Wu saw in this situation a way to extend his temporal authority over the religious community by punishing its miscreants. But Zhizang would have none of it, telling Emperor Wu to keep his non-home-leaving hands out of the church's internal religious problems.

In Zhizang's biography we find the recorded exchange between the two, in which the emperor declared, "What is it about such problems that they can't be rectified by the imperial control?"

Zhizang's somewhat insolent answer was that "The emperor's role is to rectify relations amongst family relatives [a Confucian idea]. As for the affairs of the Tathagata [the Buddhist community], you have no authority to manage them!"

This was apparently an ongoing argument, for, on another occasion when Emperor Wu tried to seize administrative authority over Buddhist monks, Zhizang declared, "The Buddha Dharma is a great sea. Non-home-leavers cannot know of it." According to the record, Emperor Wu did not take offense at this rebuff and ceded authority to Zhizang without complaint. Yet it shows that a real contradiction existed between the Buddhist community and the prerogatives sought by the growth of Imperial-Way Buddhism.

33. The Poem by Crown Prince Zhao Ming (Xiao Tong)

IN THE HISTORICAL records of Emperor Wu's Liang dynasty, there is no mention of Bodhidharma. However, I think that a poem written by Crown Prince Zhao Ming holds a clue about whether a meeting between the emperor and the sage took place. Before I look at this question in detail, let's take a look at the prince's poem, "On a Dharma Meeting at Kaishan Temple":

> Before the roosting birds have soared at dawn,
> I order the carriage to leave the villa,
> The horse ascends the winding path,
> That weaves up Ram's Gut Road,
> The ancient forest barely visible,
> We glimpse the dim outcroppings,
> And the great trees on Falling Star Mountain.
> Through the morning fog the sun starts to rise,
> While geese swim in a dark pond,
> And a frigid wind spreads the night's last frost.
> This truly solitary place,
> This peaceful and spacious place is where Dharma is taught,
> Jade trees and agate waters,
> Conceal the place of the Dharma seat,
> Somewhere amid the black bamboo and coral-colored earth,
> Are the sage's robe and a "bright moon" earring,
> Entangled in lichens we descend some rocky steps,
> Then we pull on osmanthus branches and grab pine tree limbs
> To cross steep gullies where the sun is hidden,
> Then in the mists appears the half-hidden pavilion.

How could a thousand ceremonies surpass this event?
A hundred generations will honor our emperor!
The spiritual truth here radiates limitlessly,
Like a boundless clear mirror,
The Dharma Wheel illuminates the dark room,
The wisdom ocean is crossed,
And the long-defiled dusty world,
Is drenched in light.

Who was the lecturer whom the Crown Prince got out of bed early to hear at Kaishan Temple that day? Historical evidence points to it being the monk Zhizang, the most famous of the house monks who taught the emperor and his court and who defied the emperor's edict by sitting on his Dharma seat. He is also recorded to be the monk who officiated at a ceremony where the author of the poem took his Bodhisattva Precepts. The probable date of this Dharma talk, however, also suggests that Bodhidharma's oldest disciple, Sengfu, lived at Kaishan Temple when it was given. It's quite plausible, if not likely, that Sengfu was in attendance on the cold morning the prince traveled up the mountain to hear the Buddhist sermon offered by the unnamed speaker. The proximity of Sengfu to this event is tantalizing.

Emperor Wu doted on his son and crown prince. As a boy Zhao Ming devoted himself to Confucian and Buddhist study under his imperial tutors. When he came of age, Emperor Wu gave him charge of the Eastern Palace, a hall on the east side of the Tai Cheng Palace complex where famous religious and literary men of the day lectured to the emperor and his court. Zhao Ming was also familiar with, if not involved in, the multiple sutra translation projects and organization of scriptures that Emperor Wu ordered to be carried out. He was probably intimately involved in assembling the library in the Flowered Woods imperial garden. All this activity, under the direction of the famous prince, was at one of the great intellectual centers of ancient times. Foreign and domestic Buddhist masters and other scholars flocked to the Tai Cheng Palace at imperial invitation.

Zhao Ming not only compiled the first anthology of Chinese literature, but also personally wrote commentaries on important Buddhist texts such as the Diamond Sutra. He extolled the poetry of Tao Yuan-ming, one of Huiyuan's famous friends in the "Three Laughs" incident at East Woods Temple.

Zhao Ming's fame in his own lifetime as a literary figure was wide-spread. Moreoever, from the sophistication of the poem shown above, Zhao Ming must have been at least in his late teens or early twenties when he wrote it. During the last years of his life, Zhao Ming moved to a place east of the capital city to live. From this we can surmise that this poem was very likely written between the years 518 and 525, a time that overlaps the time when Emperor Wu took his refashioned Bodhisattva Precepts in 519, when Bodhidharma reportedly set up his temple in not-too-distant Tianchang (522), and Bodhidharma's senior disciple Sengfu died (524).

Given the Crown Prince's exalted position, why didn't the monk he went to hear that morning instead hold audience in the Tai Cheng Palace, the usual venue for giving sermons to the court? We know that both Sengfu and his teacher Bodhidharma were noted for their refusal to visit the court. Zhizang, whom Chinese historians credit with having given this talk, was not a stranger to the palace. So I wonder whether Chinese historians may have it wrong, and someone other than Zhizang gave the talk at Kaishan Temple that day. Could it have been a monk that refused to go to the palace to speak? This may be a stretch. But what is not speculation is that Bodhidharma's oldest disciple, Sengfu, lived in the same temple where this talk was given, likely at the time it happened. Later, when Sengfu died, he was honored with an epithet for his monument by Zhao Ming, author of the poem. Remember that Zhao Ming was called on by his sister Yong Xing to laud Sengfu when he died.

Zhao Ming claims that that the event he attended that day surpassed a thousand religious ceremonies in importance. He also lavishes praise on his father, Emperor Wu. Whether this was genuine praise or just a formulaic insertion required by the Crown Prince's political position, it implies that Emperor Wu arranged the meeting that day but was not the speaker.

The speaker himself is described to be giving his talk in a dark room, and Zhao Ming makes a metaphoric connection between the speaker's shining Dharma words and the sunrise that is gradually

illuminating the world outside the door. The entire poem both literally and metaphorically moves from the darkness to the light; it
describes an "enlightenment" experience. The speaker's words illuminate the room while the sun rises outside to drench the red earth of
the mountain.

And the words hold other clues helpful to the search for Bodhidharma. More on this later.

34. Stone Fortress and Refreshing Mountain

THE WEATHER HAS WARMED, and I'm wearing only a light sweater against the morning chill at the bus stop for the number 6 line near my hotel. The morning traffic is heavy. It takes me nearly an hour to make the two-mile bus trip across downtown Nanjing to the Stone Fortress Park, a string of low hills that rise above the north side of the Qin Huai River before it empties into the Yang-tse. The Qin Huai River, part of Nanjing's old defensive perimeter that looped under the city, witnessed some of the city's most cataclysmic battles. Accounts relate that during some battles the bodies of the city's attackers and defenders filled the waterway such that one could walk across them like a bridge. The river bank and modern park where I'm headed is due west from where the ancient Tai Cheng Palace once stood. Rebels of ancient times set up their command posts there to lay siege to the palace.

In *feng shui* parlance, Stone Fortress Park was the "tiger" of ancient Nanjing's defenses. In old China the four cardinal directions were each associated with a mythical animal. The west was associated with the militarily symbolic white tiger. The place has the *feng shui* and astrological position of military might.

I get off the bus and walk across the street into the park. Almost at first glance it's easy to see why the Stone Fortress was really the "tiger" of the city's strategic positions. A ridge runs along the river, providing high ground to any defenders. Old bricks and columns sometimes jut from the ground. The exposed roots of large trees clutch old bricks. China's history is everywhere like this—things buried, exposed, reburied, forgotten, remembered.

I go back to the street and walk a hundred meters or so toward the old city center. There, on the last of the hills along the river, is Qing Liang ("Refreshing") Mountain. Nanjing's connection to Bodhidharma connotes the birthplace of the Zen tradition. But this forested hill in the same city is connected not with the beginning, but with the end of Zen's classical period. Until modern times a place called Refreshing Temple was located here. And now, after that temple's all but complete destruction in the twentieth century, it is again being rebuilt. A famous Zen master named Fayan (885–958) once lived here.

Fayan was the archetypical Zen teacher of ancient times. He was brilliant and deeply knowledgeable about the tradition. He taught with famous flair and creativity. His cryptic observations are still widely remembered. "A monk asked [Zen Master Fayan], 'What is the thing toward which an advanced student should pay special attention?' Fayan said, 'If the student has anything whatsoever that is regarded as "special," then he shouldn't be called "advanced."'" Fayan's temple has been destroyed and rebuilt repeatedly since he lived here. The Cultural Revolution was only the latest of the catastrophic events to occur on these premises. The only hall standing today with a connection to earlier times was built in the late Qing dynasty (1644–1911). Records say the monastery was once among the country's largest, and old drawings depict it as beautifully designed. But if its ancient halls are gone, one landmark of those times remains. That landmark is the Baoda Spring, a source of pure water that Fayan and his disciples personally dug at the site. A story about the spring appears in classical Zen records. It is an example of how Zen often used the metaphor of an "eye" to refer to the nature of consciousness and the mind:

> Once, when sand filled in and obstructed a new spring that was being dug at the temple, Zen Master Fayan said, "The mouth of the spring is obstructed by sand. When the Dharma Eye is obstructed, what is it that obscures it?"
>
> The monks were unable to answer.
>
> Fayan said, "It's obstructed by the eye!"

The same "eye" metaphor was used by the Buddha in his talk on Vulture Peak, as told in Zen's founding myth, when he said, "I possess the Treasury of the True Dharma Eye, the signless mind of nirvana . . ." The emperor actually granted the old Zen master the name *Fayan* after Fayan died. It means "Dharma Eye."

The location of the spring in the landscape indicates that it may have been located in front of where the temple's original Dharma Hall sat, symbolizing the source of the signless Dharma. Like Bodhidharma's famous wells at Hualin and True Victory Temples, such places are often connected to Zen teachers. Water is characteristically a sort of "signless" (i.e., lacking special flavor) ingredient of life. I've noticed that Dharma Halls are positioned behind old springs at several old temple sites in the country.

Now, Refreshing Mountain Park surrounds the old temple site. It is a botanical garden containing many recently replanted native species. However, the religious significance of the place is not yet lost. A third-generation disciple of old Zen Master Fayan, a monk named Yongming Yanshou (904–975), transmitted Fayan's Zen line to Korea. Now South Korean monks return to Refreshing Mountain Temple here in Nanjing to honor the origin of their Zen sect. They are working with local authorities to restore the temple, the mother temple of the Fayan Zen school.

Zen Master Yongming must be credited with spreading Fayan's teachings not just to Korea but throughout China as well. But at the same time, that disciple of Fayan did much to mingle Zen teachings with other Buddhist schools and dilute its unique character. After Yongming, Zen was never quite the same. The emphasis on "pointing directly at mind" that served as the theme of early Zen was diluted by burying it more deeply in the practices of other Buddhist sects like the Pure Land and Tiantai traditions. Yongming's ecumenical work led to the watering down of Zen's original emphasis, and in my view, wittingly or not, he obscured the power of Bodhidharma's simple instructions. Other Zen masters of later times followed suit. This led to a famous Zen master named Foguo (1063–1135), author of a well-known Zen book called the *Blue Cliff Record*, to say, "In ancient times Bodhidharma just taught 'directly pointing at mind.' Where was the forest of words we have to deal with now?"

Above the area where the old halls of Refreshing Mountain Temple once stood, a flat and carefully landscaped plot sits beneath broad ginkgo trees. Their gold leaves glitter in the autumn sun. It's obvious that the landscaped gardens and paths beneath the trees once held ancient monuments of the Zen teachers who lived and taught here. No doubt

Fayan's own stupa once stood here. Maybe it still rests a few meters beneath the surface where old folks now gather to chat and enjoy the fall day in the shade of a gazebo.

THE MEETING

The orthodox story of Bodhidharma's meeting with Emperor Wu, as it appears in texts written many centuries after the alleged event, goes like this:

> After sailing for three years, [Bodhidharma] arrived at Nanhai [Guangzhou]. The date was the twenty-first day of the ninth [lunar] month of [the year 527]. The governor of Guangzhou, [named] Xiao Angju, received him ceremoniously and made his arrival known to Emperor Wu. When the emperor learned of this report, he dispatched an invitation [for Bodhidharma to come to the capital, Nanjing]. [On the first day of the tenth lunar month of 528] Bodhidharma arrived in Nanjing.
>
> The emperor asked him, "Since I've assumed the throne, I've built temples and written scriptures, plus I've brought about the ordination of an incalculable number of monks. What merit does this [activity] have?"
>
> Bodhidharma replied, "No merit whatsoever."
>
> The emperor then asked, "Why does this have no merit?"
>
> Bodhidharma said, "These are matters of small consequence in the affairs of men and gods that are caused by transgressions [literally, *outflows*]. It's like shadows chasing form, nothing real about it [literally, *although it's there, it's not real*]."
>
> The emperor then asked, "What is genuine merit?"
>
> Bodhidharma said, "Pure wisdom of sublime perfection, experiencing one's [personal] solitary emptiness, seeking nothing in the world."
>
> The emperor then asked, "What is the first principle of the holy truth?"
>
> Bodhidharma said, "Across the vastness, nothing holy."
>
> The emperor said, "Who is facing me?"

Bodhidharma said, "I don't know."

The emperor did not understand, and Bodhidharma knew that they were not in accord with one another. On the nineteen day of the month, he retreated to the north of China. On the twenty-third day of the eleventh month, he arrived at Luoyang. In the third year of the reign of the Wei emperor Xiao Mingdi, [Bodhidharma] took up residence at Shaolin Temple and sat in meditation facing a wall, remaining silent day and night. No one could fathom him, and he was known as the "wall-gazing Brahman."

This version of events has problems immediately apparent to scholars. The most obvious is that Bodhidharma is said to have arrived in China in 527, but thereafter he is said to have arrived in Luoyang in the third year of the Northern Wei emperor Xiao Mingdi, which was actually the year 518. Such problems with the mentioned dates are only some of the reasons scholars reject this account as an invention created centuries later. For this reason many say that a meeting between Bodhidharma and Emperor Wu simply didn't happen. Western and Japanese scholars take it as a given that this was a legend that simply advanced the cause of a faction of Chan Buddhism with the emperor of the Tang dynasty about two hundred years after the Bodhidharma lived (more on this later). Thus this story of the famous meeting, which is regarded by Chan practitioners and much of China as a foundational event in Chan and Chinese cultural history, is largely dismissed as a fiction by scholars in East and West.

This is strange. The meeting between Emperor Wu and Bodhidharma is regarded as a critical, if rather obscure, event of the Zen tradition. Is it possible that the scholars are wrong, and that the event really did occur, even though early records do not show clearly that it happened?

As I've already taken pains to point out, the relatively reliable *Continued Biographies* offers an account much at odds with the account shown above. It says that Sengfu was Bodhidharma's oldest disciple and that he enjoyed great fame at the very center of Emperor Wu's empire and capital city during a time starting about thirty years before 527, when the traditional account claims Bodhidharma arrived. Moreover, our trip to Tianchang City, at least, suggests there is tangible evidence, including historical records that are not easily discountable, that Bodhidharma lived in the vicinity of Nanjing during the period in question. But even if Bodhidharma did live in Tianchang during that time, what could have brought the Indian sage and the Chinese emperor together? This is especially hard to understand given that Bodhidharma and his disciples all seemed to take pains to avoid meeting emperors.

In my view it seems likely that if Sengfu died in the year 524, as the *Continued Biographies* indicates, and Bodhidharma was anywhere in the vicinity of Nanjing, that he would have come to his disciple's funeral. It seems unlikely he could have ignored that event. When he came at last to the court of Emperor Wu, the emperor likely seized the chance to meet the famous teacher from India who had long avoided him. Perhaps after a grand funeral ceremony at Tongtai Temple, the emperor invited Bodhidharma to visit him in the Flowered Woods Garden, a quiet place where they could speak in private.

Perhaps their meeting went somewhat like traditional accounts of that event. Bodhidharma may have said a few words that revealed an awkward distance between the two men's views of Buddhism. Bodhidharma may have regarded the Imperial-Way Buddhism of Emperor Wu as little different from the court religion he left behind in North China. And then, after the meeting, Bodhidharma may have decided he must retreat from the public spotlight and avoid the annoying acclaim directed toward him by Imperial-Way Buddhism. Perhaps he decided to return again to someplace removed from "imperial sway" and so made his way back up the Yang-tse River to faraway regions.

Bodhidharma and his followers appear to have clung to the idea of being a home-leaver in a very literal sense, not accepting Emperor Wu's dilution of the ideal by expanding the Bodhisattva Vow and extending it equally to lay people. Bodhidharma's possible resentment toward the laicization of organized Buddhism would not have been unique. We've already seen that Zhizang, foremost among the most honored of the emperor's house monks, deeply held and publically displayed this same attitude.

Sengfu's biography also reinforces this view. While Sengfu's moral example was honored by Emperor Wu's court, as his biography shows, Sengfu himself appeared unconcerned, if not contemptuous, of Imperial-Way Buddhism. That the emperor and his family honored him so greatly shows that the home-leaving ideal still held powerful sway as a model. The fact that Emperor Wu at least nominally "left home" on several occasions confirms that the ideal endured despite attempts to dilute it. The idea behind Huiyuan's treatise "A Monk Does Not Bow to a King" continued to hold sway despite Emperor Wu's grab at supreme religious authority, and Bodhidharma and his disciples seem to represent, to later generations, the greatest example of resisting the dilution of Buddhism's most honored practice, that of leaving society behind.

As I mentioned before, in the *Continued Biographies* the author Daoxuan wrote a long passage of text that described monks of the Zen tradition. Among his comments about the most famous monks of Emperor Wu's age, he refers to Bodhidharma, saying that he "did not stay in places of imperial sway, and those who loved to see him could not draw him to them." This description fits not only with what we know about Bodhidharma, but about his disciple Sengfu as well. The attitude appears to extend down through several generations of Bodhidharma's disciples, with the Fourth Ancestor's refusal to respond to the emperor's summons being a shining later example of this refusal to submit to imperial authority.

35. Dingshan Temple

IT'S THREE O'CLOCK in the afternoon. I've wasted nearly an entire day. I set out this morning to find Dingshan Temple, located inside Laoshan Forest Park, which the map indicates to be across the Yang-tse and about ten miles upriver from Nanjing. First I spent a couple of hours trying to negotiate the bus system to get to Laoshan Park. But I made the mistake of getting on a bus to the Six Harmonies district, believing I could make a transfer once I crossed the river. But the bus didn't stop anywhere I could do this, so I ended up taking a taxi from a distant spot to the Pukou bus station. Pukou is a development zone a few miles from the Laoshan Park. At the station, I learned that a number 380 bus would take me to Laoshan and also to a hot springs resort that the map indicated is inside the park. That looked good. But I didn't realize the bus passed through the wrong side of the park and then made its way into the countryside far from Dingshan Temple, my intended destination. Two or three people on the bus decided my being there was a good chance to practice their English, and it took me a long time to realize that Laoshan Park was now far behind me. I got off the bus and crossed the road to catch one going back to where I came from.

According to old records, Emperor Wu established Dingshan ("Samadhi Mountain"; remember that *samadhi* means, roughly, "meditative concentration") Temple in the year 503, just a year after he came to power. He set up the temple to honor a monk named Fading ("Dharma Samadhi") who, according to the same record, was devoted to a life of "rigorous denunciation practice" and who "taught in the south and north" of the country (戒行精严,锡周南北). This aroused my suspicions. The year 503 would coincide with the time when the war between Xiao Yan (Emperor Wu) and Baojuan was not long finished. Emperor Wu would have barely taken the throne. The country was nearly broke, and civil order was barely restored. So who was this mysterious monk of "rigorous denunciation practice" who taught in the south and the north of China? Could Bodhidharma have adopted an alias to avoid persecution and followed Xiao Yan down the Yang-tse as he fought his way to the capital to overthrow the boy emperor? This may be a stretch, but the only other reference I can find to a monk of this name is about one who practiced recitations of prajna scriptures a hundred thousand times. That doesn't sound like the normal meaning of "vigorous renunciation practice" to me. A monk out in a forest doing serious meditation in the forest is what I associate with "rigorous denunciation."

But whether or not the monk Dharma Samadhi was actually Bodhidharma perhaps doesn't matter, because Dingshan Temple figures into the Bodhidharma story anyway. The temple's old records claim that Bodhidharma lived at the place for (variously) one and a half or three years, during the time right after he met Emperor Wu and crossed the Yang-tse. Such an account is impossible to square with Bodhidharma's traditional story. It also means he would have arrived at Shaolin Temple much later than anyone thinks he did (more on Shaolin later). If he meditated at Shaolin for nine years, as stated in his traditional story, then his time there would extend to the year 540. That contradicts both the traditional story as well as the more plausible story I've been investigating. So what does this mean?

Following the idea that Bodhidharma left Luoyang in the year 494, as is indirectly suggested by Sengfu's bio in the *Continued Biographies*, then Bodhidharma may have arrived in the Nanjing area on or before 503 and lived there for much of the next twenty years. Dingshan Temple, across the river and in a forested area away from Nanjing, might have been a good place to stay for at least part of that time. The temple claims to have various rocks and ledges where Bodhidharma sat in meditation, with vestiges of his wall-gazing still evident for visitors to see. Interestingly, the place also has a Plant the Staff Spring, reputedly discovered when Bodhidharma struck the ground with his staff and pure water gushed out—another connection between Bodhidharma and springs. Plus, the action of discovering such a spring by striking the ground is typically connected with the founder of a temple. The Sixth Ancestor Huineng and others have similar legends related to finding springs at their teaching places. The spring at Dingshan is still flowing sweet water today.

I first visited Dingshan Temple a few years ago with my friend Eric. Since the remains of the temple were destroyed during the '50s, there is little there in the way of an active Buddhist temple today. A few recently constructed buildings house a few monks, and much of the place has been given over to archeological research.

Eric and I arrived unannounced and spent a few hours exploring the place with the old monk in charge. He explained the significance of the temple in light of the traditional story, saying that Bodhidharma stayed there for three years after meeting Emperor Wu. He showed us the spring and other landmarks, making a point of showing us a Ming dynasty (1328–1644) stone stele that is thought to have the earliest engraving of Bodhidharma's likeness, older than anything at Shaolin Temple. An archeological dig was ongoing around the time we were there. The monk said the archeologists had uncovered an old foundation dating from the Song dynasty (960–1278). This didn't seem very interesting to me, since the Song dynasty occurred five hundred years after Bodhidharma supposedly came to the place. By that time, all the myths about Bodhidharma were several centuries old. A Song dynasty foundation doesn't offer any evidence about whether old "blue eyes" ever visited here or not.

During our first visit to the temple, I didn't get an exact sense of its location, as the roads leading to it were under construction and we seemed to weave through various hills. But later I read press reports on the Internet that the temple had been designated a "Bodhidharma Research Site." Unsure what that meant, I decided it was worth another visit to find out if anything new had turned up.

So now I'm standing at a busy intersection wondering which direction to go. A traffic cop is gazing languidly at passing traffic, not seeming very busy. I approach him and ask politely whether he knows of a place called Dingshan Temple.

This draws a blank. "What Temple?" he asks.

"Dingshan Temple," I say again firmly.

"There's no Dingshan Temple around here," he says.

I retreat toward the bus stop I came from a few minutes earlier. Some motorbikes are hanging around waiting for customers. Often the cheapest and fastest (if also most dangerous) way to get around in China's urban areas is on such bikes. They often hang around bus stops offering lifts home to pedestrians. For $1 or less, they'll transport you the last mile to your place and may even have a basket to hold your groceries. If you have a motorbike in China, you have a business.

I approach a woman on such a bike and ask her if she's heard of Dingshan Temple. She hasn't. Then a man on a bike nearby says he's heard of it.

"Dingshan Temple? You've heard of Dingshan Temple?"

"Yes," he says, "I know where it is."

With the day growing late I decide to throw caution to the wind and jump on the back of the man's motorbike. After I'm firmly aboard, we roar off into the chaos of Pukou's rush hour. I'd hoped we would be traveling into the park area, but that's not the case. Instead we're soon weaving in and out of traffic on the city's main thoroughfare, heading directly back toward Nanjing.

A few brushes with death later, the driver pulls onto a curb by a big intersection. He calls to a woman cleaning dishes at a small restaurant, asking if she knows where Dingshan Temple is located. She doesn't. I've about decided that my chances of finding Dingshan Temple again, at least today, are hovering near hopeless. I tell the motorcycle driver that he should take me to the Nanjing bus stop. But no sooner than the words leave my mouth when the woman's daughter emerges from behind a rack of dishes to say, "Dingshan Temple?" It's right up that road!" She points down a street that heads north toward the hills.

Off we go again, weaving in and out of traffic until, a few intersections later, things start to look a little familiar. Then I recognize the landscape, but where just two years ago there were unfinished roads and bare dirt, there are now many very modern-looking condos, semidetached houses, and a golf course. Soon we see some signs pointing to the temple, and as we come into a valley I definitely remember, we overtake a monk riding on a bicycle. We slow down and ask him where the temple is. He points up the road and smiles.

As the sun approaches the western mountaintops, I at last find myself in one of the shacks that now passes for Dingshan Temple, sitting across a table from the monk we encountered on the bicycle moments earlier. His name is Chenguang ("Morning Shining"), and he's about thirty years old.

Dingshan Temple sits below Lion Peak, in a valley of very auspicious *feng shui*. It faces south, the sacred direction, and is protected on three sides by hills. Best of all, it has a lake out front. It seems possible that in ancient times the lake was a "Liberate Life Pond" that often sits in front of temples and serves as a place to free fish and turtles saved from the market. Thus the temple complies perfectly with the adage "Mountains behind, water in front," the *feng shui* ideal. Bodhidharma's spring sits exactly where you'd expect it to be if it were in front of an old Dharma Hall.

I ask Chenguang about the spring. He says, "Yes, the spring is still there. It's where we get all the fresh water for our temple." He offers me a cup of hot water.

I explain to him that I came here two years ago but have seen recent news reports saying the place is now a "Bodhidharma Research Site." However, from the looks of things, not much has changed since my last visit. Have excavations continued?

Chenguang says that a lot of archeological work has been done on the site, but it has stopped for the time being. He says, "All the things they've found here have been taken away and are kept elsewhere."

I mention that I saw the Ming dynasty stele on my previous visit, and he says that it has been removed from the site for cleaning.

"Have any more interesting things been found?" I venture.

"A lot has been found here."

"Any old stone tablets?" I ask.

"They've found an old stele," he says.

"Do they know when it was set up?"

"It's from the Liang dynasty," he says. I try not to show my excitement and surprise at his answer.

"Does it talk about Bodhidharma?"

"Yes, it records something about Bodhidharma, and it dates from the Liang dynasty."

What he says is pretty earthshaking. I've been sifting for clues about Bodhidharma's early whereabouts for many years, but a reliable record about him from his own time has been impossible to come by. I feel like someone who's spent his life looking for a cure for cancer hearing about a new therapy with an 80-percent cure rate. I feel like Indiana Jones. "Really? They've found something from the Liang dynasty that records Bodhidharma's life here? Where is the stele now?"

Chenguang now realizes that he may have inadvertently let a cat out of the bag. He pauses and then says, "It's a secret."

China is full of secrets. Of course there are the normal, garden-variety secrets like military secrets and state secrets, but there are many others as well. Many secrets have to do with the whereabouts of important things, especially things related to historical events. Two centuries of looting by Chinese and foreign treasure hunters, domestic and foreign wars, plus assorted political upheavals have made people wary of revealing the whereabouts of important things. It's quite understandable. At the Fifth Zen Ancestor's temple in Huangmei there is a "True Body Hall" where the body of the Fifth Zen Ancestor is said to have remained until it was "lost during World War II." Different stories about the body's whereabouts continue to circulate. I've always felt that someone knows exactly where it is but won't give a straight answer about it.

If there really is a newly discovered Bodhidharma stele, it's anyone's guess as to why it might be kept secreted away somewhere. Perhaps there's a political fight between government entities about who should be in charge of it. Maybe the local government wants to keep it on the site in order to display it to attract tourist money, whereas the Nanjing City or provincial governments might want to remove it to a place they control, like the Nanjing museum. Or perhaps, in this case, scholars just want to have time to study the stele quietly without interruption. Anyway, given the amount of interest in and out of China in such an object, it's a little surprising that some information about it hasn't come out. Maybe Chenguang is mistaken. Perhaps he thought that something taken from the site was from the Liang dynasty, Emperor Wu's own time, but it was in fact from much later. Until knowledgeable authorities are willing to speak about such an object, we can only guess about it.

I can't conceal my interest, and I tell Chenguang that I know how earthshaking such a discovery would be regarded and sympathize with the idea of keeping it out of the public eye for a time. He seems nervous and now doesn't seem inclined to reveal any more information than he has already.

"What institution is in charge of the stele?" I ask.

He tells me there are several different groups involved, including the local Pukou government and the Nanjing cultural relic bureau. I know that I've already gotten more information than I'm entitled to know, so

I don't press my host to compromise himself any more than he has.

After some more polite conversation, I thank Chenguang for his hospitality and take my leave. I take a few more photos of recent excavation areas, then brace myself for the Mad Hatter ride back to the Pukou bus station.

DAOXUAN'S VIEW OF NANJING IN THE AGE
OF BODHIDHARMA

In some general comments about the Zen school in the *Continued Biographies*, Daoxuan suggests clues that indicate Emperor Wu would have sought to meet Bodhidharma. For example, he describes the popularity of the Zen movement that spread in sixth-century China and offers information about the situation in Nanjing in particular:

> In its initial stage of flowering and being established, Zen naturally reached the court of Emperor Wu. He looked everywhere to find those who studied mind, assembling them in the capital [Nanjing] and judging the strengths or weaknesses of their different arguments. Moreover, he utilized the upper and lower Samadhi Forest Temples on Bell Mountain, where he arranged for monks who practiced stilling the mind to reside and practice.
>
> At that time, although Buddhism flourished, there was much learned argument, and the swords of words surged like towering waves. This led to an incalculable amount of contention for supremacy. One can say that these monks became very famous, and the result was a genuine belief in true mind.
>
> If someone were to ask, I'd say that the Zen practiced and promoted [in Nanjing] was the true appearance of Buddha's teaching. Yet now, at this later time [about 125 years later], the threads of those arguments are no longer spoken of. Now we are in what is called the "Dharma-ending age," in which adherence to the precepts is our practice. This [precepts practice] is now paramount. And if you ask me to explain this, then I must say that the true teaching that reached China due to the great function of those former [Nanjing] masters was

not understood or practiced correctly. As a result within the teachings there developed two types of believers. There was a division between those who are clever and those who are not. If we all could return to the source and experience the profound truth [of Buddha's teaching], then the virtue of those who study [mind] and the rest of the Buddha world could be unified, as in the true Dharma of the first thousand years [of Buddha's teaching]. And this would be called realizing the unending true enlightenment of Buddha.

Daoxuan's comments offer a unique view of the Buddhism of his age, a time he called the "End of Dharma" (Chinese: *mofa*). Daoxuan describes the problems of that age. In particular, he says that the importance of observing "mind" was being forgotten, and devotional practice and precepts were essential Zen practice. Daoxuan also described how this undermining of the Dharma would only get worse: "The Zen doctrines will [soon] be corrupted and then propagated everywhere, their meaning diluted with polluted ideas such as 'form illuminates emptiness,' which is already much talked about, or [the idea of] 'experiencing chaos is peace.'" Daoxuan's reference to "form illuminates emptiness" is apparently an oblique criticism of the Heart Sutra, which Buddhologist Jan Nattier and others have shown to have gained currency in Chinese Buddhism about the time of Daoxuan's writing.

Daoxuan obviously thought that the "Dharma-ending age" had already arrived, and he predicted it would promulgate more false teachings. He states that various false doctrines would enter the religion. This was the time surrounding the creation of tablets at Yunju Temple that I described earlier. To Daoxuan and others, saving the Dharma through such actions was paramount.

What follows in Daoxuan's text is noteworthy. He specifically praises some of the other "former masters" of the Zen school:

A large number of records tell of those [Zen] teachers' different doctrines, their arguments and thinking . . . During the period of the first [Northen] Qi emperor [circa 550–560 CE] [the monk] Seng Chou [the third abbot of Shaolin Temple] was unique, whereas the [Northern] Zhou dynasty [circa 570] in the northern plain [Shanxi and Hebei] honored [a teacher named] Seng Shi. These monks in high places brought [Zen's] influence even to the powerful, causing Emperor Xuan Di [ruled 550–559] to give up power and hide out at Cloud Gate [Mountain] and Prime Minister Meng to lose his position and take refuge at Fu Temple.

Then Daoxuan speaks specifically of Bodhidharma (I quoted some lines of this passage earlier, but the complete passage is especially important):

> Another [monk] of this sort was Bodhidharma. He converted [people] and established the Zen doctrines in the Yang-tse and Luoyang regions. His "wall-gazing" practice of the Mahayana is the highest [teaching]. Those who came to study with and honor Bodhidharma were like a city. But while there were many who lauded Bodhidharma, only a few really understood [his teachings] and dedicated themselves to their practice. He had a loyal following who would listen to him speak. His teachings were not of good and evil. One might describe his teaching to be that the truth and the false [affairs of the world] are like two wings, [or] two wheels on the cart of emptiness. Bodhidharma would not remain in places of imperial sway. Those [in high places] who desired to see him could not draw him near. His plan was quiet contemplation, and so he ceased speaking. He regarded the two doctrines [meditation and scripture] as two tracks from the same vehicle, and [Bodhidharma] was honored in the [pure practice Zen teachings] of Seng Chou [Shaolin's third abbot].
>
> Bodhidharma's Dharma was the mysterious and deep doctrine of emptiness. It should be honored [as the principle whereby] the emotional affairs [of people's lives] are quickly exposed [as to their actual nature]. But the nature of [Bodhidharma's] deep principle is difficult to fathom. Therefore things [of the world] entrap people. If one can utilize [a proper understanding of] mind, then it will stop outflows [delusions] and make them like billowing clouds. Using such a method

will resolve one's difficulties. [Bodhidharma's] method is far from [what is found in] scriptures. It can be effective. When you compare it to the "Ten Stages leading to Bodhisattvahood" [a doctrine then widely studied] you will find the latter to be inferior and slow.

Those who enter the Zen gate in the morning expound it in the evening. It is said that it is the source of everything. Attaining this profound spiritual samadhi [one can] illuminate and penetrate hindrances. It is the ultimate limit of what can be understood or realized through wisdom and knowledge.

There are no delusions of the mind that this [teaching] cannot illuminate. It reveals the mind tossed in the karmic waves, and it calms the swells of fear, manifesting samadhi. It is thus called the knowledge that arises through samadhic power.

[Bodhidharma's teaching] maintains that an external doctrine only leads to confusion, and will not easily allow one to solve one's obstructions [to gaining enlightenment]. I personally often practice [Bodhidharma's teaching]. The doctrine he espoused is the truth. Through it, delusions of true and false, death and difficulty, are understood. It is difficult to penetrate and eliminate [ideas of] true and false, form and delusion. Delusive states are avoided only through understanding "mind only." Clinging to what is before one is not the practice of mind. All [Bodhidharma's disciples] were able to speak of the Way through [knowledge of] this practice.

Daoxuan seems to be of two minds about Bodhidharma's teachings. On the one hand he says that Bodhidharma's teaching is "difficult to fathom." Yet he also says that "Those who enter the Zen gate in the morning expound it in the evening." Here we see the same Sudden Enlightenment teaching idea that is associated with the Southern Zen school, the line regarded as springing from Bodhidharma that passed down through Chinese and East Asian history.

Notably, this passage of the *Continued Biographies* offers a rare insight into the state of Zen during and immediately after Bodhidharma's life. It indicates that Bodhidharma must be considered a central player in the debate about the nature of the mind, a debate that

Emperor Wu entertained and encouraged. It should be pointed out, however, that Daoxuan, who was not a Zen monk, held an understanding of Bodhidharma's teaching that was not the same as that of later generations of Zen teachers. The latter appear to have avoided talking about emptiness because they realized that such metaphysical doctrines unduly confuse people. Daoxuan's view that Bodhidharma's teaching was the "mysterious and deep doctrine of emptiness" may indirectly indicate that later Zen evolved away from Bodhidharma to become something less metaphysically oriented. Daoxuan himself provides the reason why this evolution would occur when he criticizes the idea of "form illuminates emptiness." This may be an oblique criticism of the metaphysically heavy Heart Sutra that gradually gained a foothold in the Zen tradition. When Daoxuan wrote these words around the year 650, the Prajnaparamita Sutra promoted extensively by Emperor Wu was widely studied. Daoxuan's criticism may have been directed against the metaphysical nature of that and other scriptures. Ironically, its text, still widely chanted in the Zen world, says "form is nothing other than emptiness, emptiness nothing other than form." In my view, Daoxuan declares that Zen's true meaning and teachings, as taught by Bodhidharma, would be widely corrupted and undermined by this idea during Daoxuan's life and the ages that followed.

It is particularly surprising that Daoxuan, who was the most important monk of the Precepts school in his era, compares that school unfavorably to Zen teachings on the nature of the mind. He indicates that sole reliance on the precepts is inferior to the Zen masters who came previously, and that this turn toward the precepts is indicative that the "Dharma-ending age" had now arrived.

How did Daoxuan, a towering figure of China's Precepts school, gain such a deep appreciation for doctrines about the nature of "mind"? During the period after the year 640, when Daoxuan wrote his *Continued Biographies*, he resided in China's capital city of Chang An (now the city of Xian). Daoxuan personally assisted the famous monk Xuan Zang in translating new Yogacara (Yogis) teachings that the latter had brought back from India. Thus, Daoxuan's exposure to "mind" teachings was extensive, and he understood the relationship between such Yogi ideas and the Zen school. He seems to have understood that Zen was the best vehicle for the spread of "mind" teachings in China.

Thus, textual evidence left by Daoxuan reveals a Zen tradition that, in its origins, was truly "outside of scriptures." Even Daoxuan, who was not of the Zen tradition, honored early Zen highly and deplored that its mind teachings were forgotten after Bodhidharma and its other early teachers passed from the scene.

36. Changlu Temple

The sun shines on the solitary green peak.
The moon floats above the cold creek waters.
When the sublime mystery of the ancestors is understood,
You will never again turn to your small mind for peace.
—*Zen Master Qingliao (1089–1151) of Changlu Temple,*
addressing the monks

长芦清了禅师上堂日:

日照孤峰翠
月临溪水寒
祖师玄妙诀
莫向寸心安。

"The entire great earth is a gate to liberation. If you push on it, you can't enter it. How can the white-haired monk standing before you compel you to enter? When you reach this place, why do you let your nostrils be in someone else's hand?" The master paused, and then said, "If you want to see the moon in the sky, put down your oar."
Zen Master Miaojue (taught circa 1170 CE) of Changlu Temple

尽大地是个解脱门，把手拽不肯入。雪峰老汉抑逼人作么？既到这里，
为甚么鼻孔在别人手里良久曰：贪观天 上月，失却手中桡.
长芦妙觉禅师

THE YANG-TSE RIVER, clear of fog and smog, spreads wide beneath the Nanjing Bridge. The white rocks of the Mufu Mountains along the southern bank of the river stand out in the bright noon sun. The 606 bus line is tightly crowded with people, pressing on me from all sides.

I'm on my way to the remains of Changlu Temple in the Six Harmonies district. It's the place on the far side of the Yang-tse River from the Mufu Mountains where I visited Bodhidharma's Nanjing cave. It lies in an ancient (first records date to 559 BCE) fishing and farming area, but is not too heavily populated now. It was by Changlu Temple that, according to legend, Bodhidharma came ashore after crossing the Yang-tse river on a "single blade of grass," escaping from Emperor Wu's agents. According to the book *Temples of Nanjing*, there's only one building left from the old temple, and the site now houses a middle school.

Six Harmonies is named after a mountain in the area, which in turn is named after an old Taoist cosmological idea that divided the universe into six directions (up, down, and the four compass points of west, south, east, and north). So *Six Harmonies* means, in effect, "everything" in harmony.

And everything would be in harmony today, except the bus seems to be belching exhaust fumes up past the trap door that covers the front-mounted engine. I suppose that the U.S. antismoking laws have made me more than normally sensitive to any kind of air pollution, for I seem to be the only person gagging on the smell. Luckily I'm squeezed close to an open window at the right front of the bus and can hang my head outside to catch a few gulps of fresher Yang-tse River air.

We travel the wide, four-lane divided road for about twenty minutes. When I boarded the bus, I asked the ticket seller to tell me when my stop appears, and now she waves at me to let me know that the upcoming intersection is my goal. There's no real pull-over spot on the four-lane road, so I hustle off the bus quickly, afraid to let it stop for long in the fast traffic while the traffic light is green. There's a taxi sitting near the intersection waiting for a fare, so I hop in and tell the driver to take me to Changlu Middle School. He turns the car around and heads south across flat land toward the Yang-tse River, the Mufu Mountains now a distant crest on the horizon. The countryside is open, and there are some large industrial plants dotting the area. I judge them to be petrochemical processing plants with a lot of large white tanks and pipes, topped by flare stack towers that flame brightly even at midday.

"There's a lot of industrial plants out here," I say to the driver.

He nods. "This place is all becoming an industrial-production area," he says. "There's more plants here all the time." He's surprised I speak

Chinese and wants to learn what I'm up to. "Why do you want to go to the school?" he asks.

"I want to see what remains of the old temple that was at that place," I tell him. "It's supposed to be a famous place where Bodhidharma crossed the Yang-tse on a single blade of grass. Have you heard of that legend?"

The driver smiles broadly. Then I notice the little Kwan Yin statue on his dashboard.

"I know," he says. "I grew up near here. Are you a professor?"

"No. Just someone interested in history. I like traveling around and visiting places like this."

We enter a small town. There's a sign on a modern looking building that says LONG REED VILLAGE MEDICAL CENTER. I notice a slight chemical smell in the air. A few moments later the driver turns east and almost immediately we roll up to a gate next to a sign that says LONG REED MIDDLE SCHOOL. Since it's Sunday, both the school and the gate are closed. However, there's a guard shack at the side of the gate. I tell the driver he should wait, and then I get out to talk to the guard. When I explain what I've come to do, the guard seems unimpressed. He says there's no way I can go into the premises on a Sunday. The taxi driver, who has gotten out of the taxi and is now listening to the conversation, chimes in and supports my story, saying that I'm a foreign guest and it shouldn't hurt for me to go in and take a look around.

After some give-and-take the guard turns and picks up a telephone through the window of the guard shack. He dials a number and then talks for a minute to someone on the other end. Then he hands me the phone and tells me that the principal of the school is on the line. I say hello, and a woman asks me who I am and what I'm doing. I explain that I'd like to see any remains from the old temple that used to be on the premises. I tell her I do research about old temples and this one is particularly interesting. We talk for a minute more and her initial hesitancy seems to dissolve. Finally she says that since I've come to see their place, they should be flattered that I'm interested. She tells me to hand the phone back to the guard. A minute later he puts down the phone to tell me that he'll give me a tour of the premises himself.

The taxi driver joins us, and the three of us walk through the gate into the school grounds. Although this old temple site is supposed to be where Bodhidharma came ashore after crossing the river from Nanjing, the river is too far away across the flatland to be seen. The guard explains that the course of the river has changed, and now it's a few miles away, off toward the Mufu Mountains that sit in the distance. Anyway, he says, he thinks the original location of the temple may have been abandoned after a flood washed it away.

We walk into a garden area in front of the school buildings where a gazebo sits among some potted chrysanthemums. The guard points at a few objects on the ground and says, "That's from the old temple."

It's obvious that there's almost nothing left of the temple that was on the site previously. Next to the gazebo there are some pieces of granite, broken temple colonnades and odd pieces of stone décor all scattered next to some chrysanthemum beds. There are also some stones that mark where the temple's old well was located. On two sides of the garden alcove are a covered walkway and wall that displays some engraved works of calligraphy inside picture frames.

"Those are all poems written centuries ago about the temple that was here," says the guard. He points at one on the end of the row and says, "Look, there's one written by Li Bai."

Li Bai was the famous poet who wrote the "Night Thoughts" poem I quoted before. He lived during the middle of the eighth century. I look closer and see that not only did Li Bai write a poem about this place, but several other famous poets did as well.

"I read that there is one hall remaining from the old temple," I say. "Is it still here?"

The guard leads us through the center of the school grounds past an enormous gingko tree. As we pass it, the guard says, "This tree is hundreds of years old. It was a big feature in the middle of the temple."

The enormous old tree is really gorgeous, its fall leaves shimmering like gold in the light wind. A sign in front of the tree declares it to be the "symbol of Long Reed Middle School's special spirit." We walk on toward the rear of the school, and the guard points out a brick building. "That's the only building still regarded as part of the old temple," says the guard.

There's not much to see. The brick building was clearly recently rebuilt and looks more like a storehouse than a temple hall. The double front door is closed and locked. I peek in through a crack in the middle of the door and see that the hall is empty.

Old records of the Six Harmonies area describe how Changlu Temple was once one of the largest temples in Southern China. It contained an assortment of special halls with names related to Bodhidharma, such as the Single Reed (blade of grass) Hall, the Directly Pointing Hall, and the Standing in the Snow Hall (a reference to a story about his main disciple that I'll tell later). During the Song dynasty (960–1278), more than a thousand monks lived here. The place had imperial support and was widely famous, as evidenced by the wall of poems written over a twelve-hundred-year period.

"What happened to the old temple?" I ask the guard.

He pauses for a moment, then says, "It burned down."

It was common for temples in old China to catch fire and be destroyed. Incense and lamps would periodically cause accidental fires. Hardly any temple in China hasn't been rebuilt numerous times.

"Was it an accident?" I ask.

The guard only shrugs. "I'm not sure," he says. He doesn't seem to want to say anymore.

We walk back toward the taxi, and I take a last look out across the wide valley toward the river. Of course, the story of Bodhidharma crossing the river on a "single reed of grass" is just a myth, part of the pious orthodoxy invented well after he lived. But I'm feeling pretty melancholy as I take my last look at the place. The destruction of the temple that commemorates Bodhidharma's river crossing seems incredibly sad, portending that something important is slipping out of our grasp, out of the collective memory of China and Zen culture. The sight of the petrochemical plants surrounding Six Harmonies Village is also depressing. They seem to say that not only is Changlu Temple unimportant, but also there's no chance that it will ever be remembered and rebuilt. Any remnants of the place will soon yield to the need for making more polyvinyl chloride for New China.

As I ride back to the bus stop, I ask the taxi driver if he knows anything more about how the temple was destroyed. He's only about twenty years old. He says he doesn't know what happened to it.

As the bus goes back over the Yang-tse River into Nanjing, I'm really feeling let down. I decide to get off the bus and walk through the northern part of the city, near the old Bell Tower, an area not far from Nanjing University. For a couple of hours I walk along some alleyways and explore a few old bookshops. Finally I notice it's starting to get late and I should have something to eat. There's a Ramada Hotel nearby. I notice through the window that they have a nice-looking salad bar, and to lift my spirits I decide to have my first fresh green salad in several weeks. Once inside I tell the waiter that I want a salad buffet but will skip the meat-heavy dinner buffet and order an entrée from the menu. They have one vegetarian dish available, a vegetable curry. I get my salad and start eating.

My curry arrives, and a couple of minutes later a young man in a chef's hat appears at the table. He smiles at me and asks, "Are you a vegetarian?"

I confirm that I am and ask him if he is a cook here in the hotel.

He says yes. Then he says, "I'm a vegetarian also."

It's a strange conversation but I play along.

The young Chinese man then takes off his chef's hat and says, "I'm also a Buddhist. "I notice that his head is closely shaven. He says, "I'm going to take my vows soon and become a monk."

I feel a little surprised at how this conversation is proceeding. "Congratulations," I say. "Did you know I'm a vegetarian because of what I ordered from the menu?"

He then admits that one of the waiters said there's a vegetarian foreigner in the dining room. He decided to come say hello.

"What are you doing here in Nanjing?" he asks.

I explain to him that I'm here visiting places related to Buddhist history. I'm especially interested in places related to Emperor Wu and Bodhidharma.

He says, "Have you been to Long Reed [Changlu] Temple?"

"I was just there today! Do you know that place?" I speak without disguising my surprise. The temple and its tiny village are far out of town and certainly unknown to nearly all of Nanjing's general population.

"That's where I went to school," says the cook. "I was a student at Long Reed Middle School."

It takes a moment for his words to sink in. "You went to Long Reed Middle School?"

"Yes," says the cook. My family comes from Long Reed Village.

Greater Nanjing has a population of about seven million people. From the looks of Long Reed Village, where the medical clinic I passed earlier in the day is located, it has at most a few hundred people.

The cook tells me his name is Shao, and we exchange cards. I tell him I'm highly pleased to meet him. I'm curious to ask him why he's about to become a home-leaver, but then I remember the unwritten rule of Chinese religious etiquette that you shouldn't ask a monk why he decided to leave the world. Instead I ask him to sit down and talk with me for a few minutes. "What happened to the temple?" I ask him. "The place was important to Zen history. Why did they build a school on the site? Do you know what happened there?"

Shao smiles and starts to explain. "Have you heard of the Nanjing massacre?"

"Of course," I tell him. "Everyone knows about it."

"Well, when the Japanese came and occupied Long Reed Village, they burned down the temple. Some monks who were living in the temple tried to save it, but they were driven away and some were killed."

"How do you know this?" I ask him.

"My grandmother worshipped at that temple and she saw what happened. She told me about it."

"Why did they burn down the temple and kill monks?" I ask. "That doesn't make any sense."

"That happened a lot. When the Japanese came, they wanted to get rid of the Chinese Buddhist clergy in the temples and put their own monks in charge. They installed their own Japanese monks to be in charge of the temples and told the population they had to follow *them* now."

I sit silent for a few moments, trying to grasp the import of what Shao was saying. Finally I say, "You mean the Japanese army killed the Chinese Buddhists and put Japanese monks in charge of the temples? Why would they do that? How could Buddhists do such a thing? Isn't Buddhism about peace?"

Shao shrugs his shoulders. "They just wanted everyone to follow them now. This was true for everything. Even religion."

"Is there any proof about this? Has anyone written about what happened at Long Reed Temple?"

Shao shakes his head. "I don't know. Anyway, it's better to forget all this now. There's enough that's been said and done. There's the memorial museum."

Shao's words roll over me like a ocean wave. For a few minutes I feel a little disoriented. I really don't know what to say.

Then Shao speaks again. "I should go back to work now. If you come to Nanjing again, I will have my head shaved and be wearing monks' robes."

I get up and shake Shao's hand and ask him to pose for a photo. Then he steps back and bows slightly to me, his hands together. He turns and walks toward the back of the dining room.

I order a coffee and sit looking at the traffic outside while the day grows dark. I'm stunned about the strange meeting I've just had. I'm also struck by the fact that when Shao told me about the Japanese burning down Long Reed Temple and killing or driving away the monks there, he had no rancor or hatred in his voice. There was no malice or desire for revenge in his words. His face had a calm look, and his voice was steady as he described those awful times.

Maybe the problems that China has experienced before and since World War II also inform Shao's demeanor and maturity. Politics, greed, hunger, betrayals, and countless other heartaches have been part of China's society, not just in recent history, but for longer than history can remember.

With his calm words, Shao revealed his personal answer to these tragedies. His is the path of leaving the world and its troubles. He leaves not just its humiliating defeats and pain, but its intoxicating victories as well. He'll renounce and leave behind the famous "three poisons" of greed, hatred, and folly. His personal answer is to live without rancor or resentment. He has mentally already "left home." He'll soon show his complete devotion to this ideal with the act of shaving off the rest of his hair, publically shedding the final vanity that identifies him with the samsaric world. He'll be someone who does not bow to a king.

37. Train to Wuhan

THE TRAIN GLIDES silently out of the station and accelerates out of town, slipping quietly over the Yang-tse and speeding into the countryside with none of the boisterous noise I've learned to expect from a Chinese railway. The train from Nanjing to Wuhan looks and moves very much like Japan's old Shinkansen, the bullet train operating in that country since the 1960s. I take a last distant look at the Mufu Mountains and the forested hills where Bodhidharma's cave sits hidden in the woods. The passengers are as quiet as the train. For the next few hours I can consider some of the facts that my trip along Bodhidharma's trail has turned up and what they might mean.

When I resolved to come to Nanjing, I hadn't included the Nanjing Massacre among my reasons for doing so. Yet in some strange sense that event now looms over my journey. For the last several nights I've researched this and related events that make up the history of Japan's occupation of Nanjing on the Chinese Internet. I especially wanted to see if there were any accounts of the destruction of Long Reed Village and Changlu Temple.

What became clear to me as I searched through the many stories available is that the meta-narrative for Japan's invasion of China in World War II included, in no small part, the propaganda that it had a sacred mission to "liberate" China. This supposed liberation had both a physical and spiritual component. Japan would free China from the clutches of Western imperialism and the threat of Soviet Communism, plus it would "unite" with China and other Asian countries to purge the scourge of liberal democracy from East Asia.

The spiritual component was, put simply, that the emperor was divine.

For a period of about one hundred years prior to World War II, certain of Japan's intellectuals developed, and the country came to deeply embrace, the ideology of *kokutai* (国体). The term is translated as "national identity" or "national polity" but has in the Japanese context the further implication of meaning "national essence." Japan's *kokutai* fused together components of Japan's ancient origin myths, including the myth of an unbroken and divine line of emperors, with modern nation-state chauvinism. A big dose of metaphysical claptrap was thrown into this heady *kokutai* brew for good measure. The result was something akin to a master race theory, complete with rituals, with the emperor acting as master of ceremonies. *Kokutai* became the political "theory," loosely defined, that underpinned Japanese militarism and expansionism.

The mythical beginning of "divine emperors" supposedly started with a goddess named Amaterasu, though the earliest-dated emperor, according to Japanese mythology, was Emperor Jimmu, who purportedly lived around 600 BCE. However, it should be noted that the historical "record" of the earliest Japanese emperors was not actually recorded in writing until after Buddhism brought that skill to the country much later. Scholars generally cite the earliest written records about the ancient Japanese emperors to the early eighth century (around the years 710–715 CE). Buddhist scriptures and the means to write history appeared in Japan more than a thousand years after the ancient Emperor Jimmu reportedly lived. Thus it seems likely that the early imperial histories were a part of the process of inventing the Japanese nation, the uniting of contending clans under unified rule.

It turns out that Buddhism played a central role in this process. The Japanese ruler Prince Shotoku (573–621), a key figure in the building of a unified Japan, famously created a "constitution" based on Buddhist and Confucian principles for the governing of the country. He lived during the Yamato period, the time when Japan's identity as a unified country took shape. During World War II, the term *Yamato* was synonymous with Japan's self-described unique national spirit or essence. One symbol of "Yamato spirit" was the country's biggest battleship of that era. Japan's largest warship, the *Yamato*, was sunk by American planes in the closing days of World War II.

The first few lines of Prince Shotoku's constitution read as follows:

Harmony [*Wa*, 和] must be upheld and conflict avoided. All men have biases, and few have farsighted vision. Thus some disobey their superiors and fathers and feud with others. But when superiors are harmonious and inferiors are friendly, then matters are discussed quietly and correct views are the basis of action.

The Three Treasures, which are Buddha, Dharma, and Sangha [the "Sangha" is the community of Buddhist believers], must be highly honored, for they are the true refuge for all beings. Few are so evil that they cannot realize the truth.

Obey the commands of your Sovereign. He is to be compared with heaven, while the vassal is like the earth, which supports heaven. When heaven and earth assume their correct place, the seasons naturally follow their course, and everything's correct nature is preserved.

But if the Earth attempts to overthrow heaven, then heaven is corrupted [and unnatural order results]. Therefore the inferior listens when his superior speaks and obeys the superior's words. Thus when you hear the commands of your superior, carry them out faithfully lest ruin will come to pass.

The ideas set forth in these passages came directly from China. Besides the references to Buddhism's "Three Treasures," the idea of the sovereign being the intermediary between heaven and earth is quintessential Chinese Confucian philosophy.

Buddhism entered Japan meaningfully in the sixth century when a powerful clan called the Soga gained ascendency over other clans vying for dominance. The Soga had strong ties to one of the three kingdoms then ruling Korea called the Baekje Kingdom. The Baekje, in turn, had ties directly to the Liang dynasty court of Emperor Wu. These ties were a major route for introducing Chinese culture to Japan, and they contained a heavy element of the Buddhist-Confucian philosophy that Emperor Wu expounded. It was not long after Emperor Wu's model of the "Bodhisattva [and Confucian] Emperor" entered Japan that the Soga clan utilized it as their ruling ideology. They were the entity that placed Prince Shotoku in power and espoused the Buddhist/Confucian ideology revealed in his constitution.

The official Chinese history of Emperor Wu's dynasty, the *Book of Liang*, tells how the Korean Baekje Kingdom sent many delegations

to Emperor Wu's court to study Chinese culture. The record specifically says that these delegations from Korea, in an earnest desire to
learn more about Buddhism, requested copies of the Lotus and Nirvana
Sutras. Emperor Wu granted their request and thus those sutras officially entered Korea during the 530s. In Japan, according to historical
records, after the Soga clan seized power in 531, the Soga chieftain
named Soga no Iname imported these and other Buddhist scriptures
through his close ties to the Korean Baekje Kingdom. Thus the Soga
clan embraced the same heady mixture of Buddhism and Confucianism that Emperor Wu used to rule his Liang dynasty, and these ideas
provided the ideology underlying Japan's clan unification, as well as
the key role of Japan's emperor in the country's unified society. In light
of this, Emperor Wu's court directly gave rise to the supposedly unique
Japanese "polity," the ideas underlying Japan's political cohesion and
establishment as a country.

But there was an even earlier and even more direct path by which
Emperor Wu's Buddhism was passed to the Soga clan and thus dif-
fused in Japan's ruling circles. In the year 522, soon after Emperor Wu
received the Bodhisattva Precepts at Flowered Woods Garden, one of
his subjects, a Buddhist sculptor named Sima Dadeng (司马达等), traveled to Japan as a Buddhist missionary and artist. He took up residence
in what was then Japan's power center, located in the area of modern
Sakurai ("Cherry Blossom") City in what is now Nara Prefecture. There
he created a Buddha Hall and sculpted Buddha statues to be placed in
it. His Buddhist proselytizing caught the ear and patronage of Soga no
Iname. Thus Japan's powerful Soga clan first learned of the great ruling wisdom of Emperor Wu and his empire through the person of the
sculptor/missionary Sima Dadeng. To the Soga it appeared clear that the
religio-political power of Emperor Wu's great empire must have resulted
from his Buddhist and Confucian devotion. Soga no Iname took this
lesson to heart, became the patron of Sima Dadeng, and spread the new
Buddhist doctrines in Japan.

Sima Dadeng's sculpture was carried on by his descendants in Japan
and became the basis of what is known as Asuka-period Buddhist sculpture. The earliest existent Buddha statue in Japan, said to be sculpted
by one of the descendants and dated to 609, still stands at Asukadera,
Japan's first Buddhist temple.

Sima Dadeng's Buddhist and Confucian gospel laid the basis for the Soga clan's ruling ideology. Perhaps just as important, Sima Dadeng brought written scriptures that introduced writing to the country. The Soga used the new ideology to unify the country and instituted writing using Chinese characters. This helped them defeat their rivals, the Mononobe clan, and thus gain ascendancy as the first unifying political clique in Japan.

The Soga clan thus embraced Sima Dadeng's Mahayana Buddhism even before its widely heralded introduction to Japan by way of Korea in 538. But it is clear that the transmission of Buddhist culture originated at Emperor Wu's court.

Emperor Wu's brand of Imperial-Way Buddhism, including the bodhisattva ideal and the Mahayana doctrines of "Buddha nature," were transmitted to Japan during the time when Emperor Wu most fervently and publically embraced these ideas. This was the same time period when Bodhidharma may have lived in the city of Tianchang north of Nanjing, and when his disciple Sengfu lived at Kaishan Temple.

The divinity of Japanese emperors, their "god" status at the center of the Japanese *kokutai* and the Yamato spirit, must be seen to be at least partly as a result of the Soga clan's embrace of the Imperial-Way Buddhism of Emperor Wu and the "Buddhist" exaltation of the Japanese ruler that started with Prince Shotoku. In China, Korea, and then Japan, Buddhism was not just a religion of home-leaving monks, but the ideology of ruling circles as well. In Japan, Imperial-Way Buddhism was first seen by the Soga clan with an eye to how imperial power could maintain "harmony" among the warring clans, and thereafter to make sure that the populace would obey their emperor. Once power is obtained, "harmony" is needed to maintain it.

Nara, Japan's ancient capital, remains today as a foremost site of ancient Japanese culture. Within Nara Prefecture is Todai Temple, an immense wooden structure that was first built around the year 752 and was the center of Imperial-Way Buddhism in early Japan. That temple, from its inception, has symbolized Buddhist ideology's protection of the Japanese state.

Reflecting on this information, I finally solve a puzzle whose answer had long eluded me. I've always wondered why it was that Zen finally took root in Japan only many centuries after it was popular in China.

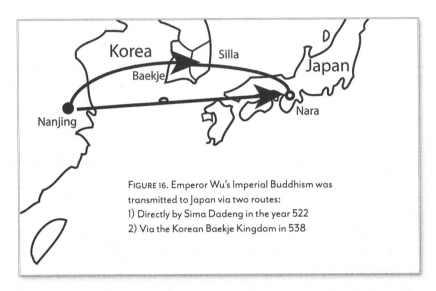

FIGURE 16. Emperor Wu's Imperial Buddhism was transmitted to Japan via two routes:
1) Directly by Sima Dadeng in the year 522
2) Via the Korean Baekje Kingdom in 538

Japan started importing Buddhism around the time Bodhidharma lived, in the early sixth century, but Zen was not established in that country until seven centuries later. Korea and Vietnam, on the other hand, embraced Bodhidharma's Zen quite early during its historical development in China. According to Zen tradition, a disciple of Zen's Third Chinese Ancestor named Sengcan transmitted Zen to Vietnam before the year 600, while Korean Zen claims to have been established when a Korean disciple of Zen's Fourth Ancestor Daoxin returned to his native land. The big difference between the time of the acceptance of Zen in Japan and in those other countries now does not appear to be an accident of history. The difference stems from the fact that from its earliest introduction in Japan, Buddhism was used to serve the interests of the state. Bodhidharma's Zen, with its antimetaphysical, anti-imperial outlook, and its avoidance of emperors, was antithetical to this political role and may not have taken root in Japan for this reason. In Japan, Buddhism has served the needs of the state from the time of its introduction into that country. Zen, by the thirteenth century, was a political pawn in Chinese politics. It was then that Japan could accept it into the special Japanese "polity."

Becoming part of the Buddhist clergy of Imperial-Way Buddhism, whether in Japan or China, could not be the quick "accepting Jesus into your heart" approach, the simple act of "directly observing mind."

It instead was a path that demanded scriptural study, especially of the Lotus Sutra, the Nirvana Sutra, and other Buddhist scriptures. Sects of Buddhism that used such sutras as the basis for their teachings were acceptable to Japan's ruling elite, and subsequently those sects flourished in Japan. Sutras that exalted bodhisattvas were exploited to enhance the prestige of ruling circles, and especially a bodhisattva sovereign, not unlike Emperor Wu.

Zen finally took root in Japan when it had evolved in China to become a fully orthodox, Imperial-Way Zen. It was only after Zen had degenerated to a point where it was compatible with and fully integrated into China's imperial system that it was also acceptable to Japan. In the thirteenth century, when Zen was studied and transmitted to Japan by Japanese monks who visited the Chinese region around Hangzhou, that area was the very center of Chinese imperial power, and Imperial Zen was its central ideology. The Five Mountains System of late Song dynasty (around 1200 CE) Chinese Zen, a system whereby Chinese Zen was administered by five central and imperially established Zen monasteries around Hangzhou Bay, served as a model for a similar system devised in Kyoto after that city became Japan's capital.

Certain of the founders of Zen in Japan seem to be aware of the problem that Imperial Zen posed, and attempted to avoid its "imperial sway." The nominal founder of Soto Zen in Japan, Eihei Dogen, is known to have avoided contact with the shogunate, the warrior rulers that exercised political power behind the façade of the emperor's throne. As it spread in Japan, Zen became more and more the handmaiden of the state. Zen's embrace of militarism during World War II is simply the culmination of Zen's evolution in Japan.

Japan's Soga clan successfully used Emperor Wu's brand of Buddhism, but not Bodhidharma's Zen, to help them consolidate imperial rule. Later, the Soga clan lost power, but the doctrine of the emperor's divinity that would in modern times underlie the creation of militant Japanism and *kokutai* had become a permanent part of the Japanese emperor's mystical identity. This essentially Buddhist identity set the stage for the emperor's mystical political position from the time of Prince Shotoku until modern times.

Since its introduction fourteen hundred years ago, Buddhism has played a critical role in Japan's view of itself. All Buddhist sects in Japan have acknowledged the role their religion must play in "protecting the country." Buddhism, in both the court of Emperor Wu as well as on the Chrysanthemum Throne of Japan, was not just a religion, but also a tool for the spreading of feudal ideology and propaganda.

Of all the Buddhist sects in Japan, it was perhaps the Nichiren School that embraced the imperial Buddhist mythology of the country most fervently. This school of Buddhism was based on the teachings of the Japanese monk Nichiren (1222–1282). It was an offshoot of the Pure Land Buddhist school that originated at Huiyuan's East Woods Temple aside Mount Lu, the temple I could see from my perch high on that mountain. Ironically, this was the same temple where Huiyuan penned the words "a monk does not bow to a king."

Using the Lotus Sutra as the basis of his philosophy, Nichiren was devoted to an extreme version of the "bodhisattva ideal." Nichiren thought himself to be a supreme bodhisattva, or even a Buddha. Based on hazy passages of the Lotus Sutra that were interpreted as prophesies, the Nichiren sect saw a divine "Buddhist" hand behind Japan's uniqueness, its *kokutai*.

My search of the Chinese Internet turned up a particularly interesting article. A Chinese scholar named He Jinsong has researched and written about the role that Japanese Buddhists played in the occupation of China during World War II. According to Professor He, many Buddhist sects provided the "spiritual" propaganda that accompanied occupation. He quotes statistics from Japanese historical sources that show that the most fervent of all the Buddhist sects supporting Japan's imperial policy was the Nichiren. But he points out and offers statistics that reveal that all the sects of Japanese Buddhism established or took control of a total of 266 temples in the state of Manchukuo, Chinese Manchuria, during Japan's occupation of that region. Among these, the two Zen sects of Soto and Rinzai together accounted for the administration of 45 temples. In a phrase that is oddly reminiscent of accounts of foreign "comfort women" that were forced to serve Japan's military troops as prostitutes, such temples were tasked to cater to the "spiritual needs" of the occupying Japanese forces. That Japanese Zen clerics were directly involved in the running of Zen temples in occupied Manchuria, and subsequently in occupied China, is a thought painful to consider.

Another article on China's Internet is perhaps even more surprising.

One of the adherents of the Nichiren sect was the Japanese World War II general leading Japan's forces in Manchuria, a lifelong military man named Kanji Ishiwara. Ishiwara saw Japan's conquest of North China as a step in the fulfillment of a Lotus Sutra prophesy that he believed foretold an era of cataclysmic war in which Japan would be ascendant, followed by a thousand years of peace. Ishiwara planned, created a pretext for, and commanded Japan's 1931 invasion of Manchuria. His policies set the stage for the invasion of the rest of China in 1937. Ishiwara believed in the need for an alliance between Japan, China, and other Asian countries to oppose Soviet Communism. After that menace was dealt with, he thought, the East Asian alliance could take on America and rid the world of the pernicious threat of liberal democracy.

The Nichiren sect to which Ishiwara belonged is highly controversial even in Japanese Buddhist circles, for it claims an absolutist position with respect to Buddhist truth, denouncing all other Buddhist sects as false. This absolutist position, combined with the belief that Japan's emperor embodied the ideal of the transcendent bodhisattva, represents a truly bizarre interpretation of Buddhist teachings.

That the Lotus Sutra, a scripture that Emperor Wu transmitted to Japan, ultimately became a tool of war ideology is clearly revealed in another passage of Brian Victoria's *Zen at War*. In discussing the rise of Imperial-Way Buddhism in Japan, Victoria quotes the principles set forth by the Nichiren Buddhist sect during the World War II era as follows:

> Imperial-Way Buddhism utilizes the exquisite truth of the Lotus Sutra to reveal the majestic essence of the national polity. Exalting the true spirit of Mahayana Buddhism is a teaching which reverently supports the emperor's work. This is what the great founder of our sect, Saint Nichiren, meant when he referred to the divine unity of Sovereign and Buddha . . . That is to say, Imperial-Way Buddhism is the condensed expression of the divine unity of Sovereign and Buddha . . . put into contemporary language. For this reason the principal image of adoration in Imperial-Way Buddhism is not Buddha Shakyamuni who appeared in India, but his majesty, the emperor, whose lineage extends over ten thousand generations.

Tragically, it would therefore appear that Emperor Wu's Imperial-Way Buddhism directly sowed the seeds that would lead to the exaltation of Japan's divine emperor. It was Emperor Wu who skillfully fused Buddhism with Confucianism into a heady metaphysical mixture of imperial divinity, a strange irony whereby a home-abiding emperor became the most exalted of spiritual beings.

But even more ironic is the sobering fact that the Nanjing Massacre occurred directly atop the site of Emperor Wu's ancient palace, the place where Imperial-Way Buddhism reached its zenith, and from where it was transported to the Land of the Rising Sun. Emperor Wu himself transferred a metaphysical Imperial-Way Buddhism to Japan that would, so many centuries later, provide the metaphysical theories justifying imperial war against China. The idea that Buddhist doctrines originated in Emperor Wu's court and were transmitted from there to Japan, then came back many centuries later armed with bayonets to commit mass murder and rape on the precise grounds of its origin, is a dark and shocking idea. Nevertheless, I propose that the awful events that occurred in 1937 and 1938 in and around Nanjing throw a spotlight on the final act of a drama that started when a real figure named Bodhidharma met Emperor Wu. The drama that started with an obscure event in an ancient court in China continued not just in the village of Long Reed, across the Yang-tse River some miles away where Emperor Wu's court stood, but on the very streets that now lie atop Wu's forgotten home. The Rape of Nanjing transpired above the place where Bodhidharma and Emperor Wu allegedly met. The meeting has more meaning than even Zen masters in the world today can remember or imagine.

Nanjing City's agony was one of many large stages for this tragedy. But one small stage was Long Reed Village, the place where Bodhidharma purportedly sought refuge from Emperor Wu's Imperial-Way court.

On June 15, 1938, according to what the cook Shao told me, Japanese occupiers killed monks at Long Reed Temple in the course of destroying it. There are reports that monks were killed at other temples during the invasion and the seven-year Japanese occupation of the area, so Shao's story of these occurrences can't be dismissed as implausible. Moreover, on the Web I've found accounts of Long Reed Village's destruction in Chinese records. Articles describe the burning of Long Reed Village itself. On that particular June night in 1938, Japanese imperial troops garrisoned at Xi Chang Gate, a place a few kilometers from Long Reed, invaded the village on intelligence reports that someone in the Chinese resistance forces was operating from there. Once the area was surrounded, a signal shot was fired, and then three invading columns of troops marched on the village. A massacre ensued. Eye-witness reports say that the entire main street of the village was turned into a "sea of fire." Many who hid in their homes to avoid gunfire died in the conflagration. On that night, it appears, Changlu Temple was also destroyed. It may be that monks were killed along with other civilians. Japanese troops knew that resistance fighters sometimes masqueraded as monks, so Buddhist clergy could be subject to the same brutal treatment as civilians who were suspected of fighting against the Japanese occupation.

This was not the first time, even in modern history, that war destroyed Changlu Temple. During the Taiping Rebellion that rocked China during the early 1860s, there were wide-ranging battles along the Yang-tse River near Nanjing. Those disturbances also laid waste to the temple. Local records indicate that by the year 1922 efforts to rebuild the temple had succeeded in creating five new halls, with a large amount of money dedicated to installing new Buddhist statues there. Those were the halls and contents destroyed by Japanese troops.

After World War II, no further serious attempts to rebuild the temple occurred, and it later became the site of the middle school that I visited and that Shao attended. Sadly, even what remains of Changlu Temple will soon be gone, making way for new industrial chemical plants planned for the area.

38. Xiangfan City

Yi's quiet meditation hut,
He built beside the empty grove,
Outside its door's a lovely peak,
Midst terraced gullies deeply wove,

Full rain poured down throughout the night,
Till an empty garden's moon did find,
A lotus pure which met my sight,
And then I knew unblemished mind.

—*"On Yi's Zen Meditation Hut" by Meng Haoran (689–740)*
of Xiangyang (now called Xiangfan) City

题义公禅房　　孟浩然著

义公习禅寂，
结宇依空林。
户外一峰秀，
阶前众壑深。

夕阳连雨足，
空翠落庭阴。
看取莲花净，
方知不染心

LIGHT IN THE HOTEL WINDOW signals that the day has arrived. I peer through the blinds to see that snow is falling and three inches has accumulated on Xiangfan City roofs. The alley I walked last night to reach the hotel is a lake of slush.

The author of the above Chinese poem, Meng Haoran, once lived here. He is among the most famous of the Tang dynasty poets. In his day the city was still called Xiangyang, as it was when Xiao Yan prepared to topple Emperor Baojuan. I arrived here by bus late last night. The four-hour bus trip from Wuhan to Xiangfan passed without a rest stop, and I arrived in Xiangfan as the sun went down. I lost my hat. I stumbled through the evening rain looking up and down alleys for the little hotel. My throat hurt in the cold. I went to bed after eating some pistachios and a Snickers bar.

Xiangfan (pronounced *Syong-fan*) is one of those huge Chinese cities (population 5.8 million) that almost no one in the West has heard of. It straddles the Han River about two hundred miles upstream and northwest from where that tributary enters the mighty Yang-tse. If Bodhidharma followed the established migration route from Mount Song to Nanjing, then he likely sailed past this city on his way south and maybe again on his return north decades later. Maybe he passed here many times during nearly fifty years of missionary work in China.

After I've had breakfast, a taxi sweeps me through the slushy streets to a bridge that crosses the Han River. The river is far larger than I had imagined it would be, and clearly wide enough to be a major travel and communications route to North China. It could easily accommodate deep-draft vessels. On the far shore I see the wall of the old city, the place where Xiao Yan presided over the area as military governor more than fifteen centuries ago. A few minutes later we pass into the old city area by crossing an ancient moat and then under a traditional Chinese city wall. We weave along a few small lanes, and the driver pulls the car up to the curb.

"That's it," says the driver. "That's the Zhao Ming Tower."

A two-story Chinese wooden pavilion sitting atop a four-story brick blockade is visible through the fog and light snow. The driver has parked next to a pedestrian street that runs from the base of the imposing structure toward the river a couple hundred meters to the north. Beneath the Zhao Ming Tower's imposing architecture is a museum of ancient Chinese art and artifacts. Stretching the length of the street in front of it are shops with traditional façades. It's clearly a tourist area when the weather is better.

The Zhao Ming Tower is named after Crown Prince Zhao Ming, the oldest son of Emperor Wu and the author of the poem examined earlier. It rests on the approximate spot where Xiao Yan's governor's office stood a millennium and a half ago. It's also where Zhao Ming was born, a year or so prior to Xiao Yan's successful overthrow of Baojuan. Although Zhao Ming lived at this spot during only the first year of his life, the city still remembers and honors his illustrious name, keeping it at the center of its old geography and equating it with its past glories.

Exiting the taxi, I point my umbrella into the blowing sleet and head toward the river along the wet pavement. Along the way a few people are buying scarves or mittens at street stalls. A number of people crowd around a man selling bowls of hot noodles. A boy bundled in a blue snowsuit rides on his father's shoulders and looks shocked to see a foreigner walking along behind him.

A passageway through the old wall of the city leads me to the south side of the wide, fast-flowing Han River. Flowing from the north, the river turns east to pass where I am standing on its southern shore and then turns south again. It looks to be a full half mile across.

The area where I'm standing on the bank is a wide pedestrian walkway and park built up several meters above the water. What is immediately obvious is why the old city was situated where I'm standing. Ships swept south on the river's current could take advantage of its turn eastward to easily land on its right bank. Grain barges and other cargos coming from North China would here find an ideal spot to land and unload. Similarly, shipping coming from the south could sail or pole its way along the north shore and then let the current sweep it into the south shore docks. Geography explains a lot.

Because of the same geography, invaders coming from the north would be at a disadvantage, their ships pushed by the bend in the river toward the starboard shore, coming within range of defenders' catapults and crossbows. The city's Web site tells how its strategic position has been the site of innumerable battles for at least three thousand years. It relates that when the Mongolians invaded China in the thirteenth century and fought their way from the north to the south of the country, it took the Great Khan's experienced army two years to overcome this historic spot's excellent defenses.

Clearly, this river was a suitable way for Bodhidharma to make his way south from the region south of Mount Song and sail all the way to Nanjing. This key part of the Bodhidharma puzzle is clear from the size and role of the Han River.

I walk west along the river a short distance and then turn left and walk south. Soon I reach Sandalwood Road. Local records say that it lies along the area where a large stream, called Sandalwood Creek, once ran. Now nothing remains of that stream due to centuries of floods and silting from the Han River. But the street is still subject to severe flooding if the Han River overflows its banks.

According to Chinese records, Governor Xiao Yan (Wu) secretly laid up stores of wood in that ancient Sandalwood Creek. When he launched his rebellion to overthrow Emperor Baojuan, he used the wood as armor on the grain barges that lined the river, creating troop transports. From here, he led his army down the Han and Yang-tse waterways, the current at his back, to win naval and land victories over Qi dynasty defenders.

Along the same Sandalwood Creek where Xiao Yan hid his timbers there was a Buddhist temple called Gold Virtue Temple. It was established by a famous Buddhist monk named Dao'an during the fourth century. Dao'an was instrumental in establishing Buddhism in China. He started the Chinese custom of naming Chinese monks with the surname Shi (pronounced *sure*) that designated them as members of the family of Shijiamuni (Shakyamuni), the historical Buddha. He was also instrumental in bringing a famous sutra translator named Kumarajiva to China from Central Asia. When Dao'an lived here in old Xiangyang, he once received a massive amount of copper as a donation to his monastery. With it, he build a sixty-foot statue of Buddha at Gold Virtue Temple, which was somewhere around where I'm walking. This imposing landmark was visible to greet beleaguered migrants that made their way down the river from Northern China. Undoubtedly, most of them stopped to take on provisions as they traveled south. It seems possible, given the timeline of Bodhidharma's possible passage along the river, that Bodhidharma stopped and stayed at that same temple located where I am now. Then it sat aside Emperor Wu's stockpile of war preparations. In any case, if Bodhidharma did indeed teach in the "south and the north" and in the region of "Luoyang and the Yang-tse," he likely stayed and taught along these banks. Perhaps it was here, even while Xiao Yan was governor of the region, that his followers numbering "like a city" crowded the banks of Sandalwood Creek to hear him speak. It's a narrative worth considering, even if any traces of his life in this area have long been swept away by the Han River's currents.

39. Mount Song and Shaolin Temple

Beside long reeds and swift clear stream,
My leisured horse and carriage track,
The creek tries to accompany
the flocks in evening winging back,
Old ruins by the river's ford,
Fall's sunset hills illuminate,
Far 'neath Song Mountain's dimming peak,
Arriving home, I close the gate.
—*"Returning to Song Mountain" by Wang Wei (699–759)*

归嵩山作　　王维著

清川带长薄，
车马去闲闲。
流水如有意，
暮禽相与还。
荒城临古渡，
落日满秋山。
迢递嵩高下，
归来且闭关

LONG BEFORE BUDDHISM arrived in China, the country's ancient Taoist philosophers had designated five sacred mountains in the country. Each mountain sat in one of the five cardinal directions of Taoist cosmology, the north, south, east, west, and the sacred center. Mount Song was the mountain at the middle, the peak of the "central" direction. Westerners don't normally think of the "center" as a direction, but this idea reflects a long-established way of thinking in Chinese culture. The name *China* itself means the "middle kingdom." In Confucianism, an

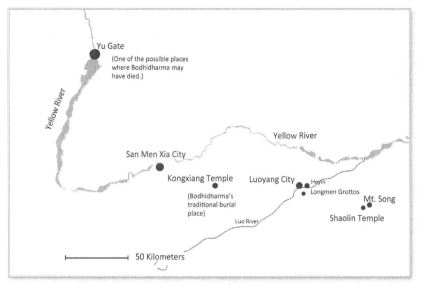

FIGURE 17. Map of Luoyang/Mount Song Area.

important idea is the "doctrine of the center." Thus when Buddhism came to China advertising itself as a religion of the "middle way," the idea found receptive ears.

Mount Song is not a single mountain but an area that holds two large mountains and some lesser peaks and valleys. The largest peak, which in Chinese may be called either "Mount Song" or the "Big House," is said to be where a grand residence of Yu the Great, the first great unifier of China, was located. Legends say that sometime around 2000 BCE, Yu tamed the raging Yellow River by dredging and using dykes. The smaller peak of Mount Song, called "Little House," is where Yu reportedly set up a smaller residence for his wife's younger sister. From the Chinese term "little house" (*shao shi*) comes the name for Mount Song's most famous temple, Shaolin (meaning "Little Woods"), which was set amid the forest by the Little House Mountain slopes.

Not far from Mount Song is the city of Luoyang, a city that served as the capital of many of China's ancient dynasties. From the country's earliest times, emperors came from there to worship the nation's gods on Mount Song's slopes.

The city of Dengfeng, which rests amid Mount Song's peaks and valleys, now offers hotels for the legions of tourists that flock to visit the place's most famous site, Shaolin Temple. The city is also famous for forty or so boarding academies that serve both as schools and training centers for young Chinese martial arts students. The city's name, Dengfeng, literally means "Ascendant Fiefdom," but locals say this name is derived from an earlier term with the same pronunciation. In ancient times China's only empress, named Wu Zetian, loved to come from her court in Luoyang to visit and pay honor to Mount Song's Buddhist teachers. She would "ascend the peak," which also is pronounced *deng feng* in Chinese. Wu Zetian, having never traveled too far from Luoyang, thought Mount Song to be the world's highest mountain.

Shaolin Temple is not simply the legendary home of the world's *kong fu* practitioners. It is known as the "birthplace" of Zen in China. According to the prevailing story, Bodhidharma came here after failing to come to an understanding with Emperor Wu and remained here for nine years, practicing his Zen meditation in a cave near Shaolin Temple.

Soon after I arrived last night on a bus from Zhengzhou City, a snowstorm blanketed the area. This morning the street in front of the hotel is frozen, and the few cars and pedestrians brave enough to venture out carefully inch their way along. Despite this, some taxis are still pursuing their livelihood, and I wave one to the side of the huge roundabout intersection near my hotel. We set off slowly into the mists toward the base of Song Mountain.

40. Shaolin Temple

ALTHOUGH THE TERM *kong fu* usually means "martial arts," it may refer to any great skill or capacity. In Chinese there is an old verse about Bodhidharma that goes like this:

> Bodhidharma came from the west with a single word, "*Mu*!,"
>> The nature of mind was his only *kong fu,*
>> Trying to grasp Dharma by using written words,
>> You'll drain Poting Lake to make the ink, but it still will never do!

达磨西来一字无，
全凭心意下工夫，
若从纸上寻佛法，
笔尖蘸干洞庭湖。

The word *Mu* in the verse is a double entendre, since it literally means "no" or "none." Thus the verse on the one hand means that Bodhidharma didn't bring a single word with him to China (no scriptures to study). But later the single word *mu* became the focus of a famous *mu koan* of Zen. In Japan and the West, many Zen students concentrate on this single word, *mu*, as part of their Zen training. So the verse above is a typical Chinese play on words with a clever twofold meaning. This *mu* reference is also about the same word that the Japanese militarist Sugimoto employed to explain his worship of the Japanese emperor.

Shaolin Temple claims, through its connection with Bodhidharma, to be the home of both Zen and Chinese *kong fu*. From its earliest days, Shaolin was connected to the imperial court. Its founder, the Zen teacher

Fotuo, reportedly established the temple in 496 under the command and support of Emperor Xiao Wen of the Northern Wei dynasty, and thereafter Shaolin long represented the unity of the imperial throne and the Buddhist religion.

Like Emperor Wu, Emperor Xiao Wen devoted himself to Buddhist sutra study, issues of doctrine, building temples, and ordaining monks and nuns. He proclaimed himself to be the Tathagata (Buddha), and he actively took part in religious life. In the year 476, for example, he ordained a group of a hundred monks and nuns, personally cutting their hair and enrobing them in a grand ceremony. He also sponsored vegetarian banquets for the Buddhist clergy. In 478, during one such banquet, he pardoned the country's condemned criminals. In 493, he established forty-seven precepts required to be taken by those entering monkhood.

Old records make clear that Emperor Xiao Wen was devoted to the study of Buddhist doctrines. He did not, however, forsake the study of Zen, as indicated by his enthusiasm for the Zen teacher Fotuo who established Shaolin Temple. Even before Shaolin temple was established, Emperor Xiao Wen built a large Zen monastery near his old northern capital city of Pingcheng where Fotuo could teach.

How can the fact that Bodhidharma is called the First Ancestor of Zen be reconciled with the fact that his contemporary Fotuo, who was also a non-Chinese of South Asian origin, was a Zen teacher? An explanation for this can be found in the Chinese Zen tradition itself. Fotuo is described as an advocate of Hinayana ("Little Vehicle") Zen, as opposed to the more lofty Mahayana ("Great Vehicle") Zen. But the alleged difference between Zen before Bodhidharma and Zen after Bodhidharma may simply be the result of politics. The earliest major Zen advocate in China was a monk named Anshigao who lived three centuries before Bodhidharma. He based his Zen practice on the Yin Chi Ru Sutra. A rendering of this scripture's name in English might be "Entering [the Way by] Practicing [supporting] the Mysterious [darkness]." The scripture taught "stillness [meditation] and observing." Since Bodhidharma's own teaching was "observing the nature of the human mind," through meditation, the alleged difference between early Chinese Hinayana Zen and Bodhidharma's Mahayana Zen seems to be not too great. Bodhidharma's purported practice of "observing mind" doesn't look that much different from what came before him. Perhaps Bodhidharma, in line with his times, embraced the Bodhisattva ideal as indicated in his "Two Entrances and Four Practices" cited above. In any case, claims that Bodhidharma was the first Ancestor of Zen seem to have much to do with politics. The clear demarcation between his Zen and Emperor Wu's Imperial Zen is stark.

Under the Northern Wei Emperor's orders, Fotuo officially founded Shaolin Temple in the year 496. Presumably it took about two years to build the temple, so the date surrounding its establishment matches with the time when Bodhidharma's disciple Sengfu is recorded in the *Continued Biographies* to have departed from the same area. Bodhidharma and his disciples are said to have lived at a spot about a mile from Shaolin Temple that is now a small nunnery. In light of the *Continued Biographies* timeline that claims that Sengfu left the area in 494 and again in 496, the date recorded for when Shaolin Temple was built, the possibility that Bodhidharma and his monks were living at the place and decided to move when construction on the new temple began is worth considering. Tellingly, despite his association with the place, mention of Bodhidharma cannot be found in Shaolin Temple's early records. Also, there is no trace of him found in the court history of Emperor Xiao Wen. It seems he wasn't in the area, or at least had dropped out of sight, by the time that temple's construction was finished.

Yet strangely, since the sixteenth century or so, the temple has claimed that Bodhidharma not only started Zen at this place, but *kong fu* as well. Where did the *kong fu* connection come from?

Popular folklore and some solid historical clues do connect Shaolin Temple to Chinese *kong fu* from early in its history, yet there is no evidence that Bodhidharma had anything to do with this. Scholars have suggested, and recent archeological evidence supports, the idea that the temple's *kong fu* began with a disciple of the temple's founder, Fotuo. That monk, named Seng Chou, one of the great Zen teachers cited and praised highly by Daoxuan, seems to have learned to defend himself from tigers in the mountains using a staff. This may be the origin of Shaolin Temple's famous *kong fu*.

SHAOLIN TEMPLE AND IMPERIAL-WAY BUDDHISM

Uncertain folklore and *kong fu* notwithstanding, Shaolin Temple's close ties with China's emperors is a prominent feature of the temple's history. During the battles that established China's most illustrious and famous Tang dynasty (713–905), a handful of Shaolin's monks assisted the future Tang emperor Tai Zong (ruled 627–650) by stealthily capturing an enemy general. Later, this brave martial act was commemorated on a stele erected by that emperor, its text still proudly displayed at Shaolin Temple today.

If the Tang emperors who lived long after Bodhidharma wanted to make a show of embracing his Zen tradition and co-opting it into their political sphere, then connecting him to Shaolin Temple in legend makes sense. It's easy to see why they would push that idea. By taking over the Zen tradition and declaring its origin to be in the imperial monastic system, they could bask in the light of Bodhidharma's popularity and also put an end to his tradition's irritating independent streak. Claiming that Bodhidharma was part of a place synonymous with Imperial-Way Buddhism helped consolidate imperial authority over that wayward religious element.

In this light, Shaolin's association with Bodhidharma reveals not the origin of Zen but his tradition's political capture by China's emperors.

Back in the present, my taxi creeps along the icy road and under a gray overcast and light snow. "Stop at the gas station on the left before we get to the temple," I say. "My friend will meet me there."

A young European man in the long thick winter frock of a monastic stands on the other side of the road next to the gas station. He is tall and has the bald head of a monk.

It must be Shanli. He greets me with a handshake and waves toward the back entrance gate of Shaolin Temple. "This way," he says, his breath making a big cloud of steam in the winter air.

We set off into the valley where Shaolin Temple and its many related structures sit. The guard waves us past the side entrance gate where residents go in and out.

We begin to get acquainted by talking about our obvious common interest, Shaolin Temple history.

"Seng Chou, the third abbot of Shaolin, was the person who actually started the *kong fu* tradition," says Shanli. "There's no evidence that Bodhidharma had any part in it."

"That's exactly what I've been telling people in my lectures for the past year," I say. "You're the first person I've ever met that also says that!"

Shanli tells me how he arrived in China at the age of sixteen. In Leipzig, his home in what was previously Communist East Germany, he was an accomplished pianist, a student at the Bach Institute. When he arrived in China, he thought he would spend a year or so here. After two days in Beijing, he traveled to Shaolin Temple, where he has remained now for nearly twelve years. Now, at twenty-eight, he's spent long years in *kong fu* training, meditation, esoteric Buddhist practices, and learning to speak both Chinese and English fluently. He was only seven or eight years old when the Berlin Wall came down. He detests the society he lived in as a young child.

"The Stasi [East German secret police] were the best spies in the world," he says. "They had informers and files for everyone. People say I gave up living in one Communist society to come live in another one. But the truth is that my guru—is that the right word? There should be a better one—anyway, my guru is transmitting something very special to me, and I don't dare leave now."

We arrive at the main temple complex, and Shanli leads me to a side gate. We enter a small compound with a bronze statue of a bare-chested monk in the center of a courtyard. Chinese characters on the statue's torso depict the locations of energy meridians, all important for both *kong fu* and traditional Chinese medicine. At the side of the courtyard we enter a guest reception room.

"Have a seat!"

We sit at a burled wooden tea table, and two Shaolin monks already seated there serve us Chinese tea.

"That's Shaolin's finest," says Shanli.

The hot tea pierces the frozen landscape of the deep winter day.

During the course of the afternoon, Shanli and I take a walk to a waterfall that is nestled in a nearby mountain gulley. The whole scene is covered with snow, and the water of the creek is frozen solid. It's obvious why Buddhist monks faced a living problem when they tried to establish Buddhism here in North China. No one could live outside in conditions like this. It's just way too cold. But while Fotuo sought and used the emperor's funds to build Shaolin Temple and take refuge from the frigid winter, Bodhidharma was sitting in a cave somewhere up on the mountain behind us. No cushy politically compromised monastery for him!

FIGURE 18. Shanli, near Shaolin Temple, 2009.

Shanli talks about what it's been like to live as a foreigner amid Shaolin's ancient traditions.

"Back in the day there weren't many people living here. Back then I knew everyone. We practiced *kong fu* every day and the food wasn't good. The toilets were especially horrible. Sometimes they were over-flowing with sewage and filled with maggots. In some of them there was literally a couple inches of shit covering the ground. Conditions were really bad. And food poisoning! I got food poisoning a lot. In fact that's probably what caused me to suffer appendicitis. The abbot saved my life. He personally got me into a hospital in Zhengzhou to have an operation. His bodyguards carried me in and made sure I got care. The facilities were unbelievable. There were buckets and rags lying around the operating theatre. The doctor asked me before the operation if I had any final messages to send to loved ones before they put me under. I told him my only request was that they don't let me be awake during the operation!"

Shanli's story reminds me about the fact that taking "final requests" seems to have been a Chinese custom at least until recently. During my early years traveling in China, I heard stories that "final messages" were collected from any airline passengers unlucky enough to be on an airplane experiencing in-flight difficulties. I didn't believe this until a Chinese business friend told me his experience. He was on a flight that had engine trouble. The flight attendants handed out paper and pens to people and then told them to put their "final messages" in a metal strongbox, apparently kept on hand just for this purpose. My friend said that the sight of the box caused many people to scream and pass out from fright.

Shanli continues, "But I woke up anyway. I was lying there, and though I couldn't feel much pain, I could feel the surgeon cutting on me. When he pulled out my appendix, I asked him to give it to me, and he did. There I was holding my appendix in my hand!"

I thought of my own experience in a Chinese operating theatre and decided not to mention it. "Have you been the only foreigner here or have there been others?" I ask.

"Early on, when living here was particularly difficult, some foreigners would come and stay for a while and then leave. The conditions were just too much for them to deal with. There was a Frenchman who came here. He was really into the mystique of the whole thing and was pretty crazy. He did the martial arts for a while but never advanced very far. There was a young Malaysian man here at the same time. A young woman was here doing research, and they were both interested in her. The Frenchman was a lot taller than the Malaysian, and he'd stand over him and say, 'Listen to me! I am zee volf! And zis is my territory!' Later the Frenchman wanted to get a tattoo on each of his forearms, one of a dragon and one of a tiger. But he didn't want a real tattoo, he actually wanted outlines of these animals burned into his arm using hot metal, like, what do you call it? A brand! He had two pieces of metal shaped like a dragon and tiger. He insisted that we help him do this at a bar outside the monastery. He asked me to hold him down while another friend stuck the hot iron on his flesh. We told him he was crazy, but he got some others to agree to do it, and I went along to watch. After having some drinks, they heated the brand in a charcoal burner, and he said, 'Okay! Do it!' Someone started to press it against him, and he started screaming. The guy pressing the brand against him passed out from fright. He fell on the floor. They botched it up real bad, and the Frenchman ended up with a horrible wound that didn't look like a dragon or anything. He went back to France and had operations to repair the damage."

Shanli looks at the top of my head and suddenly says, "I can tell you don't practice *mizong* [Esoteric Buddhism, a tradition of "secret" teachings]. There's no energy coming out of the top of your head. People who practice *mizong* can see each other's energy."

I counter that as a Zen Buddhist I take care to be sure there are no signs associated with my Buddhist practice.

Shanli is happy to tell me about his long experience at Shaolin, and we talk through the long afternoon. Before I know it, night has fallen, and Shanli says it's time for dinner. It will be served shortly at the upper monks' dining hall.

If you visit an old temple like Shaolin on a warm summer day, you might not sense the age of the place. Even sitting in the meditation hall of some old temple may not give you the feeling that you've connected with the ancients that practiced there long ago. But if you walk on a dark winter's night through a temple's silent, icy pathways, snow on rooftops, steps dimly lit, your feet feeling your away along, then you have an intimate connection with every monk who's ever felt his way to the dining hall to get a hot meal on a frozen night. The carved stone tortoises in the silent temple courtyard bear witness.

Near the kitchen, Shanli knocks on a door where some monks reside, and one opens it to greet him. They exchange some words and invite us in. One of the monks, who looks to be no more than sixteen or seventeen years old, sits on his bed, a blanket wrapped around his neck.

"His neck is affected by the intense cold here," says Shanli. "It penetrates the neck muscles and is extremely painful. I suffered from this myself before. You wouldn't believe how cold it can get at night in this place. What he's suffering from is almost unbearable."

Shanli has brought some special medicine for the young monk, an herbal salve of some sort. The monk follows us to the nearby monastery kitchen, where the evening meal is being prepared. The steam from many hot water taps, large vats of vegetable soup, and steaming *mantou* buns warms the long room where the evening meal is being prepared. Shanli sits the monk on a stool out of the way of the cooks and rubs the Chinese herbal medicine on the boy's neck. The warmth and light of the kitchen and Shanli's efforts cause the boy to visibly relax. After several minutes of strong rubbing, Shanli takes a medicated patch and applies it to the boy's neck. The world of monks is a world of mutual brotherly support. On such a night in the winter, a famous temple like Shaolin is still little more than a lonely outpost, its inhabitants a mutually supportive family.

Shanli and I, as lay persons, sit on the outermost tables of the hall during the evening meal. The days of poor sanitation and poor food are clearly gone, for the mushroom and vegetable soup served by the kitchen staff is full-bodied and deliciously filling. Meals are eaten in silence. Bowls are held in the left hand and chopsticks are held with the right. I wonder if any of the monks is left-handed. Left-handedness is still thought to be sort of a defect here, and there is little or no accommodation for left-handed people.

After dinner, having crunched through the frozen snow and returned to Shanli's quarters, Shanli calls a friend to have him come and return me to my hotel. But the roads are completely frozen, and he's not sure if his friend can make it to the temple. We set out toward the side temple gate, located a kilometer or two from the temple complex, walking carefully on the frozen road. A taxi appears that has brought some monks to the temple. We wave it down, and the driver agrees to drive me to the city. When we call Shanli's friend to inform him of this, we discover his car has broken down and he can't come to get me anyway. Agreeing to meet the next day, I bid Shanli good-bye and soon emerge onto the icy road in front of Shaolin's tourist area. Four large trucks have slid and collided on the ice within a mile of the temple entrance. They block most of the road. Emergency vehicles sit flashing. One of the cabs on a truck is smashed and twisted.

The following morning, I take another taxi to Shaolin and go knock on the door of Shanli's private room so we can make plans for the day. He's working at his laptop computer when I arrive.

"Here, take a look at this." On the computer he brings up a digital photo of an extremely scary-looking, very large insect of some type. "I photographed that right there, in the corner of my room. There are some bugs here you wouldn't believe. Huge things that will visit in the coldest part of winter to get some of the warmth of the room. There's one bug that can run so fast I can't take its picture. You could never catch it. Its bite is extremely poisonous."

I look warily along the rafters of the room.

"Look at these," says Shanli. On the floor next to his computer are a pair of furry, high ankle slippers with wires running out of them. They are plugged into the power strip by his desk. "These are my electric shoes. It's so cold here that my feet get frozen while I sit at my desk. I just bought these to try to ward off the cold."

FIGURE 19. Shanli's Electric Shoes to Withstand the Freezing Shaolin Winter.

I'm starting to respect more than ever Bodhidharma sitting in his lonely frozen cave just up the hill from here.

"It's cold today," says Shanli, "but it's nothing compared to what will come in the middle of the winter. During those times I've woken up half frozen to death and just lay there waiting for daylight to come." Shanli turns on an electric water pot and it soon begins to hiss. "Here's my solution to the cold."

On Shanli's desk sits a big jar of Nescafé and an equally large container of honey. When the water is boiling, he fills two coffee mugs each halfway full of coffee and honey and then pours in the steaming water. He hands one of the mugs to me. It looks like boiled sludge. I swallow a mouthful of his special tonic and can't suppress an involuntary shudder. But within a few minutes I notice that it is definitely effective. I wonder if monks of old also had some elixir like this to bolster their Qi.

I tell Shanli that I want to visit the Second Ancestor's Hut, a spot about a mile from the temple proper. He suggests we first visit the "Waiting in the Snow Pavilion" within the temple itself. That's the place where the Second Ancestor allegedly stood waiting in the snow to receive Bodhidharma's teaching. We drink some more hot coffee to steel ourselves against the cold, then walk into the courtyard and go through a passage to the center of the temple complex. At its upper reaches, past the old abbot's quarters, is the Waiting in the Snow Pavilion.

Shanli explains that, according to tradition, the Emperor Tai Zong of the Tang dynasty visited the temple sometime in the mid-600s. He was shown this spot where the Second Ancestor was said to have stood in the snow and cut off his arm to show his spiritual resolve. The emperor commanded that a pavilion be built to commemorate the spot. But didn't Bodhidharma sit in the cave that is up on the mountain? Why would Huike be standing here in the middle of the temple? My guess is that the emperor wasn't about to climb the mountain, so they just said that the legendary event happened here, a place convenient for an emperor to visit.

On the terrace in front of the little pavilion, there are a couple of young men who appear to be foreign tourists also looking at the scene. One pulls out a cigarette and starts digging in his pocket for a match. Shanli offers him his lighter and we start a conversation. The three of them light up smokes, while I rotate my position slightly to stand upwind. One of the two men, who introduces himself as Marc, says he is from the United Kingdom and is in China doing doctoral research about the situation with orphans here. The other man, named Hashlik, says in somewhat broken English that he is from Ukraine. They are friends and have just come to Shaolin for a visit.

The conversation turns to cigarettes. Marc says that cigarettes have opened a lot of doors for him in China. Despite the increasing public-smoking bans, smoking is still a sort of social ritual that is quite pervasive. We agree. Smoking is deeply entrenched in Chinese culture, but especially its business culture. It's one especially obnoxious habit that China has imported from the West. Some people know that the English forced the Chinese to import opium grown in British India by means of the famous Opium Wars of the mid-1800s. What is less known is that in the early 1900s the British American Tobacco company (BAT) widely introduced tobacco to Chinese farmers for them to grow as a cash crop. BAT then bought the tobacco from the farmers, made cigarettes with mechanized production, and sold the product by the millions to the armies fighting in World War I. For a short time, Chinese peasant farmers prospered like never before, and their farmland was widely given over to tobacco cultivation. But when the war ended and demand suddenly ceased, the economy of the Chinese countryside collapsed almost overnight just as other natural disasters came about that hurt the food supply. The situation turned grave. Millions died of starvation during the following years. After that tobacco became a widespread and permanent part of China's social fabric.

We invite Marc and Hashlik to join us on a hike to the Second Ancestor's Hut on a nearby mountain. Under Shanli's lead we all set off.

The Second Ancestor of Zen, Huike, is sometimes referred to as the First Ancestor of Zen in China. Since Bodhidharma was a foreigner, it follows that his most famous Chinese disciple, who received the Zen "mind to mind" transmission from him, was the first Chinese Ancestor. Legends about Huike are varied and obscure. Some claim that he once served as the abbot of Shaolin Temple, although that is unlikely. In any case, the big body of Zen historical texts called the *Lamp Records* relate that only Huike understood the essence, literally the "marrow," of Bodhidharma's teaching. After that, he is said to have lived on one of the mountains that surround Shaolin Temple.

It's been several years since Shanli last visited the Second Ancestor's Hut, and he leads us up a trail hardly perceivable under the winter snow

now beginning to slushily melt in the midday sun. I notice that Hashlik is wearing sneakers, and his feet are almost immediately soaked from snow.

"There must be a better trail than this one. Are you sure there isn't an easier way?" I ask Shanli.

"This is it," he says. "This is the trail."

For about forty-five minutes, we climb steadily through the light forest and snowy slopes of the mountain. Hashlik, his feet growing wetter and colder with each step, frequently declares he is going to go back, but Shanli always dissuades him, assuring us all that we are almost at the top of the mountain. We pass the collapsed towers of a cable car that once served the mountain, the cables now winding through the low forest. The climb gets more difficult and the trail hard to follow in the heavy brush and snow. At last, after crossing an area of deep snow and reeds ("Be careful," says Shanli, "I think there's a pond under the snow here"), we emerge at the top of the mountain.

The Second Ancestor's Hut is in a small compound. The gate is locked, and there's no one around. We walk another hundred yards or so to a lookout with an expansive view of Mount Song's peaks. Next to the railing, Shanli and Marc stop for a smoke.

Shanli takes a big drag on a "gaff" (what he calls a cigarette) and blows smoke into the clear mountain air. Behind him the snow-covered peaks of Mount Song shine radiantly in the winter sun. He looks like some bizarre advertisement for an Alpine cigarette.

Nearby, a simple statue of the Second Ancestor stands in the snow, portraying a scene from his legend.

Shanli points to a distant valley in the Song Mountains west of the peak where we stand. There appears to be a village nestled between the slopes of the snowy valley. Shanli says it's not a village, but a big mining operation that exists out of sight of the tourists and visitors. He says the pollution from the site has been a big issue, but it hasn't been closed down.

The pollution problem in China gets a lot of press but not much action. China's coal production is a huge source of pollution both because of mining activities and due to CO_2 emissions. The poster child of China's pollution problem is probably Lake Tai, a huge body of water near the famous garden city of Suzhou. So many factories and cities dumped waste into the lake that it erupted into a massive algae bloom, destroying its ancient fishing industry and causing a foul-smelling mess. Local politicians, protecting their industries and jobs, ignore national pollution laws, and the result is that one of China's most famous scenic areas is blighted. After central government officials praised local environmental activists that fought against Lake Tai's pollution, the local officials threw them in jail anyway.

Soon it's time to go back, as Marc and Hashlik need to catch a train that evening from Zhengzhou. Shanli leads us back toward where we emerged onto the mountaintop in the deep snow. Suddenly we notice there is a work crew working at the mountain's old cable car terminal building. We stop to learn that there's a plan to resurrect the easy way up the mountain. There are several workers standing around. I realize there must be a good path down the mountain, one used by the work crew to transport materials. Happily, this is the case. It's been too many years since Shanli climbed this mountain, and he didn't know about it. This is great news for Hashlik's feet, which are spared a further drenching in the wet snow. We find that the path down the mountain, though well-traveled, is compressed snow and pretty slick. For a while we slide along, grabbing tree branches and shrubs to keep from falling. Somehow the conversation turns to the poetry of Charles Bukowski. Despite our widely divergent backgrounds from four different countries, we've all read that poet. We're still swapping our favorite stories about him when we reach the base of the mountain.

41. Bodhidharma's Cave

THE NEXT DAY under a bright sun, Shanli and I depart the monastery for a final hike in the mountains.

The path to Bodhidharma's famous cave is well-constructed with stone and mortar. The problem is that it leads up a pretty steep mountain, so you should be in reasonable shape, or at least not be in a rush, to visit the place.

"As part of our *kong fu* training, we used to run up and down this mountain several times in one morning," says Shanli. "Once when we were doing this, some members of the hip-hop group Wu-Tang Clan were visiting. They were impressed when I ran up and down the mountain but were more impressed to see me light up a gaff when I finished."

I guess Shanli's ability to do impressive physical feats while smoking has something to do with his study of Esoteric Buddhism. But I recommend against trying this at home.

The path from Shaolin Temple to Bodhidharma's cave takes us past a little temple compound called "Bodhidharma's Hermitage." It's a place at the foot of the mountain where he is said to have lived. Now it's a small nunnery surrounded by a high wall. The gate at the front is open, so we enter to take a few photos in front of a small Buddha Hall that serves as a place of practice for the nuns. The building, built seven hundred years ago, is by far the oldest building still standing around Shaolin Temple. It is in a traditional Chinese style with fishtail eaves. Inside on the walls, barely visible in the darkness, are painted frescoes of the first six Zen Ancestors. The paintings are faded, and the characters that accompany them are hard to read. I ask a nun who is in the building how old the old paintings are, but she says she doesn't know.

Outside near the front door is a tall cypress tree. A sign next to it says it was planted by the Sixth Zen ancestor, Huineng, when he came to visit this famous place connected to Bodhidharma. Behind the little Buddha

Hall on an elevated area is a living compound for the nuns. In several visits here over the years, I've found the nuns to be very friendly and happy to meet foreigners. However, their director discourages such contact, and people aren't allowed to venture near their living quarters.

Big icicles hanging from the edge of the roof are glistening and dripping in bright sunlight. The day is warming rapidly. We exit the Bodhidharma hermitage and continue our walk to the cave.

On the new steps up the mountain, there are places to stop and enjoy the view. The general landscape, which includes a view of Shaolin Temple tucked between Big House Mountain and Little House Mountain, is about the same as what Bodhidharma saw when he stayed here fifteen hundred years ago. Of course the rest of the world is entirely different. Still, the world offers a lot of reasons why leaving it behind and moving onto this quiet mountain could be appealing. Before too long, but with some effort, we reach the level terrace constructed in front of Bodhidharma's cave. It measures about ten by thirty feet or so, and is partly covered in snow. The sun, low in the winter sky, casts long shadows over the quiet mountains. The silence and light plus the space and snow all support the timeless feeling of the place. Behind the *paifang* that marks the small cave is an alcove where some old monuments rest. Looking into the cave itself, I see that the nun who usually comes up the mountain to guard against taking pictures inside the place is gone today. We take advantage of this opportunity to photograph each other in the cave next to a statue of its famous inhabitant's likeness.

The traditional Zen story of how Bodhidharma instructed his famous disciple Huike about the "no-self-nature" of mind describes an event that allegedly happened in front of this cave.

According to the story, which appears in various late texts including the late-thirteenth-century *Compendium of Five Lamps*, which tells the "official story" of Bodhidharma, Bodhidharma practiced meditation within the walls of this cave every day. Huike, an earnest seeker of the Dharma, stood outside the cave in the snow, waiting for Bodhidharma to emerge. Finally, Bodhidharma emerged from the cave, and Huike seized his chance, saying, "My mind is troubled. Please pacify it!"

Bodhidharma then replied, "Bring me your mind, and I'll pacify it."

This answer gave Huike pause, and he finally said, "Although I've looked for my mind, I can't find it."

FIGURE 20. Bodhidharma's Cave near Shaolin Temple.

Bodhidharma then said, "There! I've pacified it!"

You might think Bodhidharma was trying to be cute. His point was that an individual's mind does not exist as an entity that can be separated from external experience. Bodhidharma was pointing out that no matter how hard Huike would try to find something that could uniquely be called his personal "mind" or "soul," he would never be able to do so. The perceptions of the mind cannot be divorced from perceptions and memories that originate "outside." What is mistakenly thought to be a genuinely existent, some sort of separate "self" may be sought for a lifetime or more. But no such "self" will ever be found. There is, in this Buddhist view, no soul. There is no individually existing mind that exists outside of the arising of the "other."

I examine the cave. I think Bodhidharma may have really sat here. But my view is that he did so sometime during the years 475 to 494, when Shaolin Temple did not yet exist, or at least was not yet a formally established temple. The Bodhidharma hermitage down at the base of this mountain is a mile or so away from Shaolin. Bodhidharma may have lived at the place where the hermitage now sits at a time predating the temple's establishment or, if after the temple was established, with only a tenuous connection to the temple itself. He "avoided places of imperial sway," and he likely regarded Shaolin as just such a place after it was officially established by imperial decree. Anyway, that Bodhidharma sat in a freezing cave and not in the warm temple attests to his avoidance of the place.

Back on the terrace in front of the cave, Shanli starts doing a set of *kong fu* movements to the entertainment of a handful of tourists. He's obviously a real master of this "Chinese boxing." He does a martial form of the exercises, not the slow meditative form that is better known. His arms and legs move so fast that they seem little more than a blur in the crisp mountain air.

We hike past the cave and climb the final fifty yards or so to the top of the peak. There, a large white statue of Bodhidharma gazes out over peaks and valleys of Mount Song. In the other direction, the view from the back side of the mountain stretches toward Luoyang City, just out of view behind hills in the west. Shanli does more *kong fu* movements, and I snap his picture with the big Bodhidharma, the purported First Ancestor of *kong fu*, in the background. As the sun begins to set, we turn to go back.

42. Huishan Temple

WHILE SHAOLIN IS the most famous, it certainly is not the only important Buddhist temple on ancient Mount Song. Huishan Temple, which sits at the base of Big House Mountain—Mount Song's highest and most prominent peak—was originally a mountain palace retreat for the Wei emperor Xiao Wen, the same emperor who moved his capital to Luoyang from the north of China and may have forced Bodhidharma to leave the Mount Song area. As I described previously, Emperor Xiao Wen was of the Tuoba people, a "barbarian" nationality that conquered Northern China. He wanted his foreign Wei dynasty to not only rule and control all of China but also to fully accept and embrace China's superior civilization. Both his Tuoba people and the Han Chinese they conquered were dubious about this fusing of cultures. By moving his capital to Luoyang from the cold north, Xiao Wen enhanced his Chinese bona fides by occupying the imperial grounds of many ancient Chinese dynasties. With this move he took control of the sacred center, the symbolic location from which emperors who had received heaven's mandate should properly rule. By building a branch palace on Mount Song itself, which subsequently became Huishan Temple, he presented himself to the Tuoba and Chinese people alike as the true and rightful ruler of the Middle Kingdom. Appearances and symbols mattered, and Emperor Xiao Wen did his best to appropriate the key symbols of Chinese culture. He then leavened his political authority, like Emperor Wu who came later, with Buddhist doctrines, so that he would appear to occupy the moral high ground.

After Emperor Xiao Wen died in the year 499, his palace on Mount Song was converted into a temple. Thereafter, it was home to several famous monks of various Buddhist schools. Most important, it may be the place where the Southern Zen school of Huineng came face-to-face with Buddhist establishment of the northern court in Luoyang. Mount

Song's Huishan temple may have been an important battleground in the struggle between Imperial Zen and the Zen of Bodhidharma, the Fourth Ancestor Daoxin, and Huineng, the Zen of just "observing mind."

The parking lot at Huishan Temple is covered with snow. My taxi rolls gingerly into the virgin whiteness, and I negotiate a suitable fee to have the driver wait for me on an icy fall morning. From the parking lot, I ascend some steps and pass under a *paifang* that leads to the temple halls. But the place is no longer a practicing temple. It is now a museum that houses exhibits about some of Mount Song's most famous ancient monks. I make my way up the slope toward what was once the Heavenly Kings Hall. In front of it stand two bare-branched but nonetheless magnificent old gingko trees. According to the temple's records, they are more than fifteen hundred years old, which means they were planted when Emperor Xiao Wen established his palace here. Recently these and more than a hundred other ancient ginkgo trees that remain on Mount Song have been given special attention in order to preserve them. Like the tree I saw at Changlu Temple, they silently watch over Mount Song's ancient Buddhist sites. The earliest such gingko trees are at Fawang ("Dharma King") Temple farther up the mountain. That place is another example of the Dharma King idea that long preceded Emperor Wu— the Dharma King Temple on Mount Song was established in the years immediately following Buddhism's "official" introduction to China. The two Indian monks who legendarily brought Buddhism to China were present when those trees were planted in the first century.

But Huishan Temple's main hall and museum are closed today. The museum staff has wisely decided that no one is crazy enough to try to come for a visit with so much snow on the ground (not taking into consideration a history-obsessed foreigner). So further investigation about the mysterious monk who lived here, named Jingzang, will have to wait.

What I know already adds some interesting bits to the puzzle of Bodhidharma's Zen.

A few years ago I visited Huishan Temple for the first time and spent an afternoon studying displays about its famous monks. Among them was a monk named Lao An ("Old An"). *An* means "peace" or "safety." He was a student of Zen's Fifth Ancestor, Hongren, whose temple is near Daoxin's at Huangmei.

Ancient records say that Wu Zetian (China's only empress, to whom I referred earlier) respected Old An very highly, and she came to Mount Song on three occasions to honor him. She thereafter renamed this temple Anguo ("Peaceful Nation") Temple. During about that time, Bodhidharma's Zen became a mainstream Buddhist religion at the nearby Tang dynasty "Eastern Capital" of Luoyang. There the monk Shenxiu, the leader of what was to be called the Northern and Gradual Zen school, along with his disciples, was expounding his Zen teachings. He taught at Luoyang's imperial court over the course of several years and reigning periods. Shenxiu would be known as the "Teacher of Three Emperors."

I probably first read about Huishan Temple in the book *The Northern School and the Formation of Early Chan Buddhism* by the American Zen scholar John McCrae. In his book McCrae briefly discusses the obscure Zen master named Jingzang ("Pure Storehouse") and the fact that his burial stupa is located at Huishan Temple. However, the temple really didn't catch my attention until years later when I was searching the Chinese Internet for texts from old Zen monuments. One fascinating stele was from Huishan Temple, where it was inscribed on Jingzang's burial stupa. What was fascinating was that the stele lists Jingzang as Zen's Seventh Ancestor and a student of the famous Sixth Ancestor Huineng. This was surprising, because Huineng had several famous students, but nowhere did I remember reading or hearing about one named Jingzang. He is a virtual Zen unknown. Naturally, after finding out about this burial stupa, I wanted to take a look at it and learn more about this obscure Seventh Ancestor of the Bodhidharma Zen tradition.

Thereafter, during my first opportunity to visit Huishan Temple, I asked the staff there to tell me exactly where Jingzang's old stupa was located so that I could take a look at it. They explained that the stupa was nearby but that it was closed to public viewing. When I asked if I could arrange to visit it, I was politely refused. I then explained that I was deeply interested in the history of this unknown Seventh Ancestor and furthermore I would be returning to the temple in about three weeks with a group from the United States that would want to see the stupa. This was actually true, as three weeks later I was scheduled to bring a group from the Los Angeles Zen Center to visit the area. I had not yet told the group about the stupa, but I was sure they would want to see it. The man in charge at the museum gave me his card and told me he would see if this would be possible.

During the days after that first visit to Huishan, I contacted some local friends who served as tour guides for groups I had previously brought to the area. I knew a local guide named Winston Wang, a young man who was also a Buddhist and who often accompanied my tour groups on visits to Shaolin Temple. If it were possible to visit the stupa, Winston could surely arrange it.

A few weeks later when I returned to Huishan Temple with the Los Angeles group, Winston accompanied us. He had contacted the local government antiquities bureau and arranged for one of its officials to meet us at Huishan Temple. Strangely, we were again politely told that visiting the stupa would not be possible because it was closed. I got a little animated, explaining to the local official that I had done research work concerning Jingzang and furthermore our group had traveled all the way from the United States to visit the place (along with many other places, of course). After they gave us more polite refusals, it finally came to light why the stupa was "closed." Immediately west of Huishan Temple there is a Chinese military police base, and the stupa happens to rest within its boundaries. Allowing a group of American tourists to visit such a place was probably unprecedented if not unthinkable. Yet after more arguing, the local antiquities official, who apparently was well-acquainted with the base commander, seemed of two minds. He said it might be possible to ask the appropriate officials whether we could simply enter the base and visit the stupa, which was near the front gate, and not take pictures of anything except the stupa itself. I readily agreed with this idea. After a few mobile-phone calls, the official said we had received permission to enter the base and view the stupa.

It so happened that my friend Bill Porter, who is well-known in Chinese Buddhist circles, was helping me lead this particular group in China, and our group was being filmed by a Chinese television film crew that was documenting his experiences. The crew had been with us for several days. Naturally, they were forced to remain behind as our group made its way along a road and up a hill to the military base's front gate. There, the guards who had been informed of our arrival literally crouched on top of their German shepherd guard dogs, muzzling their mouths to keep them from barking as our group passed under the gate and into the restricted area.

Happily, the stupa was not within sight of any military facilities but simply sat right next to the base entrance road. I was walking at the rear of the group to make sure everyone got into the place without any problems and then hurried forward to catch up. The road made a sharp left turn, and when I came around the corner I saw an astonishing sight. Even from a long distance I could see that Jingzang's stupa was far bigger than I was expecting. Its photo on the Internet did not convey its size. It was way bigger than an individual monk's stupa would normally be from that era, larger than any such stupas in the famous "Pagoda Forest" at Shaolin Temple or scores of other temples I had visited. I started yelling "Look at that! That's a big stupa! Look at the size of that thing!" Others in the group looked at me as if I were a little strange. I suppose they didn't know how big such monuments normally were and didn't realize what we were seeing.

Jingzang's burial stupa is nearly ten meters tall and sits on a base about six meters wide. Chinese archeologists say its special octagonal architecture, which came from South Asia, is all but unknown elsewhere in the country. While the famous murals in the Dunhuang Caves, far out on the Silk Road, depict stupas of this ancient design, almost none remaisn in existence. One of the few exceptions was this stupa.

What was most amazing is its great size, which naturally means the person it honored must have been considered especially important. Suddenly the claim of Jingzang being Zen's Seventh Ancestor seemed plausible, a claim that might be more than hyperbole written by grief-stricken disciples.

For the next fifteen minutes or so we examined this ancient, virtually unknown relic of the Zen tradition. Traces of ancient carvings could be seen on the different faces of the stupa. Obviously, when it was built it was not only big but also elaborately carved and decorated. We circumambulated the structure and took multiple photos. I was the most excited of anyone in the tour group. I had a sense that we were seeing the symbol of a genuine mystery of great importance. What could that importance have been?

Jingzang's stupa may reveal that he was a unique, even pivotal, figure of his time. This could have big implications for Bodhidharma's Zen

FIGURE 21. Stupa near Huishan Temple, Mt. Song, for Jingzang, Zen's Unknown Seventh Ancestor.

and its historical meaning. No similar stupa remains in the area, and, as I said, no other stupa of similar purpose compares to Jingzang's in size and design. Moreover, constructing such a structure required lots and lots of money. Who paid for it? We have little record about this teacher except the text that was left on the memorial itself.

After that visit I did more research on the stupa and the text that it held. Although the original stele is now nearly unreadable, the original text was, happily, recorded in various books and historical records that remain available today. I found some scholarly works about these old records and managed to get a copy of the stele's original text. There are some key discrepancies in the three records generally available for scholarly research. Despite this, an outline of Jingzang's story can be teased out of the textual evidence.

The stele is a contemporary record of a monk directly connected to the Sixth Ancestor Huineng. This is unique, since other records of his students are all from secondary sources. The stele directly states that Jingzang was Huineng's Dharma heir.

But Jingzang's stele also has some confusing, somewhat contradictory information, especially with regard to dates. It seems likely the disciples who engraved the stone were uncertain of exactly when certain events happened in the course of his life. Nevertheless, I think the basic information on the memorial must be a more or less genuine account of this mysterious "Seventh Ancestor" of Zen.

The stele relates that the monk Jingzang was born in the year 675 and died in the year 746 at the age, by Chinese reckoning, of seventy-two (Chinese traditionally count someone as one year old upon the first New Year's Day after their birth). Jingzang became a home-leaving monk at the age of nineteen and studied the Diamond, Lankavatara, and other sutras. He then traveled to Mount Song where he studied under Old An, the monk I introduced earlier, who was honored by the Chinese empress Wu Zetian. The stele says he remained with his teacher Old An for more than ten years. Then, after Old An died in the year 708, Jingzang traveled south to Nanhua Temple to become a student of the Sixth Zen Ancestor Huineng. The stele says that when Jingzang asked Huineng about the Buddha Way, Huineng responded in a manner that caused Jingzang to "flow tears" (indicating an awakening experience). Thereafter, Jingzang traveled to a place called Jingnan (an area of north Hunan Province that sits just south of the Yang-tse River). There he studied for a time under an otherwise unknown teacher named Du. Jingzang then returned to Huineng's Nanhua Temple where he received full transmission as a spiritual heir, "receiving the seal [of transmission], the Dharma, and the lamp" (a term for Zen's so-called mind-to-mind transmission of the Zen Way). He then lived at a place called Jade Buddha Woods on Great Hero Mountain (I don't know if this is the same Great Hero Mountain where Baizhang Temple is located).

Jingzang's reputation then spread widely, and he ultimately returned to Huishan Temple on Mount Song and took up residence in a hall named after his previous teacher Old An. There he remained during the last years of his life, "converting the area of Luoyang and the Yellow River," and becoming "widely known as the Seventh Ancestor that has arisen from Mount Song." The stele claims, significantly, that Jingzang did not fear undertaking exhaustive efforts to spread his teaching and advanced the doctrine of Sudden Enlightenment, the line of Zen represented by Huineng, Baizhang, and other Southern school teachers of Bodhidharma's main lineage.

It's impossible to say with certainty how much of the account is true and how much is the exaggeration of admiring disciples. But the point worth noting is that Jingzang is said to have proselytized in the area around Mount Song and Luoyang. At that time Luoyang was the "Eastern Capital" of the Tang dynasty, and an immensely important center of imperial power.

To my knowledge there is no record of Jingzang having preached to the court in the Eastern Capital. Yet other important monks who lived at this same Huishan Temple at about the same time are clearly described in Luoyang court records, the dynastic histories of the times. So we find in Jingzang a situation similar to that of Bodhidharma's oldest disciple, Sengfu. Here is a monk of Bodhidharma's tradition who lived near the imperial capital in the same place as monks who taught at the imperial court. Yet Jingzang, like Sengfu before him, is not known to have ever taught his Bodhidharma Zen to the emperor and his officials. In contrast to Jingzang, two other monks from Huishan Temple, who lived there at the same time, are well-known in official histories. Their great fame is worth noting in more detail, because they highlight the strange fact that it was Jingzang and not they who seems to have commanded the biggest memorial.

One monk, named Yixing (683–727), whose name means "Single Practice," was an early astrologist/astronomer whose observation of the heavens greatly advanced this Chinese science. Due to his prediction of an eclipse, the Emperor Xuan Zong of the Tang dynasty honored him highly.

The second important monk related to Huishan's history was named Yijing (as opposed to Yixing above—sorry that the names can be so confusing!). The history of this monk is quite remarkable indeed. Yijing was a monk of the Precepts school who was inspired by Xuanzang, the famous Chinese monk who traveled to India in search of Dharma. Yijing set off across the South Seas and traveled to India on roughly the same route that Bodhidharma used to come to China. After intermediate stops at what is now Indonesia and other places, he reached India and there learned to read Sanskrit, the language of the Buddhist scriptures. Eventually he returned to China with many sacred writings that filled gaps in the library that Xuanzang had brought back from India more than fifty years earlier. The emperor himself met Yijing upon his return to the country. After bringing back new scriptures from India, this monk reformed the precepts being used in Buddhist ceremonies, and he enjoyed immense fame and reputation at the Tang imperial court.

So why, when such notable and imperially recognized worthies as Yixing and Yijing lived at Huishan Temple, is the largest memorial there dedicated to a monk unmentioned in official records of the time?

The intriguing possibility is that Huineng and his student Jingzang adhered to the teaching of not remaining in "places of imperial sway." Jingzang, like Bodhidharma, Sengfu, Daoxin, Baizhang, and other Southern Zen masters, appears to have avoided the court so that his "observing mind" practice could remain untainted by Imperial-Way Buddhism and its doctrines. The huge stupa dedicated to the mysterious ancestor Jingzang may be another reflection of the split symbolized by Bodhidharma and Emperor Wu's legendary meeting. In the shadow play of Chinese politics, the grand size of the stupa for a monk unconnected to the emperor may have powerful, if hidden, political meaning, set up as a counterpoint to the spread of Imperial-Way Buddhism.

Traditionally, the main Zen tradition in China is described as having split into two factions. One, the Southern school, was represented by the Sixth Ancestor Huineng, and the other was the Northern school faction, led by Shenxiu, the teacher of three emperors. Usually, the difference between these two factions is described to be the difference between groups who believed in Gradual Enlightenment (symbolized by the Northern Shenxiu faction) and the Sudden Enlightenment faction of Huineng and his successors. The evidence so far suggests, however, that it was not simply different ideas about how quickly one experiences enlightenment that marked the difference between these two groups. Instead, a main difference between them seems to be that the Southern faction made a point of carrying on Bodhidharma and his immediate descendants' practice of avoiding the court. The Northern faction, on the other hand, was deeply intertwined with the imperial court of the Tang dynasty.

Jingzang's religious mission around Luoyang and Mount Song may have played a role in the doctrinal split between these two groups of

Zen, the reason for which was nominally the Sudden and Gradual differences described above. A real and essentially political reason for the underlying argument between the two factions was to remain unspoken. Around the time Jingzang died, another monk, named Shenhui, who lived in the vicinity and also is alleged to be a student of Huineng, attacked the Northern school of Zen that was then being promulgated by Shenxiu's disciples as illegitimate. The ostensible reason for Shenhui's attack on Shenxiu and his Dharma heirs was that they advanced the Gradual approach to enlightenment instead of the Sudden Enlightenment doctrine of Bodhidharma. Shenhui declared Huineng, the Sixth Ancestor, as the authentic heir of Bodhidharma's Zen, and he declared the Northern Gradual faction of Shenxiu to be a heresy.

Was the size and grandeur of Jingzang's stupa an indication that his Southern and Sudden teaching was highly popular outside the royal Buddhist establishment among monks who despised Imperial-Way Buddhism? The text from the stupa does not hint of any criticism of a Gradual Buddhist school, yet it explicitly claims that Jingzang was a Dharma heir of Huineng and that he expounded the Sudden Enlightenment teaching.

How Huineng's Southern and Sudden teachings, as taught in the Platform Sutra, spread through China is a serious bone of contention amongst scholars. Some Japanese and Western scholars think the Platform Sutra itself was not written by Huineng or even his immediate disciples but was compiled by later generations of Zen monks to advance their sect's interests. Yet a possible role for Jingzang in this argument has been missing. Could he have been the first to bring Huineng's Platform Sutra to the Luoyang area? Or could he have even been the one who wrote that text, based on lectures he heard Huineng deliver? In any case, the size of his stupa indicates that he had important and even wealthy supporters as he spread the Sudden doctrine in the precincts of China's emperor.

I have to admit that what I've suggested remains conjecture. There is no clear evidence for an important early role for Jingzang in Zen's development aside from a stupa text that appears on a very large and strange memorial. I'm hopeful more evidence will someday come to light about this unknown "Seventh Ancestor." That evidence may indeed portray Bodhidharma and his spiritual heirs in a new historical light.

43. Ordination Platforms: The Battle Ground between Imperial and Bodhidharma Zen?

THE MOST HOTLY disputed turf that lay between Bodhidharma's Zen and Imperial-Way Zen may have been the ordination platforms where monks took their vows. On reflection, the reason why these places caused controversy is obvious. Emperors wanted to maintain control of the Buddhist clergy by controlling the "gate" to becoming a monk or nun. As I mentioned earlier, the Buddhist clergy were not individually subject to taxation (though temples came to be taxed as institutions), and monks were not subject to military service or conscription to work in corvée labor gangs. From the emperor's viewpoint, keeping control of the "gate" through which young men could avoid government service and taxation was vital. Would-be home-leavers had to pass a tough examination system to qualify for ordination. The emperor was partial to doctrinal interpretations of Buddhism not simply because of his personal interest in such subjects but also because keeping the religion "mysterious" and understood by a select few provided the rationale for exclusion. If anyone could freely take vows and then bail out of the tasks of soldiering and guarding a section of the desolate and miserable Great Wall for decades on end, who wouldn't be tempted to become, at least nominally, a monk?

The ordination platform, where individuals underwent the ceremony to become home-leavers, thus was a key battleground in the clash between Bodhidharma Zen and Imperial-Way Buddhism. What a monk must know to be a "legitimate" Buddhist, along with the vows he took on the ordination platform, affected the interests of the state.

The ordination platform itself was much like the platforms where emperors performed state ceremonies and were also politically symbolic of the unity of church and state. We've already seen how Emperor Wu ascended the platform of political rule by infusing religion into the ceremony. The religious platforms where monks took their vows had political overtones as well. The actual structure of the platform where Emperor Wu declared his imperial rule was little different from the ordination platforms used by home-leaving monks. Indeed, Emperor Wu pointedly blurred distinctions between the two different ceremonies.

In this light, where did the ordinations of Huineng's Southern school and his famous Signless Precepts take place? Did monks wanting to take those precepts submit to imperial demands that all ordinations must take place on Imperial-Way-sanctioned platforms?

The records of many famous Zen monks indicate that they were compelled to take public vows on an ordination platform on Mount Song, a central platform that was imperially sanctioned. Among such monks was the famous monk Mazu, as well as Mazu's spiritual "grandson" Zen Master Zhaozhou, both of them solidly in the Bodhidharma Southern Zen faction. Yet, if these and other Zen monks were required to memorize sutras and take the officially recognized precepts, where did the Signless Precepts of Huineng or how exactly did the Bodhisattva Precepts come into play after Emperor Wu modified them? The political struggle between Imperial-Way Buddhism and Zen was a factor in what vows were recited in the home-leaving ceremony. Imperial-Way Buddhism prescribed certain types of precepts, while the Bodhidharma Zen tradition, at least, had other ideas.

Chinese scholars have for decades tried to find archeological remains of the official ordination platform that was on Mount Song. Logically it should have been around Shaolin Temple. But while Shaolin is famous as the home of Zen, during its history it was primarily a temple of Imperial-Way Buddhism, a Buddhism that emphasized not Zen but the practices of the Buddhist Precepts sect. This remained the case for many centuries after Bodhidharma and Emperor Wu lived. Zen, though famously associated with Shaolin, was second in importance to the Precepts school for most of the temple's history. Zen abbots predominated there only after the religion was compromised and absorbed into the imperial ideology of the state.

This is not to say that Zen didn't figure in the propaganda of the temple from early on. The temple's founder, Fotuo, was regarded as a

Zen master, as was the third abbot of the temple, Seng Chou. Despite this, most subsequent abbots, under imperial control, adhered not to Zen but to Precepts school rites and beliefs. One exception to this trend occurred around the year 680, when one of the Zen monks of the Northern school, named Faru, was briefly the abbot of Shaolin Temple. Faru (like his Dharma brother Shenxiu) thereafter taught East Mountain Zen on Mount Song and at the nearby court of Luoyang. While the East Mountain school of Daoxin is known to have used the Bodhisattva Precepts, what were the vows taken by monks on Mount Song during the time of Faru or Lao An? In fact, there is evidence of a struggle between Bodhidharma's Zen and Imperial-Way Buddhism over the ordination platforms themselves during that time.

Historical documents indicate that in the year 704, an ordination platform was constructed on Mount Song under imperial command. Yet Chinese archeologists, searching around Shaolin Temple for many decades, haven't found any trace of such a platform. The archeologists have naturally assumed that because Shaolin was the most famous of Mount Song's temples and arguably the main symbol of the imperial-religious establishment, then naturally it would have been the home of the country's central ordination platform.

A reason to think that the new ordination platform of 704 was at Shaolin Temple is that we have the text of a memorial set up to commemorate the occasion of the platform's inauguration, its "blessing." That text's contents explain that the platform was set up to replace one previously used at Shaolin Temple, although it doesn't say the new platform was actually located at Shaolin Temple as well.

Recently a Chinese scholar named Zhang Jianwei, researching this question, published a paper that examines the text of the memorial stele made to commemorate the setting up of the ordination platform. Although the stele itself is lost, its contents were preserved in old Tang dynasty documents that have survived to modern times.

According to those Tang documents, the stele's text was composed by the monk Yijing. I described Yijing earlier. He was the famous Precepts school monk who lived for a time at Huishan Temple and traveled to India to later return with Buddhist scriptures. He composed the contents of this stele in 504, long after his triumphant return to China from India.

A rough translation of the stele is as follows:

On today's date [seventh day of the fourth lunar month of the year 704], the director of this temple, Yijiang, along with its head monk, Zhibao, Zen Master Faji of the Imperial Religious Directorate and the mass of disciples, in order to reestablish the Shaolin Temple ordination platform, now have rebuilt this ordination platform, so that it can serve as a place of religious atonement and be honored by everyone. [This is done so that] everyone beneath the [leadership] of the [imperial] capital may come to this mountain gate. Here today, besides myself, are Precepts Master Hu, Zen Master [unintelligible], Zen Master Si, Zen Master Xun, Precepts Master Hui, Precepts Master Ke, Precepts Master Wei, and others who have all come to this temple. By common agreement this [ordination platform] will be known as a permanent symbol of the *small vehicle* [Hinayana], *and this is not to be doubted* [emphasis added]. Many worthy protectors of the precepts have come here today without being summoned. You heroes prepared the ground for this event, with more than a hundred of you taking time from your schedules to assemble here, walking for a month to come here, then appearing like a string of pearls in the practice of meditation and walking together. Among you are abbots who practice the Four Reliances [four traditional virtuous behaviors], who traverse emptiness and take refuge in the real, and who unceasingly transmit the great teaching. In this world of change we here set up a long-lasting stone foundation. In the myriad transformations this is a golden place where the fearsome world is transformed into the spacious blue void of the sky, a transforming place where delusion is left behind. This monument declares that where the karmic world is, the Dharma is not lost. The gray brick [of the platform] is transformed to gold. Here we abide and pay honor. The eye sees the [truth of] the western lands [India], but the staff strikes the ground of the East [the teaching is set up in China]. From this glorious work happiness will follow. And so we record this short text.

To understand whether Bodhidharma's faction was present at this ceremony sponsored by the "Imperial Religious Directorate," we need to take a look at the names.

One of the Zen Master's names is unintelligible. This is unfortunate, as one is left to wonder whether it may have been Lao An, the monk of extremely high reputation who was honored by the then Empress Wu Zetian and who died in 708.

Also, the stele refers to monks present by only one of the characters of their Dharma names. It refers to a "Zen Master Si," who could logically be a Zen master named Miao Si, who was a disciple of Faru and thus a member of the Bodhidharma-derived East Mountain school of Daoxin. If this indeed was Miao Si, then it means that monks of the Bodhisattva Precepts tradition (Great Vehicle Buddhism) were joining with traditional Hinayana Precepts school (Small Vehicle Buddhism) monks to honor the ordination platform.

So if this Imperial-Way Buddhism ordination place was dominant, did any Bodhidharma faction monks really use the Signless Precepts expounded by Huineng? Perhaps it was allowed that the Zen monks could have their own local precepts ceremonies using other precepts, and thus peace between the imperial center and the independent Zen of distant places was maintained. Such a development would have no doubt caused conflict with the Precepts school, which saw itself as the true guardian of the genuine Buddhist precepts.

If the ordination platform here described was indeed the central platform for the country, then it would likely have been the place where Zen Master Mazu took his official vows at Mount Song sometime around the year 730. Thus, soon after Yijing set up the platform, monks of the Southern school of Zen took their vows there.

Details of this aspect of official and Imperial-Way Buddhism's attempts to maintain central control over Zen may be revealed by future research. For now we are left with questions about whether the monks in attendance agreed on what vows would be taken on the platform. Was there an argument between the Precepts and the Zen school? Some Chinese scholars claim that this conflict existed and that Precepts sect monks would not recognize the Zen monks' right to administer any sort of precepts whatsoever, Bodhisattva, signless, or otherwise. That Yijing had both Zen monks and Precepts monks attending the platform ceremony suggests that they were trying to bridge the gap between them.

But a possibly mysterious clue about the controversy surrounding this ordination platform is that it was established, but then left unused, for about ten years before the memorial inscription written above was placed on the site. This might indicate that political infighting surrounded the platform's role in Buddhist circles, and that the hidden struggle between Imperial-Way Buddhism and Bodhidharma's lineage was protracted but not openly acknowledged.

One more claim by the scholar Zhang Jianwei about this platform is worth noting. He claims that the actual location of this ordination platform may not have been at Shaolin Temple at all. Instead, it was at Huishan Temple, where the remains of just such an ordination platform have recently been unearthed near Zen Master Jingzang's stupa. Zhang points out that the Shaolin and Huishan Temples were often referred to synonymously, as closely bound sister temples, and thus were sometimes seen to be the same institution.

Imagine that the emperor, through his representative Yijing, required that the Hinayana precepts, the long version that required long training and practice, were to be universally embraced. Imagine also that Zen Master Si, and later Zen Master Jingzang, represented the Bodhisattva Precepts, or even the Signless Precepts that tradition attributes to Zen's Huineng. Finally, imagine that when Jingzang died, his huge memorial was a symbolic gesture from the ascending Southern faction, which claimed allegiance to the Sixth Ancestor Huineng and declared that Bodhidharma's true Zen, the independent Zen of individuals who followed the internal light, was alive and growing in the center, the very heart, of the great and imperial Tang dynasty. The memorial, not noted in official records, sits only a few feet from the recently unearthed ordination platform. Was it meant as a stick in the emperor's eye?

44. The Temples of Luoyang

From incalculable eons in the past until now, through all the events of the universe, all periods of time, and all places without exception, none of it has been other than your own mind, all of it none other than your own Buddha. Mind is Buddha, and it has always been thus. Apart from this mind there is no other Buddha to be understood. Apart from this mind there is no other place where wisdom and nirvana may be found.
—*From the* BLOOD VEIN DISCOURSE, *a text attributed to Bodhidharma*

血脉论　　达磨祖师著

从无始旷大劫以来，乃至施为运动一切时中，一切处所，皆是汝本心，
皆是汝本佛。即心是佛，亦复如是。除此心外终无别佛可得；
离此心外觅菩提涅槃无有是处.

EARLY IN THE MORNING I get up and sit meditation, then make ready to travel by bus to Luoyang. Shanli has expressed a desire to travel there with me for the day, as he wants to visit the ancient site of Yongning Temple, a site connected with Bodhidharma. I learned the location of that temple on previous trips to Luoyang and am happy to repay Shanli's hospitality by taking him there.

While Shaolin Temple is not far from Luoyang, Shanli doesn't travel there often. For many years an expressway has connected the two places. When I mention this to Shanli, he says he's never traveled on that road. He has only taken the old highway that passes through the mountains near Shaolin Temple. That's the bus route we will take together on a public coach.

"We don't want to leave too early," says Shanli. "The highway can be icy."

The following morning the sun is shining and snow that had collected around the hotel during recent days is melting rapidly. I call Shanli at 9:45 to tell him I'm leaving for the bus station, located only a few minutes from my hotel. The bus to Luoyang will stop at Shaolin Temple on the old highway, so Shanli can simply get on the bus there. I tell him I'll buy him a ticket in Luoyang and save him a seat on the bus. He agrees and says he'll need to walk from the temple proper to the bus stop by the highway, a twenty-five-minute walk. I tell him I'll call when I find out what time the bus leaves. Arriving at the Dengfeng bus station at 9:55, I buy two tickets for the ten o'clock bus and call Shanli again.

"I've got tickets on the ten o'clock bus."

"Okay!" he says. "I'm leaving the temple right now! I'll hurry to the gate."

It's about a five-mile drive from Dengfeng station to Shaolin Temple, so Shanli is worried the bus will pass the temple before he gets to the main gate to catch it. But true to form, the bus doesn't manage to actually leave the station until ten fifteen. Then it proceeds slowly through Dengfeng City. It stops to pick up passengers several times. Things are going slowly. My phone rings. It's Shanli.

"I'm at the temple gate!" he says. I haven't missed you, have I?" I can hear him panting between sentences. Obviously he ran all the way to the gate of temple.

"This is China!" I yell into my phone over the loud noise of the bus engine. "We're twenty minutes late already. We won't get to Shaolin Temple for another twenty minutes!"

"I ran all the way here!" he says breathlessly.

Twenty minutes later we finally arrive at Shaolin Temple, and Shanli hops aboard the bus. It's only a short distance to the mountain pass that leads to Luoyang. Within minutes we arrive there, and I'm surprised to notice that on the shady north side of the pass there is still a layer of frost on the highway. It's a steep drop toward the Yellow River plain several hundred meters down the side of the mountain, and it's clear that the highway is still icy and dangerous.

Shanli has brought along his little video camera and now starts shooting the ride down the mountain. A few trucks and cars have slid on the ice and collided. They've been pushed to the side of the road. Some big trucks are coming up the mountain, and a few cars going the opposite way, throwing caution to the wind, are actually passing us, speeding downhill despite the unsafe conditions. It's obvious the bus driver is nervous.

As we wind carefully down the twisting road, Shanli starts interviewing me with his video camera.

"Have you ever felt in danger during your travels in China?" he asks, the camera a few inches from my face.

"Constantly!" I joke.

In almost the same moment the bus suddenly lurches sideways as a truck coming up the mountain appears from around a curve. The truck is passing a car coming slowly uphill, and it is now within a few feet of the bus, coming head on. Our bus driver jerks the bus hard to the right, and we all tumble. Brakes screeching, we pass within inches of the massive truck loaded down with a mountain of rocks. Our driver screams out some obscenities as he yanks again on the wheel and narrowly avoids the ditch, swerving dangerously back into the center of the road. We feel the bus sliding on the ice. But somehow the driver keeps us from smashing into the truck, going into the ditch, or careening over the ledge on the other side. Thankfully, within a few minutes we've descended far enough that ice no longer covers the roadbed. Slowly regaining our wits, we start breathing normally again.

The old highway between Shaolin Temple and Luoyang City passes near some of China's earliest historical sites. Chinese scholars believe that the capital of the Xia, China's legendary first dynasty, was located in this area around 2000 BCE. A major Xia archeological dig to uncover the ancient capital is near a little village called Erligou (pronounced *Ar-li-go*) close to the highway on which we're traveling. The palace of the ancient Shang dynasty, circa 1600 BCE, is also near the highway. As we travel along, we pass the home village of Xuanzang, the famous seventh-century pilgrim who braved the desert and successfully traveled to India to bring back Buddhist scriptures in his "Journey to the West." His village has a big Buddhist temple to honor its famous son.

Luoyang played a vital role in China's earliest history. Besides these two earliest of China's dynasties, several other important dynasties used the city as their capital up until the end of the Tang dynasty, around 900 CE. Located near the south bank of the Yellow River, Luoyang sits in the area where Yu the Great tamed that river's floods and created conditions that helped spawn Chinese civilization. The area is truly the original source of China's culture. Through Shaolin Temple and the nearby Longmen Grottos, the place rightfully retains a high profile in the Chinese cultural sphere.

Luoyang's place in early Chinese history can hardly be overemphasized. As I explained above, it is where Emperor Xiao Wen of the Wei dynasty lived after moving his capital from Pingcheng in the north. Here, like Emperor Wu, he embraced the metaphysical doctrines about "Buddha nature" and the Bodhisattva ideal. If Nanjing represents the dissemination of Buddhism in South China, Luoyang played the same role in the north. And Luoyang's connection to Buddhism goes far deeper than Emperor Xiao Wen and the place's close proximity to Shaolin Temple. The main legend of how Buddhism arrived in China relates that the religion came first to Luoyang during the Han dynasty, around the year 67 CE. At that time, says the legend, the emperor Han Ming established White Horse Temple to house sacred scriptures that two monks brought from India on a white horse. Scholars in China have found evidence that Buddhism had several contacts with China prior to, perhaps even long before, when this legend claims Buddhism was introduced to the country. Nevertheless, Luoyang is still widely regarded as the birthplace of Buddhism in China.

Arriving at the Luoyang bus station, Shanli and I set off toward the city's train station just a few blocks away. Shanli's friend Ronan has arranged to meet us in Luoyang at that location. Shanli has written some accounts of Shaolin Temple's history, and Ronan has edited Shanli's work. Ronan came to Luoyang by train this morning from his home in Zhengzhou City to accompany us to Yongning Temple. Happily, we quickly find him waiting for us in front of the train station. Both Shanli and Ronan will return to their homes this evening. After I find a hotel room near the Luo River, we set out by taxi to visit the remains of Yongning Temple. Yongning Temple is reputed to be where Bodhidharma once lived in Luoyang. It is located northeast of the modern city, a place where old Luoyang City stood in ancient times. Emperor Xiao Wen's palace was there, along with White Horse Temple, where Buddhism is said to have arrived in China.

After forty-five minutes or so, we pass in front of ancient White Horse temple. Just a mile farther we reach an overpass where an exit sign says REMAINS OF ANCIENT YONGNING TEMPLE. Within sight of the road we see the temple's ancient foundation amid fields of millet. We follow a dirt road to the temple's entrance, a stone gate that is in a high protective brick wall. The gate is open, so we drive in and park the taxi. Suddenly a woman appears to greet us. We tell her why we've come.

"The temple isn't open yet," she says. "Later when it opens, you can come to visit and pay admission to view it."

Our taxi driver, who knows that we've come from far away, starts arguing with the woman to let us come in. She is hesitant. I tell her I've come all the way from the United States and want to see this old temple and that my friends have wanted to come here for many years. She finally relents, and we walk on a stone path leading to the old temple's foundations. The entire "temple" is little more than a large square block of sod and brick, purportedly its old foundation. The whole edifice is about sixty feet square, with a smaller square of sod and brick sitting atop the first. It leaves a lot to the imagination. I'm extremely suspicious that such a sod and brick remnant was not eroded away long ago. I know that near here there is a good deal of rubble from what used to be the walls of ancient Luoyang City. Those ruins are barely discernable in the landscape. It seems hard to believe that the foundation of this old temple could have remained uniquely intact, even if the location where it sits is accurate (another dubious proposition). A scam? Maybe that's why the place hasn't been allowed to open yet. Maybe the authorities do not want to let such an obviously fake "ruin" defraud a gullible public.

Ancient information about the real Yongning Temple comes from a document called *Temples of Luoyang*. The text, written only about twenty years after Bodhidharma died, includes a passage that Zen scholars and practitioners have long assumed to be a firsthand account about the author's meeting with Bodhidharma. Furthermore, the text is the source of the legend that connects White Horse Temple to Buddhism's appearance in China. Composed around the year 540 by an official named Yang Xuanzhi (pronounced *Yang Swan-jer*), the document hints at Luoyang's ancient glory by providing glowing descriptions of the city's most famous temple landmarks during the period between the years 520 and 527 CE.

Yang Xuanzhi, the writer of the text, played a key role in Bodhidharma's legends for various reasons. His *Temples of Luoyang* is often cited as the earliest impartial historical text that mentions Bodhidharma by name. But later texts, such as the *Compendium of Five Lamps*, connect Yang Xuanzhi to Bodhidharma in other ways. Such late texts claim that this same man named Yang visited Bodhidharma just before the latter died. So, on the face of it, anything we can glean about Yang's life may help prove or disprove parts of Bodhidharma's legend.

In *Temples of Luoyang*, Yang Xuanzhi first describes the layout of the imperial palace and its surrounding wall and gates. He then moves on to Yongning Temple, which was located close to the palace and was clearly the grandest of all of the hundreds of temples in Luoyang at that time. The description Yang provides of Yongning Temple is detailed. It includes, for example, a description of the temple's nine-storied pagoda that stretched ten *zhang* (about one hundred feet) into the air. The pagoda was ornately decorated with figures of the Buddha, and the roof tiles of the temple, decorated with gold leaf, glistened in the sun. After he describes the temple, Yang tells about meeting a monk named Bodhidharma who was at the place and was marveling at the splendor of the temple. This is the reference that many people, including many scholars, take as an authentic early reference to Bodhidharma. Yang's account of the monk reads as follows:

> There was a monk from Western Regions named Bodhidharma. He was a foreigner from Persia. He traveled from distant regions to China. He observed the sun and clouds reflecting from the golden tiles [of the temple], the precious bells pealing far and wide in the wind, and [he] exclaimed that it was a wondrous sight, saying, "I'm 150 years old and have traveled throughout all countries. I've seen everything, but the beauty of this temple surpasses anything in the world. Throughout the Buddha realms there is nothing to compare to this!" The monk clasped his hands and chanted *namu* [homage] for days on end.

The story purports to show an encounter with the monk that occurred in the mid-520s, before the temple was severely damaged in a windstorm around the year 527. As such it places a monk named Bodhidharma in Luoyang prior to that year. Furthermore, the monk claims to be 150 years old. This text therefore seems to be the source of Daoxuan's claim about Bodhidharma's age that appears in the *Continued Biographies*.

Yet there are clearly aspects of this story that make it suspicious. The monk named Bodhidharma is described as being from Persia, not from South India, as related in the *Continued Biographies*. The Southern India origin for Bodhidharma is widely deemed more reliable, since the *Continued Biographies* says he came to China by sea. If he came directly from Persia, it seems more likely he might have come across the Silk Road. The monk also claims to have traveled throughout the "Buddha realms." Despite the obvious hyperbole of the statement, it nonetheless seems reasonable to assume that if the monk came from Persia, he did so on a route that passed through the many Buddhist kingdoms of that area. Thus the term "Buddha realms" implies the places in question to be west of Luoyang, not the South Seas.

It's critical to note that Yang Xuanzhi authored the *Temples of Luoyang* more than twenty years after this purported meeting with Bodhidharma took place. This casts their alleged encounter in a suspicious light. Another very odd detail of the account is the manner of the monk's practice. He is said to have "clasped his hands and chanted *namu* for days on end." Frankly, that doesn't sound like the Bodhidharma that is described in the *Continued Biographies*. Nowhere in that text are Bodhidharma and his disciples described as continuously chanting *namu*, a Pure Land Buddhist style of practice. Quite the contrary, he and his disciples are described as devoted to meditation practice.

All this makes the text rather suspicious. Yet, in the *Continued Biographies*, it is obvious that the author Daoxuan has used this account in the *Temples of Luoyang* to cite Bodhidharma's age as 150. What this means is that confusion about Bodhidharma apparently started quite early, and Daoxuan must have been at pains, at least initially, to nail down his real story. In light of all this, can *Temples of Luoyang* and its description of Bodhidharma be taken as describing a real event?

Yang Xuanzhi, the author of *Temples of Luoyang*, was not a Buddhist, and his meeting with a monk named Bodhidharma is described in the context of Yang's description of one of Luoyang's most famous, if very short-lived, temples. At the time that Yang wrote his account, Yongning Temple, indeed most of Luoyang's Buddhist Temples, had already been completely destroyed. Luoyang itself was largely in ruins, the result of a war that ended the Northern Wei dynasty and divided it into the contending Eastern and Western Wei dynasties in the year 534. In the *Temples of Luoyang*, Yang Xuanzhi compares the situation in Luoyang before and after the war, saying, "In the city where more than a thousand temples stood, now a bell is hardly heard."

After reviewing the historical evidence about this alleged meeting, I've concluded that the monk described in Yang Xuanzhi's description was not the person of Bodhidharma I've been looking for in China these past weeks. I'd go so far as to say that I think the encounter was instead a fabrication by Yang Xuanzhi to enhance his story about the beauty of Yongning Temple. It's plausible there were holy men who honored Yongning Temple in some manner as Yang describes. But the story he provides, written twenty years after the fact, seems to be an amalgam of events assembled by his memory and imagination. He may have invoked the name Bodhidharma, which likely had some currency in that age, simply to enhance his unlikely story. A chance encounter between Yang and Bodhidharma, on reflection, seems to strain credulity.

Besides the *Continued Biographies*, Daoxuan wrote another text called the *Guanghong Mingji*. Although largely a religious treatise, it includes biographies of some famous figures of the age, including a description of Yang Xuanzhi himself. Daoxuan makes it clear that Yang Xuanzhi was not sympathetic with Buddhism. Moreover, Yang's description of Luoyang's temples was clearly not nostalgic. It was meant, instead, as part of a political critique of Buddhism, an attack on the religion. Yang resented the extravagant expenditures that went to building temples and supporting the religion, money that he thought would have been put to better use to maintain order in the empire and uphold Confucian ideology. The *Temples of Luoyang* had a political purpose, which was to attack Buddhism as a religion harmful to the state. Given the political purpose of the text, it seems likely that the depiction of Bodhidharma in *Temples of Luoyang* was meant as a caricature, and Bodhidharma's name was used in this instance because Yang wanted to faintly denigrate him and his followers with an unflattering portrait.

In sum, I doubt that the account of Bodhidharma in *Temples of Luoyang* is authentic. Chinese scholars have shown that at least one other monk named Bodhidharma lived in China at the time in question. If there was an encounter between Yang Xuanzhi and a monk named

Bodhidharma (which I doubt), then the account suggests that some other Bodhidharma was at Yongning Temple that day.

All these doubts notwithstanding, here we are taking multiple pictures of Bodhidharma's alleged home, Yongning Temple. Shanli convinces the woman guarding the old temple site to let us look around for ten minutes or so. I shoot a few photographs of Shanli and Ronan standing on the ruins (if the bricks were genuine, would such a thing be allowed?). After Shanli and Ronan are satisfied, we clamber back into the taxi.

Our driver pulls out of the Yongning Temple entrance road, and I ask him to stop atop the highway overpass that crosses some train tracks just nearby. On the overpass we get out of the car for a look around. The east-and-west-running track appears to pass approximately along the same line where the southern wall of the old Luoyang palace of Emperor Xiao Wen once sat. Remembering old maps of the place, I point out to Shanli and Ronan where the palace probably stood and where the old walls and gates were likely positioned.

From our high vantage point we can see many temporary buildings sitting among the farmers' fields to the north. The taxi driver tells us that archeologists are indeed now exploring the whole area due to some recent important finds here.

I then look east from our vantage point and ask the taxi driver if he knows where a place called Heyin ("South of the River") is located. He says he's never heard of that spot.

An incident in the year 528 occurred somewhere near where we're standing, possibly to the east, near where the Luo River now flows. In that year there was a power struggle between the Wei emperor Xiao Ming and a faction led by his mother the Empress Dowager. A general named Er Zhurong took advantage of the political upheaval to convince the emperor to summon officials to Heyin, a place near the Luo River, for an imperial ceremony of sacrifice to heaven. Er Zhurong, seeking to eliminate obstacles to taking power, then unleashed his troops on the crowds of officials and others assembled there, slaughtering up to two thousand people. Because of this flagrant act of terrorism, the aristocracy of Luoyang fled the city in fear, and the emperor ceded power to Er Zhurong. Some scholars have speculated that Bodhidharma was among those killed in this massacre at Heyin. This idea comes from the fact that in the biography of Bodhidharma's main disciple, Huike, Daoxuan writes that he "buried [Bodhidharma's] remains on the banks of the Luo River. Also, the year 528 fits well into the same account's approximate time of Bodhidharma's death. The text says Huike expounded Bodhidharma's teaching after the latter's death and then left the area in the year 534. This Huike biography contradicts what Daoxuan wrote about Bodhidharma himself, however, for in that passage he wrote that the place of Bodhidharma's death was unknown.

Without a clear explanation for the discrepancy between these two accounts written by the same author, we can only guess why they differ. At least one Chinese scholar says it is likely that Huike's biography was written many years after Bodhidharma's, when Daoxuan had met some of Huike's disciples and gained new information about Bodhidharma's life. Perhaps someone claimed that Bodhidharma died in the Heyin massacre, and Daoxuan decided that the idea was credible. So he thereupon added the report that Huike buried Bodhidharma on the banks of the Luo River to the *Continued Biographies*.

My own view is that it is unlikely that Bodhidharma died in the Heyin incident. Other evidence about him indicates he avoided royal assemblies, and it is hard to imagine that he would have wanted to take part in the event, or even be found in the vicinity, of the imperial court city of Luoyang. Heyin, despite theories and timelines that support the idea, was probably not the place where Bodhidharma died.

45. Empty Appearance Temple

IN THE YEAR 2002, the Buddhist author and authority Bill Porter (Red Pine) and I decided to try to find Bodhidharma's grave (which is not believed to be the same place where he died). We had only a vague idea of its location. At the time I had not yet studied the memorial to Bodhidharma that references Bear Ear Mountain as his burial place. But that location is mentioned in some later records I was aware of. I had no idea where Bear Ear Mountain was located. I had an old map that indicated the place to be an entire range of mountains, not simply one mountain, in an area southwest of Luoyang. But other places in China have the same name, and I was in dark about where to look for it. Bill Porter seemed confident that the place was indeed southwest of Luoyang and thought he had a good idea where it was. So I contacted some travel-business friends in Luoyang and explained that we wanted to find the place. Amazingly, my friends not only quickly found its location, but also arranged for a van and guide to take us there.

So on a foggy morning in the spring of 2002, we set off with a few other traveling companions from Luoyang on an expressway that heads west from that city. The road runs parallel with the east-flowing Yellow River that lies twenty miles or so to the north. The entire area is part of the broad Yellow River watershed. After about an hour we reached an exit called Kwan Yin Hall and got off the expressway. From there we traveled south. After bumping along a few miles on a country road, Bear Ear Mountain loomed before us.

The mountain is more like a bare rocky peak but does actually look, from a distance, like a bit of bear anatomy. Later I saw that behind the mountain is a second one that looks very similar, and the two together give the impression of a bear's head. On that day, as we approached the first mountain, I noticed that it rose on a walkable slope all the way up to a wide rock outcropping that passably looks like a bear's floppy ear. As we approached the peak in our van, we could see a white ring surrounding the lower flank of the mountain's north side. Getting closer we could see that the white ring was a whitewashed stone fence, and there was activity going on inside it. Soon we clambered out of the van in front of a construction site where cement mixers and workers toiled to build a new temple gate. Laborers carried sand in buckets on shoulder poles, while an assortment of machinery caused a din. The most prominent thing on the broad lower flank of the mountain in front of us was an old stupa. It stood just past the construction area on the right. Our local guide informed us it was Bodhidharma's burial stupa. When we asked its age, the guide explained that the current stupa was built in the fourteenth century to replace an original that was destroyed prior to that time.

Farther back on the site, about seventy-five meters or so, was a newly constructed building in traditional style that was not yet open. It stood locked and shuttered.

The local guide explained that the place, called Empty Appearance Temple, was under reconstruction. He said it is a subtemple of Shaolin Temple, and that that temple's abbot, Shi Yongxin, was working with the Chinese Buddhist Association and the Japanese Bodhidharma Association to rebuild what was once a large monastery here.

The site had something else to offer. Between the front gate under construction and the distant hall, we saw four stone monuments sticking jauntily out of the ground. According to the guide, one of these old monuments was a copy of an original purportedly created by Emperor Wu to commemorate Bodhidharma's death.

That was news to me. Up to that point I didn't know anything about such a memorial written by Emperor Wu to praise Bodhidharma. I was shocked that such an important thing, if it was real, wasn't more widely known.

The guide then explained that Emperor Wu created three such monuments, all with the same text. Copies of the other two steles also still exist, one located at Yuanfu Temple in North China and one at Shaolin Temple. Yuanfu Temple is the place where Zen's Second Ancestor Huike was buried.

The words that comprise this temple's name, *empty appearance* (*kong xiang*), offer a typical Chinese play on words. While they literally mean "empty appearance," they also sound like the words for *empty chamber*. This name refers to an old legend that claims Bodhidharma got out of his burial crypt and returned to India, leaving an "empty chamber" behind. The legend says that a monk returning from India spied Bodhidharma walking toward the west while carrying a single sandal. When the monk returned to China and reported this strange event, the emperor ordered Bodhidharma's crypt to be opened. Nothing remained inside but a lone sandal, one he forgot and left behind.

46. Bodhidharma's Memorial Stele: Written by Emperor Wu?

THE TEXT OF THE MEMORIAL placed at Bodhidharma's burial place, purportedly composed by Emperor Wu, is worthy of attention by Zen practitioners and modern scholars. While the *Continued Biographies* may offer the most reliable information about Bodhidharma's life, Bodhidharma's memorial claims an even earlier origin. As I mentioned above, three copies of this memorial exist, each a reproduction of a previous tablet that was destroyed sometime in the past. The text on each of these large stone memorials is nearly the same. They extol Bodhidharma, express regret that Emperor Wu didn't understand his message, and make other exclamations praising the old sage.

That Emperor Wu could have any connection with these steles is an intoxicating thought. If that were true, then so much of importance could be confirmed and understood. Yet, like so much about Bodhidharma, the situation is not that simple. Scholars inside and outside China have debated these stone tablets' authenticity. A definite conclusion is still out of reach.

Although the monuments self-proclaim their origin to be at the time of Bodhidharma's death, there is some agreement among Chinese scholars that the monuments were originally engraved around the years 728–730 CE, about two hundred years after Bodhidharma died. Nevertheless, these old steles seem intimately connected to Bodhidharma's life, and they also provide fascinating information about the early years of Zen. Based on my study of the memorials' text and knowledge of Zen records of later times, I believe that Zen masters of the ninth and tenth centuries were familiar with them. Some widely known Zen stories refer to phrases and words that appear on the monuments. They are an extremely important source of information about early Zen, whether or not they were composed by Emperor Wu.

The tablets provide intriguing and specific information about Bodhidharma. They tell about a relationship with Emperor Wu that in some ways fits the traditional story and suggest that Bodhidharma's impact in China was very great. They also provide a date and clues about the place of his death. Although each tablet suffers wear and damage that makes its contents difficult to read, taken together their contents can be reconstructed, and a translation is possible. Here is a translation that relies mainly on the text of the stele that remains at Shaolin Temple, the best-preserved of the three old monuments.

The text of the memorial allegedly composed by Emperor Wu for Bodhidharma reads as follows:

> I have heard, that within the blue sea, there is a black dragon with a lustrous white pearl, and that neither gods nor men have ever seen it. But my teacher has done so, the great teacher Bodhidharma. He is said to have come from India, though his home is unknown. We don't know his family name. This great teacher took mind to be the essence and the yin and yang as the device. His nature was provided by heaven and his wisdom given by gods. His bearing was like the sea and the mountains, his spirit like billowing clouds. He possessed Udana-like clarity, with profound learning like Dharmaruci. The entire Buddhist canon was within his mind-stream. The five skandhas are transported on the sea of words. Riches turn to dust, and golden speech [scriptures] fall short. Vowing to spread the Dharma, he came east from India, planting his staff in China. He expounded the wordless truth, like a bright candle in a dark room, like the bright moon when the clouds open. His words reverberated through China, and his path passed through ancient and contemporary. When the emperor and his court heard his name, they honored him like the vast heavens. He was like a leaping fish in the sea of wisdom, startling the birds in the Zen river; his Dharma upholding the heavens and the Buddha sun in their high brilliance. Such was the nourishment he gave the world; [his teaching was] the moistureless Dharma rain that invigorates the body-field. He expounded the dharmaless Dharma, illuminating the bright truth. With

a single phrase he directly pointed to "Mind is Buddha" [and thus] cut off the ten thousand causes, annihilated form, and revealed the body apart from the myriad bodies. Form and emptiness, mundane and sacred, all sublimely illuminated in a single instant of time due to [realizing the nature of] mind. [With the understanding of] no-mind [mu], the sublime truth instantly attained. [But with only an understanding of self-existent] mind, people remain in a state of ignorance. Mind exists without existence. No-mind [mu] is not [to be understood as] Nonexistence. [With this knowledge] the wise have penetrated the "Nonexistence" [mu] obstruction. The numinous extends inconceivably, unsurpassably vast, unsurpassably small, united in nonexistence, manifested in existence. Our true teaching! Now it spreads like clouds, and those who study it [are as numerous] as raindrops. Though the seeds are scant, the flowers are many. The only one who understood [Bodhidharma's essential teaching] was Zen Master Huike! The great teacher [Bodhidharma, upon passing the Dharma to Huike] at last relaxed and exclaimed, "My Mind is complete! The great teaching has been carried out. The entire true teaching is now possessed by Huike!" Bodhidharma instructed Huike to clasp his hands, and then transmitted the light, the principle that is apart from the affairs and things [of the world]. When consciousness comes, it abides in a body. When consciousness travels on, the body is lost. [Upon receiving this teaching, Huike] cried out, exclaiming that [the true] age [of consciousness] surpasses [the age of] heaven and earth, and it transmigrates like [the light of] the sun and moon. It gives rise to the eternal flows of the Dharma seas and endlessly bathes the dark mystery. It eternally pours forth the Zen River, which ceaselessly cleanses away impediments. [Bodhidharma] declared accumulating merit is not beneficial! What was the emperor's error? The moon [lies above] the mysterious Zen garden, the [mental] winds obscure the road of awakening, [but then] the Dharma rafters break, wisdom waters are submerged in the currents, the dark flows hide the boat, the tides and waves surge, and no strategy can help. When suddenly it happens! [Because] mind and form have no difference, color and appearance appear as eternal, and at that time the earth and all things are purified. Heaven is vast and blue. Wild beasts cry out. Sweet springs gush forth! Another cry! Non-action arrives, and all action is gone, the Way is manifested, and birth and death are exposed. Bodhidharma died on the fifth day of the twelfth month in the early morning hours at Yu Gate. His age was unknown. He was buried ceremoniously at Bear Ear Mountain. His disciples were grief-stricken. Their lamentation moved heaven and earth, and their tears drenched their bodies. They were overcome, mourning as though their fathers and mothers had died. All the disciples, their eyes closed, mourned in this manner. The Dharma realm came as one [to his burial], there being none who did not attend. Though his body was interred there in a grave, his appearance traveled to the western regions. [It was as if] he came but did not come, left but did not leave. None [known as] holy or wise have attained [Bodhidharma's] wisdom. My [imperial] actions lack merit and [only comprise] unworthy karma. Above [this karma] has harmed [heaven's] yin and yang. Below it has damaged the happiness of all [beings]. At night I am greatly troubled and unable to eat. Within all that are great [functions], there is [essentially only] Buddhism's Mind. Though I have not gained [the merit] of nine years [of sitting meditation] to benefit beings, [I] still seek the meaning of Dharma, this eternal and miraculous gate. Practiced in peace it is the essence, the sublime. [Those who] transmit it by word and deed [literally, "ear and eye,"] are the Great Teacher's progeny. Alas! I saw him but didn't see him! Met him but didn't meet him! I have only regret and distress about the past and present. Though I am but an ordinary person, I dare take the role of teacher [and say that] which I have not attained in this life will create the conditions for my future [rebirth]. One cannot engrave mind onto a stone, [so] how can the Dharma be demonstrated? I fear heaven will change and the earth will be transformed, and then teachings of the Great Teacher will not be heard. So I'll venture to establish

this monument for those who come here to see, and I compose
the following verse:

From Mount Lanka's peak a jeweled moon appears, inside
    a Golden Man unfurls his silks,
His appearance like the earth, his true body empty,
Unblemished, unadorned, in eternal purity,
    he penetrates the cloud and fog of Mind,
A lotus which, with majestic form, brings eternal joy to each
    in their situation,
Not of existence or nonexistence, not coming or going, the
    learned and talented can't explain,
[Ideas of] real and empty don't matter, and all great and small
    affairs are cut off,
In an instant attaining sublime awakened Mind,
    the leaping fish in the Wisdom Sea surpasses the former sages,
The principle is in the eternally coursing Dharma, whence has it
    ever ceased to flow?
Within the Black Dragon's pearl is a mind-light, whose bright
    rays dull every opposing blade,
New followers scurry about, their Compassion Eye closed,
    but through residing in Zen River currents, their roof beams
    break,
No going, no coming, no is or isn't, it is here that body and
    mind part ways,
Abiding or moving all return to perfect stillness, so from where
    have cries ever issued?
Telling him to clasp his hands, he passed the lamp, birth and
    death, coming and going, are all like lightning,
Yet unwavering Mind remains, not destroyed [even] by the
    aeonic fire,
Only [Hui]ke gained possession of true Dharma, his ignorance
    dispelled.

Many things are striking about the memorial's text. It is filled with
metaphors and pieces of stories widely associated with Bodhidharma.
Some of the memorial's words are closely connected with Zen teachings

still used today. The memorial offers commonly used metaphors like the moon appearing from the clouds, or "rafters breaking" upon experiencing enlightenment. The text offers an early reference to "nine years" of meditation, perhaps the nine years Bodhidharma is credited to have sat in his cave at Shaolin.

The text's passages suggest they were not composed by Emperor Wu. Early in the text, there is an odd reference to the emperor using a third-person expression. I translated the text as "What was the emperor's error?" But the characters that are used here to refer to the "emperor" (皇天) are not typically found in such a context. This compound word is widely defined as being analogous to the word *God*, or *the creator*, and is not a word normally found when the emperor refers to himself. The text thus appears to be meant to flatter the emperor and was therefore likely written by a third person.

Other passages seem to indicate an origin well after Bodhidharma, and even Emperor Wu himself, died. The stele at Kong Xiang Temple self-proclaims that it is signed by Emperor Wu, yet the name Wu, which means "Martial," was not connected with the emperor until after his death. As such, the text could not have been written, as it claims, upon Bodhidharma's death twenty years or so prior to the emperor's own death in the year 549. Another clue rests in the phrase "Though his body was interred there in a grave, his appearance traveled to the western regions," which appears to be a reference to the legend that Bodhidharma was seen walking back to India at a time after his death. Obviously, a memorial composed immediately after the time of his death could not contain such information.

Another reason Emperor Wu likely didn't write the text can be found in the passage that claims that Bodhidharma was Emperor Wu's teacher. The text says, "But my teacher has done so, the great teacher Bodhidharma." This might be a perfunctory expression of praise, not an actual description of the relationship between Emperor Wu and Bodhidharma. The Zen tradition itself claims they had no such relationship. Yet, could it indicate that Bodhidharma had some as yet undefined relationship with the author of this text, if not Emperor Wu?

Later, the text hints at Emperor Wu and Bodhidharma's legendary estranged relationship when it says, "Alas! I saw him but didn't see him! Met him but didn't meet him!"

For these and various other reasons, Chinese scholars and others believe the memorial was created for political reasons long after Bodhidharma died.

With careful dating and analysis, a Chinese scholar named Ji Huazhuan has argued that the monuments were likely created between the years 728 and 732. The main reason Professor Ji offers this conclusion is that a tally of all the memorials existing at Shaolin Temple was taken just before that time, and this memorial by Emperor Wu was not listed among them. Other early sources, such as a reference to the memorial in the works around 733 of the monk Shenhui, confirm that the monument certainly existed by the year 732. Professor Ji also argues that the monuments were likely composed by a Northern school Zen monk named Jingjue. That monk is the known author of a text called the *History of the Lankavatara Masters*, and Professor Ji points out similarities in style between the two texts.

Professor Ji maintains that the creation of the memorials, plus the *Lankavatara Masters* text authored in this time period, were part of the political propaganda meant to give credence to the Northern school of Zen in the court of Emperor Xuan Zong of the Tang dynasty. The moral lesson the steles impart is that emperors will regret it if they reject the Zen tradition. The steles seem to say that Emperor Wu only belatedly realized the meaning of Bodhidharma's teaching and regretted that he earlier failed to comprehend its truth ("I saw him but didn't see him! Met him but didn't meet him!"). Thus the memorials' not-so-subtle message was that then emperor Xuan Zong and others should not make the same mistake Emperor Wu made. They should not fail to recognize Bodhidharma's importance, and they should support the Zen tradition associated with him.

Without going into all the details of Ji Huazhuan's arguments, it must be acknowledged that on many levels he makes a strong and well-constructed case about the memorials' origin and purpose.

If the story of Bodhidharma meeting Emperor Wu wasn't established until the time of the carving of the memorials, in the early 700s, then political motives may have been what gave rise to the story of their meeting. Yet here, like in everything about Bodhidharma, the clues do not lead directly to that conclusion.

There are references in the memorial that connect it to famous

Zen stories and suggest it may have been their origin. For Zen students the most obvious and interesting connection is the reference to "penetrate[ing] the nonexistence [*mu*] obstruction." This seems to be a reference to the same famous story called "Zhaozhou's *Mu*!" that Zen students are familiar with and that the Japanese Sugimoto used to expound on emperor worship. The memorial is a reference to the story that appears in a Zen context at least a hundred years before Zhaozhou lived. Another Zen text claims a connection to this text prior to Zhaozhou, but the memorial is the earliest use of the *mu* story in the Zen tradition that I am aware of. Another example of the text's connection to a later Zen story may be in its reference to an "aeonic fire." This appears to parallel another later Zen story, a subtle and interesting teaching attributed to a Zen master named Dasui (878–963).

A monk asked Zen Master Dasui, "When the aeonic fire engulfs everything, is 'this' annihilated or not?"

Dasui said, "Annihilated."

The monk said, "Then it is annihilated along with everything else?"

Dasui said, "It is annihilated along with everything else."

The monk refused to accept this answer. He later went to Touzi Datong and relayed to him his conversation with Dasui.

Touzi lit incense and bowed to the [statue of] Buddha, saying, "The ancient Buddha of West River has appeared." Then Touzi said to the monk, "You should go back there quickly and atone for your mistake."

The monk went back to see Dasui, but Dasui had already died. The monk then went back to see Touzi, but Touzi had also passed away.

This story appears on its face to contradict the teaching set forth in the steles. The steles indicate that "this" (which in Zen refers to the mind, or consciousness) is not exterminated in the "aeonic fire" that ends the universe. Yet Dasui appears to contradict the words on the memorial by saying that "this" is indeed annihilated. The monk then goes to the Zen Master Touzi, who highly praises Dasui's answer and tells the monk to return and "atone for your mistake" (of not accepting Dasui's answer). But then the monk returns to find that Dasui has died. When the monk subsequently returns to see Touzi, he discovers that Touzi has also passed away. Both teachers are now "annihilated." So Dasui's answer that "this" is annihilated, from the perspective of the inquiring monk, has a peculiar irony and a subtle twist not untypical of Zen stories.

In his analysis of the memorials, the Chinese scholar Ji Huazhuan cites several eighth- and ninth-century texts that reference their existence. Clearly, these memorials attributed to Emperor Wu served as source material for some later and important Zen teachings. An exhaustive study of their content is beyond the scope of this discussion.

If the monuments were created around the year 730, does it follow that their content was also fabricated at that time? I think not. Certain phrases in the text seem to suggest that at least some of the passages were originally authored at the time of Emperor Wu. It is this possibility to which I'll now turn.

During the time period when Professor Ji claims the memorials were created, Zen was already a well-established religious tradition whose legends were known at China's imperial court. The main disciple of Daoxin, the Fourth Zen Ancestor, was the Fifth Ancestor Hongren. At least three of that Zen ancestor's disciples are known to have taught at the Tang dynasty court. This means that at the time these memorials were carved and set up, the Zen tradition of Bodhidharma was already widely known and honored not only by the emperor but also by many people in Chinese society.

For that reason I think it's unlikely that information put on Bodhidharma's monuments were made up out of thin air. The text on the memorials was not simply fabricated by the monk Jingjue. At least some of the stories on these monuments must have been in circulation before their creation and may even stretch back to Bodhidharma's time. It seems likely that at that time there were other written records related to Bodhidharma. Those other records are now lost, but they must have contributed at least certain portions of what was carved on the long-lasting stone monuments that remain now.

The way the old text was written seems to show that it was not composed at one sitting or even by one author. Oddly, the time and place of Bodhidharma's death are provided at the middle of the text. Typically such information would be placed at the end. This raises the possibility that the latter part of the text was added at a later time. The content of this latter portion of the text seems to support this idea. The description of the monks' mourning and the great attendance at Bodhidharma's funeral seems formulaic and lacking in genuine detail. Bodhidharma's disciples are not described with individual names, but rather by the phrases "their tears drenching their bodies" and "mourning as though their fathers and mothers had died." These expressions look as if they were added to heighten the drama. Another late entry in the text says that "his appearance traveled to the western regions," which appears to be a reference to the legend of Bodhidharma returning to India with only a single sandal. This legend appears in the later *Compendium* version of Bodhidharma's death and other much-later texts. Obviously, if the memorial was written at all once right after Bodhidharma died, then this old legend would not yet have been known.

Thus there is the possibility that at least part of the text that appears before the passage citing the date of Bodhidharma's death was written much earlier, and the latter text was added at the time the memorials were created.

The *Continued Biographies* account of Sengfu, Bodhidharma's senior disciple who lived in Nanjing, says that upon his death he was greatly honored by Emperor Wu and his court. It states that Emperor Wu's daughter, Princess Yong Xing, approached the Crown Prince Zhao Ming and invited him to compose the laudatory memorial to be erected in Sengfu's honor. This suggests that Zhao Ming, the son of Emperor Wu and a very famous literary figure, composed such memorials for teachers of high reputation, perhaps on behalf of his father. What is even more interesting is that there seem to be clues in the first part of the Bodhidharma memorial that could link that part of the text to Zhao Ming himself.

The main clues may lie in two phrases that are found in both the stele and in the poem I earlier translated that told of Zhao Ming's visit to Kaishan Temple in the early morning. Certain phrases in each text, metaphorical passages, are quite similar.

In Zhao Ming's poem about a Dharma talk he attended at Kaishan Temple is the phrase "The Dharma Wheel illuminates the dark room." This passage has a double meaning. The speaker that day at Kaishan

Temple sat in a dark room at the break of dawn, and the poem correlated the scene that morning to the illumination of darkness with the teacher's Dharma words. Therefore, Zhao Ming's phrase in the poem *was not* a general metaphor used in other Buddhist poetry or prose but a description of a specific place and time, a talk on a particular morning at Kaishan Temple on Bell Mountain.

On the memorial stele we find the following phrase that refers to Bodhidharma and his teaching: "He spoke the unspeakable Dharma, like a bright candle in a dark room." What this indicates, to my thinking, is that the author of the steles knew of Zhao Ming's poem and incorporated a similar metaphor. Again, this metaphor is not a general metaphor for the nature of the Dharma, like other metaphors I've described earlier, but is a specific reference to the event described in Zhao Ming's poem.

There is only one other use of this metaphor that I have found in Buddhist poetry, and it tends to confirm the link. In a poem titled "Receiving the Precepts in Flowered Woods Garden," the prince Xiao Wang, Emperor Wu's second son and Zhao Ming's younger brother, uses essentially the same phrase. The poem describes a ceremony of receiving the Bodhisattva Precepts in the same garden where some say Emperor Wu met Bodhidharma, the garden of the same name as Hualin Temple in Guangzhou. A few lines of Wang's poem highly praise the words of the preceptor of the ordination ceremony, but they don't identify him. In his poem the prince uses almost the exact phrase found in Zhao Ming's poem about Kaishan Temple and on Bodhidharma's memorial stele. And he adds a twist that seems to draw the poem even closer to the Bodhidharma style of teaching. A passage in his poem reads as follows:

A true Mind shines wondrously,
The ferried boat honors the profound teaching,
Drawing near this, imperial affairs drop away,
And the light of the mind illuminates a dark room.

The last line's metaphor adds weight to the idea that a composer of the first part of Bodhidharma's stele at the very least was intimately familiar with the poetry of the Liang dynasty princes. It may also suggest that Wang accompanied his older brother Zhao Ming to visit Kaishan Temple that dark morning.

But the illumination of a "dark room" metaphor is not the only correlation between the steles and the poetry of the Liang princes. Right after the occurrence of the metaphor I've described above, the memorial says of Bodhidharma, "He was like a leaping fish in the sea of wisdom." Similarly, the term *sea of wisdom* appears in Zhao Ming's poem when he says, "Here the sea of wisdom is crossed." The term *sea of wisdom* is not a widely used Buddhist expression. It would be somewhat familiar to persons conversant with Buddhist literature. Here, the occurrence of the term in both Zhao Ming's poem and Bodhidharma's stele may lend weight to the idea that the author of the steles knew the princes' poetry.

One other clue may lie in the use of the phrase used for "emperor" that I mentioned earlier. Zhao Ming used extremely flattering language whenever he mentioned his father Emperor Wu. In the Kaishan Temple poem, he flatters his father with the following line: "Countless tributes for a hundred generations will go to my emperor!" It makes sense that many people may have talked like this in an age when an emperor could have your head removed on a whim. Still, the flattery used in each instance is unusual. The phrase of high praise for Emperor Wu that is in the Kaishan Temple poem strikes a tone similar to the deference shown to Emperor Wu in the memorial text. This again points to the writing style of the Crown Prince Zhao Ming.

There is yet another piece of evidence to consider. Zhao Ming also composed a separate poem about an unidentified monk who gave a talk to an audience at Tongtai Temple. That was the special temple built behind Tai Cheng Palace where Emperor Wu lived during times when he had renounced the imperial throne. In that poem about a monk talking at Tongtai Temple, Zhao Ming first refers to Vulture Peak, the place in India where Buddha taught and that was the legendary origin place of the Zen sect, the place where Buddha held up a flower. The reference to Vulture Peak may suggest not only a link to Zen, but also that the lecturing monk was a foreigner. Here's a translation of the first few lines of the "The Virtuous Talk of a Monk at Tongtai Temple" by Xiao Tong (Zhao Ming):

> Illumination flows from the world of Vulture Peak,
> The scriptures hide the Buddha realm,

The source reaches its end, returning from light to what is
  nameless,
When people hear it they reach the solitary stillness . . .

Overall, the tone of this poem and of his poem of the meeting at Kaishan
Temple is similar. Moreover, the phrase "scriptures hide the Buddha
realm" can be taken to mean that the speaker that day, whoever he was,
counseled against relying on scriptures to understand the Dharma. This
suggests a link to Zen's mind teachings, the practice that relied on "just
observing" and that avoided the metaphysics of the sutras.

Connections between Bodhidharma's memorials and the poetry of
Zhao Ming and his younger brother do not prove that Zhao Ming
composed even a portion of the memorials. But taken altogether, the
first part of the memorials text and Zhao Ming's poetry are suspiciously
of the same flavor.

Yet there is a major reason why the Zen tradition and many scholars
will not accept that Zhao Ming could have composed any part of the
memorial to Bodhidharma. That problem lies in the fact that the date
given for Bodhidharma's death that appears on the monuments, the fifth
day of the twelfth (lunar) month of year 2 in the Datong era, or 536,
occurred five years after Prince Zhao Ming himself is known to have
died (531). This contradiction is found in some other old records.

There is a text called the *Baolin Biography*, generally thought to have
been composed around the year 801. The *Baolin Biography* agrees with
the date offered on the Bodhidharma memorials for his death, yet the
text also specifically claims that Bodhidharma's memorials were composed by Crown Prince Zhao Ming. One or the other, or both, of these
facts must be wrong.

How can these confusing and contradictory accounts be reconciled?
Remember that the *Continued Biographies*, the earliest datable account
of Bodhidharma and his disciples' lives, places his death sometime
prior to 534, the time when Huike left Luoyang and traveled to the
territory of the Eastern Wei dynasty. If that account is roughly accurate, and it is the best account we have regarding the times involved,
then Bodhidharma's death could have occurred as much as three years
or so prior to Prince Zhao Ming's death due to illness in 531. In that
case, Zhao Ming could indeed have composed, or helped compose, a

document memorializing Bodhidharma before his own untimely death in the year 531.

The appearance of the phrase "Mind illuminates a dark room" in Prince Xiao Wang's poem raises another possibility. That is that the memorial was composed not by Zhao Ming but by Xiao Wang, Emperor Wu's second son. In that case, it may have been composed long after the death of both Bodhidharma and Zhao Ming. Xiao Wang lived until the year 551, even ascending the dynastic throne for a brief period under difficult circumstances two years before his own death.

Could Jingjue or some other author of the steles have added the 536 date to an earlier text? And why would he do so? I believe there was a great deal of confusion about the precise date that Bodhidharma died. The *Continued Biographies* offers contradictory information on the year, and this confusion is revealed in later records.

For whatever reason, the "official" story of Bodhidharma, the story that the steles provide as a cautionary tale, places his death in the year 536. Later accounts that say Bodhidharma arrived in China in 527 appear to be calculated by subtracting the nine years he reportedly spent meditating in a cave from the listed date of his death on the memorial steles, namely 536.

What seems plausible, but not provable, is that Emperor Wu and the rest of his court met Bodhidharma on one or more occasions on or before the year 524. Bodhidharma and Huike both may have come to visit Bodhidharma's ailing oldest disciple, Sengfu. Or they may have come to visit during the grand funeral described in Sengfu's biography. Then, perhaps Bodhidharma at long last consented to give a talk at Kaishan Temple or even to the court at Tongtai Temple or Flowered Woods Garden. Upon Sengfu's death, Emperor Wu's oldest daughter, Princess Yong Xing, declared her allegiance to his teachings and petitioned the Crown Prince Zhao Ming to write his memorial. Could Xiao Wang, younger brother to the same crown prince, have already received the precepts from Sengfu or Bodhidharma at Tongtai Temple, thus honoring their ideal of not entering the actual palace that stood across the street from the temple's front gate?

And what if there was a meeting? What if Bodhidharma did in fact come to visit Sengfu from his little temple in Tianchang, sixty miles away? Perhaps Bodhidharma told the court that it was Huike, not

Sengfu, who really understood his teaching. Then, to avoid their new celebrity, Bodhidharma and Huike left the area and returned to the north either on foot or by sailing up the Yang-tse and Han Rivers, returning to the area where Bodhidharma first took Sengfu as a disciple thirty years earlier. Bodhidharma may have thereafter had even more stature because of an encounter with Emperor Wu. Then, around the time 528 to 530, Bodhidharma died. Although Emperor Wu had not grasped what Bodhidharma had said during their encounter, he may have still tried to share the spiritual limelight with the famous Indian sage by declaring him to be his teacher. Prince Zhao Ming, assigned to issue a proclamation of praise for Bodhidharma, wrote something along the lines of the first half of the memorial text, and this was, or served as the basis for, the text used when the steles were carved and erected in the early 700s.

This version of possible events conforms and takes into account the narrative of the *Continued Biographies*, the best available source about Bodhidharma's life. It also suggests an origin for Bodhidharma's memorial steles that was not fabricated out of thin air. Yet the date given for Bodhidharma's death on the steles, 536, cannot be reconciled with the version of events provided in the *Continued Biographies*. The mystery continues.

There are other unanswered questions here. If the phrases about illuminating a "dark room" and references to a "sea of wisdom" were only added to the memorial steles because the author, two centuries after Bodhidharma lived, was aware of the poems by the Liang princes and tried to give authenticity to the steles, why are there no other allusions to those princes or their writings on the steles? This implies that the writer of some of the steles was one of the princes. And could it mean that the year 536 given for Bodhidharma's death is, after all, reliable, and that Xiao Wang, not his older brother Zhao Ming, was the author?

But Daoxuan, author of the *Continued Biographies*, did not make any reference to the 536 date of Bodhidharma's death, although he worked on the *Continued Biographies* over a twenty-year period and had access to disciples intimate with Bodhidharma's Zen tradition.

In my view, the memorial steles attributed to Emperor Wu have a connection to the Liang Court, though the exact nature of the connection is obscure. The text indicates that Emperor Wu's sons influenced, directly or indirectly, the first part of the memorial's contents. It appears that certain legendary aspects of Bodhidharma's life, such as his "nine years" of sitting meditation, his mythical return to "western regions," and his meeting with Emperor Wu, were known and widely circulated at the time the stelae were made. The contents also suggest these old memorials were not composed in a single sitting by a single writer.

Scholars contend that different religious factions, whether Buddhist, Taoist, or Christian, advance mythologies that will enhance their political positions with the state. This is clearly true. Bodhidharma's story, based on impartial historical accounts and relatively reliable records, also suggests a political element was central to the plot, but not a political element of ingratiating his life to emperors and their families. Indeed, his story seems to indicate just the opposite. Bodhidharma's life, related in the *Continued Biographies* and the memorial steles, and even possibly by the poetry of the Crown Prince Zhao Ming, was of a life devoted to solitary practice that avoided emperors and perhaps even the religious metaphysics that darkened his age.

47. Bodhidharma Memorial Ceremony

As THE SUN slowly brightens the morning fog, I sit in a late-model black sedan waiting to be driven to the Bodhidharma memorial ceremony at Empty Appearance Temple. This Dharma meeting takes place every year on the fifth day of the tenth lunar month, usually falling sometime in early November by the Western calendar. At the first such convocation, which occurred in the autumn of the year Bill Porter and I sought out the place, more than fifty thousand people attended. Every year since then on that date, monks from around China and even other countries have joined with lay people to commemorate Bodhidharma in big public observance at the same site.

The celebration features groups of lay people who have traveled from afar, bands of peasant musicians and dancers, demonstrations by young martial arts practitioners from Shaolin Temple, and other colorful sights. There's an art exhibition in one of the temple halls that is devoted to Bodhidharma, a few speeches by government officials and high-ranking monks praising "Bodhidharma Culture," and general China country fair festivities.

Every year at this Dharma convocation, there is a contingent of lay Buddhist women from Luoyang City who attend. Wearing beautiful lay Buddhist robes, they carry a banner announcing their group, and they take an active part in the celebrations. I saw them during my first visit to the ceremony. They were coming up the road to the temple in a long procession. Every three steps they'd make a full prostration on the road, followed by three more steps and another prostration. They always seem, to me, the most dedicated and enthusiastic supporters of this blood vein of Zen culture, this link to China's "cultural essence."

A half mile or so from the temple is a big *paifang*, a wide gate that arches above the entrance road. This morning I ask the driver of the sedan giving me a ride to the celebrations to stop there. I get out and stand watching while the lay ladies of Luoyang pass in their slow, noble procession of bowing and devotion. When they have finally all passed the *paifang*, I fall in behind them and follow suit.

48. Train to Shanghai

THE TRAIN FROM Luoyang to Shanghai is a communications trap. It leaves at 9:00 PM, so I need to book an extra half day, at least, on my hotel room in Luoyang. Crowds stretch across the plaza in front of the train station. I arrive more than an hour before I need to because my time in my hotel has run out. I stand in the cold wondering if the scene inside the station is more depressing than the square in front of it. Should I go in or not? Then, even though I have a first-class ticket, I find there's no first-class waiting room, so I place my backpack and suitcase in some strange unknown liquid beneath the only seat I've found open in the Number 4 Waiting Hall. The words *Number 4 Waiting Hall* are themselves dehumanizing and a cause for melancholy. I listen to the same songs on my iPod that I've heard a thousand times, and time drags on to the appointed hour. Finally a surge in the crowd signals that the lights indicating "Shanghai, Ticket Inspection" are now flashing. My suitcase is four times larger than any other traveler's, and I strain to get it down the long flight of steps leading to the train platform without letting it slip and roll free, crushing some child innocently clutching her mother's hand on the steps below me. The sound of the suitcase wheels on the cement platform—*rrr, rrr*—and the sound of the train whistle in the distant night convey the loneliness of a Johnny Cash ballad. I climb aboard and find I must rearrange things in the top pocket of my suitcase so it will fit under the sleeper. My compartment mates arrive: a young couple with a little boy, maybe two years old, who looks at me with wide eyes, probably seeing his first foreigner up close. I make my usual jokes: "*Wa, a laowai!*" ("Look how big his nose is! Terrifying!")

The mother is friendly and smiles. They all wave to someone standing outside on the platform. She says, "Say good-bye to Uncle."

Soon I rearrange my blanket and pillow and search for sleep. But I can't sleep. Instead I mull over the things I read on the Chinese Internet last night, the things that helped make a Chinese train station assume its bête noir atmosphere.

At 4:00 AM the train stops. I notice we're in the city of Xuzhou. We've come pretty far. Maybe they were exaggerating when they said we'd arrive in Shanghai at three thirty the next afternoon. If we're already in Xuzhou, it shouldn't take that long to get to Shanghai, should it? I get up and open the door into the empty train corridor. You can't use the restroom while the train is stopped at the station. I wait. I watch. The train finally pulls away from the station. I use the restroom and go back to the compartment. I feel anxious and can't go back to sleep.

After another sleepless hour or two, dawn breaks. The dining car is the next car down. For twenty yuan, you can have a "buffet breakfast." I find there's only one dish out of ten or so that looks vegetarian-palatable. But I pay the twenty yuan and fill a small plate. I start to sit down at an empty table before I notice that a sign on it that indicates it is reserved for Islamic passengers eating their halal food.

At around eight in the morning, the train rolls across the long trestle above the Yang-tse River, indicating we've reached Nanjing. The couple with the little boy pick up their bags, give me a nod and a smile, and get off the train, leaving me alone in the compartment. Will it really take another seven and a half hours to reach Shanghai? It's less than two hours away if you take a high-speed train. As the sun rises, the landscape can't shake off a low fog. The train begins a slow crawl south, pausing frequently. The Chinese authorities are building superfast trains, some even have maglev technology, but you still can't buy a ticket that lets you transfer to a faster train when you reach a given station.

I settle in to pass the seven-hour trip to Shanghai. I try to read, but thoughts about Nanjing, Emperor Wu, and Bodhidharma weigh on me.

NANJING IN CONTEXT

Is it fair to say that Buddhist metaphysics actually caused the aggressive imperial adventures Japan undertook in World War II? On balance, I do not think it is fair to do so. The causes of the war are naturally deeper than the propaganda used to justify it. Such causes are certainly atavistic, which is to say they are connected with deeper historical antagonisms with social, geographical, and biological origins. One cause historians point to is the scourge of extreme nationalism, in which Japan and other nations got caught up, that has accompanied the rise of the modern nation-state. Modernization, along with the rise of resource-hungry capitalist economies, ethnic rivalries, and other causes, all create a tinderbox easily ignited by the odd case of megalomania or just plain old jingoism. Buddhist metaphysics was largely just window dressing for more fundamental forces. Ideological fanaticism of every stripe, perceived national insult, and simple arrogance and its accompanying delusions have long spurred elites to propagate hatred and violence toward other groups. The experience in Japan is not unique, nor is it even the most recent extreme example of this problem. Fanatical belief has walked hand in hand with the history of conflict of every age, and Darwinian impulses abound. Historians have noted that in the case of Japan, the very acceptance and embrace of the philosophy of social Darwinism by Japan's intellectuals helped promote *kokutai* thinking.

While Buddhist metaphysics only decorated deeper forces, it also provided excuses for some of the extreme manifestations of the tragedy. Social elites politicized the religion in a long historical process. Then, at a critical juncture, it failed its mission of offering a counterpoint or remedy for the impulse toward war and empire. Instead, it contributed to war mania. This failure must be acknowledged and understood.

ON THE TRACK TO SHANGHAI

The snow is gone. The train rumbles slowly along, with many long stops.

Once, when I get up to stand in the corridor, an Asian man with gray hair passes in the corridor. He's well-dressed. Later I look through the train passage into the dining car and see him sitting at a table and smoking. I close the door between the train cars to help keep his cigarette smoke from drifting my way. Twice I've caught bronchitis after breathing cigarette smoke in China.

When Shanli and Mike and Hashlik and I climbed the mountain to the Second Ancestor's hermitage, Mike said he wanted to make a movie about cigarette culture in China. He said he was talking to a man about an orphanage connected with his organization in the United Kingdom.

The project hadn't gotten funded, and the Chinese man was depressed about this. Mike said the man couldn't admit what the problem was until Mike realized that something was wrong and offered him a cigarette. Then the man opened up and talked freely. This is one part of Chinese culture in which I won't ever be able to participate.

While I'm sitting in the train compartment, the gray-haired man comes by and sticks in his head. He says something to start a conversation. He sits down. He's Japanese, and his home is in Nara, Japan's ancient capital. Even stranger, his name is Sakurai, the same name as the place near Nara where Sima Dadeng lived. He tells me his wife has a very big heart. She likes foreigners. Come and stay at our house, he says. One month. Two months. However long you like. I tell him I've been to Nara a few times. It's a beautiful place. I remember some Japanese. "*Nara wa, aki ni naru to, utsekushi desu nee!*" ("Nara! When fall comes, it's beautiful!") He says he's in the bamboo-flooring business. He buys the bamboo material in Thailand and imports it to China for manufacture and sale. He says he can't sell it in Japan. Business is bad. We make more small talk. After a while he excuses himself and leaves.

I sit looking out at the slow-moving landscape and thinking about Nara.

I daydream. Maybe if Buddhism is to survive in the West, it should get rid of its metaphysical baggage and go back to what Bodhidharma originally stood for. Western philosophy has managed to rid itself of much metaphysics, and Bodhidharma's Zen, as it appears in the West today, might benefit from the same attitude. The West is about rationalism. In a certain sense, so was Bodhidharma. Where should the Bodhisattva Vow, a big part of Zen in the West, fit into the whole picture?

The morning drags on. Then Mr. Sakurai again appears in the door and says he wants to show me something in his train compartment. I follow him there. He has a big wooden box. Inside is a piece of Chinese pottery, heavily glazed and oddly shaped, a tall cylindrical vessel that looks like a bumpy pipe with stubby wings. Its glaze displays a twisted and bumpy amalgam of green, blue, and pink hues.

"A business partner gave me this as a present."

I'm struck with a sudden realization that he's hoping he can give it to me.

"It's big," I say. "You can't carry it."

Sakurai shows me that there's a little sticky price tag on the thing that says it costs eighty thousand yuan, more than ten thousand dollars. Now I'm really afraid he wants to give it to me.

I tell him, "If you take it back to Japan, your wife won't like the color."

He laughs. He knows I don't want it.

"Everywhere I go in China people give me big books," I say. "It's impossible to carry them."

I examine the thing more closely. It's awful.

"Too bad that in Japan you have sliding doors and not hinged doors," I tell him. "You could put umbrellas in it and keep it out of sight behind the door."

Sakurai breaks out laughing. He closes the box.

We walk back out into the train corridor together, and he suggests we have a beer in the dining car. We take the few steps to that car and sit at a table. Sakurai orders a beer, and I order a coffee. I haven't had any beer or wine, any alcohol of any kind, for a long time. He lights a cigarette. I decide I should accept the world a little more, and so I sit there uncomplaining while he smokes, hoping I won't catch bronchitis. After my coffee is gone, I order the first beer I've had since I can't remember when. We talk about the world and how hard the recession is for everyone and what it's like to try and survive in business. Finally we arrive in Shanghai. He's made me promise, and I agree, to meet him for a drink that evening. Cigarettes or not, Sakurai is really an engaging, friendly man. Nara is a beautiful place. I'd like to go there again, maybe for a month or two.

That evening I find my way to Jenny's Blues Bar near Huaihai Road to meet Sakurai. When I arrive he is already there, sitting at the bar. I pull myself up on a bar stool and order a beer, wondering if there will be a live band. I like blues and have even seen some great Chinese blues musicians perform in Hong Kong and China over the years. Two girls behind the bar take my money and give me the beer. There's no live music, they say, just recordings. They are interested that Sakurai and I can speak Chinese, and we all chat for a while. Then a young woman appears walking among the customers. She's dressed in a Tiger Beer outfit, including a bright yellow sash with the Tiger Beer logo on it. She sees that I've ordered an American beer and pitches to me that my next one should be a Tiger. I promise her I'll order Tiger next time.

Sakurai is a little drunk. We continue chatting with the bartenders, and I notice that an older woman, who appears to be managing the place, is interested in our conversation.

Sakurai frequents this place and has his own private bottle of whiskey that he drinks whenever he comes here. He talks about Thailand. He says he likes the Thai people a lot and starts talking about how polite they are. The older woman stands nearby, listening to Sakurai. She has a deeply pained expression on her face. She obviously is the boss, as she directs the girls working behind the bar about various small tasks. I wonder why she looks so aggrieved and exhausted.

Sakurai notices that one of the girls working behind the bar is new and asks her where she comes from. She says she's from Anhui Province. Then she asks me if I know where Anhui is located. I say that of course I do, for that's the place where the sacred mountain of Dizang Bodhisattva, one of the four great Bodhisattvas of Chinese Buddhism, is located.

Then the older woman chimes into the conversation. "Have you been to that place?" she asks.

"Yes," I say. "Quite a few times."

She's surprised I know about the mountain. "Do you know what is special about Dizang?" she asks.

I say, "He goes into hell and liberates beings that are there."

Oddly, it seems that both the older woman and the girls tending the bar know all about this bit of Buddhist lore.

The woman's face is almost contorted in pain. Obviously she wants to talk about something. Finally she tells her story. Recently she began following a Buddhist path. She tells me this directly, as I gather that Sakurai already knows her story, as do the girls behind the bar. She has a teacher, she says. Her teacher is in the Mizong ("Tantric") Buddhist tradition like the one Shanli follows. Then she seems to break down, and the story floods out. She's owned the bar since 1994 when she divorced her philandering husband. Her twenty-nine-year-old son, named Bao Jun, died a few months ago of a heart attack. They were eating ice cream on Huaihai Street near Shanghai's famous Cathay Theatre. She thought the pain he was experiencing was from the cold ice cream. Then he was dead. He was her only child. The woman's face takes on an incredible expression of tragedy as she speaks about her son. She describes how his personality was outgoing and kind, and he worked on projects to help people, like a new school that she was helping him establish for poor children. She shows me his photos on a computer screen that sits at the end of the bar. He appears smiling and happy in each photo. His sudden death has caused his mother to doubt everything. Now she seeks answers in Buddhism and bodhisattvas. She tells me she asked her Buddhist teacher if she could continue selling alcohol. He said she could, but she must be very careful. Now she avoids letting any customers get intoxicated. She tells me more about her son. He managed his own coffeehouse where he made a point of paying people high wages and treating them well. He was a little overweight. She jokes that he was a *pangzi* (an endearing term meaning "fatty"), but he wasn't that much overweight, really just average on the American scale. Look, she says to me, at his open, deep eyes, that showed an acceptance of everything, nothing held back.

"When he died, I stayed in my house for five days and didn't come out. They all came to get me."

I notice that as we are talking the girls working behind the bar have drawn near and are listening to our conversation intently, and the girl in the Tiger Beer getup is doing the same. Perhaps they hope I can offer some solace to this woman, who is their boss, whose world has collapsed and who has turned to Buddha.

"I have money. I have everything I need," she says. Then she pauses. "I just feel that . . ." She pauses and then continues, "Everything in the world is dirty."

We talk for a while about Buddhism. She says she will go to Jiuhua Mountain in Anhui Province and pray to Dizang, the bodhisattva that travels into hell to liberate the unfortunate beings there. She will take the precepts with her Buddhist teacher. She's not sure how much longer she will do business. She asks me, a foreigner who she thinks knows a little about Buddhism, why her son died.

THE DEATH OF EMPEROR WU

During the Heyin Massacre of 528, when the general Er Zhurong slaughtered hundreds of government officials and others of the Northern Wei Court, a young military commander named Hou Jing escaped the carnage by fleeing to a Buddhist temple and hiding out there. Said by Chinese historians to have been a crude opportunist, and sporting the nickname Little Dog, he inveigled a command in Er Zhurong's forces and then, possessing the unprincipled ruthlessness necessary to such a position, was appointed to a high rank in his army. Subsequently, along with Er Zhurong, he led marauding troops in victories over rival forces in North China. Within a short time Er Zhurong himself was killed through betrayal, but Hou Jing, ever the opportunist, parlayed his battlefield successes and reputation to become a commander of new political factions. He made a point of sharing the spoils of his conquests among his troops, especially by rounding up all the women in a defeated countryside and giving them to his soldiers for their amusement. After the establishment of the Eastern Wei dynasty in 534, the emperor ordered his general Hou Jing to occupy and govern the area of Henan, which bordered Emperor Wu's Liang dynasty to the south. During this time, Little Dog learned of the weakness and corruption that had spread in Emperor Wu's empire. He proclaimed, "I'll call on my troops to roam everyplace beneath heaven. I'll cross the [Yang-tse] river, capture that old-timer Xiao Yan, and make him the abbot of Great Peace Temple!"

The emperor of the Eastern Wei well knew Hou Jing's wide-ranging ambitions and feared that when he died his dangerous general might try to deny the emperor's son the throne and take it himself. So, prior to his death, the Wei emperor took steps to make sure his son could stop any power grab by Hou Jing. His preparations were successful, for when the emperor passed away, his son did stop Hou Jing's attempt to seize the throne. Now isolated and seen as an enemy of the Wei, Hou Jing appealed to his southern enemy, Emperor Wu, offering to turn his back on the Wei and place his territories under Emperor Wu's Liang dynasty. Although most officials in Emperor Wu's court were horrified by the idea, the eighty-three-year-old Emperor Wu decided to accept Hou Jing's offer. Suffering mental decline, the emperor claimed that he had a dream in which he took control of China's Northern Plain. Sycophants in his court proclaimed the dream was a harbinger of Emperor Wu unifying the country, and the emperor chose to follow this fateful path.

Emperor Wu received Hou Jing and his territories with a ceremony worthy of China's mythical kings Yao and Shun, declaring him the king of Henan and commander of his northern forces. Before long, Hou Jing quietly put into effect his plan to take over the Liang dynasty. With his own troops now nominally a part of Emperor Wu's forces, he was soon able to advance on the capital virtually unopposed and before long took control of the city with little meaningful resistance.

Emperor Wu finally realized his mistake but was unable to marshal enough forces to stop Hou Jing from taking control of the country. The only thing left guarding the emperor was his reputation as a bodhisattva, and, surprisingly, this seems to have been worth something.

Hou Jing, instead of deposing Emperor Wu and claiming the throne, kept him as a figurehead. While the rebel general outwardly paid honor to the emperor, he kept the monarch under house arrest in the palace, gradually starving him to death. Emperor Wu's popularity, and his symbolic importance, saved him from being summarily executed. The situation was similar to what prevailed in Japan, where shoguns opted to keep the emperor as the symbolic head of the country, all the while retaining real power for themselves. This method of rule proved especially useful in Confucian societies where the emperor is supposed to lead by example. A virtuous emperor like Wu could be kept as a figurehead while those with real power could rule outside the public eye. Appearances were maintained with propaganda like the "mandate of heaven," "Bodhisattva Emperor," or, in the case of Japan, the "Divine Emperor." In truth these high-sounding ideals were a perfect cover for debauchery, graft, and, in the case of 1930s Japan, imperialism.

Ultimately the grand rule of Emperor Wu literally ended with a whimper. The *Book of Liang* portrays the old man dying in bed, his power and prestige evaporated. He asked for some honey. But there was no honey or anything else left to succor the dying emperor. No one responded to his request, and so he died.

Hou Jing made a show of honoring the emperor in death, even allowing his son to nominally take the throne as emperor. But Hou Jing also moved into the palace and directly grasped the levers of power. There, like the Qi emperor Baojuan Emperor Wu had once deposed, Hou Jing feted his friends and established his own imperial harem. The people of the capital city deeply hated the usurper and suffered much at the hands of Hou Jing and his court clique.

But Hou Jing's shogunlike rule of the country did not last long. The *Book of Liang* relates that a strange monk became part of Hou Jing's palace coterie. One night, after a bout of drinking, the monk stabbed the drunken general. The cleric then ran from the palace crying, "I've killed the slave! I've killed the slave!" According to the historical record, some people of the city dragged Hou Jing's body into the street where they cut it up, boiled it, and devoured it to show their hatred for him.

49. Bodhidharma's Fate

THERE IS AN ACCOUNT of Bodhidharma's death that appears as a fully embellished story in the thirteenth-century *Compendium* (added as an appendix to this book). The odd story in that text purports to detail the sage's death, but the account is highly suspicious and can't be confirmed by any early sources. The story says his death occurred at a place called Thousand Saints Temple. But there is no record of any such temple in Chinese historical records, and no one knows where it might have been. Even more strange, the account says that before he died Bodhidharma was visited by the official Yang Xuanzhi, the same official who wrote the *Temples of Luoyang* and whom Daoxuan described as hostile to Buddhism. It says Yang came seeking Bodhidharma's teaching, and the sage obliged him with a lecture on the nature of mind and the nature of Zen. Then Bodhidharma died. The story also says that Yang was then the prefectural governor of Biyang City, a place a few hundred kilometers south of Luoyang. But no records I have found indicate that Yang served in that position there. The story retells a legend saying that Bodhidharma was poisoned by his jealous detractors. This unsupported idea may have arisen because of Daoxuan's account of bitter criticism to which Bodhidharma was subjected during his life.

The *Compendium* account confirms that Bodhidharma was buried at Empty Appearance Temple near Bear Ear Mountain. That place, since at least as early as the seventh century, has laid claim to be his burial spot. Because it has made the claim from such an early time, and is where the memorial purportedly composed by Emperor Wu is located, at least that part of the story seems plausible.

Taken as a whole, the *Compendium* account of Bodhidharma's death is heavy on legend and light on verifiable fact. As I've already mentioned, Yang Xuanzhi, mentioned in this account, composed *Temples of Luoyang*, and Daoxuan described him as hostile to Buddhism. Thus this account of Bodhidharma's death, though of great interest as folk-lore and as a representation of how Bodhidharma was honored by later generations, cannot be taken as accurate. See a complete translation of the *Compendium* account of Bodhidharma's death in the appendix of this book.

DRAGON GATE: DID BODHIDHARMA DIE NEAR CHINA'S ABANDONED HEART?

"Who among you is an adept of the Dragon Gate? Right now, is there anyone that can enter? Hurry up and go in so that you can avoid a wasted life."
—*Zen Master Fengyang (947–1024), addressing assembled monks*

The Yellow River is named for the yellow silt it ferries from central Asian Deserts and the North China Plain to the sea. It creates rich soil all along the river's course, and ancient farmers prospered there. The surpluses of good farming allowed for trading, markets, and the accumulation of wealth needed for civilization. But the river's constant silting also caused disastrous floods. Four thousand years ago, the legendary Chinese ruler Yu the Great led the ancestors of the Han people in the fight to survive along the Yellow River's banks. He built dikes and dredged the river, taming its unbridled floods.

Forever honored for his labors, Yu is remembered as China's first hereditary king, whose progeny maintained continuous rule for sixteen generations. Yu was the primogenitor of the legendary Xia (Hsia) dynasty.

Perhaps Yu's greatest river-control project took place where the Yellow River emerges from the Dragon Mountains into the dusty soil of the Yellow River basin. That place, called Dragon Gate, concentrated the waters of the river to run through white rapids before they reached the plain. Today the waters there still course through massive boulders and outcroppings, but now a constructed lake just downstream has slowed the flow and controlled the shifting silt deposits that caused floods. Yu also controlled the waters at this critical point where the river exited the mountains, a place also called Yu Gate. Dragon Gate and Yu Gate are names applied to this same place.

A legend intimately tied to China's origins says that Yellow River carp traveled upstream through this spot, struggling and leaping through the rapids to reach their spawning grounds. Their heroic efforts were likened to Yu's efforts to tame the river. Yu's labors secured him the dragon throne. Thus, metaphorically, fish that conquered these rapids were likewise thought to become dragons. The painting I purchased years ago in Hong Kong depicts their struggle. In the painting, among three leaping fish, the one that leaps the highest clears the rapids and changes color, turning orange. Like Yu, when the fish conquered Dragon Gate, it changed into a dragon. In China and Chinatowns throughout the world, the scene of *li yu tiao long men* ("fish leaping through Dragon Gate") is still displayed on all types of Chinese folk art, an echo of the mythical beginnings of China. The bright orange color of goldfish was bred into carp by ancient Chinese fish breeders to reflect the transformation of carp into dragons at Dragon Gate. When Zen Master Fengyang, quoted earlier, challenged his disciples to show they were adepts at Dragon Gate, he evoked the metaphor of the carp who could successfully transform themselves to become dragons.

Was this also the Yu Gate where Emperor Wu's memorial says that Bodhidharma died? One clear and dry autumn morning, Eric and I decide to find the place and see for ourselves. We hire a car in Xian and set off.

North of Xian, the Wei River flows from west to east on its way to join the Yellow River. This area of the Wei and Yellow River basins gave rise to China's earliest legendary kings, such as the Yellow Emperor, and the area is considered to be the original homeland of the Han Chinese.

Not far from Xian, we cross the Wei River and proceed northeast through the fertile flatlands that spawned China's earliest history. Our goal is the place where the Yellow River enters the area from the north.

After a couple of hours' drive, we reach Hancheng, a newly industrialized city ringed with chemical plants that lies against the low-lying hills of an encroaching range of mountains. The air, heavy with industrial haze, is further fouled with a yellow cloud kicked up from new road construction. The loess dust of the area, the source of Yellow River silt, covers the countryside. The chemical process plants of Hancheng look like the same type that encroach on Changlu Temple near Nanjing, leaving the same taste on the tongue as you pass them.

After bouncing our way through the road construction around the Hancheng industrial zone, we soon reach Yu Gate, where the Yellow River emerges from the mountains. The river runs from north to south at this location and serves as the border between China's confusingly named Shaanxi and Shanxi Provinces.

My first view of Yu Gate is disappointing. The place seems forgotten. Some enormous boulders remain at the place where the Yellow River exits the mountains, and a bridge spans its waters. The old boulders at this spot help form a natural ford across the river. Historical accounts indicate ancient armies crossed the river at this location to travel to the North China Plain, thus the place had strategic significance on the chessboard of China's old battlefields.

It was these boulders and the rapids just upstream from there that gave rise to the grand rapids of legend. But upstream, on the far shore of the river, a modern gravel pit has gashed a big hole in the side of the Dragon Mountains. As a result, it appears that gravelly detritus has filled in the waterway, taming the white water where fish once turned into dragons. We gaze up and down barren landscape. Only a few scrub trees break the pale monotony of the steep rocky slopes that plunge toward the now placid river.

Sometime in recent history, an entrepreneur, or maybe the local tourist board, tried to make a go of the place. At the side of the road, a badly rusted sign still advertises the FISH JUMPING DRAGON GATE in faded characters. Also barely readable are signs pointing toward the place's EIGHT FAMOUS SIGHTS, among which are the GARGLING JADE SPRINGS, the ROCK LANDINGS, and the THUNDEROUS THREE-LEVELED RAPIDS. But the signs have fallen against the hillside. No tourists but us are around, and no gargling springs or three-tiered rapids seem anywhere apparent. There is only the thin, quiet river on a fall afternoon, meandering meekly through bare mountains. Upstream, at a distance, are some low, gentle rapids.

A few dilapidated buildings next to the road indicate that something remains of a village that once stood here. A man standing in front of one of the shacks waves to me, and I walk over to ask him about the place. He greets me with a toothless smile and motions toward a sign indicating that the old building is in fact a restaurant.

"Is there any legend about Bodhidharma coming here?" I ask.

No, he tells me. There is only the legend of the Great Yu. He doesn't know anything about Bodhidharma coming to this place. And no, he has never heard of Thousand Saints Temple.

"Wasn't there a temple here before?"

The man nods. "It's gone now," he says. "Everything is gone. But we have a photo of the old days." He motions me toward the broken door that hangs on the front of the building. "Go take a look."

I am uncertain whether this is just his ploy to get some customers. But I follow the man's invitation nonetheless and walk through the shabby entrance of the little eatery.

I enter the darkened room where a couple young men slurp noodles at one of the four or five tables in the little restaurant. In the dim light I can make out, on the back wall, a blown-up photograph. It is huge, maybe ten feet wide, and covers the entire back wall of the little eatery. Maybe it was taken in the 1930s or 1940s. It shows, in full detail, the grandeur of Dragon Gate before modernity laid waste to it. The panoramic photo displays a wide and deep river, full of fishing vessels and cargo junks, all moored or anchored near a grand shrine dedicated to Yu the Great. The huge shrine perches like a bird above the deep river waters, its Ming-style roof curving upward like a bird taking wing over the waves, or maybe like a fish leaping to become a dragon.

That evening when Eric and I return from Dragon Gate, we pass and stop at Empty Appearance Temple to talk to its abbot, the monk Shi Yanci. He meets us at the front gate and then leads us into the temple reception room for tea.

"Do you have any idea where Thousand Saints Temple was located?" I ask him.

"No," he replies, pouring the tea.

"It's supposed to be at Yu Gate," I say. "Today we went to the Yu Gate where the Yellow River comes out of the mountains. The place that is also called Dragon Gate."

"That's not where Bodhidharma died," says the abbot. "It's too far from here. Also, there are many Yu Gates. Yu had many projects in many places, and when he was finished, many of those places were called Yu

Gate. It may have been on the Luo River instead of the Yellow River. The Luo River flows south of here."

I remember that the Second Ancestor's biography indicated he buried Bodhidharma on the banks of the Luo River. But that account seems uncertain because it contradicts Bodhidharma's biography written by the same author, Daoxuan.

Yanci slurps a mouthful of tea and continues. "There are some places on the Luo River that were called Yu Gate. But no one has ever found a Thousand Saints Temple."

I sit quietly and sip some tea, trying to sort out the mystery.

Yanci puts down his cup and smiles. Then he says, "If you keep coming and going, you'll never find Bodhidharma."

50. Epilogue

AN IMPORTANT interpretation of Bodhidharma's historical significance is that he symbolized resistance to the politicization of Buddhism in China. Buddhist emperors, of whom Emperor Wu was one of many, used the symbols and doctrines of the religion to enhance and legitimize their political rule. Of course, the emperors who used Buddhism in this way did not always do so cynically. Emperor Wu appears to have embraced the religion on a deep personal level. Nevertheless, the politicization and resultant degradation of Buddhism, especially the degradation of the home-leaving ideal, led Buddhism to be a component of East Asian political ideology and a foundation of state power. This mixture of religion and statecraft was no less disastrous in East Asia than it has proved to be in other places.

The tools of Imperial-Way Buddhism included the following:

1. The Bodhisattva Path: The Mahayana doctrine of the Bodhisattva Path was vital to Imperial-Way Buddhism. This doctrine exalted non-home-leavers and thus denigrated the original world-leaving ideal espoused by the historical Buddha. Emperor Wu's rule signifies a high tide of this trend in China.
2. Control of the precepts and ordination ceremonies: Emperors naturally had an interest in limiting the total number of home-leaving monks and nuns. Monks were not subject to taxation, military service, or conscripted labor. Likewise, nuns were not producing citizens or carrying out the essential work that women provided to an agrarian society. Naturally, many young men or women, especially those without an inheritance or better prospects, might select a religious life if it were readily available, so emperors established stringent intellectual and other requirements to limit the number

of home-leavers. Monks were typically required to memorize long passages of scripture as part of the imperially sanctioned qualification process.

3. Funding the construction of monasteries: In China's icy winters, monks and nuns needed permanent and sturdy housing to withstand the elements. As the main source of funds for building and maintaining monasteries, emperors had the right to select their abbots. They also selected the Buddhist teachings that would be taught in the imperial monastic system. In this manner, much of Buddhism naturally became "imperial" in nature.

4. Scripture translation: Emperors, as the patrons of major translation projects, could select or approve works for translation that tended to exalt their own position and prerogatives. An example of this was Emperor Wu's focus on the King Ashoka Sutra. Another important aspect of this phenomenon was the selection of "metaphysical" sutras, scriptures that suggested the existence of a divine realm beyond ordinary life and beyond the comprehension of ordinary people. Emperors and their coteries of religious monks made political use of metaphysical scriptures by assuming a role as interpreters of "higher truths."

Bodhidharma's life represents a counterpoint to Imperial-Way Buddhism:

1. The Buddhist historian Daoxuan, whose accounts are largely credible, claims Bodhidharma purposefully avoided emperors and their courts.

2. Daoxuan also recorded that Bodhidharma's senior disciple, Sengfu, avoided Emperor Wu's court during a long time span even though he lived only a short distance from the imperial palace. His avoidance was both religious and political in nature, but in principle Sengfu did not avoid the world in general. This is evidenced by the account that Sengfu traveled, at the invitation of Emperor Wu's older brother, from Nanjing to distant Sichuan Province, where he expounded Zen teachings.

3. Some credible evidence indicates Bodhidharma himself lived in the

general vicinity of Nanjing, not far from Emperor Wu's court, for an extended period of time. If so, it would appear he also avoided the court in the manner described by Daoxuan.

4. Sengfu's record indicates that Bodhidharma did not rely on sutras but instead emphasized "observing" (the nature of mind). This is at odds with Imperial-Way Buddhism's emphasis on sutra study and metaphysical interpretations of Buddhist doctrine.

5. Later Zen teachers of Bodhidharma's lineage, particularly the Fourth Ancestor Daoxin, fought against imperial control of their religious practice. Chinese scholars believe Daoxin adopted farming as a means of survival independent of imperial sponsorship, despite the fact that farming violated the traditional precepts against monks doing manual labor or taking life (earthworms and pests unavoidably killed in the process of cultivation and food preparation). This lifestyle was further codified by Baizhang, who established the "Pure Rules" of monastic life. Chinese Zen Buddhism thus adopted the work ethic to survive.

6. Zen masters of Bodhidharma's traditional lineage, at least for a certain period of time, forcefully rejected metaphysics. The literature of most early Zen masters, but particularly key figures such as Daoxin, Baizhang, and the later Huanglong, makes this clear. This antimetaphysical position stands in clear contrast to the sutra-derived doctrines advanced by Imperial Zen. Under Imperial Zen, these doctrines (e.g., Buddha nature, the Bodhisattva Path) became not simply "skillful means" teachings. They were reified in a manner completely at odds with Southern school Zen teachings.

What seems apparent is that early Bodhidharma Zen underwent important changes to take root in China and to avoid political interference. The establishment of farming monasteries, the changes in the nature of the precepts, and the direct efforts of the Zen school to remain politically independent were all aspects of the long historical process of integration.

Chinese Zen dealt with many problems unique to China. One of these was maintaining the home-leaving ideal in a society where family was paramount and where the physical act of leaving home and entering a hostile natural environment required some external support and organization.

Bodhidharma and his Zen tradition were, from a political perspective, an adaptation to this situation. It appears that Zen valued independence and the home-leaving ideal above the strict application of the traditional precepts. It posed the "nature of the mind" as the intellectual and moral justification for farming and other nontraditional home-leaving lifestyles.

These points complement a number of questions already raised by many scholars and suggest some new interpretations for early Zen. It is beyond the scope of this book to review and examine all them all. Here are a few that come immediately to mind:

1. The Southern school of Zen was not simply the Sudden Enlightenment school but also the branch of Zen that, for a certain period, successfully avoided direct control by Imperial-Way Buddhism. The Northern school, which ostensibly represented the Gradual Enlightenment method of practice, was a branch of the tradition that violated the taboo against involvement with the emperor that Bodhidharma symbolized to his spiritual heirs.

2. Zen especially honored the Fourth Ancestor Daoxin and Zen Master Baizhang for helping maintain Zen's independence from the throne by establishing farming and labor as a means of livelihood for the home-leaving Sangha.

3. Zen eschewed sutras not simply because such literature tended to cause people to reify Buddhist concepts ("emptiness," "Buddha nature," etc.) and thus engender metaphysical thinking, but also because of their strong association with and exploitation by Imperial-Way Buddhism.

4. The idea of the "bodhisattva way," perhaps from its inception, was nurtured by monarchs as a way to laicize and subvert Buddhism's world-leaving ideals. By claiming to be a bodhisattva or incarnation of the Tathagata, kings endeavored to be the head of the church and thus maintain political control of Buddhism and its antiworldly tendencies. In the case of Emperor Wu, where this

question can be examined in some detail, it is clear that even the clergy closest to the emperor sometimes tried to counter imperial usurpation of the religion's independence.

Zen Buddhism was not always at odds with Imperial-Way Buddhism, however. For example, the adoption of the Bodhisattva Precepts served the purposes of both Imperial Zen and Bodhidharma's Zen. Emperor Wu drew on different translations and adaptations of these precepts to create the Home-Leaving, Home-Abiding Bodhisattva Precepts and thus allowed Bodhisattva Emperors to have exalted spiritual status. But Zen also had an interest in emphasizing such precepts, as they could be used in lieu of traditional precepts that Zen farmer monks were violating. An interesting facet of this is that although Zen monks undertook farming, they adhered to the vegetarian diet espoused by Emperor Wu and adopted the vegetarian lifestyle as a permanent part of Chinese Buddhism. In these and certain other respects, the interests of Imperial Zen and Bodhidharma Zen coincided.

Whether or not Bodhidharma personally sought to create or maintain a non-Imperial-Way Buddhism in China or not, I believe that later Zen generations honored Bodhidharma's politics as much as his spiritual practice. Zen's emphasis on the legendary meeting between Emperor Wu and Bodhidharma supports this idea, and the dialogue of the traditional story supports this conclusion. Moreover, when we examine the huge number of Buddhist masters who were called "Zen masters" in China prior to Bodhidharma's arrival, we need to sort out why Bodhidharma was given the title "First Ancestor" of Zen. I think that Zen's emphasis on avoiding Imperial-Way Buddhism offers at least a partial explanation of this dilemma.

If, in China, the opposition between Bodhidharma's Zen and Imperial-Way Buddhism seems clear, in Japan any antagonism between that country's Zen tradition and the throne is less obvious. There, Zen has often served the throne and the national polity. There are notable exceptions and acts of resistance to this in Japan's Zen history, such as Dogen's apparent rejection of politics or the resistance that ensued to Meiji government decrees that weakened home-leaving. Such examples show that at times the Bodhidharma/Emperor Wu antagonism was in play. In general, however, Zen was far less successful at avoiding imperial

interference in Japan than in China. Indeed, Myoan Esai did not successfully transplant Zen to Japan until it had devolved in China to be the
handmaiden of the imperial court. Bodhidharma's Zen was far from its
original position of political independence in China when Esai, Benin,
and others arrived there to carry it back to Japan around the beginning of the thirteenth century. This later, essentially neutered Zen was
acceptable to Japan's political elites. It is notable that Japanese monks
had various contact with Chinese Zen teachers prior to that time, but
none resulted in Zen taking root in the island nation.

The connections (both direct and through Korea) between Emperor
Wu's court and the establishment of Buddhism in Japan shows that
from the very beginning its success in that country hinged on politics.
Buddhism's role in politics waxed and waned there until the modern
era, when it played a prominent role in World War II. A foreign-designed
constitution separating church and state ultimately removed overt religious metaphysics from the Japanese national polity.

The metaphysical component of Japanese Buddhism, conjoined to
politics, led to a path far removed from the religion's early ideals. This
has led some modern Japanese scholars to claim that Japanese insti-
tutional Buddhism is not Buddhism at all. In my view this does not
mean that there were not authentic Japanese Buddhists who grasped
the religion for the right reasons and practiced it faithfully in every age.
Many Japanese Buddhists undoubtedly understood the significance of
the failed meeting between Bodhidharma and Emperor Wu for reasons
as I've outlined in this book.

Yet in Japan, the fusion of imperial authority with Buddhist metaphysics and institutions was extreme. The practical result of this mixing
was that the Buddhist home-leaving ideal was eventually diluted to a
degree far beyond what occurred in China, and the bodhisattva ideal
more or less replaced the home-leaving ideal completely. During the
Meiji period of the late nineteenth century, the Japanese government
chained Japan's Buddhism to the rise of the modern nation-state. New
policies reinforced trends toward laicization that permitted monks to
marry and made privately owned temples commonplace. The very existence of "priests," a word foreign to the lexicon of Buddhism in India
and China, indicates the creation of an exalted spiritual class that, aside
from their titles, were often not markedly different in their concerns

and lifestyles from those of lay Buddhists. Of course, "priests" had an additional role as the adjudicators of orthodoxy, an orthodoxy that in Japan was part of the ruling ideology. This phenomenon is especially ironic in the context of Zen Buddhism, a religion that emphasizes that differences between "sacred" and "mundane," "enlightened" and "ordinary" are in an important sense without meaning.

51. Was Japan to Blame?

AFTER WORLD WAR II, commentators criticized the Kyoto school of philosophy that existed in Japan during the war. That Buddhist-oriented philosophical group, headed by the scholar Nishida Kitaro, stood accused of providing the philosophical underpinnings of Japan's imperial misadventure. Throughout his life, Nishida tried to reconcile his perceived "essence" of Japanese and Chinese philosophy with Western science and culture. Critics said his work helped provide the philosophy behind the Japanese militarists' belief that Japan was "special" and should spread its cultural superiority to Asia and the world. Perhaps the criticism of Nishida is unfair, as he seems to have been torn between nationalist sentiments and a belief in cosmopolitanism. His writings do reflect a desire for Western and Eastern philosophy to complement each other in a global community.

But the Kyoto school that Nishida headed based its Buddhist philosophy on the metaphysical idea of "absolute nothingness." To Nishida and his fellow philosophers, the uniqueness of Eastern culture lay in this concept. Absolute nothingness was purportedly known only through a "pure experience" of reality that was not simply apart from questions of right and wrong but also *transcended* them. This absolute nothingness, it was argued, symbolized the essential Asian, and particularly Japanese, cultural insight. It found social expression in the "emptiness" of an enemy soldier or the death of a noble samurai warrior or kamikaze pilot. It found artistic expression in the "emptiness" of the beauty of a transient cherry blossom that falls from the tree in full bloom. Members of the Kyoto school praised the emperor as the ultimate expression of this transcendental metaphysic. The emperor, they said, personally embodied absolute emptiness.

"Emptiness" became a pretext for criminal actions, violating the Buddhist precepts, and violating the teachings of the religion that allowed the term into its dialogue. What I would like to point out here is that the term, though fundamental to Prajnaparamita Buddhist scripture and thought, is seldom found and is without metaphysical meaning in old Zen texts.

The old Zen masters did not want people to be caught up in "emptiness" or any other idea. This is clear from passages like the one quoted above from Baizhang, who specifically counseled against brandishing the term.

Perhaps if Emperor Wu's imperial Buddhist metaphysics did not contribute to the horror that engulfed Nanjing centuries later, then some other ideology of like-minded silliness would have done so. But we should consider that it was a historical process that ensued from Emperor Wu's court that culminated in a horrific tragedy at the same location centuries later. The irony merits our attention and meditation.

But is it fair to overemphasize Japan's role in war crimes? Japan is hardly alone, particularly in the context of World War II. The crimes committed in Nazi Germany are well-known. But also remember that British and American forces unleashed an unprecedented mass bombardment of civilian populations by aircraft in Germany and Japan as a terrorist weapon. The pervasive triumphalism of the Allies' victory often overlooks this. Are the crimes that the Japanese imperial army committed against innocents in Nanjing heavier on the scales of justice than the intentional firebombing of civilian Tokyo, Osaka, Hamburg, Dresden, and scores of other Axis cities, events in which civilians died by fire on a scale dwarfing the numbers killed in the atomic attacks on Hiroshima and Nagasaki?

Such ethical questions are further blurred by the fact that the West likely contributed to Japan's imperial misadventures in a tangible way. A recent book entitled *The Imperial Cruise*, by James Bradley, reveals how President Theodore Roosevelt, whose racist beliefs Bradley clearly exposes, urged Japan to adopt their own Monroe Doctrine toward the rest of Asia. Roosevelt saw Japan's quick embrace of Western values during the late 1800s as evidence of Japanese racial superiority. He thought Japan would cooperate to advance America's own interests in Asia by helping maintain the Open Door Policy, a name that served as a fig leaf for the United States's imperial interests in China and its subjugation of the Philippines. As Roosevelt saw it, since the United

States's colonial conquests of Native Americans were finished and had reached the shores of the Pacific Ocean, it was natural that the imperial thrust should cross the Pacific to Asia. Bradley describes how Roosevelt encouraged Japan in its colonial adventures, contributing to that country's successful conquest and occupation of Korea in 1910. This whetted Japan's growing nationalist sentiments and greater imperial ambitions in the years that followed.

When I was a youngster growing up in Oregon, we sang the Oregon State song, "Oregon, My Oregon," a paean to empire that rang forth from our innocent classrooms, a song that proclaims,

> Land of the empire builders,
> Land of the Golden West,
> Conquered and held by free men,
> Fairest [!] and the best,
> Onward and upward ever,
> Forward and on and on,
> Hail, to thee, land of heroes, my Oregon.

Roosevelt, one of the "fair" (here our state song appears to refer not just to the idea of fairness, but also to fair skin) empire builders, consciously passed the mantle of empire to Japan. This gives a special irony to the song's second verse:

> Land of the rose and sunshine,
> Land of the summer's breeze;
> Laden with health and vigor,
> Fresh from the western seas.
> Blest by the blood of martyrs,
> Land of the setting sun;
> Hail to thee, Land of Promise,
> My Oregon.

As the sun was setting in Oregon, it was rising in Japan.

Ashoka, the Buddhist king of India, embraced Buddhism and politicized its ideals. Soon after Buddhism arrived in China, that country's emperors did the same. In this light, the question becomes whether many Mahayana Buddhist doctrines were developed with specific political ends in mind. Answering that question is beyond the scope of this book, and anyway has already been suggested and discussed by some scholars. Yet no matter why they were created, such scriptures allowed rulers who were at the extreme opposite of the religious scale from home-leavers to publically embrace the religion. They thus became monarchs toward whom monks must bow, all while these monarchs need not yield their own overarching worldly power and status. The Bodhisattva Vow and the absolutist metaphysics of the Lotus Sutra and other Buddhist scriptures facilitated this development. Caught up in the hope that vast numbers of converts would result from an "enlightened" king, a big part of the Buddhist religion appears to have accepted this dangerous trend.

The defiance Emperor Wu's teacher Zhizang displayed upon being denied the Dharma seat in the Tai Cheng Palace indicates that Bodhidharma was not the only cleric resentful of Imperial-Way Buddhism. Yet Bodhidharma appears uniquely successful at remaining outside the imperial orbit while carrying out his Buddhist mission in China. He was a successful counterpoint to the politicization of Buddhism and symbolized this ideal to his spiritual successors. Whether he actually saw himself in this role is less certain, and less important, than the fact that this is the role assigned to him by the Zen tradition that honors him.

Appendix:

Traditional Account of Bodhidharma's Death
in the *Compendium of Five Lamps* (thirteenth century)

IT HAS LONG BEEN REPORTED that Bodhidharma traveled with his disciples to Thousand Saints Temple at Yu Gate. They stayed there for three days. At that time the prefectural chief Yang Xuanzhi, who had long honored Buddhism, came to visit.

He asked Bodhidharma, "Your Excellency is called the patriarch of the Five Seals of India. What is this teaching?"

Bodhidharma said, "Those illuminated to Buddha mind and who practice in accordance with this understanding, these are the ones called patriarchs."

The governor then asked, "What do you teach besides this?"

Bodhidharma then said, "You must have clarity on this Mind, comprehending its past and present, unhindered by [thoughts of] existence and nonexistence, not seeking Dharma, apart from cleverness and ignorance, without delusion or enlightenment. If you can understand in this fashion, you'll be called a patriarch."

The governor then asked, "Your disciple has long taken refuge in the Three Treasures and understood the teachings of wisdom and ignorance, but I have been uncertain about the truth. Hearing you speak, I now begin to grasp it. I ask for the master's forbearance to reveal the true doctrine."

Bodhidharma, knowing the earnestness of the request, then spoke this verse: "Without seeing evil or feeling revulsion, and without perceiving goodness or making exertions, and without forsaking knowledge or approaching ignorance, without shunning delusion or attaining enlightenment, in this way you will achieve the great and unexcelled Way. Penetrate immeasurable Buddha Mind. Don't follow ideas of ordinary or sacred, and naturally you'll become a patriarch."

When Yang heard this verse, he experienced both joy and sorrow, saying, "May the master long abide in the world and liberate people [from delusion]."

Bodhidharma said, "I will soon leave the world. I cannot remain here long. There are countless sorrows, and I've encountered many difficulties."

Yang then said, "Who among your followers comprehends the master's teaching?"

Bodhidharma then said, "I have transmitted the secret of the Buddhas that benefit those on the road of delusion that they may find peace in this teaching. As to those who would find peace, they cannot do so but for this [teaching]."

Yang then said, "If the master does not speak, then how can this penetrating light come forth?"

In response Bodhidharma only recited this prophesy: "The river swirls with jade waves, the lamplight opens the golden lock. Five persons practice together, and among ninety none are not me."

Yang heard this and said, "This I don't fathom, so I only silently hold it." He then bid farewell and left. Although at that time Yang did not grasp the master's verse, he later understood its meaning.

At that time the Wei dynastic house honored Buddhism, and Zen adepts were as numerous as trees in the forest. Vinaya Master Guang Tong and Tripitaka Master Ruci were prominent among monks. Seeing the master expound Dharma, they condemned the teaching of "pointing at mind." When they would debate Bodhidharma, they would raise [ideas of] existence and nonexistence. Bodhidharma spread his profound teaching widely, universally bringing about the Dharma rain, and because of his great celebrity they could not bear the situation, giving rise to harmful thoughts. They added poison to Bodhidharma's food, increasing the amount until they'd done so six times. When the karmic conditions of his teaching were exhausted, [Bodhidharma] passed his Dharma to others. They were unable to save him, and, sitting upright, he passed away. The date was the fifth day of the tenth lunar month of [536]. He was buried on the twenty-eighth day of the twelfth lunar month at Samadhi Forest Temple on Bear Ear Mountain. Three years later, the Wei envoy Song Yunfeng was returning from western regions and encountered Bodhidharma in the Cong Mountains carrying one sandal and traveling quickly.

Song asked, "Where's the master going?"

Bodhidharma said, "To India!"

Song returned [to China] and told his story. Bodhidharma's disciples opened his grave and found the casket empty, with only one sandal remaining there. This was brought to the [imperial] court's attention and caused much surprise. [The court] honored the remaining sandal, placing it in Shaolin Temple, where it was venerated. In the fifteenth year of the Kaiyuan period of the Tang dynasty [727], it was transferred to Huayan Temple on Wu Tai Mountain, but now its whereabouts are unknown. Previously, Emperor Liang Wudi met Bodhidharma, but they had no affinity, but then [the emperor] heard that [Bodhidharma] had gone to proselytize in the Wei [territory]. Emperor Wu [hearing of Bodhidharma's death] made haste to author a memorial tablet [to honor him]. Later the story of Song Yunfeng was heard, and [thus] the tale is complete. The [Tang emperor] Tai Zong posthumously conferred the name Great Teacher Perfect Enlightenment. The burial stupa is called Empty Perception.

Printed in the United States
by Baker & Taylor Publisher Services